Using CorelDRAW! 4

ED PAULSON

Using CorelDRAW! 4

Library of Congress Catalog No.: 93-85722

ISBN: 1-56529-124-7

95 94 93   6 5 4 3 2 1

Interpretation of the printing code: the rightmost double-digit number is the year of the book's printing; the rightmost single-digit number, the number of the book's printing. For example, a printing code of 93-1 shows that the first printing of the book occurred in 1993.

Screen reproductions in this book were created using Collage Plus from Inner Media, Inc., Hollis, NH.

Publisher: David P. Ewing

Associate Publisher: Rick Ranucci

Director of Publishing: Mike Miller

Managing Editor: Corinne Walls

Marketing Manager: Ray Robinson

Trademarks

To my parents, John and Jean Paulson, for their unwavering support of me and my writing.

CREDITS

Publishing Manager
Shelley O'Hara

Acquisitions Editor
Sarah Browning

Product Development Specialists
Jim Minatel
Kathie-Jo Arnoff

Production Editor
Heather Northrup

Editors
Kelly Currie
Kezia Endsley
Thomas Hayes
Louise Lambert
Cindy Morrow
J. Christopher Nelson
Brad Sullivan

Technical Editors
Patricia K. Gibson
Kelly Frazier

Vendor Contact Coordinator
Patty Brooks

Editorial Assistant
Sandra Naito

Book Designer
Amy Peppler-Adams

Production Team
Jeff Baker
Angela Bannan
Danielle Bird
Paula Carroll
Laurie Casey
Charlotte Clapp
Michelle Greenwalt
Brook Farling
Carla Hall
Bob LaRoche
Heather Kaufman
Caroline Roop
Amy Steed
Tina Trettin
Michelle Worthington
Lillian Yates

Indexer
Johnna VanHoose

Composed in *Cheltenham* and *MCPdigital* by Que Corporation

ABOUT THE AUTHOR

Ed Paulson has been a CorelDRAW! user since 1989. He is a member of the Austin chapter of Corel Artists and thoroughly enjoys working with CorelDRAW! and its associated applications. He is the author of numerous published articles and several technology-related books, including a telecommunications textbook, and has taught at the university level. His educational credits include bachelor's and master's degrees in engineering from the University of Illinois and an MBA from the University of Texas at Austin.

He is the executive director of Applied Concepts, an Austin, Texas based technology training and consulting company. Applied Concepts, an authorized CorelDRAW! training center, develops and markets its training curriculums to organizations around the country and is a provider of authorized CorelDRAW! training materials.

Mr. Paulson has over 20 years of high technology industry experience and has worked extensively with such notable companies as Seagate Technology, Plantronics, IBM, WANG Laboratories, and AT&T. He believes that effective training is the most expedient route to improving worker productivity and appreciates the opportunity to share his experience in print, in the classroom, and as a speaker.

ACKNOWLEDGMENTS

The preparation of a book of this scope involves the people at Corel who developed a wonderful software package, the people at Que who turned the text and figures into a beautiful final product, and the people who assisted with the writing of the various chapters. A heart-felt thank you to the many people who were integral to this project's completion.

I also want to thank those people around me who realized that writing this book required extraordinary effort and time, and gave me the space to complete it without interference. Thank you to Mike Buls, Elizabeth Purzer, and my other business associates who did not write me off their list while I was out of pocket.

I also want to thank these people from Que: Sarah Browning for pushing me and the project, Shelley O'Hara for making the outline better than it was, Jim Minatel for making the changes necessary for a final product we can all be proud of, Heather Northrup for deciphering my handwriting and coordinating the complex edits, and Don Roche for believing enough in me and this project to start the process. Thanks also to Patricia Gibson and Kelly Frazier for their helpful technical comments.

Thank you, Tracey Walicki and Janie Sullivan at Corel Systems, for your support during the Beta phase, and beyond.

These people wrote various sections of the book, and deserve a thank you for taking their work seriously and applying a professional touch under a tight deadline: Wendy Wheeler for the chapters on object drawing, using color, using TRACE and PHOTO-PAINT; Clancy Mullen for the chapter on changing object shapes; and Jan Gillespie for the chapter on CorelCHART.

Thank you for purchasing *Using CorelDRAW! 4*. Your feedback is welcome so that we can make this book an ever-improving resource for its readers.

CONTENTS AT A GLANCE

TABLE OF CONTENTS

III Working with Files

IV Becoming an Expert

V Using the Other Corel Applications

Introduction

The ability to draw and print images used to be reserved for an elite few, but with the advent of products like CorelDRAW! this drawing ability is more and more commonplace. Once you learn CorelDRAW!'s basic operation, and thinking mode, you can use a wide array of functions and features that allow you to take your imagination and translate it into computer-generated pictures.

I have been using CorelDRAW! since 1989 and have watched it evolve from its early stages into one of the most flexible graphics packages in the world. The concept of vector graphics, which saw its first major public introduction with CorelDRAW!, was a novelty in the late 1980s and is now the industry standard drawing mode. What makes DRAW different from the other packages that followed is that Corel Systems never stood still. It continually improved the package so that what you see in release 4 is a solid step in the Corel product evolution.

Who Should Use This Book?

This book is designed as a complete reference to DRAW and its associated other applications CorelPHOTO-PAINT, CorelMOVE, CorelSHOW, CorelTRACE, CorelMOSAIC, and CorelCHART. The emphasis of the book is not to treat each package as a stand-alone application, but to reinforce the synergy that exists between the packages. The Corel suite of products takes full advantage of the Windows DDE/OLE environment and allows you to use work created in one Corel application while creating a new image in another application.

If you are a beginner, start with Chapter 1, which introduces you to various CorelDRAW! 4 applications. Chapters 2 and 3 lead you through the basics of DRAW. If you are an experienced DRAW user, you will find the book a complete reference to all of the various features, options, and applications encountered with the Corel suite of applications. The organization of this book makes it easy to find the information pertinent to your needs. Personal experience based recommendations are included as they apply to the particular section.

The emphasis is not on drawing various types of pictures, although that is important. The emphasis is on informing you, in a structured way, on the uses and benefits associated with the various Corel product features. When you become familiar with the various features, use your imagination to discover new ways of using them.

The experienced user will find Chapter 21, "Combining the Applications," informative with regard to integrating the Corel applications to achieve your desired results. If you are a service bureau, keep this book around as an authoritative reference on how to make the applications perform as your clients require. Much of what you need is already included with CorelDRAW!, and it would be a shame to reinvent the wheel if an image that matched your needs was included with the clip art.

How This Book Is Organized

This book is organized to follow the natural order of learning and using CorelDRAW! 4, progressing from the basic and essential topics to more complex and often optional issues. To help you see this organization, the book is divided into five parts:

Part I	Getting Started	Chapters 1-3
Part II	Learning CorelDRAW! Basics	Chapters 4-8
Part III	Working with Files	Chapters 9-10
Part IV	Becoming an Expert	Chapters 11-15
Part V	Using the Other Corel Applications	Chapters 16-21

Part I is designed to provide the reader with information relevant to the use of this book and the overall capability of the Corel suite of products. Because CorelDRAW! is the germinating application upon which the operation of the other applications is defined, DRAW and its capabilities are covered first.

Part II introduces all of the basic drawing and image-editing techniques.

Part III deals with the various output mechanisms and how they are used in conjunction with color selection to work effectively with commercial printers.

Part IV covers the more advanced DRAW features such as Special Effects and PowerLines, with a chapter dedicated to the useful multipage document feature and the innovative Object Database Manager.

Part V introduces all of the other applications included with CorelDRAW! 4. The PHOTO-PAINT chapter shows you how to capture and modify bitmap images for use with other applications. The TRACE chapter illustrates the procedures used for changing those bitmaps into vector graphic objects that are easily scaled and modified for use in the other applications. CHART covers the creation of graphs and charts typically used in formal presentations. The CorelMOVE chapter introduces the new animation features of Corel 4. The SHOW chapter covers the inclusion of objects created in the various applications into a unified presentation.

The book also includes three appendixes. Appendix A covers Corel-DRAW! 4 installation. Appendix B presents issues that arise when using Corel with other applications. Appendix C provides tables showing the Corel codes for inserting special characters from many of the fonts provided with CorelDRAW! 4 and Windows 3.1. Also included is a short glossary of useful terms related to this product.

Using CorelDRAW! 4 gives you a tremendous graphics background that prepares you well for working with any of the Corel applications, while also laying the groundwork for understanding the technology associated with any graphically related software package.

How To Use This Book

Each chapter is designed as a complete unit, with references to those other sections of the book where specific topics are covered in more detail. New users are encouraged to work their way through Chapters 1-3 to acquire a quick introduction to the Corel application thinking process. If you are familiar with CorelDRAW!, but unfamiliar with commercial printing procedures, review Chapters 10 and 11 on printing and using color. The information in these chapters becomes important as you become more proficient with the product.

If you are an experienced Corel 3 user, you can update yourself by re-viewing the basic new features including PowerLines, non-PostScript color separations while printing, print merges, scanner support in PHOTO-PAINT and TRACE, animation in MOVE, multipage documents, the Object Data Manager, and ways to customize DRAW.

You are encouraged to bounce around in the book using the table of contents or index as a guide. You are also encouraged to read the open-ing comments in each chapter because they outline the information that follows. In addition, the overall procedures associated with a spe-cific operation are often outlined at the beginning and then explained in detail throughout the rest of the chapter.

The appendixes cover information pertaining to installation and opera-tion of the applications with other applications. They are provided as reference items.

Conventions Used in This Book

The conventions used in this book have been established to help you learn to use CorelDRAW! 4 quickly and easily. The directions are not keyboard or mouse specific. Choose the method that you are most comfortable with. Many procedures may be easiest with the mouse while others may be better accomplished with the keyboard. This is largely a matter of personal preference.

In many instances, there are three ways that you can access a com-mand: you can click on it with the mouse, you can press a letter, or press a function key. The letter you press is indicated in **boldface** in this book. Commands that require multiple letters to be chosen con-secutively will have more than one letter in **boldface**. These letters are usually underlined on the screen in Corel. Where appropriate, the func-tion key alternatives follow the command. The keys are separated by a + sign if more than one key must be pressed at once. For instance, Ctrl+F1 means to press the Control key and the F1 function key at the same time.

There are many tools represented by icons in CorelDRAW! Where ap-propriate, these icons are displayed in the book when discussing the commands.

Directions for mouse operations such as click and drag refer to the primary mouse button, which is generally the left mouse button. If you have swapped your primary mouse button to the right button, all the referrals to the right (secondary) mouse button actually refer to the left button.

Where To Find More Help

If you find yourself stuck at a particular point in CorelDRAW!, the built-in help feature may answer your questions. Help is explained in Chapter 2. In addition, you can use this book or the Corel documentation to answer most questions.

If all else fails, you can try the Corel technical support number. Call (613) 728-1990 for the Corel interactive, automated help line. If this cannot answer your questions, you can transfer to a technical support representative. You can also get automated support via fax at (613) 728-0826, ext. 3080. Other technical support options are detailed in the front of the Corel manual.

If you have a CompuServe membership, help is available through the Corel forum. Type **Go Corel** to access this forum.

Finally, as of this writing, Corel has released a maintenance patch version of CorelDRAW! 4. This addresses certain bugs in the initial version. You should call Corel at (800) 77COREL to see if you need this update. It is available to registered users free of charge.

Closing Comments

CorelDRAW! 4 is more than just a drawing package. It is now a suite of products that provide a wide array of image processing functions. As you learn the operation of the various applications, think about how you can use each in conjunction with the other applications to create images that are far beyond those you currently use. I enjoyed writing this book and intend for it to become a reference and guide to specific application sections while also providing an overall framework for using the Corel applications as a unified offering.

Thank you for making *Using CorelDRAW! 4* a part of your computer library. This is where the fun starts!

Ed Paulson

Austin, Texas

Getting Started

PART

I

OUTLINE

An Overview of CorelDRAW! 4

You can use the components of CorelDRAW! 4 most effectively if you have a realistic set of expectations about the capabilities of the program. This chapter outlines the different applications of CorelDRAW! 4 and explains how they can be used in conjunction with each other. CorelDRAW! 4 combines powerful technical drawing and illustration, animation, presentation graphics and charting, file conversion, tracing, photoshop editing of color bitmaps, desktop publishing and layout, object-oriented image database management, and screen capture applications into one software package.

CorelDRAW! does some of these things exceptionally well and others only adequately. But taken as a whole, it is one of the most comprehensive software packages on the market today. If you learn CorelDRAW! and its associated features, you are well on your way to understanding any Windows-based software application.

What To Expect from CorelDRAW! 4

The CorelDRAW! 4 name is a bit misleading because the product is really a combination of several different software application packages. CorelDRAW! is only one of the applications provided with the package. Other applications that enhance the use of CorelDRAW! or capitalize on work created in CorelDRAW! have been added as the product has evolved.

Think of the Corel suite of products as a set of image-processing tools, of which CorelDRAW! is the illustration and drawing tool. The other tools enhance the overall product by providing capabilities that are needed when working with quality images in today's computing environment. The following sections list the tools that come with CorelDRAW! 4, explain their functions, and discuss how they complement each other.

You can start any of these Corel applications by choosing the appropriate icon from within the Windows Corel Application Group.

CorelDRAW!

As the umbrella application in the suite, CorelDRAW! determines the menu structure and icon arrangement used in the other applications. DRAW is a sophisticated drawing tool that can be used to create everything from simple line art to technical drawings to complex full-color artwork. Some of the winning entries in the Corel art contest are included with this book. They were all created with CorelDRAW!, using the features covered in this book.

Basic features include the capability to draw shapes and lines and to define outline and fill attributes. DRAW provides a helpful shape tool that allows for easy yet versatile modification of those shapes into any design you might want. DRAW uses a special graphic format for all objects, so the quality of the image does not degrade as the objects are scaled or rotated.

DRAW also comes with a set of special effects that handle shading, highlights, transitions from one object to another, and envelope shaping of entire objects. With the tools provided by DRAW, you can take on the most complex drawing tasks; the possibilities are limited only by your imagination. The only restraint is that DRAW works according to well-defined rules which you must follow. Learning to use them properly will keep you from getting frustrated and discouraged.

Objects created in CorelDRAW! can be transferred to other Corel applications by exporting the appropriate files or using the Windows Clipboard. Exporting file information is covered in Chapter 9.

MOSAIC

Because these products deal with images instead of text, Corel provides MOSAIC to enable you to view images when you call up a file directory. Files are displayed as *thumbnail* images, allowing you to select files for use based on their image contents rather than their name or date of creation. MOSAIC is a separate application that can be started on its own or from CorelDRAW!. Sometimes it might slow down the file-opening process, but it can be a life saver when you are working with a number of different files and cannot remember when a file was created or what it was named.

MOSAIC can also be used to print multiple files at once. Simply select the desired files from the MOSAIC screen and then choose the desired action (Print, in this particular case). MOSAIC loads the required applications and then performs the print functions. It relieves the user of the routine tasks associated with this type of printing operation.

CorelCHART

CorelCHART is a presentation graphics chart-creation application. With it you can import or enter data that you want to present in graphical form and then select the chart style you want to use for the display. The finished charts are not actually presented by CHART; they are imported into SHOW for the final presentation. But you can use CHART to print or export your graph in file formats that can be used by other applications. CHART provides a wide variety of chart styles, including 3-D, so you should be able to find a style appropriate for your particular charting needs. Because CHART does not easily create some conventional final presentation products, such as single slides containing charts with bulleted text, it cannot be considered an equivalent to the Freelance Graphics program. But you can customize virtually any facet of a chart using CHART's image-handling capabilities.

CorelMOVE

CorelMOVE, a new feature of release 4, provides animation capability. Now you can create an object in DRAW or MOVE and design it to move around on-screen. You can add sound and user-driven cues, which make the animation interact with the viewer. The procedures required to create animation are relatively complicated; Chapter 20, which covers MOVE, takes you through them step-by-step. MOVE is an exciting new feature that you are sure to have fun with.

CorelPHOTO-PAINT

CorelPHOTO-PAINT is an editing application that allows you to scan an image, edit images with Paint tools, and apply filters (such as pointillism or fractal texture overlay) that add artistic touches to an underlying image. PHOTO-PAINT makes many types of image modifications possible; you will have fun exploring their use. Images created in PHOTO-PAINT can be used as backgrounds in SHOW or as images in the other applications.

CorelTRACE

CorelTRACE transforms a PHOTO-PAINT image into a format that can be used by CorelDRAW!, allowing you to use the full power of DRAW for editing purposes. A Realtor might scan an image of a house for inclusion in a flyer, for example, and then need to scale or modify it slightly before final printing. Using TRACE to convert the image, the Realtor can then import it to DRAW and edit it as needed. After you understand it, the entire procedure is quick and painless; the final output looks professionally created. TRACE images are stored as Encapsulated Postscript (EPS) files so they can be used in other applications.

CorelSHOW

A formal presentation requires a flow of information that is usually organized in CorelSHOW. Graphs created in CHART, logos created in DRAW, pictures scanned and edited in PHOTO-PAINT, and animation developed in MOVE can be combined with other things, such as sound, in SHOW to create dramatic effects. SHOW does not provide much intrinsic editing capability because most of the editing is done in the source applications. Consequently SHOW makes extensive use of the Windows 3.1 data-linking capability (a topic which is covered in depth later in this book). With SHOW, you can also create stand-alone presentations that do not require DRAW or SHOW to run on standard PCs.

PostScript versus Non-PostScript Issues

Some of DRAW's printing capabilities are not available on non-PostScript printers. You are cautioned in advance to verify your printer type and be aware of the limitations that a non-PostScript printer places on your final output. Not all of DRAW's textures and fill patterns are available without PostScript, but now you can create color separations with non-PostScript printers (a welcome addition for veteran DRAW users).

New Release 4 Features

Only CorelMOVE animation is completely new to release 4, but the other applications have been enhanced. Some noteworthy changes and additions include items like these:

- Non-PostScript color separation printing
- Multipage documents for desktop publishing type of work
- Object database manager that correlates background information with a screen image
- PowerLines that simulate a paintbrush for an artistic effect with line drawings
- Dimension lines for technical drawings
- The contour special effect
- Merging of text and images while printing
- Scanner support

- Expanded use of roll-up with OCR capabilities to control functions
- Increased number of clip art files to 18,000
- Increased number of fonts to 750
- Fractal textures for image enhancement (CD-ROM)

Prior DRAW users will find that things are located differently in the new release and some keyboard shortcuts have changed, so some adjustment will be needed at first. After you get used to the new layout, however, you will find that your efficiency and creative possibilities are both enhanced.

NOTE

 Look for the release 4 feature icon throughout the book to locate features that are new to CorelDRAW! 4 or that are substantial improvements over previous versions.

Summary

This chapter has provided a brief sketch of the various parts of the CorelDRAW! 4 product and an overview of how they relate to each other. If you think of these items as applications that work in conjunction with each other (rather than as separate applications), you will begin to recognize the full power of CorelDRAW! 4.

Using CorelDRAW! 4 combines step-by-step procedures with a detailed product reference. This book accommodates your level of expertise whether you're a beginner or an advanced user.

The next chapter introduces you to the basic features of CorelDRAW!. Even if you are already familiar with these features, you should probably look at this chapter as a refresher. Doing so will give you an opportunity to get into the program and see the many enhancements to CorelDRAW! 4 firsthand.

CorelDRAW! Basic Information

This chapter covers basic information that pertains to almost every aspect of Corel application operation. You learn how to start CorelDRAW! and about the various parts of the DRAW screen. This chapter also explains Corel's basic operational philosophy. A clear understanding of Corel's basis for operation allows you to understand its "thinking," which makes you proficient with CorelDRAW! at a faster rate.

Starting CorelDRAW!

The Windows Corel application group contains all the Corel-related applications. Each one is represented by a different Windows icon (see fig. 2.1). You can start each of these programs by double-clicking its associated icon.

FIG. 2.1

The Corel application group with icons.

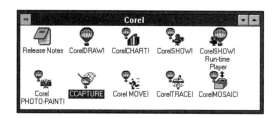

To start Corel, follow these steps:

1. Locate the Corel applications group and double-click it. The Corel group window opens.

2. Double-click the CorelDRAW! icon. The CorelDRAW! 4 application window displays as shown in figure 2.2.

FIG. 2.2

The CorelDRAW! application window.

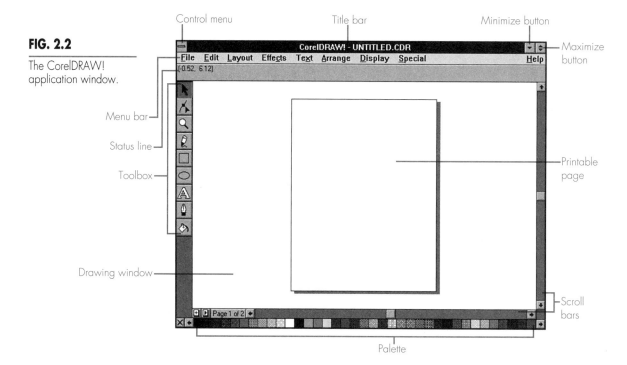

The basic layout of the CorelDRAW! toolbox and menus is similar to that used by the other Corel applications. Time spent familiarizing yourself with this setup makes the other Corel applications easier to learn.

Learning the Parts of the CorelDRAW! Screen

All Corel applications have a similar presentation and the overall operation of the windows themselves is the same. This section overviews the basic Corel screen tools and sections.

At the top of the active window is the title bar, which shows the application name. CorelDRAW! also shows the name of the file currently being edited. Because the file in figure 2.2 does not yet have a name, CorelDRAW! calls it UNTITLED.CDR.

> All CorelDRAW! drawings have a CDR extension. This extension is useful when you are trying to locate CorelDRAW! files using the Windows File Manager.

NOTE

To the left of the title bar is the Control menu, a small box with a horizontal line. Double-clicking on this box terminates CorelDRAW! and returns you to Windows.

Click the minimize button to shrink the application to an icon. Keep in mind that the application is still running even though it's shrunk to an icon.

Click the maximize button to enlarge the DRAW window so that it takes up the maximum amount of allowable screen space. To restore the window to its original size, click the restore button (a double arrow).

The menu bar, which is located below the title bar, contains the various pull-down menus used to operate the Corel applications.

The status line is located below the menu bar. The status line provides important information about the current stage of CorelDRAW! objects such as their screen location, size, line, and interior fill characteristics. The status line is displayed by default, but you can hide it by using the **Sh**ow Status Line toggle on the **D**isplay menu.

The toolbox runs along the left side of the window. It contains the drawing tools used to create and modify the basic shapes that combine to make a finished drawing. You take a detailed look at the toolbox later in this chapter.

To display the rulers, choose Show **R**ulers from the **D**isplay menu. The rulers are located below the status line and along the side of the toolbox. The ruler increments are user defined. The page origin location defaults to the lower-left corner of the page so that all measurements are positive.

TIP

Leave the origin at its default location, the lower left corner of the page, unless you have a specific reason for moving it. This way the page location numbers are all positive instead of a combination of positive and negative numbers.

The drawing window is located in the middle of the screen. This window is where the actual editing and layout of the drawing takes place. Contained within the drawing window is the printable page, which is a display representation of the currently active drawing. You can drag objects between the printable page and the drawing window.

Use the horizontal and vertical scroll bars to scroll the window. Click the arrow located at either end of the scroll bar to move in that direction. You can also use the horizontal and vertical scroll bars to move the image by either selecting the arrows and moving the viewing window in increments or using the mouse to drag the scroll box across or up and down the scroll bar to move the viewing window in larger increments.

 DRAW allows for editing of multiple-page documents. A small section is reserved at the left end of the horizontal scroll bar to display the number of the current page and the total number of pages contained in the complete file.

The color palette is located at the bottom of the window. You activate the color palette by pulling down the Display menu and choosing Color Palette. In the Color Palette dialog box, you can set different options, such as the Palette Type (for example, Custom, Process, Spot). To use a color, first select the object, and then click the desired palette color.

Viewing Your Work

You have three ways to view your work on-screen in CorelDRAW!: Editable Preview, Wireframe view, and Preview. The default drawing view is called Editable Preview. This view shows objects in full color with all their attributes, except for fills that use PostScript Textures and halftone screens (see fig. 2.3).

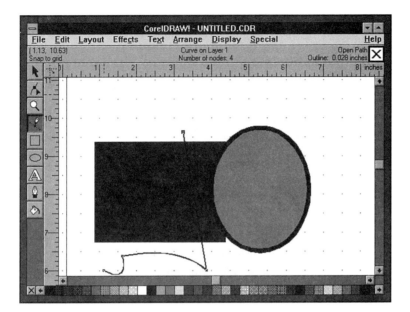

FIG. 2.3

Viewing work in Editable
Preview.

Wireframe view features quicker screen redraws because it shows only
the outline of the various objects and does not show their relative orientation or fill characteristics (see fig. 2.4). To change to Wireframe
view, open the **D**isplay menu and choose the **E**dit Wireframe option.

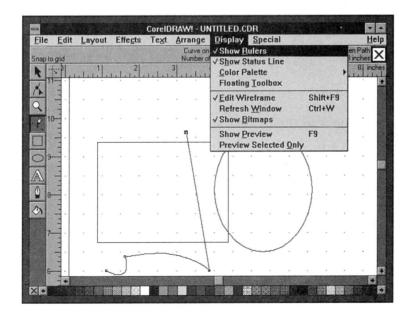

FIG. 2.4

Viewing work in Wire-
frame view.

TIP

Higher powered computers show little editing performance difference between Editable Preview and Wireframe view. Lower powered computers, however, perform better if you edit in Wireframe Preview and use Editable Preview on an occasional basis to look at the drawing.

When you edit in Wireframe view, all object characteristics are shown at the right side of the status line. Once you become familiar with DRAW operation, you may find that Wireframe view used in conjunction with the status line information provides optimal drawing performance.

Both Wireframe view and Editable Preview let you enlarge or reduce the size of the drawing so you can get an overview or zoom in on a specific detail. Both views also have scroll bars at the edges of the window so you can move your viewing window to see other portions of your drawing. You can also display facing pages on-screen, which is useful for multipage documents, in both views.

TIP

To switch between Editable Preview and Wireframe view, press Shift+F9.

Preview gives the most accurate representation of how your image will actually print.

Reviewing the Toolbox Tools

Just as a carpenter uses a box of tools to build a house, you use the Corel tools to build your drawings. The following descriptions start with the top tool and move top-to-bottom through the toolbox.

 The Pick tool is the arrow icon at the top of the toolbox. Use this tool to select, or pick, the objects on which you want to work. There are numerous ways to select an object; the most fundamental method is to click on the object you want to select.

TIP

Pressing the space bar activates the Pick tool. Pressing the space bar again returns you to the previously used drawing tool.

CorelDRAW! objects are constructed by a set of nodes. The Shape tool allows you to change the location and performance characteristics of the nodes.

The Zoom tool has a fly-out menu that provides different levels of drawing magnification.

TIP

You can set up the right mouse button to provide an automatic 2X magnification when you click it by pulling down the **S**pecial menu, choosing Pr**e**ferences, and then choosing the Mouse button. From the Preferences - Mouse dialog box, choose the **2**x zoom option.

You use the Pencil, Rectangle, and Ellipse tools for drawing lines, boxes, and circular shapes.

The Text tool fly-out menu allows you to enter artistic text and paragraph text onto the drawing. It also provides access to the symbol library.

The Outline Pen and Fill tools provide fly-out menus that allow you to easily change the drawing characteristics of the selected objects.

How DRAW Creates Objects

Early computer-based drawings were composed of a series of dots that combined to form a screen-based image. Each of the dots was an isolated black or white spot and did not see itself as part of an overall image or object. You could perform certain manipulations with the screen images, but any substantial change caused a serious degradation of the image quality because the dots did not really understand their position as part of the whole image.

CorelDRAW! uses a method of image creation called vector graphics. This technique is relatively common today, but was revolutionary when it was first introduced. Vector images see the dots as part of an overall object instead of the object being a series of dots. Corel retains information about the object (such as size, line thickness, and fill) and then combines the dots to form the desired final outcome. This idea is the essence of vector graphic imaging.

To retain this object information, DRAW recognizes the size and shape of the underlying object and then creates a mathematical model based on nodal points and the angle of the lines moving in and out of the node. The number of node points used is dependent upon the complexity of the object being drawn. When the user changes the size of the object, DRAW calculates the new nodal related information and then connects the nodes with the appropriate dots. The quality of the object is not affected by the change because all object information is contained in the nodes, which are always kept current.

In essence, a Corel drawing is nothing more than a mathematical combination of nodes that represent objects. As the objects are placed on top of each other with various attributes, such as line thickness or fill type, the final illustration desired by the user is created. Objects are simplified or made more complex based upon the number of nodes included and their type.

It is important that you think of your drawings as a combination of objects with specific attributes instead of as dots connected on-screen. Once you make this thinking transformation, the overall operation of CorelDRAW! becomes relatively simple to understand and you see the true power of this package.

Understanding Object Outlines, Fills, and Defaults

CorelDRAW! does not really know that a drawing exists. It only knows that there are a certain number of objects that each have specific defining characteristics and that it is supposed to draw these objects in a certain order and orientation.

Most objects consist of two basic components: an outline and an interior fill. The outline is a line that defines the perimeter of the object, and the interior fill determines the color and texture of the space within that perimeter.

Even text characters have both an outline and interior fill, which means that each character is individually controlled, making for some very interesting color and texture combinations. Both the outline and fill can have various designs, colors, and styles. CorelDRAW! allows you to define default characteristics for outlines and fills, which saves you time when you are creating graphic objects, artistic text, and paragraph text.

TIP

You can make your drawing life a lot simpler by setting the default Outline and Interior Fill characteristics early in your drawing's life. Defaults provide more consistency across the various drawing objects and greatly speed up the drawing process. Every time that you change the default, CorelDRAW! applies the new default to all objects you create from that point forward.

TIP

If you don't have an object selected and you choose Apply in a roll-up window or a selection made from a menu, a dialog box appears which allows the choices to become the defaults for the selected object types in this and future sessions.

Using Roll-Up Windows

CorelDRAW! provides roll-up windows that streamline the application of numerous attributes to selected objects. For example, the Pen roll-up window shown in figure 2.5 allows ready access to the fly-out menu features such as line thickness, arrows, dashing, and color. Many of the more widely used CorelDRAW! features (blend, fill, extrude, and so on) have their own roll-up windows. You can open and close the roll-up windows as you need them.

To access a roll-up window, click the roll-up window icon contained within a tool's fly-out menu or choose the desired roll-up's menu option. The appropriate roll-up window appears.

Click the down arrow in the upper-right corner to open the window. Click the up arrow to roll up the window. You can also move the roll-up window to any desired screen location by dragging the roll-up window title bar. To compress the roll-up window and move it to the upper-left corner of the editing screen, for example, click the Control menu box in the upper- left corner of the roll-up window and choose Arrange All.

TIP

You can automatically arrange the screen location of multiple roll-up windows by opening the desired roll-up windows and then choosing Arrange All under the Control-Menu. All roll-up windows are arranged as title bars and moved to the upper-left or upper-right corner of the screen.

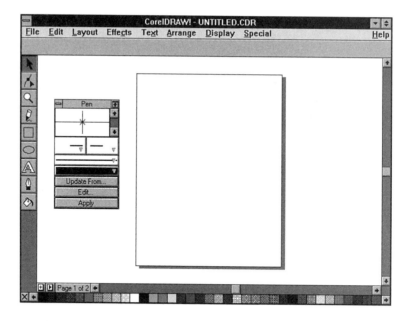

To use a roll-up window, click the attribute or attributes (such as line thickness, dashing, and color) in the roll-up window that you want to use, select the object to which you want to apply the attribute or attributes, and then click Apply in the roll-up window. CorelDRAW! applies the attributes to the selected object. Once you have chosen the attributes you want from a roll-up window, you can apply these attributes to any number of objects simply by selecting each object and clicking Apply in the roll-up window. This procedure is much easier than individually choosing each attribute for each object from a menu.

Using Roll-Up Windows and Styles

The roll-up windows provide ready access to multiple attributes that are related to the same function so that you can apply these attributes all at once instead of as separate operations. You can effectively use roll-up windows to apply a consistent combination of attributes (a *style*) to a set of objects by defining the roll-up selections, selecting the object, and clicking Apply. You can also apply styles to artistic and paragraph text.

These styles include all of the attributes needed to accurately define the appearance of the selected object. When you create a style, you give it a name. You access styles by selecting the object, clicking the right mouse button, and choosing Apply Styles to display all applicable style names. Note that styles are a combination of many different object attributes, but the other defaults deal only with one particular object aspect (for example, fill or outline). CorelDRAW! stores these styles in templates that you can access from within any drawing.

The major benefit associated with using styles is consistency of appearance. Drawings become "busy" when the various text or graphic objects contain many different appearances. Defining and applying styles speeds up your operation of CorelDRAW! and also gives your drawings a professional appearance.

Follow these steps to define a style:

1. Create the graphic object or text.

2. Apply the desired formatting characteristics.

3. Select the object and double-click the right mouse button to display the object menu.

4. Choose the Save As Style option to display the Save Style As dialog box as shown in figure 2.6. Notice the various options that a particular object's style definition includes.

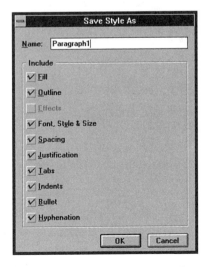

FIG. 2.6

The Save Style As dialog box.

5. Choose the various style options you want included under the style name, type in a style name, and click OK.

The style is now accessible under the Style roll-up window. You can create styles for both Corel text and graphic objects.

Getting On-Line Help

CorelDRAW! comes with an on-line help facility that truly puts a reference book of information at your fingertips. The Help lookup procedures follow the standard Windows help operational procedures, so if you know how to use Help in other Windows applications, you should be able to run the CorelDRAW! help menus.

Clicking **H**elp in the menu bar reveals a drop-down menu that contains several options: Contents, Screen/Menu Help, How To Use Help, Search For Help On, and About CorelDRAW!. Each has a useful and unique function.

Choosing **C**ontents (F1) reveals the table of contents of the help function, which is shown in icon form. Help is available on those items shown by simply clicking on the item and following the string of dialog boxes until you reach your desired topic. When you are finished, click the Back button as many times as necessary to return you to the Contents screen or close the dialog box to exit Help completely.

Choosing Screen/**M**enu Help (Shift+F1) changes the cursor to an arrow and a question mark. Moving this cursor to any currently accessible screen location or menu command (bolded, not dimmed) opens the Help information for that particular feature. This Help function is particularly handy when you are still familiarizing yourself with the screen layout.

Choosing **H**ow To Use Help reveals dialog boxes with instructions on how to use the Help function. You may find its information handy if you plan to use Help on a regular basis, but most operationally related Help topics are covered in this section of the book.

The **S**earch For Help On (Ctrl+F1) menu selection opens the Search dialog box shown in figure 2.7. You can either scroll through the topics in the display list and then double-click your desired topic, or type the name of the topic into the text entry box at the top of the dialog box and then click on **S**how Topics to reveal various topics related to your selection. They are shown in the display box at the bottom of the window. Double-clicking the topic, or selecting the topic and then clicking on **G**o To, takes you to the help section pertaining to your selection.

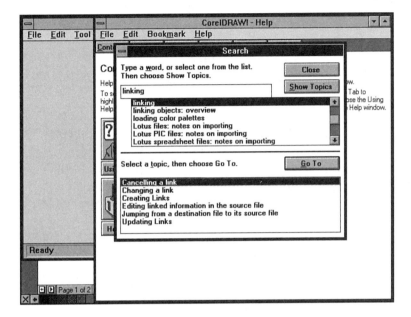

FIG. 2.7

The Search dialog box.

Finally, choosing **A**bout CorelDRAW displays a dialog box that contains information pertaining to the licensed owner, serial number, and image information such as the number of groups, number of objects, and free disk space. This information is handy as a benchmark for determining the complexity of your drawing.

Planning Ahead

The only way that CorelDRAW!'s WYSIWYG (What-You-See-Is-What-You-Get) capability can work properly is if the computer display is formatted to comply with the capabilities of the output device. If you don't consider the desired output form before you start drawing, you may have to redo a great deal of work.

It is also helpful to remember that CorelDRAW! is actually several different software packages (DRAW, CHART, MOSAIC, and so forth) sold in one box, as opposed to many different capabilities provided in a single application (Excel's database and chart features, for example). The Windows 3.1 feature called Object Linking and Embedding enables you to use the Corel packages in a complimentary way. Keeping this feature in mind early in the design process strengthens your work.

Printing Considerations (Monochrome versus Color)

Just as high-quality audio speakers determine the sound quality of a stereo system, your final drawing only looks as good as the final output device. You must design your drawing around that device's limitations.

If the final device is a color PostScript printer, you have a wide variety of high-quality print options and your imagination can soar. If the final device is a monochrome (black-and-white) laser printer, such as a Hewlett-Packard LaserJet 4, the quality is still excellent, but the screen colors may assume unpredictable shades of gray as they are converted from the screen colors to a printer-compatible format.

If you do not take your output device into consideration early in your design process, you may have to correct some of your previous design work to accommodate the final output device requirements. Simple things like choosing Portrait or Landscape printing can dramatically impact the amount of work involved with drawing creation.

The good news with CorelDRAW! is that most Corel objects are created in a vector graphic as opposed to a bitmap format. A vector graphic format allows for major changes to the size and shape of objects without negatively impacting the quality of the final output. So, if you do get caught with an output device change, you should be able to modify the drawings to accommodate the change. A little advance planning helps avoid this situation. Chapter 11 provides tips, procedures, and suggestions on creating high-quality output that is usable by commercial printers.

Object Linking and Embedding

A major benefit of working in the Windows environment is the standard Linking and Embedding feature. These features become particularly handy when working with the various Corel applications.

Object linking provides automatic updating of information created in one application file (called the source) into another application (called the destination). When changes are made to the source file contents, affected sections of the destination file are automatically updated to reflect new changes, or you can define when updates occur. Effective use of these features can greatly increase your efficiency when integrating the various Corel applications with each other and numerous Windows applications (such as Word for Windows).

You make substantial use of these Windows features in the later chapters where the various Corel applications are used in concert to make effective business-related presentations, documents, and illustrations. Whenever possible, look for ways that linking data can make your work more efficient and productive.

Summary

This chapter covers much of the basic information needed to understand CorelDRAW!'s thinking. It covers the basic screen layout, toolbox fundamentals, Corel's unique method of creating objects, and Help menu operation. You are now ready to apply this knowledge in the creation of a simple drawing. This topic is covered in the next chapter.

A Quick Start

The best way to learn a package is to perform simple tasks that enable you to work with many of the package's features. This chapter takes you step-by-step through some of the basic features of CorelDRAW! 4 so that you can immediately begin creating drawings. As you become more comfortable with the program, you will want to experiment with the more advanced concepts covered in later chapters.

Creating a Simple Drawing

The first part of this chapter introduces the basic drawing tools. In this section, you follow the steps to create the simple snowman drawing shown in figure 3.1.

Drawing Circles

If you have ever made a snowman, you probably started with the biggest ball of snow and then made smaller ones to pile on top. For this drawing, however, you are going to make the snowman's head first and then build his body. The head and body are made from circles, which are easy to draw with CorelDRAW!. You use the Ellipse tool to draw circles and ellipses.

FIG. 3.1

The completed snow-
man drawing.

Follow these steps to draw the circles that make up the snowman's
head and body:

1. Choose the Ellipse tool (F7).

2. Place the cross hairs where you want the upper-left corner of the
circle—just slightly above and to the left of the center of the page.

3. Press and hold the Ctrl key and then click and drag the mouse
down and to the right. The outline of the circle appears as you
drag.

NOTE

Holding down the Ctrl key makes the ellipse as long as it is wide, thus
creating a circle.

4. Stop dragging when the circle is the size you want, about 1 inch in
this case. Release the mouse button and then the Ctrl key. You
should have a circle like the one in figure 3.2.

TIP

The size of the circle is given on the status line above the drawing as you
draw the circle.

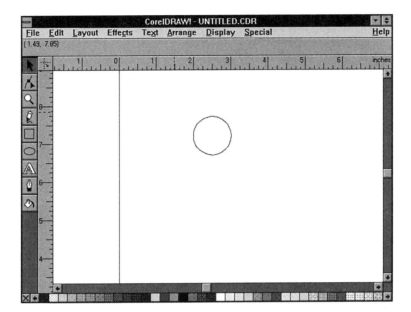

FIG. 3.2

The snowman's head.

5. Draw the middle circle for the body by repeating steps 2 through 4, except make the circle about 1.5 inches. At this point, don't worry about where the circle is on the page.

6. Choose the Pick tool. The circle you just drew should now be selected as indicated by the small black squares (handles) that appear around it.

7. If the circle is not selected, position the Pick tool so that it is touching the circle you just drew and click the mouse button once. The black boxes that appear indicate that the circle is selected (see fig. 3.3). After an object is selected, you can move, shape, or perform other operations on it.

8. With the cursor touching the circle, drag the mouse. The cursor changes to four arrows, and a dashed outline shows where the circle is (see fig. 3.4).

9. When the dashed outline is just touching the bottom of the head circle, release the mouse button.

> **NOTE**
>
> If the second circle isn't exactly where you want it, use the Pick tool to select the circle and then move it again.

FIG. 3.3

Selecting the larger circle.

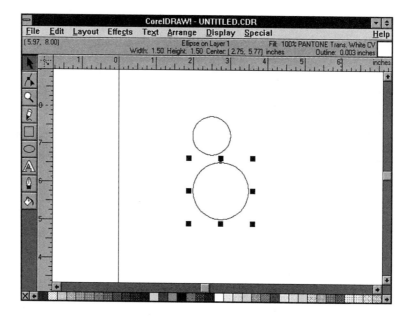

FIG. 3.4

Moving the circle.

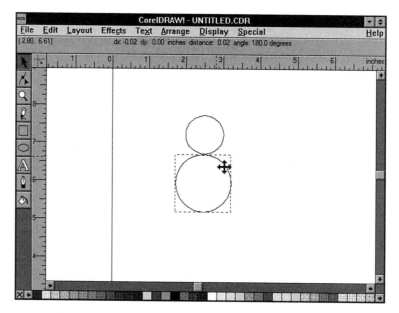

 10. Complete the snowman's body by selecting the Ellipse tool again and drawing the last circle. This one should be about 2 inches in diameter. Move it to the correct place if needed.

Shading the Circles

The snowman's head and body need some color. Although snow is white, it doesn't show up well in the drawing if you don't shade it.

To shade the snowman, follow these steps:

1. Select the Pick tool.

2. Click above and about 1.5 inches to the left of the top of the snowman's head.

3. Drag the cursor down and to the left until the entire snowman is enclosed in the dashed box that appears, as shown in figure 3.5.

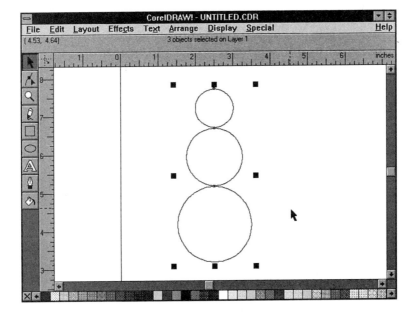

FIG. 3.5

The selected snowman.

4. Release the mouse button. Now all three of the circles are selected, and you can work with them all at once. The status line should say that three objects (the three different circles) are selected. This method of dragging a box around several objects is called *marquee selecting*.

NOTE

If all the objects aren't selected, your box did not enclose all three circles. Simply drag a new marquee box, this time being sure to enclose all three objects.

5. Fill the circles with one of the light gray shades located on the color palette by clicking the gray tone with the left mouse button.

6. Press F4 to display all drawn objects, and then press F3 to return to the prior view.

Drawing the Hat

Every good snowman needs a top hat. For this part of the drawing, you use three different tools: the Rectangle, the Pencil, and the Pen.

To draw the top part of the hat, follow these steps:

1. Choose the Rectangle tool (F6).

2. Somewhere on the blank space in the drawing area, click and drag the mouse to make a rectangle about .5 inch wide and 1 inch tall.

TIP

The Rectangle tool works much like the Ellipse tool. Watch the status line to see the size of the rectangle as you draw it.

3. Release the mouse button.

4. Select the Pick tool. The hat is automatically selected.

5. Make the hat black by clicking the black color on the color palette.

6. Click and drag the rectangle to its place on the head.

7. If you don't like the size of the hat, click one of the black boxes (handles) surrounding the hat. Drag the handle until the hat is the size you want it.

8. Click the hat again, and the corner handles change to curved arrows (see fig. 3.6). You use these arrows to rotate the object.

9. Position the cursor on the upper-left arrow and drag it slightly down and left. The status line indicates the angle of rotation.

10. When the angle is about -10 degrees (see fig. 3.7), release the mouse button.

NOTE

You may want to move the hat a little to make it sit on the head better. Click the hat again to make the arrows change back into handles; then click and drag the hat to where it should be.

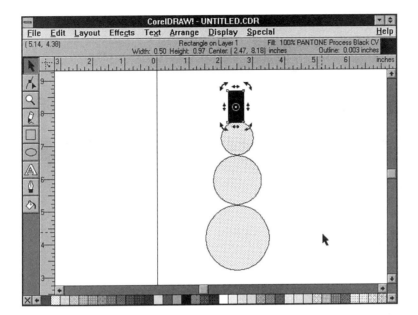

FIG. 3.6

The hat selected with the rotation arrows.

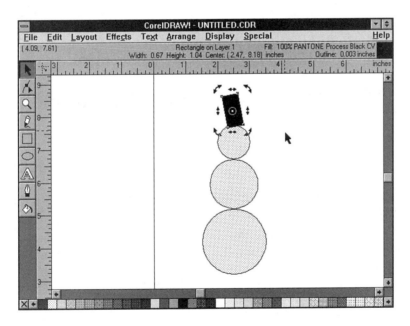

FIG. 3.7

The rotated hat.

To add the brim to the hat, follow these steps:

1. Select the Pencil tool.

2. Position the cursor in a blank area, and click once.

3. Move the cursor until the line is about 1 inch long (see fig. 3.8). Do not hold the mouse button while moving the cursor.

FIG. 3.8

Drawing the brim.

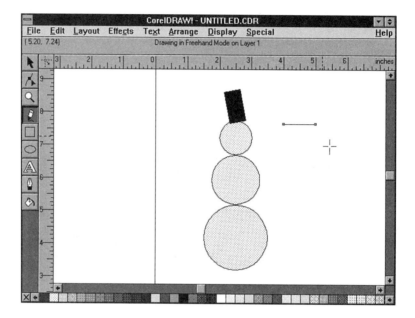

4. Click the mouse button to draw the line.

5. Choose the Outline tool (F12). A fly-out menu appears.

6. Select the third icon from the right on the top row to make the brim thicker.

7. Select the Pick tool and then rotate the brim, using the same method you used to rotate the hat, until the brim and hat are at the same angle.

8. Move the brim to the bottom of the hat.

Drawing the Face

Finally, you are ready to give this snowman some facial features. In this section, you draw two small circles for eyes, a triangle nose, and an arc for a mouth.

Drawing the Eyes

Drawing the eyes involves using many of the tools and techniques you have already used in this chapter. You also learn how to make an exact duplicate of an object in a drawing.

To draw the snowman's eyes, follow these steps:

1. Using the Ellipse tool, draw a small circle, which is to be the first of the snowman's eyes.

2. Click the black color on the color palette to make the eye black.

3. Make the eye the correct size by dragging the handles (small black boxes).

4. Move the eye to the snowman's face.

5. Duplicate the snowman's first eye by pressing Ctrl+D. An exact replica should appear a slight distance from the original eye.

6. Move this second eye to the desired position on the snowman's face.

Drawing the Nose

The nose requires a new technique. You are going to draw an inverted triangle by connecting three lines.

To draw the nose, follow these steps:

1. Select the Pencil tool.

2. Click the mouse button once, and move the cursor horizontally to the right about .2 inch.

3. Click twice, without moving the mouse, to begin a second line at the end point of the first.

4. Move the mouse down and left at a 45-degree angle with respect to the first line until the cursor rests roughly on the location of the second triangle corner.

5. Click twice, without moving the mouse, to begin a third line.

6. Move the cursor at a 45-degree angle to the first line until the cursor rests precisely on the beginning point of the first line.

7. Click once to close the loop.

8. Select the Pick tool.

9. Click the black color in the color palette to make the nose black.

10. Move the nose to the face (see fig. 3.9).

FIG. 3.9

Adding the nose.

Finishing the Face with a Smile

For the finishing touch, give the snowman a smile. The easiest way to create a simple curve, like a smile, is to modify a circle so that only a small arc of the total circle remains.

Follow these steps to create the snowman's smile:

1. Choose the Ellipse tool (F7).

2. Place the cross hairs in a blank part of the drawing area, and draw an ellipse.

3. Choose the Shape tool (F10). Your screen should now look like figure 3.10.

4. Place the point of the tool in the *shaping node* (the small box at the top of the circle).

5. With the pointer outside the circle, drag the mouse down and to the right. You should see the circle being clipped as you drag the mouse (see fig. 3.11).

6. Release the mouse button.

7. Choose the Pick tool, and rotate or size the smile, using the techniques introduced earlier in the chapter, if needed. Then drag the smile to the face.

Congratulations! You have created your first drawing in CorelDRAW!. You made a snowman, and you didn't even have to get cold doing it.

FIG. 3.10

After choosing the Shape tool (zoomed in).

FIG. 3.11

The smile (zoomed in).

Saving the Drawing

At this point, you have put a lot of work into this snowman. Not saving him would be a real shame. Maybe you will want to come back and add some arms and a corncob pipe. Or you might want to add some sunshine and draw him melting into oblivion. In either case, you need to save this drawing to disk if you want to use it again later.

To save your snowman drawing, follow these steps:

1. Choose the **S**ave option from the **F**ile menu (Ctrl+S) to display the Save Drawing dialog box shown in figure 3.12.

FIG. 3.12

The Save Drawing dialog box.

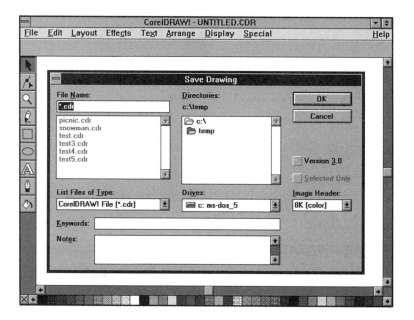

2. In the File Name text box, type the name **snowman**. CorelDRAW! automatically adds the extension .CDR.

3. Choose the appropriate directory and drive.

4. Click OK to save the drawing in CorelDRAW!-compatible format.

You can save the file again later under the same name by pressing Ctrl+S or choosing **S**ave from the **F**ile menu.

TIP

CorelDRAW! provides numerous file formats. Saving and converting these formats is covered in Chapter 9.

Creating a Drawing with Symbols and Clip Art

Two kinds of existing art are available in CorelDRAW!: clip art and symbols. The distinction between them is not absolute, but symbols are generally simpler, and clip art is usually more detailed. This section explains how you access symbols and clip art, add a symbol or clip art to your drawing, modify it, and combine it with other symbols and clip art to create a new picture.

The best way to consider the differences between clip art and symbols is to consider their place in your drawing. Clip art should usually be seen as a starting, or focal, point of a drawing, one which you probably will not want to modify extensively. The complexity of the clip art makes it harder to work with, and the drawing is typically more complete as it stands. A symbol is easier to alter and much less complex. Using a great deal of clip art can create a large file and, depending on your printer, may be difficult or time-consuming to print. Symbols use much less memory and do not significantly increase the size of your file. If you want to get "fancier" with your art work, you can combine clip art and symbols to create complex, professional-looking drawings.

Retrieving Clip Art into a Drawing

To get some practice in combining clip art and symbols in your drawing, you create in this section a flier announcing a company picnic. You begin this flier by importing a clip art image of the sun.

To import the sun image, follow these steps:

1. Start a new page by choosing **File**, **New**. Do not save the changes.

2. From the File menu, choose the **Import** option. The File Import dialog box shown in figure 3.13 appears.

3. Choose the CorelDRAW! Clipart subdirectory and then the General clip art group.

4. Choose the Sun file (SUN062.CDR), and click OK. If you get a message at this point about version 3 and 4 text spacing, simply accept the version 4 text spacing conversion.

FIG. 3.13

The File Import dialog box.

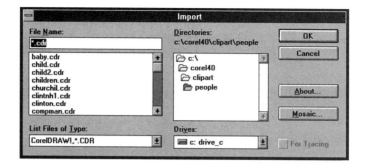

You can use multiple clip art pieces in a drawing by repeating steps 1 through 3. This process saves time and allows for quick, professional-looking drawings.

5. Before making any changes, choose **S**ave from the **F**ile menu.

6. In the File **N**ame box, type the name **picnic** and then click OK. Figure 3.14 shows the sun saved as a new drawing.

FIG. 3.14

Saving the sun clip art as a new drawing.

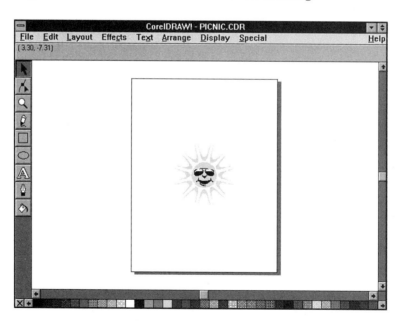

7. Size the image by dragging the control handles, as covered earlier.

Modifying the Clip Art

You may find that the clip art doesn't exactly fit your needs. Maybe your company makes sunglasses, and the glasses in the drawing look too much like the competition's. You can modify the clip art to meet your specific needs. First, to separate the parts of the sun so that you can make changes, follow these steps:

1. Choose the Pick tool.

2. Select the sun.

3. From the **Arrange** menu, choose the **Ungroup** option (Ctrl+U).

4. Deselect the sun drawing by clicking anywhere on the page. The various objects that comprise the sun are now individually accessible.

Enlarging your view of the drawing makes it easy to select objects when several are close together. Follow these steps to zoom in on and remove the sunglasses:

1. Choose the Zoom tool.

2. From the fly-out menu, choose the enlarge icon (the magnifying glass with a + sign).

3. Move the cursor (which looks like a magnifying glass) to the sunglasses, and drag a marquee box around the sunglasses.

4. Select the sunglasses using the Pick tool (see fig. 3.15).

5. Press Del to remove the sunglasses from the drawing.

6. Now choose the Zoom tool again, but this time choose the magnifying glass with the - sign (F3). The view shrinks to the way it was before, and the new sun looks like the one in figure 3.16.

Not only does Mr. Sun not have sunglasses, he doesn't have eyes either. Follow these steps to give him eyes:

1. Select the remaining white eye slits, and press Del to remove them.

2. Choose the Ellipse tool (F7), and draw an ellipse. Give it a black fill by clicking with the left mouse button on the black palette color.

3. Draw a second, smaller ellipse with a solid white fill. Place this second ellipse on the first, near the bottom (see fig. 3.17).

FIG. 3.15

The enlarged sun with glasses selected.

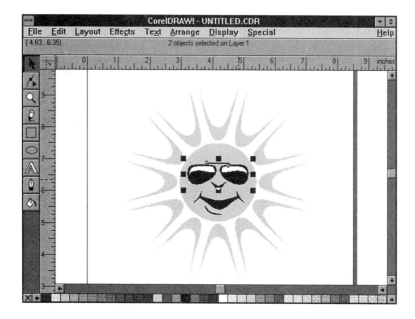

FIG. 3.16

The modified sun clip art (with sunglasses deleted).

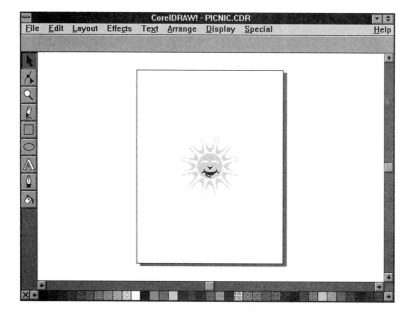

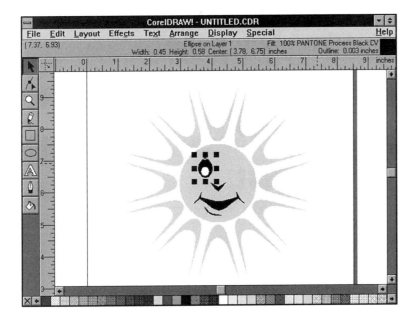

FIG. 3.17

Drawing a new eye.

4. Select the black-and-white ellipses by dragging a marquee box around them with the Pick tool.

5. From the **Arrange** menu, choose the **G**roup option (Ctrl+G) to form these two objects into a group that represents Mr. Sun's first eye.

Next you need to copy the eye group and move the copy into place as the second eye.

6. Select the first eye group. Change the size of the eye if necessary.

7. Press Ctrl+D to create a duplicate of the object.

8. Move the eyes into the desired positions inside Mr. Sun's face.

9. Select all the components of the sun drawing by choosing **E**dit, Select **A**ll. Then choose the **G**roup option from the **A**rrange menu to form the entire arrangement into a single group with preserved alignment. The results are shown in figure 3.18.

10. Because you just made a major change to the drawing, you should save the drawing again. Press Ctrl+S or choose **F**ile, **S**ave to save the drawing.

FIG. 3.18

The modified sun clip art (with new eyes added).

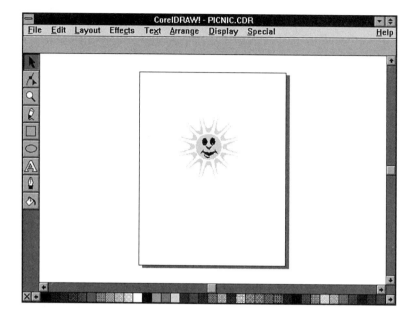

Adding Text

The picnic flier is off to a good start, but it isn't very useful without some text telling what the flier is all about. To add text to your flier, follow these steps:

1. Choose the Text tool. (If the star is displayed, click it and hold down the mouse button until the fly-out menu appears; then choose the letter *A*.)

2. Place the cross hairs above the sun you just created, and type the words **PICNIC TIME!**

NOTE

For more on working with text, see Chapter 8.

3. Move the cross hairs beneath the sun, and type the following text, pressing Enter at the end of each line:

   COME ONE, COME ALL to

   The Acme Company Picnic

Saturday June 10th at

The Old Camp Grounds

4. Click the Pick tool to add the text to the drawing.

5. Select the lower text with the Pick tool, and then choose Edit Text from the Text menu. The Artistic Text dialog box shown in figure 3.19 appears.

FIG. 3.19

The Artistic Text dialog box.

6. Choose the Center option, and click OK. If your text looks different from that shown in the figure, check the point size and change it accordingly.

> **TIP**
>
> If you see an error in what you have typed, you can correct it right on-screen by clicking at the error location within the text string, deleting the old text, and typing in the new text.

> **TIP**
>
> You may need to move the text into its correct alignment with respect to the rest of the document. Simply click and drag the text just as you would any other object.

Figure 3.20 shows the text added to your sun drawing.

FIG. 3.20

The modified sun clip art
with text added.

Creating a Border and a Drop Shadow

A border and a drop shadow will give your flier a more completed look.
To add these items, follow these steps:

1. Choose the Rectangle tool (F6), and draw a rectangle around the
   picture.

2. Select the rectangle you just drew, and make a duplicate by pressing Ctrl+D.

3. Move the second rectangle up and slightly to the right.

4. Change the fill of the second rectangle to black; then place it at
   the back of the other objects by choosing the **O**rder To **B**ack option from the **A**rrange menu.

5. Change the fill of the original rectangle to white; then move it to
   the back of the other objects by choosing the **O**rder To **B**ack option from the **A**rrange menu.

6. From the Arrange menu, choose **O**rder Forward **O**ne to place the
   white rectangle above the black rectangle and beneath the other
   objects. The results should look like figure 3.21.

7. Save your drawing by choosing **F**ile, **S**ave (Ctrl+S).

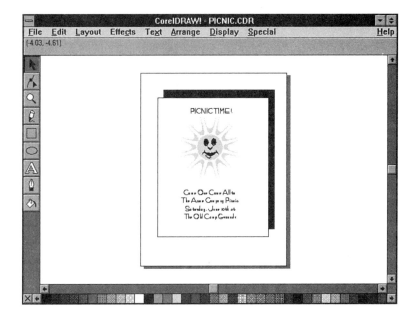

FIG. 3.21

Adding the drop shadow to the flier.

Adding Symbols

Now you can add a few related symbols to finish your flier. Follow these steps:

1. Choose the Text tool and hold down the mouse button to display the fly-out menu.

2. Choose the star symbol to display the Symbols roll-up window (see fig. 3.22).

3. Click the arrow pointing down in the upper-right corner to display the drop-down list box, scroll through the different symbol groups, and choose the Sports Figures group.

4. Choose an appropriate symbol (such as a ball player, a swimmer, or a golfer), and drag it from its location in the Sports Figures group to the upper-left corner of your drawing. Choose another symbol, and drag it to the upper-right corner.

FIG. 3.22

The Symbols roll-up window.

Previewing and Printing

You can preview your drawing at any time by pressing the F9 key. CorelDRAW! shows you exactly how your picture will print. (The only exception occurs if you do not have a color printer. Even though your drawing may have color, the resulting printout will not.) If you have a properly installed printer on line, you can print the drawing by following these steps:

1. From the **F**ile menu, choose the **P**rint option. The Print dialog box appears (see fig. 3.23). If the Preview Image box is selected, the picture displays with margin cutoffs, which appear as dashed lines near the edge of the page. (These are typically .25 inch wide all around the picture. Any portion of the picture beyond these lines will not print.)

2. Click OK.

You may want to save your drawing now by pressing Ctrl+S to update the version of the file you already saved to disk.

Considering Copyright When Using Clip Art

One final note about clip art is in order. The clip art provided by CorelDRAW! is yours to use as you like within the copyright restrictions imposed by federal law. You should always be cognizant of the copyright laws that apply to artwork and of the limitations on its use. Corel requests that all clip art be designated as Corel copyright material, but this designation is not always required if the clip art has been substantially modified. If you have any doubts about the legality of your use of a piece of clip art, consult a copyright attorney before you use the art.

Corel provides a statement pertaining to copyright licensing on the copyright pages of the user's manual. If you plan to use the clip art for professional applications, you should review this information before proceeding.

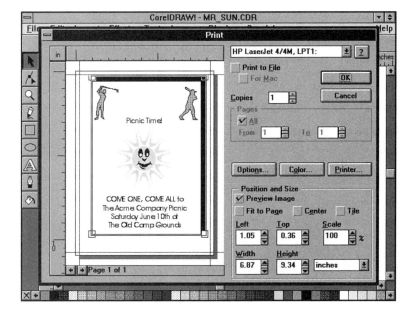

FIG. 3.23

The Print dialog box.

Summary

In this chapter, you learned some basic procedures to give you a quick start in CorelDRAW!. By creating a simple snowman, you saw how to draw basic shapes such as a straight line, a curved line, a rectangle, and ellipses. You also learned how you can make modifications to these shapes and combine them to make more complex drawings. And you learned how to save a drawing so that you can use it again later.

This chapter also introduced you to clip art and symbols, including methods of modifying the clip art to meet your specific needs. Finally, you printed your company picnic flier, complete with clip art, symbols, and text.

This chapter merely scratches the surface of the total capabilities provided with CorelDRAW! and its companion applications, and you are encouraged to delve into the more advanced features so that you can make your imagination a reality.

Proceed to Chapter 4 to learn more about drawing the basic shapes that combine to make up a Corel drawing.

Learning CorelDRAW! Basics

PART

II

OUTLINE

A Detailed Look at Object Drawing

The previous chapter introduced you to the three tools CorelDRAW! provides for drawing objects: the Pencil tool, the Rectangle tool, and the Ellipse tool. With only these three tools, you can create complex graphics and virtually unlimited illustrations. All three tools use the same technique to draw an object: click the tool, click anywhere on the page, and then drag the mouse. You have many options available to you while drawing an object and many ways to change it after you finish.

This chapter leads you through the basics of creating and reshaping an object; later chapters cover the many advanced commands and options you have when creating an illustration in CorelDRAW!, such as Power-Lines and Dimension Lines. Reading this chapter will give you an understanding of lines, shapes, and objects and will prepare you for creating your own complex illustrations.

Drawing Straight Lines

You create straight lines with the Pencil tool (accessed by pressing F5 or clicking the toolbox icon), which you can set to draw in one of two modes: Freehand and Bézier. Freehand mode is much like drawing on the screen with a pencil, but Bézier mode requires you to establish anchor points, or nodes, which CorelDRAW! then connects with lines. The two modes work very similarly when drawing straight lines, except that Freehand mode assumes that when you release the mouse, it's the end of the line. Bézier assumes that you will continue the next line segment when you release the mouse.

To change from one mode to the other, click the Pencil tool and hold down the mouse button until you see the fly-out menu (see fig. 4.1). The first button in the fly-out menu is for the Freehand mode, and the second is for the Bézier mode (the three other buttons are for creating Dimension Lines for technical drawings, covered later in this chapter); click either the Freehand or Bézier button to choose that drawing mode.

TIP

Double-clicking the left mouse button on the Pencil tool reveals the fly-out menu.

TIP

The status line on your CorelDRAW! window tells you which drawing mode you are in.

Drawing a Straight Line in Freehand Mode

Freehand is the most commonly used drawing mode because you see your line as you draw it. This section introduces Freehand drawing techniques.

To draw a straight line in Freehand mode, follow these steps:

1. Click the Pencil tool and hold down the mouse button to display the fly-out menu, or double-click on the Pencil icon.

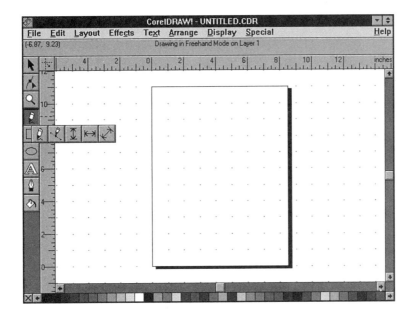

FIG. 4.1

The Pencil tool fly-out menu showing Freehand and Bézier icons.

2. Click the Freehand mode button. The cursor changes to cross hairs; however, the cross hairs do not appear until you position your pointer on the drawing area.

3. Position the cross hairs in the drawing area where you want the line to begin, and click the mouse button. Do not click and drag or you will not get a straight line.

4. Move the cross hairs, and you see a line stretching from the original point waiting for you to anchor it somewhere on the drawing area. Position the cursor at the point where you want the line to end, and click again.

CorelDRAW! connects these two points for you with a straight line (see fig. 4.2). If you hold down the Ctrl key while you draw a straight line in Freehand mode, you constrain the line to horizontal, vertical, or an angle that is a multiple of 15 degrees.

TIP

Under the **S**pecial menu, choose Pr**e**ferences (Ctrl+J) and then choose Constrain Angle to change the degree of this angle. It defaults to 15 degrees.

FIG. 4.2

Drawing a straight line
in Freehand mode.

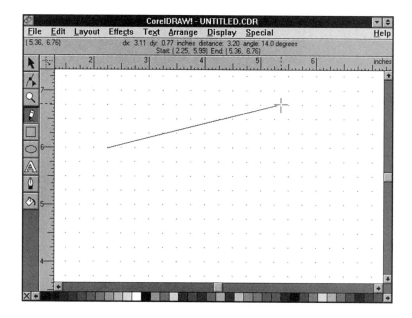

Drawing a Straight Line in Bézier Mode

Follow these steps to draw a straight line in Bézier mode:

1. Click the Pencil tool and hold down the mouse button to display
the fly-out menu.

2. Click the Bézier mode button. The cursor changes to cross hairs,
which appear once you move the cursor to the drawing area.

3. Position the cross hairs in the drawing area where you want the
line to begin, and click. Be sure to release the mouse button before you begin to move the cross hairs, or CorelDRAW! will think
you want to draw a curve.

4. Position the cursor at the point where you want the line to end
and click again (see fig. 4.3). CorelDRAW! connects these two
points for you with a straight line.

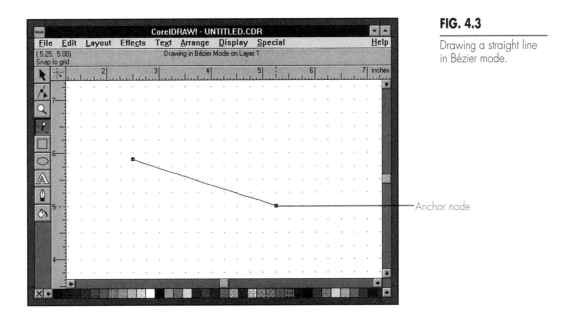

FIG. 4.3

Drawing a straight line in Bézier mode.

Anchor node

Drawing a Single Object Using Several Straight Lines

To create multiple straight lines that are connected as one object, keep using the Pencil tool and click again where you ended your last line. As long as you are within five pixels of where you ended your last line, CorelDRAW! assumes that you want the lines to be joined. If you make a mistake, pull down the **E**dit menu and choose the **U**ndo command to delete the last line segment, or press Ctrl+Z.

> **TIP**
>
> You can change the distance CorelDRAW! gives you when connecting lines and curves by going to the **S**pecial menu, choosing Pr**e**ferences, choosing C**u**rves, and adjusting the figure in the Auto**J**oin option. Make the number higher than five pixels to increase the maximum distance at which CorelDRAW! automatically connects lines.

To draw an object using straight lines, follow these steps:

1. Click on the Pencil tool and hold down the mouse button to display the fly-out menu.

2. Choose either Freehand or Bézier mode by clicking on the appropriate button. The cursor changes to cross hairs.

3. Position the cross hairs on the drawing area where you want the beginning of one line segment of the object. Click once to anchor the line.

4. Move the cross hairs to where you want the beginning of the next line segment of the object. Click twice in Freehand mode, once in Bézier mode. This completes one side of your object and anchors the line for the next line segment (see fig. 4.4).

FIG. 4.4

Drawing an object using multiple straight lines.

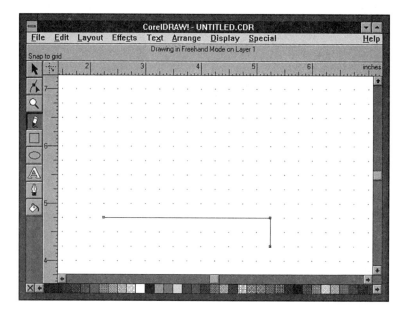

5. Continue moving your cross hairs and double-clicking in Freehand mode or single-clicking in Bézier mode to end one line and begin another.

6. When you come back to the original point of your object, or wherever you want to end the line, click one last time (see fig. 4.5).

TIP

Read the status line on your CorelDRAW! document for information on line length, angle, and so forth, to ensure consistency.

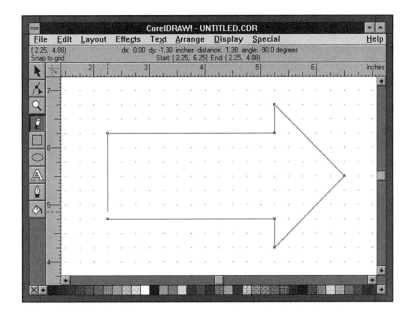

FIG. 4.5

Complete the object by clicking again on the original point, which converts an open path object into a closed path object which can be filled.

Drawing Curved Lines

You also use the Pencil tool to create curved lines. With curved lines, the mode you choose has much more effect on your control of the line. If you only need a rough drawing, use the Freehand mode. Drawing in Freehand mode is much like drawing with a pencil, but you may find the effect too rough and too many nodes to be acceptable. If accuracy is essential, use the Bézier mode. Drawing in Bézier mode gives you elegant curves with a minimum of nodes.

For more control when creating a line with many segments, pause before drawing each new segment to allow the CorelDRAW! screen to redraw so you can view the curve. Relax, and remember that you can reshape lines created in both Freehand and Bézier modes by moving, adding, or deleting a node using the Shape tool, which is covered later in this chapter.

TIP

Draw curved lines using as few nodes as possible to simplify your drawings; fewer nodes make drawings easier to work with and speed up screen refresh times. You can always use the Shape tool later to add more nodes if needed.

Drawing a Curved Line in Freehand Mode

To draw a curved line in the Freehand mode, follow these steps:

1. Click the Pencil tool to display the fly-out menu.

2. Click the Freehand mode button. The cursor becomes cross hairs.

3. Position the cross hairs in the drawing area where you want the line to begin.

4. Click and drag, drawing the curve as if you were drawing with a pencil on-screen (see fig. 4.6).

TIP

If you make a mistake before you end the line, hold down the Shift key while continuing to drag and go back over the line segment you just drew. (This technique does not work on previous line segments.) Release the Shift key to return to regular drawing.

FIG. 4.6

Drawing a curved line in Freehand mode.

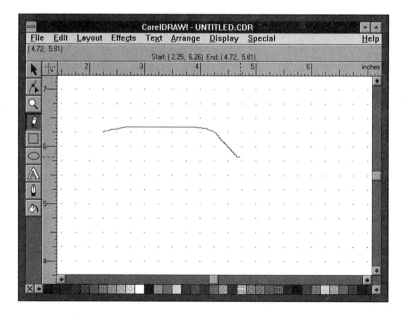

5. When you reach the end of the curve, release the mouse button. Notice that CorelDRAW! adds nodes for you at each point on the curve where the direction of the curve changes.

TIP

You can add a curve to an existing line or curve by using the Pick tool to select the curve to be changed and then using the Freehand drawing tool to click at either end node and continue drawing. Autojoin joins the curve or line segment with the one that you select.

Drawing a Curved Line in Bézier Mode

A Bézier curve is a line that you form by setting anchor points and then shaping the curve using control points. Using Bezier mode to create curves minimizes the number of nodes, but decreases the level of complexity allowed with each curved segment (see fig. 4.7).

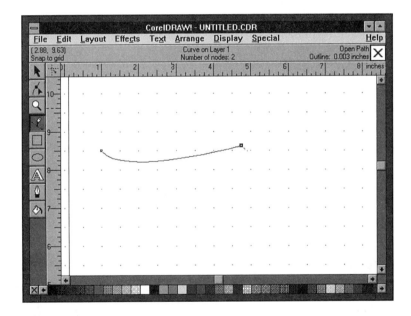

FIG. 4.7

A completed Bézier curve.

Drawing curved lines in Bézier mode may appear complex in written instructions, but a little practice can get you familiar with the process. Plus, Bézier gives you smooth curves with a minimum of nodes. Bézier curves are particularly useful when you want a precise illustration. This is the mode to use when accuracy is critical.

To draw a curved line in Bézier mode, follow these steps:

1. Click the Pencil tool and hold down the mouse button to display the fly-out menu.

2. Click Bézier mode button. The cursor changes to cross hairs.

3. Position the cross hairs in the drawing area where you want the line to begin.

4. Press once to set the first anchor point and continue to hold down the mouse button. A node appears to indicate that this is the start of the curve.

5. Still holding down the mouse button, start to drag the cursor. Two control points, one of which follows your cursor, appear on opposite sides of the node (see fig. 4.8).

To set the height or depth of the curve, make the distance between the control points larger or smaller. The larger the distance is between the node and the control points, the larger the curve. The smaller the distance is between the node and control points, the tighter the curve. The angle of the line connecting the control points determines the slope of the curve.

TIP

Hold down the Ctrl key to constrain the control points to move in 15-degree increments.

FIG. 4.8

The control points of a curve node drawn in Bézier mode.

Control points—

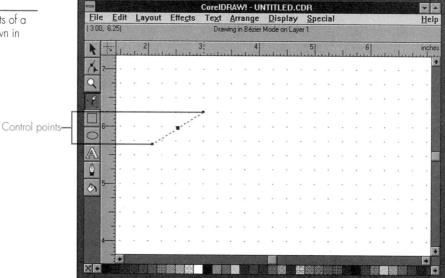

6. When the control points are where you want them, release the mouse button.

7. Move the cross hairs to the point on the drawing area where you want the line to end, and click the mouse button. CorelDRAW! places the second node at that point, and then connects the node to the first node with a curved line showing the characteristics you chose during your placement of the control points (see fig. 4.9).

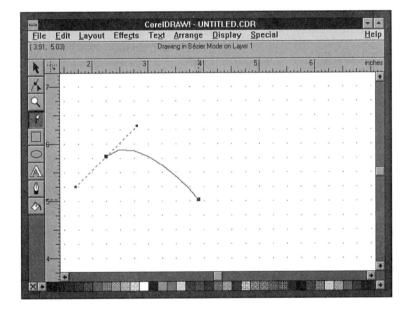

FIG. 4.9

A completed Bézier curve.

Reshaping a Curve by Changing Its Nodes and Control Points

You can come back later and make adjustments to a curve or line you created in either Freehand or Bézier mode. Every curved line in Corel-DRAW! has at least two nodes, which you can move with the Shape tool to reshape the curve end points. Each node has one or two control points associated with it. You move the control points to reshape the curve. You can delete or add nodes, or create a break in a line segment, all of which also change the curve. The control points show the nodal slope characteristics of the approaching or departing line.

Plus, you can change the curve node to a different type, depending on what characteristics you want the curve to have. There are three types of curve nodes: cusp, smooth, and symmetrical.

Changing a Curve by Moving Its Control Points

To reshape a curve by moving its control points, follow these steps:

1. Click the Shape tool.

2. Click the curve you want to reshape. The nodes of the curve become visible.

3. Click the node you want to change. The control points for the node become visible.

4. Click and drag the control points until the curve is the shape you want.

TIP

If a node overlaps a control point, click white space to end the curve and make sure no nodes are selected. Then hold down the Shift key and drag the control point out from under the node.

 CorelDRAW! 4 also allows you to drag directly on the line with the Shape tool to shape the curve. Control points don't actually need to be selected at all.

Changing a Curve by Moving Its Nodes

To reshape a curve by moving its nodes, follow these steps:

1. Click the Shape tool.

2. Click the curve you want to reshape. The nodes of the curve become visible.

3. Click the single node you want to move, or Shift-click to select more than one node to move. Nodes become filled black squares when selected.

TIP

To select the first node on a certain curve, press the Home key. To select the last node, press the End key.

4. Click and drag the node(s) until the curve is the shape you want.

Changing a Curve by Editing Its Nodes

The three different types of nodes are defined by how their control points move.

- A *cusp* node has one or two control points; the control points move independently of each other so line segments can change direction sharply on either side of the node (see fig. 4.10).

- A *smooth* node always has two control points that lie on a straight line that passes through the node so the curve stays smooth; the control points can be different distances from the node (see fig. 4.11).

- A *symmetrical* node always has two control points that are connected by a straight line, and the control points are always an equal distance from the node for a smooth and balanced curve. Symmetrical is usually the default setting for nodes (see fig. 4.12).

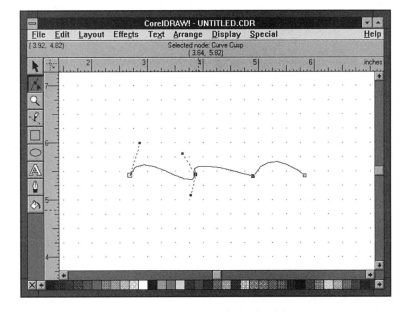

FIG. 4.10

A cusp node.

To reshape a curve by editing its nodes, follow these steps:

1. Click the Shape tool.

2. Click the curve you want to reshape. The nodes of the curve become visible.

FIG. 4.11

A smooth node.

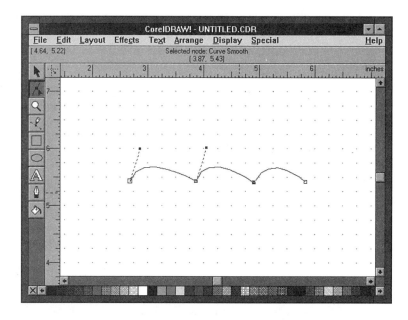

FIG. 4.12

A symmetrical node.

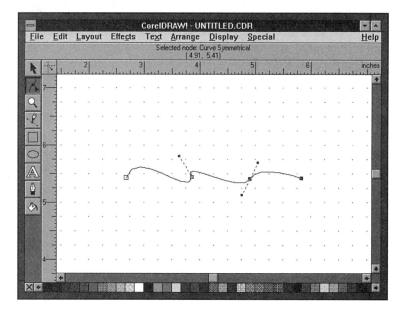

3. Click the single node you want to edit, or Shift-click to select more than one node. Nodes become filled black squares when selected.

4. Double-click the last (or only) node you want to edit to activate the Node Edit roll-up window (see fig. 4.13). Grayed options are not available. The options for editing a node or line segment are the following:

Option	Purpose
+	Adds nodes
−	Deletes nodes and segments
⟦⟧	Joins two end nodes
⟦⟧	Breaks the curve at a node
Auto-Reduce	Deletes extraneous nodes
To Line	Changes segments to lines or curves
To Curve	Converts line node to a curve node
Stretch	Stretches and changes a segment
Rotate	Rotates and skews a segment
Cusp	Makes nodes cusped
Smooth	Makes nodes smooth
Align	Aligns nodes
Symmet	Makes nodes symmetrical
Elastic mode	Makes movement of nodes a factor of how close they are to the base node (the one you drag)

Drawing a Curve-Sided Object

Drawing a curve-sided object in Freehand mode emulates drawing with a pencil: you click where you want the object to begin, hold down the mouse button, and draw. If you want to draw a closed object so that you can fill it later, make sure you end by clicking your original point again so that CorelDRAW! knows to connect all the line segments.

FIG. 4.13

The Node Edit roll-up window.

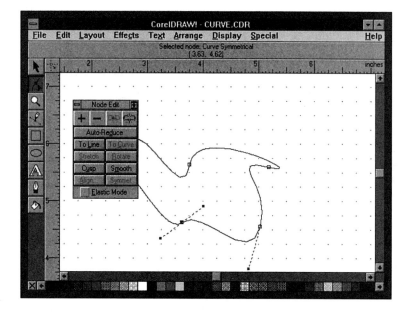

In Bézier mode, however, you repeat a series of steps to set the nodes and the curve characteristics. To draw a curve-sided object in Bézier mode, follow these steps:

1. Follow the steps for drawing a curved line in Bézier mode.

2. Still holding down the mouse button, drag to set the control points for the second curved line segment. If you want a smooth curve with one bump for this line segment, continue to drag in the direction the curve is moving in the first line segment. If you want a smooth curve with two bumps (indicating the curve has changed direction), drag in the opposite direction that the curve is moving in the first line segment.

3. Release the mouse button, and CorelDRAW! redraws the line segment to include the new node (see fig. 4.14).

4. Repeat these steps to finish the curved object. If you want a closed shape, place the final node on top of the first node. Just click within five pixels of the first node and drag.

TIP

Press the space bar twice to draw stand-alone curved line segments unconnected to the previous line.

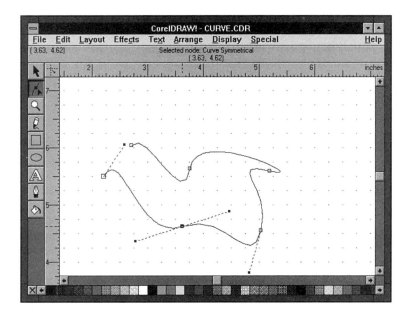

FIG. 4.14

Drawing a curve-sided object in Bézier mode.

Creating Rectangular and Square Objects

You draw both rectangles and squares using the Rectangle tool (or by pressing F6). You can build the dimensions of your rectangle or square either from one corner to its diagonal or from a center point outward. After you draw the rectangle or square, you have the option of adding rounded corners. If you decide you want square corners instead, you can easily change them back.

> The status line gives you the exact dimensions of the rectangle or square as you draw.

TIP

Drawing a Rectangle or a Square from a Corner Point

To draw a rectangle or square from a corner point, follow these steps:

1. Click the Rectangle tool. The cursor changes to cross hairs.

2. Position the cross hairs in the drawing area at the point where you want one corner of the rectangle.

3. Click and drag in any direction until the rectangle is the desired size; then release the mouse button to complete the rectangle. CorelDRAW! creates a rectangle shape with one corner fixed at the original point as you drag the cursor (see fig. 4.15).

   To create a square, press the Ctrl key while clicking and dragging the Rectangle tool. Both sides of the rectangle are sized equally to create a square when you release the mouse button.

FIG. 4.15

Drawing a rectangle
from a corner point.

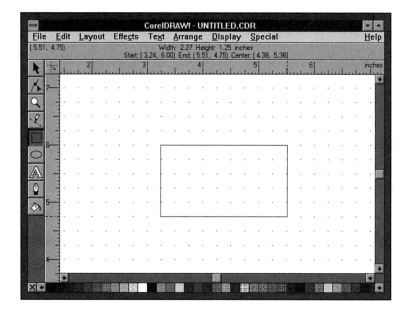

Drawing a Rectangle from a Center Point

To draw a rectangle or a square from a center point, follow these steps:

1. Click the Rectangle tool; the cursor changes to cross hairs.

2. Position the cross hairs in the drawing area at the point where you want the center of the rectangle.

3. Hold down the Shift key, and then click and drag from that center point to get the correct width and depth of the rectangle. When the rectangle is the desired size, release the mouse button (see fig. 4.16). Be sure not to release the Shift key until after you release the mouse button, or you automatically go into drawing a rectangle from a corner point.

To draw a square from its center point, press and hold both the Ctrl key and the Shift key while dragging the Rectangle tool.

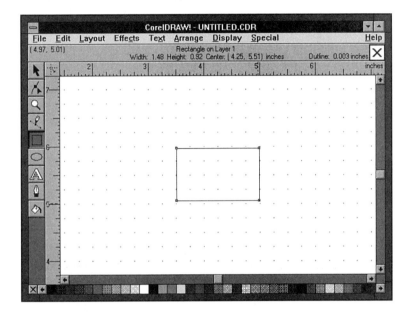

FIG. 4.16

Drawing a rectangle from a center point.

Rounding the Corners of a Rectangle or Square

TIP

Make sure the rectangle or square is the correct size before you add rounded corners. If you later size an object with rounded corners, the corners may appear distorted.

To round the corners of a rectangle or square, follow these steps:

1. Click the Shape tool.

2. Click any one of the lines of the rectangle or square you want to change so that the corner nodes appear.

3. Click any one of the corner nodes and, while holding down the mouse button, slide the node down either side of the rectangle and away from the corner. If you move one corner node, all the other nodes move at the same time.

4. When the corners of the rectangle are rounded to the correct degree, release the mouse button (see fig. 4.17).

FIG. 4.17

Moving corner nodes to make rounded corners.

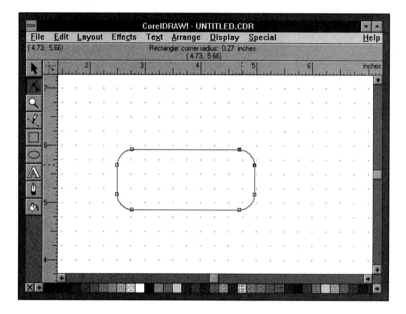

5. To return to square corners, drag a corner node back to the corner position.

TIP

To create a series of rectangles or squares all with the same corner radius, activate Snap To Grid so that the corner nodes align automatically from one grid increment to the next. Pull down the **L**ayout menu and choose **S**nap To G**r**id. The status line on your document window also tells you the radius of the corner.

Drawing Circular Shapes

You draw both a circle and an ellipse (an oblong circle) in CorelDRAW! with the same Ctrl and Shift key operations you use to draw a rectangle and square. You also use the same two methods of sizing an ellipse or circle, either from one corner to the other, or from a center point out. To figure out where exactly to put your cursor when creating a circular shape, imagine that an ellipse fits inside an imaginary rectangle and that a circle fits inside an imaginary square. Think of this imaginary square or rectangle as the defining rectangle.

Drawing an Ellipse or a Circle from a Corner Point

To draw an ellipse or circle from a corner point, follow these steps:

1. Click the Ellipse tool; the cursor changes to cross hairs.

You also can choose the Ellipse tool by pressing F7.

TIP

2. Position the cross hairs in the drawing area where you want one corner of the defining rectangle of the ellipse.

3. Click and drag in any direction until the ellipse is the desired size, and then release the mouse button. As you click and drag, CorelDRAW! creates an ellipse shape with one corner fixed at the original point (see fig. 4.18). The second click creates the opposite corner of the defining rectangle.

   To create a circle, press and hold the Ctrl key while clicking and dragging the Ellipse tool.

Drawing an Ellipse or a Circle from a Center Point

To draw an ellipse or a circle from a center point, follow these steps:

1. Click the Ellipse tool so that the cursor changes to cross hairs.

2. Position the cross hairs in the drawing area where you want the center of the ellipse.

3. Hold down the Shift key, and then click and drag from that center point to get the correct width and depth of the ellipse. When the ellipse is the desired size, release the mouse button (see

fig. 4.19). Be sure not to release the Shift key until after you release the mouse button, or you automatically go into drawing an ellipse from a corner point.

To create a circle, press and hold the Ctrl key while holding down the Shift key and clicking and dragging the Ellipse tool.

FIG. 4.18

Drawing an ellipse from a corner point.

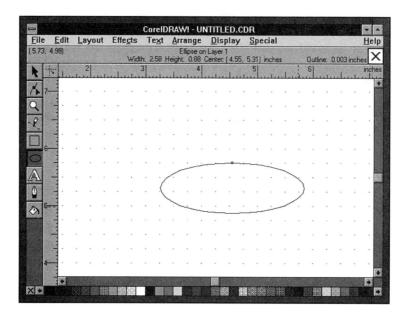

Drawing a Pie Wedge or an Arc

You can modify an ellipse to create a pie wedge or an arc. Even after you modify an ellipse into a pie wedge or arc, however, CorelDRAW! shows you the full ellipse shape in the highlight box.

Drawing a Pie Wedge

To draw a pie wedge, follow these steps:

1. Follow the steps for drawing an ellipse or circle.

2. Click the Shape tool, and then click the outline of the ellipse. A single node appears on the ellipse.

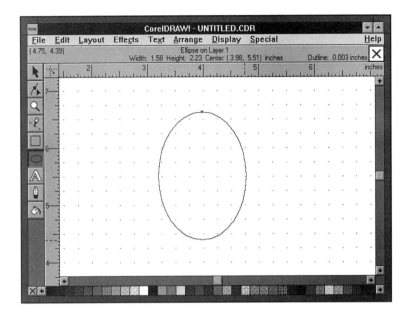

FIG. 4.19

Drawing an ellipse from a center point.

3. Click this node and drag it in either direction on the ellipse with the pointer outside of the object perimeter to create two nodes with an arc in between. Release the mouse button.

> **TIP**
>
> Hold down the Ctrl key while you make modifications to constrain the angle of the nodes to 15-degree increments.

4. Click the node and drag inside the ellipse perimeter to create a pie wedge. Release the mouse button when the wedge is the size you want (see fig. 4.20).

Drawing an Arc

To draw an arc, follow these steps:

1. Follow the steps for drawing an ellipse or a circle.

2. Click the Shape tool, and then click the outline of the ellipse. A single node appears on the ellipse.

3. Click this node and drag it in either direction with the pointer outside the ellipse until the arc is the size you want, and then release the mouse button (see fig. 4.21).

FIG. 4.20

Drawing a pie wedge.

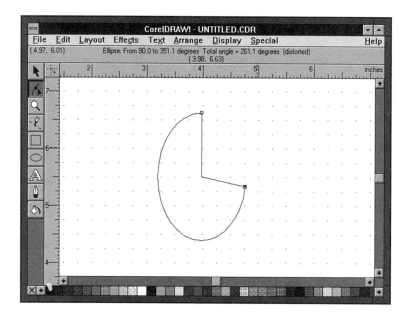

FIG. 4.21

Drawing a circular arc.

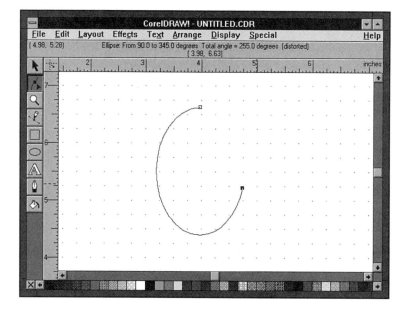

Understanding Object Components

The squares, circles, lines, and curves you create in this chapter are all CorelDRAW! objects, as are any symbols, text blocks, bitmapped art, or other graphics you may import. All objects have dimensions, starting points, and ending points, and are on a specific layer within the CorelDRAW! document. All objects also have an outline (the border around the edges), of a certain thickness in a certain color, and a fill in a certain color or pattern; objects you create are assigned default values for these outlines and fills, but you can change them later.

Determining Object Characteristics

One way to determine the characteristics of an object is to click the Pick tool, and then select the object by clicking its outline (see fig. 4.22). When you select an object, a set of eight black squares (scaling handles) appears to mark the boundary of its highlighting box. Then read the status line at the top of the CorelDRAW! window for information, such as the name of the object (if it is a shape created within CorelDRAW!), which layer it resides on, its measurements, its center point location, the thickness of the line on its outside edge, and the color of the fill, if any. You can also find out how many nodes (anchoring points) an object has.

NOTE

An X in the fill area on the status line indicates that the object selected has no fill, which makes it transparent for the objects beneath it.

Understanding Open and Closed Path Objects

The main difference between an open and closed path object is that the closed path object can accept an interior fill (a color or texture), but the open path object cannot (see fig. 4.23). Curved lines, straight lines, and some curved and polygon shapes are usually open path objects.

FIG. 4.22

Characteristics of a
selected object.

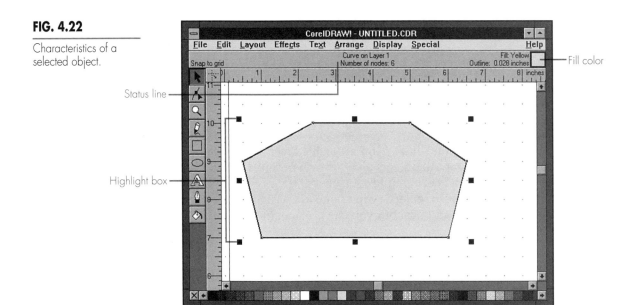

FIG. 4.23

Closed path and open
path objects.

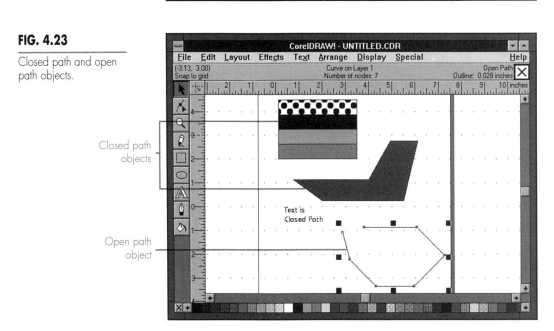

Rectangles, circles, squares, and text are closed path objects. Sometimes an object appears to be an enclosed shape or to have closed

paths, when really the line segments are open paths that merely intersect. You can check whether an object is unfillable by choosing the Pick tool, clicking on the object, and checking whether the status line says Open Path on the Fill Indicator. For example, an ellipse modified to be an arc using the previous procedure is an open path and cannot be filled. The pie shape, on the other hand, is a closed path and fillable.

The color or pattern inside a closed object is its fill. CorelDRAW! gives you a wide assortment of fills in various patterns and colors. Most fills have their own controls and special menus. You can also make or import your own colors, fills, or graphics done in CorelDRAW! or other programs. To fill an open path, you must close it first by joining the two end line segments.

Drawing an Open Path Object

To draw an open path object, use the Pencil tool in either Freehand or Bézier mode and draw a straight line object or a curved line object. Do not connect the final line segment to the original node.

Drawing a Closed Path Object

When you draw a straight line object or a curved line object and complete the shape by clicking back on the beginning node, CorelDRAW! often completes the closed path for you. If you attempt to fill the object and the status line tells you it is Open Path, you can easily convert it.

Converting an Open Path Object to a Closed Path Object

Use the Join command in the Node Edit roll-up window to join the end nodes of an open path to complete a closed path. The Join command joins two end nodes (but you can accomplish a Join command on several pairs of nodes simultaneously). Before you can join nodes on two separate objects, you must first combine the objects by selecting the objects and then choosing **Arrange Combine**.

To convert an open path object to a closed path object, follow these steps:

1. Find the end nodes on your open path object that you want to close.

2. Click the Shape tool, and then select the two nodes to join by Shift-clicking them or by dragging a marquee box around the two nodes.

3. Double-click one of the selected nodes (or press Ctrl+F10), and the Node Edit roll-up window appears on-screen (see fig. 4.24).

4. Click the Join icon in the roll-up window, and CorelDRAW! redraws the object as a closed path that can then be filled.

FIG. 4.24

Joining end nodes to make a closed path object.

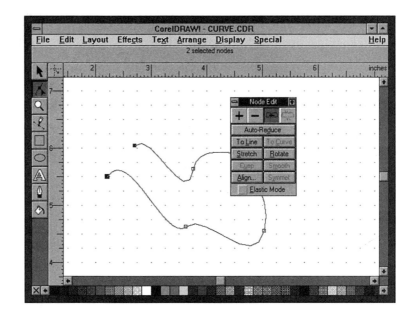

TIP

To automatically select the first and last node in a curve, first select the curve with the Shape tool. Press Home, and then press Shift+End. Then use Join to make a closed shape. The End key function is new to release 4.

You can convert a closed path into an open path by first selecting a node, and then choosing the Break icon located in the roll-up window.

Summary

In this chapter, you learned how to create lines and curves in both the Freehand mode and the Bézier mode using the Pencil tool. Revising existing lines and curves using various editing techniques was also covered. You learned how to create a rectangle and a square, and how to give these objects rounded corners. You also learned how to create an ellipse, a circle, a pie wedge, and a circular arc. Additionally, you learned about the difference between closed path objects and open path objects, and how to convert one into the other.

The next chapter describes in more detail how you can manipulate these lines and shapes to create sophisticated graphics.

Mastering Object Manipulations

CorelDRAW! gives you the ability to manipulate graphic objects to achieve artistic effect. Achieving many of the desired results requires aligning, layering, and duplicating objects. CorelDRAW! provides numerous techniques that make working with objects easy and more productive. This chapter introduces you to these basic object related operations.

Knowing how to use these techniques efficiently is a key to creating drawings in CorelDRAW!. Several sections in this chapter include some detailed examples that you can duplicate. These examples are shown in addition to the general procedures you can follow as a reference while creating your own drawings.

Selecting Objects

You must first select an object before CorelDRAW! can assign attributes to it. Corel drawings may involve hundreds of objects, so the ability to select a particular object, or group of objects, out of many is critical. This section explains the various ways of selecting objects in Corel.

The concepts are easiest to understand if you are in Wireframe view. To change to Wireframe view, choose **D**isplay **E**dit Wireframe. This chapter uses the two rectangles and two circles as shown in figure 5.1 to illustrate the procedures with a concrete example. You can practice the selection and grouping techniques on these simple objects or on any objects of your own.

FIG. 5.1

Various graphic objects.

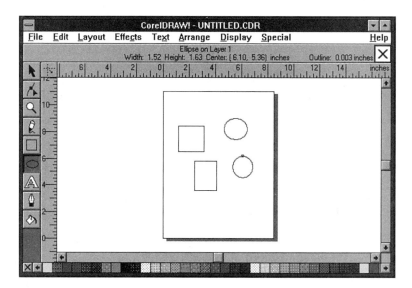

Selecting Individual Objects with the Pick Tool

To select an individual object, first choose the Pick tool and then click the desired object's outline. Once selected, the object becomes surrounded with a series of small black boxes, called handles, as shown in figure 5.2.

TIP

The cursor must be precisely on the object's outline when selecting in Wireframe mode. When in Editable Preview mode, you can click any-where on the object or its fill to select the object.

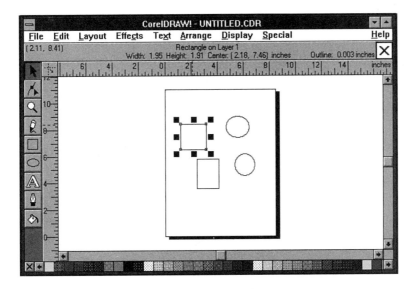

FIG. 5.2

A selected object.

Selected objects are always surrounded by this series of black boxes. In addition, CorelDRAW! also shows the corner nodes of the selected object. All CorelDRAW! objects have nodes associated with them, and these nodes appear each time that you select the object.

TIP

Remember that you cannot edit the nodes with the Pick tool; you must use the Shape tool to modify nodal characteristics.

Selecting Individual Objects with the Tab Key

You can also select an object using the Pick tool in combination with the Tab key. Select an object with the Pick tool and then press the Tab key to individually select each of the existing objects in the order of initial object creation. Pressing Shift+Tab moves you backwards through the drawing order. Keeping Tab depressed sequences the selections through each object.

This selection technique is particularly valuable when the drawing contains hundreds of closely aligned objects. Selecting an object with only the Pick tool is often impossible simply due to the proximity of the objects. Adjacent objects are often drawn in sequence, and this technique allows you to get in the neighborhood of the desired object and press the Tab key until you select the desired object.

You deselect an object, or group of objects, by either pressing Esc or clicking an empty portion of the editing window.

Selecting Groups of Objects with the Pick Tool

The Pick tool provides a convenient way for selecting multiple objects at once by enabling you to drag a marquee box around the desired group of objects.

1. Choose the Pick tool.

2. Click the Pick tool in the top-left corner of the area that includes all the objects you want to select. Drag the tool to the bottom-right corner of the area. A marquee box appears around the area as you drag the tool, as shown in figure 5.3.

3. Release the mouse button. All objects contained within the marquee are selected.

TIP

You do not need to drag from top left to bottom right, but to achieve consistency in moving, copying, and selecting objects, a top-left-to-bottom-right sequence is recommended.

You must include the entire object within the marquee before CorelDRAW! includes it in part of the selection. On the other hand, if the entire object is included in the marquee, it is selected whether you want it or not. If you want to select non-adjacent objects or if you are selecting objects in a drawing that contains many objects, you should use a different selection method.

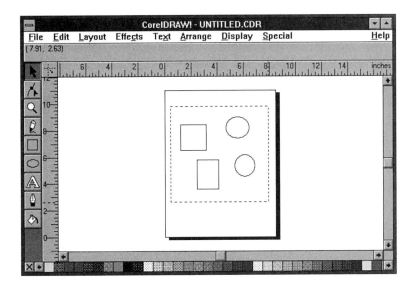

FIG. 5.3

Marquee selecting
multiple objects.

If you need some practice with marquee selection, follow these steps:

1. Draw the four objects shown in figure 5.1 if they are not already on-screen.

2. Select only the top two objects

3. Select only the bottom two objects.

4. Select the upper-right and bottom-left objects without including the other two.

Selecting Non-Adjacent Objects with the Shift Key

You can select combinations of several individual objects by using the Pick tool in conjunction with the Shift key. Use this selection technique when you cannot use the marquee method because unwanted objects would be selected within the marquee.

To select multiple objects that are not adjacent, follow these steps:

1. Select the first object with the Pick tool.

2. Press Shift and click the next object you want to select.

3. Repeat step 2 for any additional objects you want to select. The status line shows the number of objects that are selected.

To practice this technique using the objects in figure 5.1, follow these steps:

1. Select the upper-right object on-screen.

2. Press Shift while clicking the lower-left object.

A box appears around the two objects, and their nodes are displayed. Even though the marquee appears to surround all four objects, only two are actually selected by CorelDRAW!. You can tell that the other two objects are not selected because their nodes are not displayed. Also, the status line shows that two objects are selected, not four.

Pressing the Shift key while clicking a selected object (Shift-click) deselects it. For example, if you select an entire group of objects and then want to deselect one of objects placed in the middle of the marquee, just Shift-click the undesired object to deselect it. The status line updates to show one less object is selected.

3. Press Shift and click either of the two remaining objects.

The status line shows that three objects are selected and the selection box expands to include the third object. You can repeat this process for any number of objects.

Selecting All Objects on the Page

Copying and pasting entire drawings requires selecting all objects on a drawing page. You can select the entire drawing page by using the marquee method or by choosing the **Edit Select All** option. Unlike the marquee selection method, the Edit Select All option always ensures that all objects are included in the next action. This option is particularly useful when exporting drawings in various file formats for use with other applications.

Deleting Objects

The procedures for deleting objects are simple. Select the objects that you want to delete and then delete them using either the Delete key or the **Edit Delete** menu selection.

Selecting and then cutting an object to the Windows Clipboard, by choosing the **E**dit Cut menu option, removes the object from the drawing and leaves it available for pasting into other applications or Corel drawings.

If you make a mistake in deleting an object, select the **E**dit Undo (Ctrl+J) command. The number of undeletions executed by CorelDRAW! is dependent upon the Undo Levels set using the **S**pecial Preferences menu selection. The maximum number of Undo levels is 99.

Laying Objects on Top of or beneath Each Other

CorelDRAW! always places the most recently drawn object on top of the ones drawn previously. You change the position of objects with respect to each other by moving them on top of or beneath other objects. Because larger objects that contain interior fills can obscure smaller objects, the procedures covered in this section show you how to arrange objects so that smaller objects are accessible and/or visible with respect to larger ones.

If you want to move an object forward (closer to the front) in the back-to-front order of objects, follow these steps:

1. Select the Pick tool and click the object you want to move.

2. Choose **A**rrange **O**rder Forward **O**ne (Ctrl+PgUp). This option moves the object forward one place in the order.

If you want to move an object to the top (the front object) in the back-to-front order of objects, follow these steps:

1. Select the Pick tool and click the object you want to move.

2. Choose **A**rrange **O**rder To Front (Shift+PgUp). This option makes the object the top object.

The steps are similar for moving an object back. You use Back **O**ne (Ctrl+PgDn) to move an object back one place in the order and To **B**ack (Shift+PgDn) to make it the bottom object.

The following steps illustrate the use of the Front and Back commands when orienting objects:

1. Draw the objects shown in figure 5.4 and pay special attention to their relative size and orientation. Draw the large rectangle first, the small rectangle second, and the ellipse third to ensure the proper front-to-back orientation.

FIG. 5.4

Zoomed in picture of objects used for object ordering exercise.

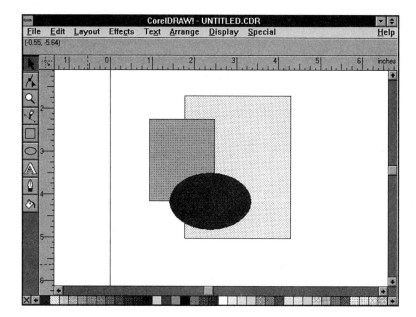

2. Select the ellipse and then choose the **Arrange Order Back One** option or press Ctrl+Page Down. The ellipse is now between the two rectangles as shown in figure 5.5.

3. Choose **Arrange Order Back One** again to move the ellipse to the back of the order. Both rectangles are now on top of the ellipse.

4. Select the small rectangle, and move it behind the other objects by pressing Ctrl+Page Down. Your drawing should look like figure 5.6.

5. Select the small rectangle and then choose the Arrange Order Front One menu option. This action moves the object forward one level.

6. Press Ctrl+Page Up to move the small rectangle on top of the other objects.

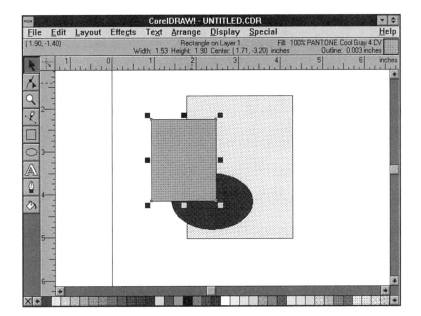

FIG. 5.5

Zoomed in picture of
the ellipse moved back
one level.

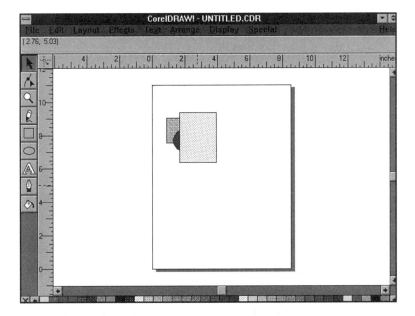

FIG. 5.6

Small rectangle moved
to the back.

To reverse the entire order of the objects, select the group of objects to
be reordered and then choose the **Arrange Order R**everse Order menu
option.

Copying Objects

The two basic types of copies are duplicates and clones. A *duplicate* is an exact copy of the originally selected object that is no longer connected to the original. A *clone* is also an exact copy of the original object, but it remains connected to the original object so that modifications to the original object are carried over to the clones. The following sections explain how to duplicate and clone objects.

Duplicating Objects

Drawings often require objects of the same general shape, but of different size and orientation. Effective use of the CorelDRAW! duplicating techniques can save you time when you work with such drawings.

All duplicating techniques follow the same two-step procedure:

1. Select the objects for duplications.

2. Duplicate the objects using any of the following three methods.

   ■ Use the **E**dit **D**uplicate command (Ctrl+D), which creates a copy a specific distance from the original.

   ■ Press the + key on the numeric keypad, which places the duplicate on top of the original objects.

   ■ Copy and Paste the object via the Clipboard.

CorelDRAW! automatically selects the duplicated objects so that duplication can happen again from the new location. A group of selected objects is duplicated in exactly the same manner as a single object.

The following steps illustrate the duplication process:

1. Choose the Editable Preview display mode and delete all existing objects. Either choose the **E**dit Select **A**ll command and delete all existing objects or ask for a new page and don't save the old one.

2. Draw a rectangular object.

3. Select the object and then choose **E**dit **D**uplicate or press Ctrl+D. The object is duplicated to the side and on top of the original and remains selected for additional operations.

4. Choose **E**dit **D**uplicate, or press Ctrl+D, again and a new copy is placed in the same relative orientation to the second object as the second object was to the first. (The position used for the duplicated object is a user-defined default setting. Setting this position is covered in the next section.)

TIP

To duplicate an object and place it directly on top of the original object, select the object and then press the + key on the numeric keypad. Even though you cannot easily see the duplicate, it is already selected and can be dragged to another screen location. If you don't use this technique carefully, you can end up with multiple objects and greatly increase the complexity of your file, so move the objects immediately after pressing +.

Setting the Automatic Duplication Defaults

CorelDRAW! provides a method for precisely defining where a duplicated object is placed. If used properly, this automatic duplication feature can greatly increase your drawing efficiency. This is particularly true when creating forms, which are essentially lines or boxes of the same shape and size copied to various screen locations.

You can specify where CorelDRAW! positions duplicates. Follow these steps:

1. Choose **S**pecial Preferences to display the Preferences dialog box shown in figure 5.7.

2. Change the vertical and horizontal values as needed by double-clicking the value and typing a new value, or by erasing the old value and then typing a new one. Keep in mind that these distances are relative to the object that you're copying.

Positive numbers place the duplicate object to the right (horizontal) and above (vertical). Negative numbers move the object in the opposite directions. Mixed positive and negative settings are allowed and often useful.

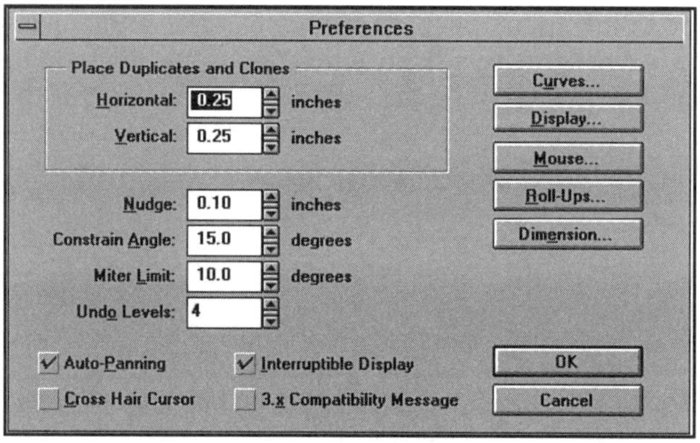

FIG. 5.7

Setting the duplicate
location default.

Preferences

Place Duplicates and Clones

Horizontal: `0.25` inches

Vertical: `0.25` inches

Nudge: `0.10` inches

Constrain Angle: `15.0` degrees

Miter Limit: `10.0` degrees

Undo Levels: `4`

Curves...

Display...

Mouse...

Roll-Ups...

Dimension...

☑ Auto-Panning   ☑ Interruptible Display   OK

☐ Cross Hair Cursor   ☐ 3.x Compatibility Message   Cancel

TIP

You can also set the values by clicking the small up and down arrows, or by dragging up or down on the space located between the up and down arrows. The cursor turns into a double arrow when located between the two arrows.

3. Click OK. The next time you duplicate an object, CorelDRAW! places the duplicate according to the settings you entered.

Cloning Objects

Cloning makes CorelDRAW! operations faster, easier, and less tedious. It is a unique method of duplicating objects so that they are related to the original, or master, object. Changes to the master affect all cloned objects.

The following steps outline the cloning procedure:

1. Select the object to be cloned.

2. Choose Edit Clone. CorelDRAW! creates the clone at the screen location defined in the Duplicate Preferences menu. You can drag the cloned object to another screen location.

3. Repeat steps 1 and 2 to create as many clones as needed.

Edit Clone is not accessible while a clone is selected. You cannot clone a clone. You can only clone the master. To determine whether an object is a master or clone, select the object and then click it with the right mouse button. The bottom of the displayed fly-out menu shows `Select Master` if the object is a clone or `Select Clones` if the object is the master.

To simultaneously make changes to all object clones, select the master object then make any changes you need. All of the clones automatically change too.

You make changes to individual clones just like any other CorelDRAW! object: select it and make the changes. However, if you change a clone's attributes, those attributes are no longer linked to the master. For example, if you change the line thickness on a clone, any changes to the line thickness of the master do not affect that clone.

To familiarize yourself with the cloning process, try the following exercise:

1. Either select or draw and select an object that includes all desired attributes.

You can clone master objects that include special effects such as Blending, Extruding, Contouring, or Powerlines and have those effects carry to the clones. Changing these characteristics on the master affects the clones as long as you originally apply the characteristics to the master *before* cloning. Adding these effects to the master after cloning does not affect the clones.

2. Choose Edit Clone from the menu. CorelDRAW! creates the clone at the Duplicate Preferences location.

3. Drag the clone to your desired screen location.

4. Modify all clone attributes by selecting the master object and changing its attributes. All clones will adopt the new master object attributes, such as color, size, rotation, and outline.

Aligning Objects

The high level of precision provided by CorelDRAW! is a mixed blessing. You can create precise objects, but small variations between objects and their alignment are painfully visible and frustrating to correct. Luckily, CorelDRAW! comes with a set of automated alignment tools that simplify the task.

Using the Grid To Ease Alignment

The grid defines specific intervals upon which object outlines can fall. The grid is particularly useful when working with rectangular objects because all four sides of the rectangle are constrained to fall on a grid line, which greatly simplifies object alignment. When drawing objects that do not require rigorous alignment, such as illustrations, you should disable Snap To Grid so that you have complete freedom in moving the objects.

Establishing the Grid

To establish the grid, follow these steps.

1. Choose **Layout Grid** Setup to display the Grid Setup dialog box shown in figure 5.8.

FIG. 5.8

The Grid Setup dialog box.

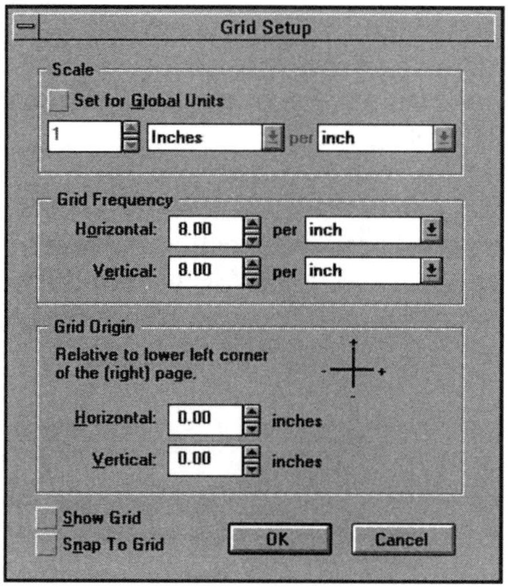

2. Enter the horizontal and vertical grid frequencies you want to use for the grid. (These options are discussed in detail in the next section, so you may just want to accept the defaults for now.)

3. Choose the Snap To Grid (Ctrl+Y) option located at the bottom of the dialog box to align newly created objects along grid lines.

TIP

You can also activate or deactivate Snap To Grid by choosing Layout Snap To Grid.

4. If you want to see the grid while you are drawing or editing, choose the Show Grid option located at the bottom of the dialog box.

5. Click OK to return to the editing screen.

NOTE

The Show Grid feature is not really valuable when viewing the entire page, but becomes very useful when you zoom in on a smaller portion of the page. The ruler units adjust and the actual grid spacing is revealed (see fig. 5.9).

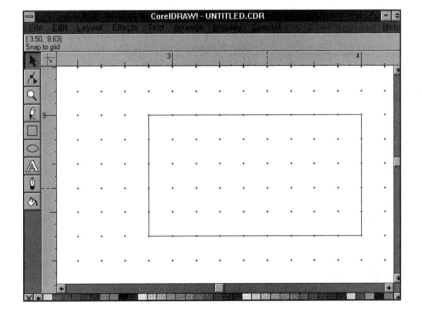

FIG. 5.9

Show Grid while using zoom.

To draw objects aligned to the grid, draw them as you normally would. The edges of the objects will now only align along grid lines.

Establishing Scale Settings

Setting the display scale so that all displayed units are in the desired form (feet, kilometers, and so on) is often useful. Using this feature in connection with dimension lines greatly simplifies the creation of technical drawings.

With the Set for Global Units option shown in the Grid Setup dialog box, you can set the display units pertinent to a particular drawing, such as one inch equals one kilometer. You can choose from various unit types by clicking the down arrow next to the unit listed to display the drop-down list and then choosing the one you want.

Once you establish these settings, CorelDRAW! calculates all display dimension units accordingly. All objects are described on the status line in the display unit you set (kilometers in the example), which makes drawing creation much simpler. This feature is particularly valuable when dealing with technical drawings.

Establishing Grid Frequencies

The horizontal and vertical grid frequencies, accessed by choosing the Layout Grid Setup menu option, establish the location of the various grid alignment lines. For example, a setting of 8 grid lines per inch (unit) creates a 1/8-inch grid network. The maximum number of grid lines per unit follow:

Unit	Grid Lines
Inch	72 lines
Pica	12 lines
Point	1 line
Millimeter	About 2.8 lines

You should establish a grid frequency for each new image and then stick with it, or a multiple of the original, to ease alignment of subsequently created objects to those created earlier in the process. Keep in mind that working with a drawing containing a very tight grid network is often difficult, and each new drawing may require a different grid frequency.

To set the grid frequency, follow these steps:

1. Choose **L**ayout Gr**i**d Setup. The Grid Setup dialog box appears.

2. In the Grid Frequency area, set the **H**orizontal and **V**ertical unit preferences.

3. Click OK.

Establishing the Grid Origin

The grid origin is the assumed 0,0 location for the drawing, and all page locations are referenced from that origin point. In general, the origin is located at the lower-left corner of the drawing so that all page locations are shown as positive numbers. Moving the origin to another page location so that all dimensions are referenced from that new location is occasionally useful.

You can either specify the precise page location using the Grid Setup dialog box, or you can drag the icon located at the intersection of the horizontal and vertical lines to the desired new origin location. All screen locations shown on the status line from that time forward show dimensions based on the new origin location.

To specify the precise location of the origin using the Grid Setup dialog box, follow these steps:

1. Choose **L**ayout Gr**i**d Setup. The Grid Setup dialog box appears.

2. Choose **H**orizontal (or **V**ertical) in the Grid Origin section of the Grid Setup dialog box.

3. Type the desired new horizontal (and/or vertical) location for the origin.

4. Click OK.

Aligning Individual Objects

This section deals with the Snap To Objects feature. Effective use of this feature can greatly increase your drawing speed.

Objects are snapped to each other by their nodes. When you enable the Snap To Objects feature, object nodes are "magnetically" aligned with each other. Keep in mind that Snap To Grid must be off (choose **Layout Snap To Grid**) for Snap To Objects to work properly because the grid overrides other features.

To use the Snap To Objects feature, follow these steps:

1. Choose **Layout Snap To Objects**.

2. Select an object.

3. Click one of the selected object's nodes and drag it toward another object. As you approach the nodes of the second object, a dashed blue line indicates the node-to-node alignment between the two objects.

4. Drag the mouse pointer toward the desired location on the second object and release the object once it "snaps-to" the correct location. Note that the object nodes are "magnetically" attracted.

Most CorelDRAW! objects have nodal points that are used as "magnets" during the Snap To Object process. These node points are located differently for different object shapes and types (see table 5.1). When node points from various objects are brought near each other, they attract each other along those node points.

Table 5.1 Node Points for CorelDRAW! Objects

Object Type	Node Points
Rectangular and square objects	Along the edge of the object in the same relative location as the scaling handles, and one in the center.
Rectangular and square objects with rounded corners	In the center of the rectangle and at the ends of each arc segment in each corner.
Closed ellipses and circles	In the center and at the end of each major and minor axis along the object's perimeter.
Modified ellipses and circles	At the same points as for the closed ellipse, and also at the endpoints associated with the removed wedge.

Object Type	Node Points
Open line paths	At the ends and at as many other locations along the path as are required to complete the curve.
Bitmaps	In the corners and center of the bitmap image.
Artistic text	At the standard scaling handle locations and in the center.
Paragraph text	At the standard scaling handle locations and in the center.

Figure 5.10 shows the node locations for each type of object.

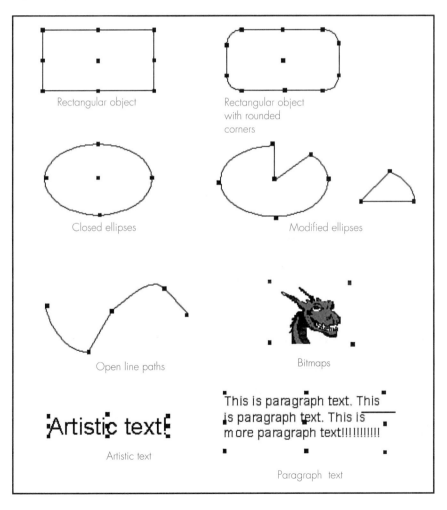

FIG. 5.10

Types of objects and their node locations.

You can use the Snap To Objects feature to automatically resize objects to each other by first dragging the two objects on top of each other and then allowing the snap to magnetism to do the rest as you drag the nodes towards each other.

1. Activate Snap To Objects by choosing **L**ayout **S**nap To **O**bjects.

2. Draw a large rectangle and a small circle on top of each other on the drawing page.

3. Select the circle with the Pick tool and drag the right scaling handle to the rectangle's right side. The sides should snap to each other.

4. With the circle still selected, drag the left scaling handle toward the left side of the rectangle. It should snap to the rectangle's mid-span.

5. Now drag the circle's top and bottom scaling handles toward the top and bottom of the rectangle, respectively, and notice that they also snap to the rectangle's side nodes. The circle is now exactly sized to fit within the rectangle.

Simultaneously Aligning Several Objects

The Align command enables you to simultaneously align several objects along their edges or center in a horizontal or vertical direction. This feature is particularly useful when the objects are of different shapes and were created with Snap To Grid deactivated.

To align objects using the Align command, follow these steps:

1. Select all of the objects you want to align.

2. Pull down the **Arrange** menu and choose **A**lign, or press Ctrl+A to display the Align dialog box (see fig. 5.11).

3. Select the arrangement option you want and click OK.

FIG. 5.11

The Align dialog box.

The diagrams shown in the dialog box indicate the relative alignment of objects performed by each alignment type. You can choose vertical options and horizontal options individually or jointly. If you only choose an option for one direction, CorelDRAW! ignores the other direction's alignment. For example, vertical center alignment causes the objects to move up or down so that the centers align, but no horizontal movement is performed. Horizontal center alignment works the same way but in the horizontal, instead of vertical, direction. Choosing both horizontal and vertical center aligns the centers of all selected objects with each other and in both directions.

The last object selected remains in place, and all other selected objects align around its location. If you selected the objects using the marquee method, all objects align around the bottom object. Because there is no definite way to determine which object is at the very bottom, you should select the objects individually for alignment. An alternative approach is to move the desired base object to the back and then select the objects using the marquee method.

CorelDRAW! also allows you to align objects to the center of the page by using the Align command with the Align To Center Of Page option activated. The object alignment selections tell CorelDRAW! which part of the objects to align with the center of the page. For example, the Vertically Bottom-Horizontally Center combination aligns the bottom center of all selected objects with the center of the page as shown in figure 5.12.

The Align To Grid option instructs CorelDRAW! to align the selected objects in the chosen orientation, but to lay the aligned objects along the closest grid line.

Using the Guidelines To Ease Alignment

CorelDRAW! provides guidelines to allow for easy alignment of objects along straight vertical and horizontal paths.

TIP

You can display the guidelines on top of the other objects by opening the Layers roll-up window and then dragging the guidelines layer to the top of the list.

FIG. 5.12

Objects aligned as bottom
center to page center.

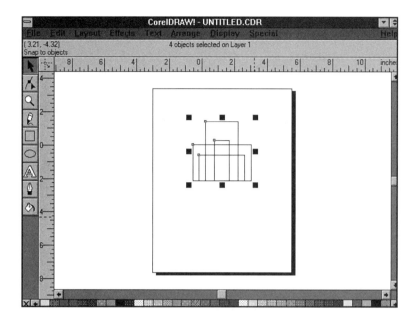

The general procedure for mouse-oriented establishment and use of
guidelines follows:

1. Click the vertical ruler and drag a guideline to the location where
   you want the guideline.

2. Click the horizontal ruler and drag a guideline to the location
   where you want the guideline (see fig. 5.13).

3. Choose **L**ayout Gu**i**delines Setup to display the Guidelines dialog
   box (see fig. 5.14).

4. Choose the **S**nap To Guides option shown at the bottom of the
   dialog box and click Close to establish this guideline criteria.

5. To align objects along guidelines you have created, drag the objects to the guideline and their nodes align along the guidelines
   (see fig. 5.13).

The Guidelines dialog box allows for creation, deletion, and precise
page locating of guidelines. These features become particularly helpful
when the overall page formatting must conform to precise standards.
CorelDRAW! stores the guidelines on their own layer.

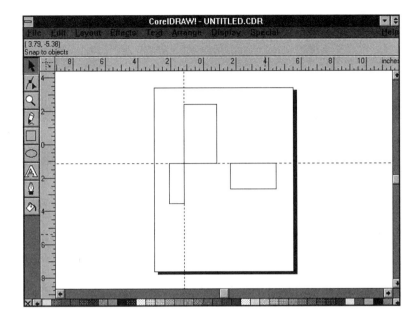

FIG. 5.13

Using the guidelines for alignment.

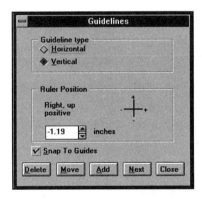

FIG. 5.14

The Guidelines dialog box.

The Ruler Position dialog box option allows you to numerically designate the guideline locations relative to the current ruler origin. Use this procedure when you require specific alignment of objects, such as with tabular data or margins. Simply select the Guideline type, enter the page location at which the guideline should appear under the Ruler Position section (positive is to the right or up), and then click **A**dd. CorelDRAW! now displays the guideline at that location. You can repeat this procedure as many times as needed.

Combining and Grouping Objects

Many times when you are drawing, you will want to work on groups of objects together as one object. Or you will have labored to precisely align all of the objects in a drawing, and you want to be able to keep them aligned even if you move or resize them. Combining objects is useful for speeding the redraw process during screen refresh because combining reduces the number of objects to be drawn.

The following sections explain how to group and combine objects and how to work with these object types. These sections also explain how to separate grouped objects.

Distinguishing between Grouping and Combining Objects

Grouping objects is used often with CorelDRAW! because alignment of separate objects to each other is often critical, hard to establish, and necessary to keep after established. Each object in a group retains its own identity, but it becomes part of a group of objects. Selecting any member of the group selects the entire group of objects.

Combining, on the other hand, creates a single object out of many different objects and is used primarily to decrease the size of CorelDRAW! files and increase drawing speed.

Grouping Objects

Group objects any time that the relationship between objects is critical and you want to maintain it. Grouping objects enables you to select a number of objects at once for actions such as rotating, sizing, or moving. You can also form groups with several subgroups, each of which is its own individual group.

TIP

CorelDRAW! allows up to ten levels of subgrouping. Look to the status line to determine whether the selected objects are part of a subgroup.

You will use grouping extensively because much of the work done with CorelDRAW! involves the relationships between groups. For example, you may create a drawing of an automobile. The windows, doors, tires, and so on are all distinct objects that create the final automobile image. Once you complete the automobile image, you work with the total automobile not just the image of the tires. The automobile group is the single image of the automobile, which is composed of many separate objects. Selecting any object within the automobile group selects the entire group. You must ungroup the group before any single object is accessible by itself.

To create a grouped set of objects, follow these steps:

1. Draw a big circle and two smaller ellipses to create a drawing similar to that in figure 5.15.

2. Select the objects to be grouped (the two ellipses in this example) using any of the previously mentioned object selection procedures.

3. Choose **Arrange Group** (Ctrl+G). The status line now indicates that this is a group of objects (see fig. 5.15).

You can now perform any standard object operations on the new object group. For example, figure 5.16 shows the results of copying a group.

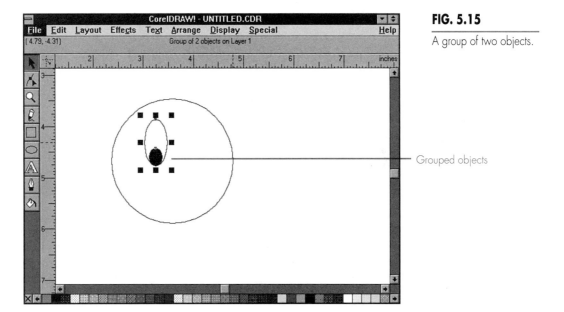

FIG. 5.15

A group of two objects.

Grouped objects

FIG. 5.16

Drawing a character
using a copied eye
group.

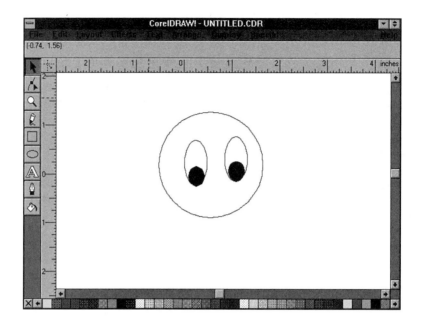

Ungrouping Objects

Ungrouping objects is simply a matter of selecting the group, and then
choosing the **Arrange Ungroup (Ctrl+U)** option. If the group is comprised of several smaller groups, you may need to ungroup each of
them also.

The primary reason for ungrouping is to make changes to an individual
object instead of to the entire group. Make sure that you regroup the
objects after making the modifications to the single object, or you can
lose the alignment of the whole group.

 ## Accessing Objects within a Group (Child Objects)

A simpler way to change the characteristics of a group member object
is to select it as a *child object*. While an object is selected as a child
object, you can treat it as though it were a stand-alone object. When
you deselect the object, it reverts to being a member of the group.

To create a child object within a group, follow these steps:

1. Select the object group.

2. Ctrl-click the object within the group that you want to make a child object. The status line indicates that a child object is selected, and the black selection squares around the group become black circles around the child object.

> You may need to Ctrl-click several times to work through the levels of the group until you can access the desired child group.   **TIP**

3. Make any changes you want to the child object.

4. Click anywhere on-screen and the child object is no longer selected, and it is again treated as part of the group.

To give you a clearer understanding of this concept, the following steps illustrate how to select and modify a child object using the drawing from the previous section.

1. Click the pupil of the left eye of the character drawn in the previous exercise. The standard scaling handles appear around the left group of objects.

2. Ctrl-click the left pupil. The black squares around the left eye group turn into small circles around the left pupil, indicating that the pupil is a child object (see fig. 5.17).

3. Change the interior fill to a shaded design, and then click elsewhere on-screen.

4. Click the left pupil again and notice that the entire original group is once again selected. However, the left pupil now has a shaded fill instead of black. Repeat this procedure and return the pupil to a black fill or choose **Edit Undo**.

Combining Objects

You combine objects when they have the same attributes and they do not need to be treated as separate objects. Cross-hatching is a good example of the benefits of combining. Each line in the cross-hatch is a separate object and must be drawn individually. This process adds time and complexity to the drawing. Because cross-hatching lines have the same attributes, you can combine them into one single object even though some of the lines are not actually touching. Combining greatly speeds up the drawing time and decreases the amount of storage space required for a drawing.

To combine objects into one, select all of the objects to be combined and then choose **Arrange Combine**. CorelDRAW! now treats the objects as a single curve with many nodes. You can separate combined objects by using the **Arrange Break Apart** command (Ctrl+K).

NOTE

Warning to users of Corel 3: Ctrl+L is now the keyboard shortcut for the Combine command and Ctrl+C is the shortcut for copy. Although this change conforms to many conventions, it can be confusing if you're used to the old commands.

TIP

A combined object has a maximum node limit between 1,000 and 2,000 nodes, depending on the printer capabilities.

FIG. 5.17

Group with a child object selected.

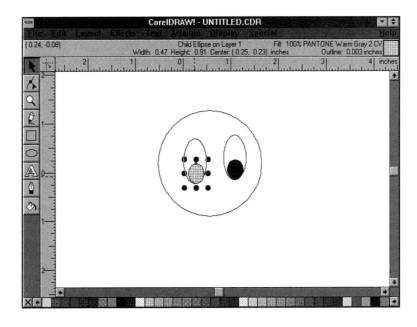

The following example gives a general idea of the benefits associated with combining objects and the basic procedures to follow. You are going to give your character creation from the previous examples some hair.

1. Choose the Pencil tool and draw a series of lines on the top of the head of the grouped object character (see fig. 5.18).

2. Draw a marquee around the hair strands. The status line displays the number of objects selected.

3. Choose **Arrange Combine**. The status line indicates that the large number of objects is now treated as a single curve with many nodes.

4. Select a hair strand. This action now selects the entire hair object because the strands are all combined into one object.

5. Choose **Arrange Group** to group this new hair object with the rest of the character to make the hair a permanent part of its personality.

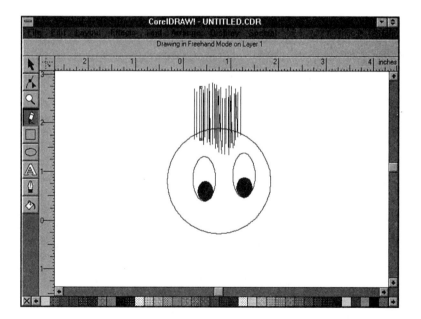

FIG. 5.18

Combining objects.

The Combine command has a few major characteristics you should consider whenever you use it:

■ Before CorelDRAW! combines an object, it first turns the object into curves. This characteristic applies to text, rectangles, ellipses, and other objects that may not have started out as curves. Once text is converted to curves, you can change it back only by using Undo.

■ Combining objects decreases screen redraw time and greatly enhances drawing efficiency.

■ All combined objects adopt the attributes of the bottom object, or the one selected last. Select the object with the desired attributes as the last object, or move it to the back and then, using the marquee method, select the objects to be combined.

■ Objects do not need to touch to be combined. Node alignment between nontouching objects is only possible after the objects have been combined.

You can use clipping holes, or masks, for impressive effects. Combine enables you to easily accomplish this otherwise complicated procedure. In this example, you create the mask shown in figure 5.19.

1. Enter the Animals text using an Arabia font type of around 30-point size. Give it a black interior fill and outline.

2. Draw a rectangle around the text.

3. Select the rectangle and the Animals text, and then choose **A**rrange **C**ombine (Ctrl+L) to make the two objects one. The combined object contains a "knockout" where the Animals text previously existed. The combined object adopted the attributes of the text because it was the last item selected.

4. Add symbols or backgrounds as needed for effect. In this case, the gorilla and kangaroo symbols were taken from the Animals symbol group. Move the symbols to the back so that they are partially masked by the combined object.

This masking technique is nicely used when overlaying a city skyline with the city's name. For example, you can place the Chicago skyline behind a combined object containing a white fill and a center knockout of Chicago text.

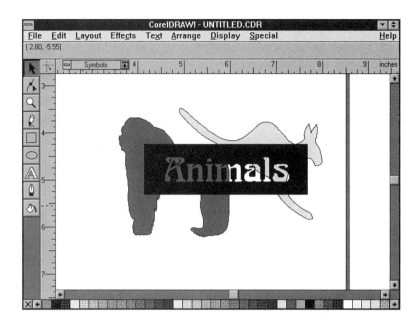

FIG. 5.19

An example of a mask.

Using Tricks and Techniques

You can combine each of the techniques discussed in this chapter to create interesting final effects. Welding provides an easy way to create complicated outlines from several objects. Nudge provides a convenient and precise way for moving objects into exactly the desired orientation using the keyboard instead of the mouse. You also can use lines for alignment even when they do not print. The following sections introduce all these techniques.

Welding Objects Together

The Weld feature is used to consolidate multiple objects into a single object that is a composite of the total outline of all objects involved. The individual objects disappear after the weld, and a single outline object remains. Weld eliminates the need to perform relatively complicated node-related actions to achieve the same effect. CorelDRAW! always applies the outline and fill of the most recently created object to the newly created, "welded" object.

To weld objects together, follow these steps:

1. Select the objects to be welded. The status line indicates the number of objects selected.

2. Choose **Arrange Weld**. The status line indicates that the separate objects are now a single object with the aggregate outline of the previously separate objects.

You can now perform any operation on this object, such as filling it.

TIP

> Trying to weld text may lock up your computer. To be on the safe side, connect the text to curves and then break them apart before welding.

The following procedure demonstrates the use of and benefits associated with the Weld feature:

1. Draw the rectangular objects shown in figure 5.20, making sure that the relative size and orientation of the objects matches that shown in the figure.

2. Select all three rectangles. The status line indicates that three objects are selected.

3. Choose **Arrange Weld**. The status line indicates that the three separate objects are now a single object with the aggregate outline of the previously separate objects (see fig. 5.21).

4. Apply a gray fill to the new, welded object.

You can also perform this procedure using the multisegment line feature, but using the three rectangles allows for quicker and more precise creation of the I-beam object. Try performing a weld using a circle and a rectangle to really see welding's benefits. You will find many uses for this valuable feature.

Moving Objects with Nudge

You use the cursor arrows to move, or nudge, a selected object a precisely defined distance. To nudge an object, select the object and then press the cursor arrow key that points in the direction of desired movement.

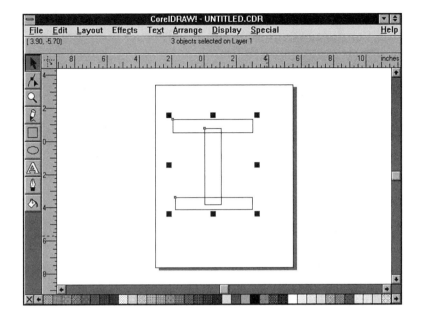

FIG. 5.20

Three objects before welding.

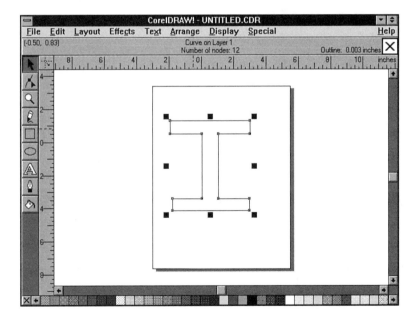

FIG. 5.21

The objects after welding.

To set the amount of offset caused by each nudge, choose **S**pecial Preferences. The dialog box shown in figure 5.22 appears. Type the new
nudge displacement value (0.25 inches for example) in the **N**udge box.

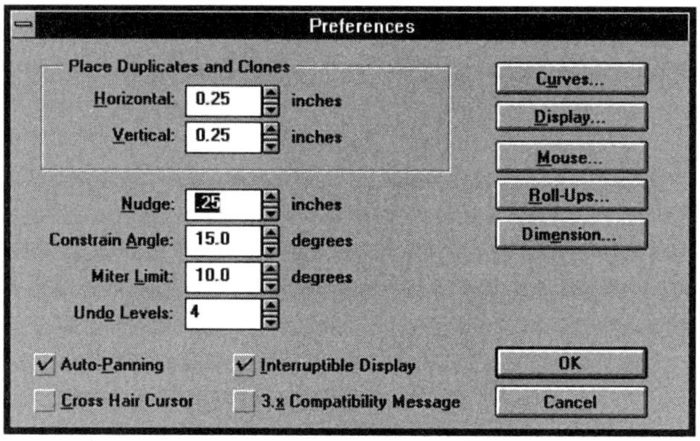

FIG. 5.22

Setting the nudge
distance.

You can also nudge a node by first selecting it with the Shape tool and
then nudging it with the cursor arrows. The same nudge displacement
preferences apply to node nudges.

Aligning with No-Color Lines

You may occasionally want to align objects along a common border,
but not necessarily show the line along which they are aligned. You can
achieve this effect by drawing the alignment line and giving it no thickness or making its color match the page color.

The alignment line shows up in Wireframe mode but does not display in
the Editable Preview mode because it has no display attributes.

Understanding CorelDRAW! Layers

Complicated drawing may involve hundreds of objects. Drawing is less
confusing and the redraw time is faster if you work with fewer objects

at a given time. The CorelDRAW! layers feature allows you to select certain objects that appear on a specific layer, or plane, of the drawing. You can then display only those layers that directly pertain to the current editing needs and display all the objects only as needed.

Think of the layers as clear pieces of plastic upon which the objects are drawn. Selecting a layer places that piece of acetate into the viewing area. You can specify overlays so that you can view specific layers in combination.

Understanding How CorelDRAW! Layers Objects in a Drawing

Layer 1 is the default layer for object drawing, the guides exist on their own layer (which you can edit), and the grid exists on its own layer (which you cannot edit).

Layers are selected, created, deleted, and objects are moved between layers from the Layout Layers roll-up window which is shown in figure 5.23. Simply click a layer name to edit objects contained in that layer.

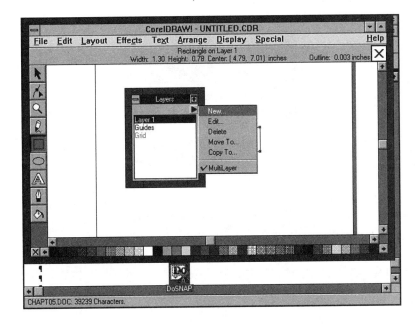

FIG. 5.23

The Layers roll-up window.

You can change the order of layers by dragging the layer name higher or lower in the layer name list shown in the Layers roll-up window. The first layer is at the top and the last layer is at the bottom. Reordering the layers may cause objects on one layer to obscure objects on another.

TIP

You activate objects added to the Guides layer by using the Layout Snap To Guides option. The ability to create custom guides is handy when creating drawings with specific layout issues such as plotting information along angular lines.

You add and delete layers using the fly-out menu displayed after clicking the small arrow pointing to the right in the upper-right corner of the Layers roll-up window. Figure 5.23 shows the fly-out menu.

The MultiLayer option contained in the fly-out menu instructs CorelDRAW! to allow access to objects contained on all layers of the drawing. Deselecting MultiLayer restricts object access to those on the currently active layer.

Clicking New or Edit displays the Layer Options dialog box shown in figure 5.24.

FIG. 5.24

The Layer Options
dialog box.

TIP

Double-clicking any of the layer names opens the Layer Option dialog box for that particular layer.

Enter custom layer names using the Layer Options dialog box. You can use up to 32 characters in the name. Clicking OK adds the new layer name in the roll-up window.

Use the Layer Option dialog box items to determine whether the layer displays, prints, or is locked so that accidental changes do not occur. Turn off the display for layers you do not currently need, and the screen refreshes faster. Turn them on again when you want to see the entire object with all of its layers.

Use the Color Override option to specify a color for a particular layer so that objects belonging to this layer are clearly displayed. Using Color Override displays the objects in Wireframe mode so only object outlines are displayed. The actual object fill and outline attributes remain untouched. The Override Color is for your benefit only. Deselecting Color Override returns the object display to its normal state.

Grouping and Combining Objects from Different Layers

You can group objects contained on different layers. The process is similar to the standard grouping procedure except that you must consider the different layers. First, select the layer on which you want the final group of objects to reside. Select all desired objects and choose **Arrange Group** (Ctrl+G). The group is now formed on the active layer.

Follow the same procedure to combine objects, except choose the Arrange Combine option after you select the objects. Selecting multilayer objects with the marquee method causes the combined object to reside on the layer of the most recently created object, not necessarily the currently active layer.

Summary

The techniques introduced in this chapter are used repeatedly in CorelDRAW!, and a thorough understanding of them helps in understanding the Corel thinking process.

You can move, align, rotate, and size entire groups of objects at once using the techniques outlined in this chapter. As your drawings get more complicated, you will benefit from the information provided in the layering section. Review these techniques until they become second nature, and you can concentrate on the task of creating your drawing.

Now that you have a handle on the basics of CorelDRAW!, you can start digging into more sophisticated concepts, such as modifying outlines and fills, which is covered in the next chapter.

Modifying Object Outlines and Interior Fills

All DRAW objects have interiors on outlines that can be colored, shaded, and/or textured. The wide variety of options provides numerous artistic opportunities for the creative individual. This chapter shows various techniques for changing object fill and outline attributes and delves into much of the detail necessary for you to effectively use color, shading, and texture to achieve your desired artistic effect. When you have finished this chapter, you will be ready to draw many of the objects needed for your work.

Modifying the Outline Characteristics

CorelDRAW! can enhance the appearance of an object's outline in many ways, with color, corner shapes, line caps, varying widths (resembling those of calligraphy), dashes, or a halftone pattern.

You can use one of the following four methods to change the appearance of an outline. To use any of these methods, first select the object outline by clicking it; then you can change its attributes. These methods all involve different options.

- The Outline fly-out menu offers selections of line widths and colors. Click the Outline tool to call up this menu. The various line widths are shown along the top row and the shades of gray are along the bottom.

- The on-screen color palette displays colors that you can assign to an outline. (For more information, see this chapter's section on "Outlining in Color.")

- The Outline roll-up window provides shortcuts for selecting line widths, line styles, line ending shapes, and outline colors. (See this chapter's section on "Using the Outline Roll-Up Window.")

- The Outline Color dialog box enables you to design and select the color for your outline. (See again this chapter's section on "Outlining in Color.")

- The PowerLines roll-up window provides an artist's brush effect to drawn lines.

NOTE

When in Editable Preview, the screen displays the object's outline appearance as it will print (except for any PostScript halftones). The Wireframe mode, however, just depicts the object as a bare outline; the object's attributes are described on the status line. (Those PostScript halftones are the only outline attribute that will not print on non-PostScript printers.)

Spot color is a term used by printers that refers to the process of applying a color to an area on the page by using a plate with the exact color of ink to match the spot color as opposed to separating that spot color into its component colors with plates for each of those colors (process colors). Spot color is often used to avoid the high cost of three- or four-color separation printing. A common use of spot color is on business cards with a one-color logo and black text.

Using the Pen Roll-Up Window

The Pen roll-up window, shown in figure 6.1, gives you a faster way to perform many functions with just a few quick clicks of the mouse button. Access the roll-up window by clicking the Outline tool and then selecting the roll-up icon (the second icon from the left on the top row of the fly-out menu). You may recall learning the basic operations of the roll-up window in Chapter 2.

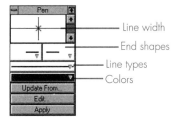

FIG. 6.1

The Pen roll-up window.

The Pen roll-up window enables you to perform the following functions:

- To specify the width of a line, click the up or down arrows at the right side of the Line Width box to increase or decrease the line width. Maximum width in the Pen roll-up is .5".

- To specify the end shapes (arrowheads) of a line, click one of the End Shapes boxes to view the selections. Then click a selection to place it in that box. Press Esc to return to the Pen roll-up window.

- To see the selection of line types, click the long narrow Line Types box. Click your choice or press Esc to return to the Pen roll-up.

- To see the color palette, click the next long narrow box, the Colors box. The color palette box appears. The More button takes you to the Select Color dialog box.

- To transfer an attribute from one outline to another, first choose the object with the Pick tool and then click the Update From button. The pointer changes to a From? arrow. Next, click the object you want to copy from. Its outline attributes will be copied to your originally selected object.

- To display the Outline Pen dialog box, click the Edit button.

- To transfer your selections (color, line width, and so on) onto the selected object in your drawing, click the Apply button.

The roll-up window shortcuts are added to many sections of this chapter and make the associated functions easier and faster.

Changing the Color of the Outline

If you are going to print to a black-and-white printer or import your drawing into page layout software that does not support color printing, use only black and gray on-screen. That way, your screen display is a close match to what prints.

You can make an outline in white, black, or any shade of gray. These shades are most visible when the outline is more than a hairline width.

The easiest way to assign any color (including gray) is by clicking an object and then clicking (with the secondary mouse button) the palette at the bottom of the screen. After you click a color selection, the outline acquires the color you selected.

NOTE

If the palette isn't currently displayed, choose the **C**olor Palette option from the **D**isplay menu. Scroll the palette one color at a time by clicking an arrow at the left or right end of the palette with the primary mouse button; scroll the width of the screen by clicking the arrows with the secondary mouse button.

The following procedures give you other ways to assign a color to an outline. Select the object with the Pick tool, click the Outline tool and the fly-out menu appears (see fig. 6.2). Then use one of these methods.

FIG. 6.2

The Outline fly-out menu.

- Choose a gray pattern directly from the options shown at the bottom right of the Outline fly-out menu.

- Follow these steps:

    1. Click the pen icon in the Outline fly-out menu. The Outline Pen dialog box appears.

2. Locate the color selector near the upper-left corner, and click the arrow in the rectangle to the right of the word Color.

3. Select a color. Your selection is shown in the color selector box and in the box on the right side of the screen.

4. Click OK and the selected color appears as the outline of your object.

■ Follow these steps:

1. Click the roll-up icon in the Outline fly-out menu to display the Pen roll-up window, or press F12.

2. Choose Edit from the Pen roll-up window.

3. Click the Color box (near the upper-left corner of the screen).

4. Click one of the color rectangles.

5. Choose Apply from the Pen roll-up window to apply that color to the outline.

■ Follow these steps:

1. Click the color wheel icon. The Outline Color dialog box appears.

2. Choose any option from the Show pull-down menu. All these options offer the means to create a shade of gray.

3. Start by selecting a gray from the custom palette at the bottom of this screen and adjusting the shade. The Outline Color screen is explained more fully in this chapter's section on "Outlining in Color" and in Chapter 11.

4. Choose OK.

■ Follow these steps:

1. Click the roll-up icon to open the Pen roll-up window.

2. Click the bar above Update From.

3. Select a color from the palette; or click More to open the Select Color dialog box, and then select a color and click OK.

4. Choose Apply from the roll-up window to put this color onto the outline.

TIP

The black, white, or gray selection from the Outline fly-out menu changes only the outline's color; it does not affect the object's PostScript halftone screen settings. If you are using a PostScript printer and want to access the PostScript halftone screen settings, specify your grays with spot color.

Outlining in Color

CorelDRAW! offers a limitless range of colors that you can apply to your outlines. In this section, you learn how to outline objects and text in color. The use of color outlines adds depth and interest to your design projects. Chapter 11 gives a full explanation of CorelDRAW!'s color capabilities.

The easiest way to assign a new color is by selecting the object with the Pick tool and then clicking (with the secondary mouse button) the palette at the bottom of the screen. The object then adopts the color you selected.

NOTE

If the palette isn't currently displayed, open the **D**isplay menu and choose **C**olor Palette **C**ustom Palette to toggle the palette display, making it visible.

Another approach is to use the Outline Color dialog box shown in figure 6.3 to choose or create a color.

First click the object you want to color with the Pick tool, and then select the Outline tool. When the Outline fly-out menu appears, click the color wheel icon. Continue with any one of the following methods. After you finish the procedure and click OK, the color you specified is applied to the outline.

■ Follow these steps:

1. Choose **D**isplay **C**olor Palette **C**ustom Palette.

2. Choose a color from the custom palette at the bottom of the window.

3. To view more selections from this palette, click the scroll arrows to the right or left of the palette.

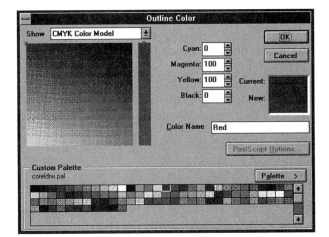

FIG. 6.3

The Outline Color
dialog box.

- Use the Show pull-down menu (at the upper-left corner of the Outline Color dialog box) to select a color palette. Click the arrow at
the right end of the Show text box, and pull down to see those
options. You should use the same option for all objects in your
drawing, if possible.

- Use the Show menu's Model options to select colors. When you
choose a Model option (CMYK, RGB, or HSB Color Model), a dot
appears in the large square box and also in the tall narrow box
that is just to the right. The dots are positioned on the color that
is being assigned. If the dots are in a red area of the boxes, for
example, the outline will have that same red color. (The chosen
new color is shown in the smaller square box at the right of the
window, along with the current color of the outline.)

- Follow these steps:

   1. Click the roll-up icon to open the Pen roll-up window.

   2. Click the bar above Update From.

   3. Select a color from the palette; or click More to open the
   Select Color dialog box, and then select a color and click OK.

   4. Choose Apply from the roll-up window to put this color onto
   the outline.

- Follow these steps:

   1. Click the roll-up icon to open the Pen roll-up window.

   2. Choose Edit.

3. Click the box next to the word Color (near the upper-left corner of the screen).

4. Click one of the gray rectangles, and click OK.

5. Click Apply to apply that gray color to the outline.

■ The Outline Pen dialog box provides yet another way to assign a color to an outline. To use this method, follow these steps:

1. Click the Outline tool to display the Outline fly-out menu.

2. Click the pen icon.

3. In the Outline Pen dialog box, locate the color selector near the upper-left corner, and click the rectangle to the right of the word Color.

4. Choose a color from this selection, or—to view other colors—use the scroll bar or click More.

Defining a Nonprinting Outline Type

CorelDRAW! enables you to not assign an outline to an object. This effect is useful when you want a fill to blend into the drawing without being separated by an outline. To create a nonprinting outline type, you can use one of several methods.

The following three methods remove the outline so that only its fill is visible when you are working in the editable preview. If no fill is included, the figure is not seen at all. (In the Wireframe mode, you cannot completely eliminate the outline; it is just reduced to a thin line.) Click the outline to select it, and then use one of these procedures:

■ Click the Outline tool to open the fly-out menu, and click X to choose no outline.

■ Using the secondary mouse button, click the X at the left end of the color palette at the bottom of the drawing screen to choose no color for the object's outline.

■ Follow these steps:

1. Choose the object with the Pick tool.

2. Click the Outline tool.

3. Select the roll-up icon from the Outline fly-out menu. The Pen roll-up appears.

4. Scroll down the up/down scroll bars near the top of the Pen roll-up window until the box to the left is filled with an X to choose no outline.

5. Click Apply.

You can "fill" an outline with a halftone screen pattern only if you are printing a spot color output to a PostScript printer. You access the controls for specifying halftone screens through the PostScript Options option in the Outline Color dialog box. Those controls are identical to those used to specify screen patterns for object fills.

Establishing a Default Outline Type for Objects and Text

When you add a new object to your drawing, CorelDRAW! draws it with the attributes that have been set in the Outline Pen dialog box. (The Outline Pen dialog box is new with CorelDRAW! 4.) As shown in figure 6.4, the attributes include color, line width, type of corner, and so on. You can change these attributes so that every new object you draw has the newly assigned attributes.

Change the default outline attributes by following these steps:

1. Make certain that no objects in your drawing are currently selected. If an object is selected, deselect it by clicking the Pick tool and then clicking a blank part of the screen.

2. Click the Outline tool to display the Outline fly-out menu.

3. From the fly-out menu, select an icon that relates to the attributes you want to assign.

4. Indicate whether you want to set these outline attributes for Graphic (thickness), Artistic Text only, or Paragraph Text only.

TIP

Use caution when applying a default outline to text. In most cases, no 6-10 outline is necessary and an outline of more than .007 will distort your letters.

5. Depending on the icon that you selected in step 3, the procedure may be completed; no dialog boxes appear on-screen. If a dialog box displays, choose the attributes that you want. CorelDRAW! assigns those attributes to all outlines that you create from this point on (until you change the settings again).

FIG. 6.4

The Outline Pen dialog box.

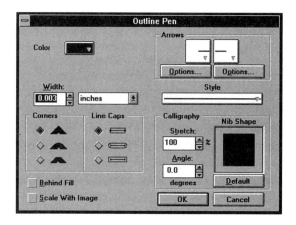

The Pen roll-up window gives you the following shortcut to this procedure:

1. Make certain that no objects are selected.

2. Select the Outline tool and the roll-up icon.

3. In the roll-up window, specify the default outline attributes.

4. Click Apply. The Outline Pen for New Object dialog box appears.

5. Indicate whether you want to set these outline attributes for Graphic (thickness), Artistic Text only, or Paragraph Text only.

6. Click OK to return to the drawing screen.

Copying Outline Designs between Objects

To bring consistency to your drawings, you can copy the attributes of an object's outline from one object to another. These attributes can include color, line thickness, corners, line caps, and so on.

To copy outline designs between objects, follow these steps:

1. Select the destination object(s)—the object(s) to which you want to copy.

2. From the Edit menu, choose Copy Attributes From.

3. Choose Outline Pen (F12) and/or Outline Color (Shift+F12); then click OK. Outline Pen copies the line width, and Outline Color copies the color of the outline.

4. Click the From? cursor on the source object—the object from which you want to copy the attributes. (If the object is filled, you can click its outline or interior.) The destination object(s) now display the outline attributes of the source object.

The Pen roll-up window gives you the following shortcut to this procedure:

1. Select the Outline tool, and then choose the roll-up icon.

2. Select the destination object(s)—the object(s) to which you want to copy.

3. In the Pen roll-up window, click Update From.

4. Click the From? cursor on the source object—the object from which you want to copy the attributes. (If the object is filled, you can click its outline or interior.) The destination object(s) now display the outline attributes of the source object.

Modifying the Interior Colors

CorelDRAW! provides beautiful colors and patterns to use as interior fills for closed objects. The variety of fills includes uniform colors or shades of gray (spot or process), fountains (linear, radial, or conical), two-color and full-color patterns (supplied by CorelDRAW! or created by you), halftone screens, and PostScript or bitmap textures.

NOTE

The editable preview shows your fill selections on-screen unless you have chosen a PostScript texture or halftone screen effect. Determine an object's fill in Wireframe mode by selecting the object with the Pick tool and then checking the status line. (Those Postscript textures and halftone screen effects are the only fill attributes that will not print on non-PostScript printers.)

CorelDRAW! gives you four ways to select fills. (When using any of these methods, you must first select the object by clicking it; then you can choose the fill.)

■ To call up the Fill fly-out menu, click the Fill tool. Then click one of the selections at the bottom of the menu (white, black, five shades of gray, or an icon [X] for removing fills). The object fills with that color.

■ Choose a color from the on-screen color palette. (For more information, see the section, "Using a Solid Fill Color.")

■ Use the Fill roll-up window for shortcuts in selecting fountains, patterns, and textures. (For more information, see the section, "Using the Fill Roll-Up Window.")

■ Use dialog boxes to assign attributes, sometimes with numerical precision. You display the dialog boxes by clicking icons in the Fill fly-out menu and by clicking the Edit button in the Fill roll-up window, or press Shift+F11. (The dialog boxes are explained throughout this chapter.)

TIP

You can make a fill in any color, including white, black, or a shade of gray. Remember, if you are going to print to a black-and-white printer or import your drawing into page layout software that does not support color printing, you need to use only black and gray on-screen so that the display is a close match to what will print.

Using the Fill Roll-Up Window

The Fill roll-up window is similar to the Outline roll-up window. It gives you a fast way to perform many functions with just a few clicks of the mouse button. Access the roll-up window by clicking the Fill tool and then selecting the roll-up icon (the second icon from the left on the top row of the Fill fly-out menu). When you first open the Fill roll-up window, it looks like figure 6.5.

FIG. 6.5

The Fill roll-up window.

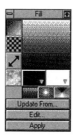

You may recall learning the basic operations of the roll-up window in Chapter 2.

Use the Fill roll-up window to perform the following functions:

■ To select the type of fill, use the four square buttons along the upper-left side of the window. The choices, all of which are discussed in detail later in this chapter, are fountain fill (see "Working with Gradated (Fountain) Fill Types"), two-color fill (see "Defining and Editing a Two-Color Pattern"), full-color fill (see "Defining and Editing a Full-Color Pattern"), and styles.

■ To display the current fill selections, click the preview box.

■ To change the size of the tile, click the Tile button, which is the second on the left. (This option applies only to the two-color, full-color, and styles.)

■ To transfer an attribute from one fill to another, click the Update From button. A dialog box appears in which you need to make selections. Choose the Update From dialog box and a From? cursor appears. You can select another object from the screen and its fill attributes will appear in the Fill roll-up. You can then change or apply these attributes to the original object you selected.

■ To display the dialog box for the currently selected fill type, click the Edit button.

■ To transfer your selections (color and so on) onto the selected object in your drawing, click the Apply button.

The roll-up window shortcuts are added to many sections of this chapter to make the associated functions easier and faster.

Establishing a Default Fill Type for Objects

You can assign a default fill to appear in every new object you create. You also can change this fill at any time so that every object you subsequently draw has the newly assigned fill.

Change the default by following these steps:

1. Make certain that no objects are selected. (Disregard this step if you intend to use the roll-up icon from the Fill fly-out menu.) If an object is currently selected, deselect it by clicking the Pick tool and then clicking a blank part of the screen.

2. Click the Fill tool to display the Fill fly-out menu.

3. From the fly-out menu, select an icon that relates to the attributes you want to assign. Unless you select the roll-up icon, the screen displays the Uniform Fill dialog box (see fig. 6.6).

FIG. 6.6

The Uniform Fill dialog box.

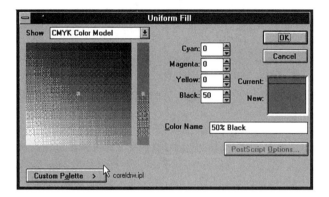

4. In the dialog box relating to the attribute chosen, indicate whether you want to set these outline attributes for Graphic (thickness), Artistic Text only, or Paragraph Text only. (These dialog boxes are new for version 4.)

5. Depending on the icon that you selected in step 3, the procedure may be completed; no dialog boxes appear on-screen. If a dialog box is displayed, select the attributes that you want. CorelDRAW! assigns those attributes to all objects in that category that you create from this point on (until you change the settings again).

TIP

The Fill roll-up window gives you a shortcut to the previous procedure. Just choose the icon that corresponds to the type of fill you want, select the fill, and then click Apply.

Using a Solid Fill Color

In addition to black, white, and shades of gray, you can give a fill a solid color of any imaginable shade. The easiest way to assign a new color is by clicking an object and then, using the primary mouse button, clicking the palette at the bottom of the screen. After you click a color selection, the object changes to the color you have selected.

Another approach is to use the Uniform Fill dialog box (see fig. 6.6). This dialog box gives you several ways to choose or create a color.

You can access the Uniform Fill dialog box quickly by first selecting an object and then pressing Shift+F11.

TIP

To choose or create a color, using the Uniform Fill dialog box, follow these steps:

1. Click the object you want to color.

2. Select the Fill tool to display the Fill fly-out menu.

3. Select the color wheel icon. The Uniform Fill dialog box appears.

4. Click a color box in the custom palette at the left of the dialog box; then click OK.

After you finish the procedure and click OK, the color you have specified is applied to the fill. (For more detailed information on the Uniform Fill dialog box, refer to Chapter 11.)

Creating Objects with No Fill

An object is not required to have a fill. One advantage in not using a fill is being able to view items beneath the objects. (This question of fill is only for use in Editable Preview; fill is not seen at all in the Wireframe mode.) It also makes your files smaller and printing times shorter.

To create objects with no fill, select the Fill tool to open the Fill fly-out menu; then choose X. Any new objects that you create afterwards will have only an outline and no fill.

To remove the fill from an existing object, select the object, select the Fill tool, and choose X from the Fill fly-out menu. Or select the object and use the primary mouse button to click the X at the extreme left of the on-screen color palette.

Copying Fills between Objects

You can copy a fill from one object to another to bring consistency to your drawing. The fill includes the color and pattern and any PostScript halftone settings. To copy a fill between objects, follow these steps:

1. Select the destination object(s)—the object(s) to which you want to copy.

2. From the Edit menu, choose Copy Attributes From.

3. Choose Fill, and click OK. A From? cursor appears.

4. Click the From? cursor on the source object—the object from which you want to copy the attributes. The destination object(s) now display the fill attributes of the source object.

The Fill roll-up window gives you a shortcut. Follow these steps:

1. Select the destination object(s)—the object(s) to which you want to copy.

2. Click Update From in the roll-up window.

3. Click the From? cursor on the source object—the object from which you want to copy the attributes. The roll-up now shows the fill you have selected.

4. Click Apply.

Using a Patterned Fill

A fill can contain patterns that have two or more colors. This feature enables you to become more creative in assigning fills.

The procedures for defining and editing two-color patterns and full-color patterns are similar. The next section, "Defining and Editing a Two-Color Pattern," describes the basic procedure that generally applies to both types of patterns. The subsequent section, "Defining and Editing a Full-Color Pattern," explains the methods that are unique to the application of full-color patterns.

Defining and Editing a Two-Color Pattern

You can select two-color patterns from CorelDRAW!'s library, import them from a paint program, create them from the bitmap editor, or create them with the software's drawing tools.

Selecting a Two-Color Pattern

To select a two-color pattern from the library, follow these steps:

1. Select the object to which you want to apply a pattern.

2. Select the Fill tool to open the Fill fly-out menu.

3. Click the checkerboard icon on the flyout menu. The Two-Color Pattern dialog box shown in figure 6.7 appears.

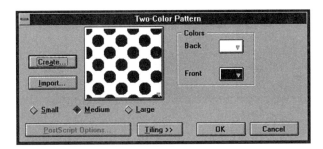

FIG. 6.7

The Two-Color Pattern dialog box.

The large preview box displays the selected pattern.

4. View the palette of patterns by clicking the triangle in the corner of the preview box; use the scroll bar to view more patterns.

5. Select a pattern by double-clicking it, or by clicking it and then clicking OK. The selected pattern appears in the preview box.

6. Apply the pattern to the selected object by clicking OK.

The Fill roll-up window gives you the following shortcut to this procedure:

1. Select the object with the Pick tool.

2. Select the Fill tool and the roll-up icon to open the Fill roll-up window.

3. Click the checkerboard icon.

4. Click the preview box. A palette of full-color patterns appears.

5. Double-click a pattern to select it. The pattern is displayed in the roll-up window's preview box.

6. Click the Back or Front Colors buttons to choose a background color and foreground color of the pattern.

7. Click Apply to apply the pattern to the selected object.

With the Two-Color Pattern dialog box, you can change the existing patterns in many ways—by changing colors, tile size, offset, and so on. The following sections explain the dialog box options in more detail.

TIP

Because bitmap and vector fills take a long time to display and print, add them as the last step in your drawing process.

Create a palette of temporary objects that have the color and pattern of fill and outline you want, then use the Copy Style From command to copy their color arrangements into other objects.

Importing a Pattern

You can create patterns from scanned images and graphics that were created in such programs as CorelPHOTO-PAINT or any other format that CorelDRAW! imports.

If the imported graphic has more than two colors, your pattern may not turn out well because those objects are rendered as dithered black-and-white images. Specifying foreground and background colors is possible, but you cannot change the shape. Do any editing in the software package in which the image was created.

Two-color patterns are imported at the same resolution in which they were created, unless they exceed 256 x 256 dots (pixels) per inch. Any patterns exceeding this limit are changed to 256 x 256. The resolution must be lowered to 64 x 64 if you plan to edit with CorelDRAW!'s bitmap editor, but the bitmap quality is poor at this low resolution.

TIP

White space around a pattern is part of the pattern and influences the pattern's size when tiled. Before importing the pattern, you may crop any unwanted white space with your paint program.

1. Select an object with the Pick tool.

2. In the Two-Color Pattern dialog box, click the **I**mport button. The Import dialog box appears (see fig. 6.8).

3. Select the drive. Select the path where the image you want is saved from the **D**irectories window.

4. Make a selection for the List Files of **T**ype option.

5. Select the file name.

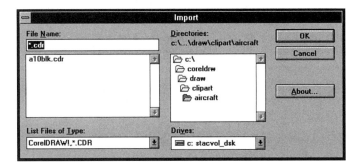

FIG. 6.8

The Import dialog box.

6. Click OK to apply the pattern to the Pattern Preview window.

7. Click OK to apply the pattern to the selected object.

The Fill roll-up window provides a shortcut to this procedure. Follow these steps:

1. Click the checkerboard pattern.

2. Click the preview box. A selection box appears with a menu at the top.

3. Open the File menu.

4. Choose the Import Pattern option. The Import dialog box appears, to enable you to import patterns to use as pattern fills.

5. Choose the drive and path, and enter the file name in the File Name box.

6. Click OK. The file you selected is imported and added to the end of the two-color pattern palette.

7. Click on Apply to apply the two-color pattern to the selected object.

Creating a Pattern

Click the Create button in the Two-Color Pattern dialog box to display the Two-Color Pattern Editor dialog box. This bitmap editor enables you to create patterns and edit existing patterns.

Choosing Foreground and Background Colors

You can designate the foreground and background colors in the Two-Color Pattern dialog box when you create a two-color pattern. To choose your colors, follow these steps:

1. Click the Back button if you want to choose your background color, or click Front to choose your foreground color.

2. Select a color from the palette, or—if you want to view more selections—use the scroll bar. Click More to enter a Two-Color dialog box similar to the Uniform Fill dialog box. (If the existing colors don't interest you, create new colors, using the instructions given in Chapter 11.)

   The preview box shows the appearance of the colors you have chosen.

3. Click OK to apply the colored pattern to the selected object.

The Fill roll-up window provides another way to perform this procedure. Follow these steps:

1. Select the object and choose the Fill tool. The Fill fly-out menu appears.

2. Click the roll-up icon to access the Fill roll-up window.

3. Click the checkerboard to select a pattern. Click the down arrow to display the drop-down list.

4. Select the pattern for which you want to change the colors.

5. To select a foreground color, first click the *left* color button beneath the preview box to reveal a palette. Click a color to select it. (Pressing Esc cancels and returns to the roll-up.)

6. Select a background color by first clicking the *right* color button beneath the preview box and then clicking a color to select it. (Pressing Esc cancels and returns to the roll-up.)

7. Click Apply to apply the pattern to the selected object.

Specifying Tile Size

A pattern is made of *tiles* that repeat across an object in much the same way that tiles repeat on a floor. The Tiling button in the Two-Color Pattern dialog box enables you to specify the tile size and starting location. Follow these steps:

1. Select the object that contains a two-color pattern.

2. Select the Fill tool, and then choose the checkerboard from the fly-out menu

3. Click Tiling in the Two-Color Pattern dialog box. A Tiling dialog box appears.

4. Adjust the tile width and height by entering a value in the Width and Height boxes, or scroll to the values you want. To the right of this value is a box in which you can specify the measurement in inches or another unit. You can change the settings more easily by simply clicking Small (1/4"), Medium (1/2"), or Large (1").

The changes are reflected in the sample tile as you adjust the width and height settings.

5. Click OK to apply the new tile size to the selected object.

As you may have guessed, the Fill roll-up window gives you a shortcut. Follow these steps:

1. Select the object that contains the pattern.

2. Invoke Fill roll-up by selecting the Fill tool and choosing the roll-up icon from the fly-out menu.

3. Click the checkerboard to select the two-pattern fill.

4. Click the Update From button.

5. Click the Tile button. The two squares that appear on your object represent adjacent pattern tiles in your object.

6. Make the pattern larger or smaller by dragging the node in the bottom-right corner of the left square.

7. Click Apply to make the changes to your object.

The patterns are bitmaps, so the selected tile size may affect the pattern's appearance when printed. If the tiles are too big, curved and diagonal lines seem jagged. If the tiles are too little, they take longer to print.

A pattern's default width-to-height ratio might be changed when you import or create the pattern. A pattern that is much longer in one dimension than the other may seem stretched or compressed. Change the tile size to re-create the correct proportions.

The on-screen tiles may not truly portray what will be printed, because screen resolution and printer resolution are different. Get the best representation of what will be printed by zooming in on the pattern before you print.

Controlling the Tile Offset

The First Tile Offset option enables you to shift the entire tile pattern horizontally or vertically across the object. To control the tile offset, follow these steps:

1. Choose **T**iling in the Two-Color Pattern dialog box. The First Tile Offset box appears on the right side of the screen. The X control is for horizontal shifting of the pattern, and the Y control is for vertical shifting. Shifting can resolve the problem of partial patterning along a border of the object that contains the pattern.

2. Specify the amount of offset as a percentage of the tile height and width. A pattern of one-inch tiles that is vertically shifted 50 percent, for example, moves downward one-half inch. A 50-percent horizontal shift moves the pattern one-half inch to the right.

3. Click OK to apply the value to the pattern.

Controlling the Row/Column Offset

Using the Row/Column Offset option, you can move individual rows or columns of a tiled pattern in relation to the adjacent rows or columns. Follow these steps:

1. Choose **T**iling in the Two-Color Pattern dialog box. The Row/Column Offset box appears near the lower-right corner of the screen.

2. Indicate whether you want to offset rows or columns by clicking the appropriate selection.

3. Specify the amount of offset as a percentage of the tile height or width. A pattern of one-inch tiles that is offset 50 percent in columns, for example, moves each column one-half inch downward in relation to the column on its left.

4. Click OK to apply the value to the pattern.

Defining and Editing a Full-Color Pattern

You can apply full-color patterns to a fill directly from CorelDRAW!'s library, or you can edit them to the colors and shapes you want. Many of the procedures involved in defining and editing full-color patterns are identical to defining and editing two-color patterns. The following paragraphs describe those procedures that are unique to four-color patterns.

Selecting a Full-Color Pattern

To select a full-color pattern, follow these steps:

1. Select the object.

2. Choose the Fill tool to open the Fill fly-out menu.

3. Choose the double-arrow icon to open the Full-Color Pattern dialog box shown in figure 6.9.

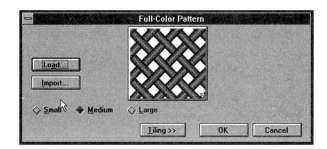

FIG. 6.9

The Full-Color Pattern dialog box.

The large preview box displays a sample tile of a pattern.

4. View the palette of patterns by clicking the preview box.

5. Select a pattern by double-clicking it, or by clicking it and then clicking OK. The selected pattern appears in the preview box.

6. Apply the pattern to the selected object by clicking OK.

In the Full-Color Pattern dialog box, you can change the existing patterns in many ways—by changing tile size, offset, and so on. Notice that the Full-Color Pattern dialog box is similar to the Two-Color Pattern dialog box. Two features from the Two-Color Pattern dialog box are not present in the full-color version, however: Create and Back/Front. The unique features of the Four-Color Pattern dialog box are explained in the following paragraphs. The rest of the options operate the same as the Two-Color Pattern dialog box options, so refer to the section on "Defining and Editing a Two-Color Pattern" for more information.

Loading a Pattern

The screen that appears when you choose the Load button is virtually identical to the Import dialog box that you use when importing a two-color pattern. The difference is that you use the Load button for full-color patterns. The Import button allows the import of patterns created in other applications.

To load a full-color pattern, follow these steps:

1. Click the Load button to display the Load Full-Color Pattern dialog box.

2. Specify the drive and subdirectory in which the PAT files are located. (Full-color patterns are stored with the file name extension PAT.) By default, this directory is the Corel40\Custom directory.

3. Select a pattern file name from the File Name box. Click the file name once to view the pattern in the preview box to the right.

4. Click OK to accept the pattern and to return to the Full-Color Pattern dialog box. Notice that the selected pattern appears in this preview box.

5. Click OK to apply the pattern to your drawing.

Editing Full-Color Patterns

You can edit existing full-color patterns or those that you create. Editing can include changing the colors and reshaping the elements.

To edit a full-color pattern, follow these steps:

1. Choose the Open command from the File menu (Ctrl+O). The Open Drawing dialog box appears (see fig. 6.10).

FIG. 6.10

The Open Drawing dialog box.

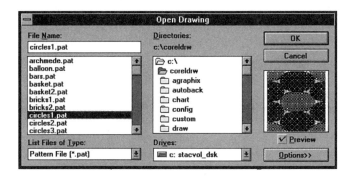

2. Designate the drive and file name of the pattern you want to edit.

3. Choose PAT in the List Files of Type box.

4. Click the PAT file you want to edit and click OK, or double-click the PAT file.

5. Click OK.

6. Edit the pattern using CorelDRAW! toolbox tools.

7. Save the pattern by choosing the Save **As** command from the **F**ile menu. Rename the file with the .PAT extension. Choose Corel40\Custom directory as the path. The revised pattern is now in the selection list of the Load Full-Color Pattern dialog box.

The pattern on the drawing page is enclosed in an invisible bounding box. The size and location of the bounding box window stay the same— and it is not affected when the pattern is moved, stretched, or scaled using the toolbox tools.

If you move, stretch, or scale a pattern of any size, save it by choosing the **C**reate Pattern command from the **S**pecial menu. Once you invoke this command, cross hairs appear. Drag these cross hairs to indicate the rectangle area to be saved as a pattern. A Save Full-Color Pattern dialog box appears. Name the pattern file and click OK.

Using PostScript Textures

You can fill objects with PostScript fills if your printer is a PostScript printer or you are sending your files to be printed on a PostScript driver machine. PostScript textures are very complex. As a result, they print very slowly. Use them with caution. To use PostScript fills, follow these steps:

1. Select the object with the Pick tool.

2. Select the Fill tool to open the Fill fly-out menu.

3. Choose PS to open the PostScript Texture dialog box.

4. In the PostScript Texture dialog box, select the name of the texture you want; use the scroll bar if necessary. When you click the name, the screen displays parameters of the texture. These parameters define the texture and are unique to each texture.

5. Customize the texture by changing any of these parameters—by scrolling to a different number or typing the number.

6. Click OK.

In the drawing window, the texture is not displayed. Instead, the object is filled with a pattern composed of the letters *P* and *S*. A printout is the only way to view the selection. To print only the objects filled with a PostScript texture, select the objects, choose Selected Objects Only in the Print dialog box, and then click OK.

NOTE

> PostScript textures print as black and opaque when you are printing color separations.

Using PostScript Halftone Screens

To access the PostScript screen controls, you must have a PostScript printer installed as your currently active printer. You can apply half-tone screens to objects or to an entire drawing. (A *screen* is a pattern of dots or lines applied to an object for the purpose of commercial printing or special effects.) You can assign special screen characteristics to specific objects while the other objects in your drawing are printed with the printer's default screen settings as set in the Print Options dialog box.

To apply a screen to an object, follow these steps:

1. Select the object that is to receive the screen.

2. Click the Fill tool to display the Fill fly-out menu.

3. From the Fill fly-out menu, select the color wheel. The Uniform Fill dialog box appears.

4. Click the PostScript **O**ptions button, which is available only with certain color palettes. The PostScript Options dialog box shown in figure 6.11 appears.

   Screens have three attributes that you can adjust to achieve particular effects: screen type, screen frequency, and screen angle.

5. In the PostScript Options dialog box, specify the screen frequency and angle. Click OK to apply the attributes to the object. These attributes don't appear on-screen, but they do appear when the object is printed. These attributes are discussed in the following paragraphs.

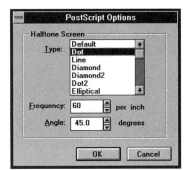

FIG. 6.11

The PostScript Options dialog box.

Setting Screen Type

Screen types include line, dot, circle, and others. Halftones have the best effect at 40- to 60-percent tint.

Notice that your computer monitor does not display halftone screens; you must make a printout to see their appearance.

Setting Screen Frequency

Altering the frequency (lines per inch, or lpi) can cause an increase or decrease in the number of grays. It can also make the screen type visible or invisible. Follow these guidelines for setting screen frequency:

- Use a value of 100 or more if the output is going to a high-resolution device (such as a Linotronic) and you don't want the screen pattern to be apparent.

- Use a value between 60 and 80 if you are printing on a 300-dpi laser printer; a higher value doesn't allow many gray levels when you print.

- Use a maximum value of 60 dpi if your output is to be photocopied.

The following table shows the relationship between screen frequency and the number of gray levels.

LPI and number of shades of gray are closely linked. The number of shades of gray is (resolution divided by LPI) squared. As you increase the LPI, you reduce the number of grays you have to work with. At some point is the optimum value where you have lots of grays and your

LPI is still high enough to produce reasonable quality. Corel sets this frequency automatically depending on your printer's resolution. The only reason to change this setting is to create a special effect, such as granularity of a pattern or a very smooth rendition of a logo (in one single pantone color).

Setting Screen Angle

This option enables you to control the angle of the screen. Be cautious when using coarse line screens (those with a low frequency setting); when you rotate, skew, scale, or stretch the object, the effect may become very different because the screen angle remains the same. The following examples demonstrate the printed results when you change the angle on a halftone with a 45-percent tint:

Line @ 90 degrees	10 per inch
Line @ 60 degrees	10 per inch
Line @ 0 degrees	10 per inch
Line @ 0 degrees	40 per inch
Line @ 0 degrees	100 per inch
Dot @ 90 degrees	10 per inch
Dot @ 60 degrees	10 per inch
Dot @ 0 degrees	40 per inch
Dot @ 60 degrees	60 per inch
Dot @ 0 degrees	100 per inch

Overlaying Objects for Masks or Holes

This feature creates transparent "holes" that enable you to see whatever is behind an object. The space in the middle of the letter *O* is an example of a hole. Every typeface character provided by CorelDRAW! has transparent holes.

Learn about this feature by trying the following procedure:

1. Make a line from one side of the page to the other.

2. In another part of the screen, draw a rectangle with a circle inside it.

3. With the Pick tool activated, drag the cursor (and the dotted rectangle it creates) across the entire rectangle that is already on-screen. With this movement, you select the original rectangle and the circle.

4. From the Arrange menu, choose **Combine** (Ctrl+L).

5. Click the Fill tool to open the Fill fly-out menu, and select a fill. Notice that the circle contains a transparent hole. Move the combined rectangle/circle on top of the line to see that the hole is transparent (see fig. 6.12).

Working with Gradated (Fountain) Fill Types

Fountain fills blend two colors or tints of colors. The effect is similar to the shading of a rounded object. This feature gives the designer easy three-dimensional shading to achieve realistic effects.

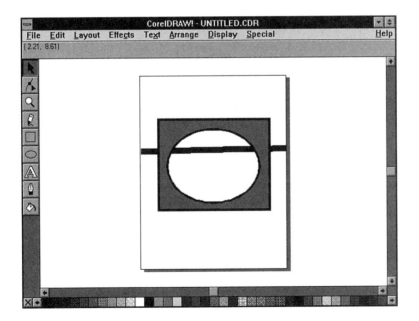

FIG. 6.12

A transparent hole.

Using the Fountain Fill Dialog Box

The Fountain Fill dialog box, as shown in figure 6.13, enables you to select the colors, offset, and other features for your fountain, also known as gradient fills.

FIG. 6.13

The Fountain Fill dialog box.

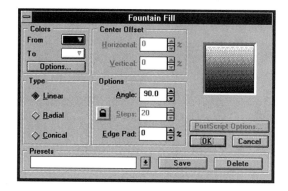

To create fountain fills with the Fountain Fill dialog box, follow these steps:

1. Select the object you want to fill.

2. Press F11 to display the Fountain Fill dialog box. Or click the Fill tool and then the fountain fill icon (the third icon from the left on the top row).

3. Select the appropriate options (described in the following paragraphs).

4. Click OK.

Choosing Colors

To select colors for your fountain fill, you use the Colors options in the upper-left corner of the Fountain Fill dialog box. These selections determine the range of colors to be used in the fountain.

TIP

When using spot color to make color separations, create fountains between two shades of the same spot color. You can ignore this rule when printing directly to a color printer like the HP PaintJet.

Fountain fill effects begin with one color and end with another. Select the beginning and ending colors by following these steps:

1. Click the From color button.

2. Select a starting color from the palette.

3. Click the To color button.

4. Select an ending color from the palette.

You can specify intermediate colors or apply a rainbow effect by using the Fountain Fill Color Options dialog box. For more information, see this chapter's section on "Using Fountain Fill Options."

Choosing the Fountain Type

You can create three types of fountain fills: linear, radial, and conical fountains. A *linear* fountain is made of up to 99 colors drawn in parallel lines. A *radial* fountain starts from a center point and blends into another color as it progresses outward. A *conical* fountain looks like a bird's-eye view of a cone where two colors are shining onto opposite sides of the cone.

To choose your fountain type, click one of the buttons in the Type box of the Fountain Fill dialog box. Selecting a type enables you to view its effect in the preview box; then you can click OK to apply the fill to your drawing.

Controlling the Fountain's Bands with the Edge Pad Option

With the Edge Pad option in the Fountain Fill dialog box, you can adjust the placement of the fountain's bands within an object. When placed into an object, a fountain is really put into a highlighting box behind the object. If you have an oddly shaped object, the peripheral bands tend to fall outside the object. With edge padding, you can keep all the bands visible by increasing the amount of start and end color in the fountain.

Use the Edge Pad option to specify the percentage of the object's highlighting box you want filled with the start and end colors. The maximum value is 45 percent. The default value is 10 percent, and 20 percent is a typical value setting.

Controlling Printing with the Steps Option

The Steps option in the Fountain Fill dialog box enables you to specify how many stripes you want the printer to use to print the fountain fill. *Stripes* is a term used to describe one color value.

To set the stripes, follow these steps:

1. Click the lock icon beside the **Steps** option.

2. Enter a value in the **Steps** box. This value overrides the Fountain Stripes settings in the Print Options and Preferences dialog boxes.

NOTE

The number of steps you enter in the Steps box of the Fountain Fill dialog box affects the appearance of a custom fountain fill. The custom fountain is made of the start and end colors and those specified at each step division. If you specify 3 in the Steps box, for example, the custom fountain uses the colors at the 0-percent, 50-percent, and 100-percent positions in the preview box. You can specify a color at the 50-percent position or allow the fountain to use whichever intermediate color is there.

The default number of steps is 20; entering a different number overrides this amount. If you don't enter a number in the Steps box, CorelDRAW! uses the setting for the Preview Fountain Steps option in the Preferences dialog box. Keep in mind, however, that the Fountain Stripes option of the Print dialog box overrides the number in the Preferences dialog box.

Specifying the Angle of Linear and Conical Fountains

With the Angle option in the Fountain Fill dialog box, you can specify the angle at which the two colors meet in linear and conical fountains. If you rotate an object with a linear or conical fountain fill, the fountain angle changes to maintain its original angle relative to the object. Use one of these methods to set the angle:

- Enter the angle in the **Angle** box. Possible angles range from 360 degrees to 0 degrees to –360 degrees. Notice the change in the preview box.

- To adjust a linear fountain, you can position the cursor in the preview box, click the mouse button, and drag the cursor to where the angle should be. Hold down the Ctrl key while dragging if you want the angle to change in increments of 15 degrees. The numbers change in the Angle box and when you release the mouse button. Notice the angle changes in the preview box.

■ Use the second method in the Fill roll-up window rather than the Fountain Fill dialog box. The preview box in the roll-up window responds just like the preview box in the Fountain Fill dialog box.

Offsetting the Center of Radial and Conical Fountains

The Center Offset options in the Fountain Fill dialog box give you a way to offset the center of radial and conical fountains so that the fountain center does not align with the center of the object. This feature gives flexibility to the designer to choose the direction that light bounces off an object. Use one of these methods:

■ Enter percentages in the Center Offset **H**orizontal and **V**ertical boxes. Negative numbers move the center of the fountain downward and to the left; positive numbers move it upward and to the right.

■ Position the cursor in the preview box, click the mouse button, and drag the cursor to where you want the center. (Hold down the Ctrl key while dragging if you want the angle to change in increments of 10 degrees.) The numbers change in the Angle box, and when you release the mouse button, the angle position changes in the preview box.

■ Perform the second method in the Fill roll-up window. The preview box in the roll-up window responds just like the preview box in the Fountain Fill dialog box.

Using PostScript Options

The PostScript Options button in the Fountain Fill dialog box is available only if you are using spot color to create the fountain. Use the PostScript Options dialog box to designate the halftone screen used to print your fountains (and to show whether you want to overprint them). For more information, see the section "Using PostScript Halftone Screens" earlier in this chapter.

Using the Fill Roll-Up Window To Create Fountain Fills

The Fill roll-up window gives you a shortcut for creating a fountain fill. Follow these steps:

1. Select the Fill tool to open the Fill fly-out menu.

2. Select the roll-up icon.

3. Click one of the three buttons above the Update From selection. Click the left button to select a linear fill, the middle button to select a radial fill, or the right button to select a conical fill.

4. Choose the fountain fill's starting color by first clicking the left color button below the preview box and then double-clicking a color. (Or, if you want a larger selection of colors to choose from, first click More to access the Fountain Fill dialog box.)

5. Choose the ending color by clicking the right color button below the preview box and then double-clicking a color.

6. Click Apply to apply the color to the object.

Using Fountain Fill Options

Customizing fountain fills gives you the opportunity to create the specific fills you need to complement your designs. From the Fountain Fill dialog box, choose Options. The Fountain Fill Color Options dialog box appears, with three types of custom fountain blends that determine the intermediate colors of a fountain (see fig. 6.14).

FIG. 6.14

The Fountain Fill Color Options dialog box.

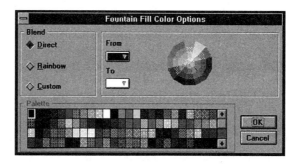

Direct is the default type. The intermediate fountain colors are taken as if a straight line were being drawn across the color sheet from the start color to the end color.

Rainbow gives a wide spectrum of colors to the fountain, because the intermediate colors are taken from a path around the color wheel. Click the clockwise or counterclockwise directional icons to the left of the color wheel. The path is shown by a line on the color wheel.

The Custom blend option enables you to select up to 99 intermediate colors from the palette near the base of the dialog box.

To specify intermediate fountain colors in custom blends, follow these steps in the Fountain Fill Color Options dialog box:

1. Click a square at either end of the preview box, the varied band of color. A color location marker (shown as a triangle) appears on the bottom of this box; the marker stays filled while it is the currently selected marker.

2. Move the marker by dragging it to the location where you want to place the color. Notice the changes in the preview box as you move the marker; you also can enter that percentage value manually, causing the marker to move accordingly.

TIP

You don't need to drag the existing marker; you can simply position the cursor where you want to add the color and double-click.

3. Select a color from the color palette. The color is blended at the location of the currently selected marker.

4. Repeat steps 1 through 3 if you want to add other colors.

5. Click OK to return to the Fountain Fill dialog box.

6. If you want to save the fill, click the Save button.

You can access a list of saved custom fountain fills from the Fountain Fill dialog box. Select a custom fill by clicking on the down arrow beside the Presets dialog box and then clicking the preset fill name you want. Then click OK, or if using the Fill roll-up window, click Apply.

Avoiding Banding in Fountain Fills

If your artwork contains fountain fills and will be separated for offset printing, you need to take some precautions to avoid banding in your fountain fills. *Banding* is the effect created when the transition from one fill percentage to another is clearly visible in the fountain.

PostScript creates up to 256 shades of each of the four process colors. The true number of shades that you can use, however, depends on the resolution of your output device (in dpi, dots per inch) and the frequency of the halftone screen (in lpi, lines per inch). The equation (dpi/lpi) squared reveals the number of shades available. You can create better fountains if you know the number of shades you have available.

(If the fountain covers less than the full range of 1 percent to 100 percent, the number of available shades is proportionately less. A gradation from 30 percent to 80 percent, for example, creates a range of 50 percent of the 256 shades—that is, 178 shades.)

The range of colors you cover in a blend can make it difficult to determine the percent change in a shade. Take the color that changed the most and use that color as the color that determines your percent change. Never use two Pantone colors in a blend. All you can do with Pantone is to blend from a color to an absence of color. Using a different color is bound to create a very strange effect if you have high-resolution output because the screen angles are not adjusted to reduce mories or muddiness.

Design a fountain by following these steps:

1. Measure between the end points of your blend. This distance is expressed in points.

2. Determine each step size (in points) with this equation: divide the distance (in points) by the number of gray levels or shades.

A result greater than one may lead to banding. Prevent banding by lessening the distance, raising the percentage of gradation, increasing the output resolution, or diminishing the screen frequency.

Summary

Without the techniques described in this chapter, the objects in your drawing look like stick figures. Using CorelDRAW!'s outline and fill features give aesthetic enhancement and substance to your outlines and their interiors. Those objects also gain practical value because the enhancements help to distinguish one object from another; one color, for example, can represent a certain unique value in your drawing.

Now that you have read this chapter, you should understand how you can modify objects by modifying outlines and creating and manipulating fills. You should also know the different types of fills and the options associated with them. Chapter 7 discusses how you can modify objects by scaling, rotating, and distorting them.

Scaling, Rotating, and Distorting Objects

The major advantage in using vector graphics is that you can substantially modify an object without sacrificing image quality. In this chapter, you learn how to use CorelDRAW! to enlarge and reduce objects, rotate them, and distort them by stretching, skewing, and making mirror images. Using these operations, called object transformations, helps you create the images you want.

This chapter begins with an introduction and guide to the basic tools and techniques used to transform objects. These include the Pick tool, the Effects menu, the Stretch & Mirror mouse mode and dialog box, and the Rotate & Skew mouse mode and dialog box. The later sections provide detailed examples of the five types of object transformations.

The chapter concludes with an exercise that lets you practice using the transformation techniques in combination to create an unusual image from a simple object.

Learning the Basic Tools and Techniques

This section introduces you to the basic tools and techniques used to transform objects. In figure 7.1, each transformation has been applied to the character string that represents its name. This chapter covers the following object transformations:

- Scaling an object, which changes both dimensions proportionately (makes it larger or smaller)

- Stretching an object, which changes one dimension (makes it longer or shorter)

- Mirroring an object, which flips it over to create a reverse image

- Rotating an object, which turns it in a clockwise or counterclockwise direction around a specified center of rotation

- Skewing an object, which causes it to slant at an angle

FIG. 7.1

Object transformations.

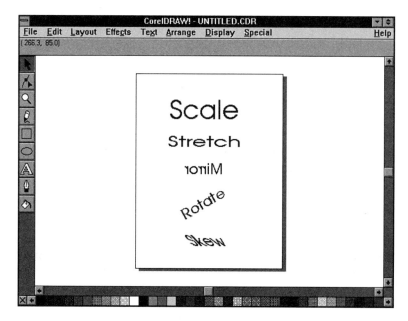

You can apply object transformations to all objects, including text strings and open line and curve segments. You can apply them to a single object or to a group of objects. However, you cannot apply object transformations to only part of an object.

Before you can transform an object, you must first select it. The simplest way to select a single object is to click its outline or fill with the Pick tool. For more information on ways to select single and multiple objects, refer to "Selecting Objects" in Chapter 5.

Using the Pick Tool and the Effects Menu

You can transform objects by using the Pick tool and the mouse or by entering precise values in the Effects menu. The Pick tool method is the quickest, but it is imprecise. Repeating the results of the Pick tool method with other objects is difficult.

CorelDRAW! divides object transformations into two categories: Stretch & Mirror and Rotate & Skew. You can use each feature with the mouse or a dialog box, as described in the following sections.

Scaling, Stretching, and Mirroring Objects

Making an object larger or smaller, or changing its scale, is one of the most common and useful of all object transformations. Scaling an object changes its size without affecting its shape.

You may want to change the size of an object in only one dimension. For example, you may want to make an object taller without increasing its width. This object transformation is called *stretching*. Stretching an object increases (or decreases) one dimension of an object (its length or width). With the Stretch transformation, you can quickly lengthen or shorten a line segment, transform a circle into an ellipse, or change the appearance of text.

Having the capability to create a mirror image of an object is often useful. You can easily create a precisely symmetrical object, for example, by making half of the object and then creating a mirror image of it. Creating a mirror image of an object is really just a special application of the Stretch transformation.

To scale, stretch, and mirror an object, you first activate the Stretch & Mirror mode by selecting the object. You can select an object by clicking it with the Pick tool. After you select an object, eight black squares, called handles, appear around the object (see fig. 7.2). With the Pick tool, drag the corner handles with the mouse to proportionally enlarge or reduce (scale) the object. To stretch an object, drag the side handles in the direction you want to stretch the object. Look at the status line to see the X and Y scale percentages.

You create a mirror image by dragging the vertical or horizontal handles across the object until the outline depicts the desired size. When the status line shows a negative number, you are creating a mirror or reflection. When you release the mouse button, a mirror image of the original object is drawn.

TIP

Holding down the Shift key as you drag the handles stretches or scales the object from the center. Holding down the Ctrl key as you drag the handles stretches and scales the object in 100-percent increments. If you hold down both Ctrl and Shift keys at the same time while dragging the handles, both actions are applied.

FIG. 7.2

The Stretch & Mirror mode.

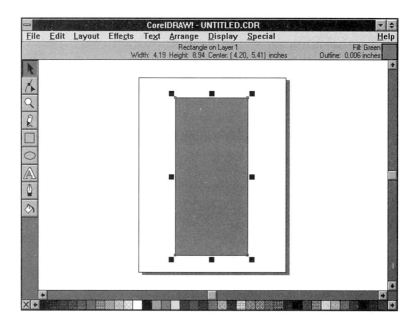

Unlike mouse transformations, you can perform more than one transformation at a time using menu commands. For example, you can simultaneously stretch an object horizontally and vertically.

To scale, stretch, or mirror an object using menu commands, follow these steps:

1. Select an object

2. From the Effects menu, choose the **S**tretch & Mirror option; or press Alt+F9. The Stretch & Mirror dialog box appears (see fig. 7.3).

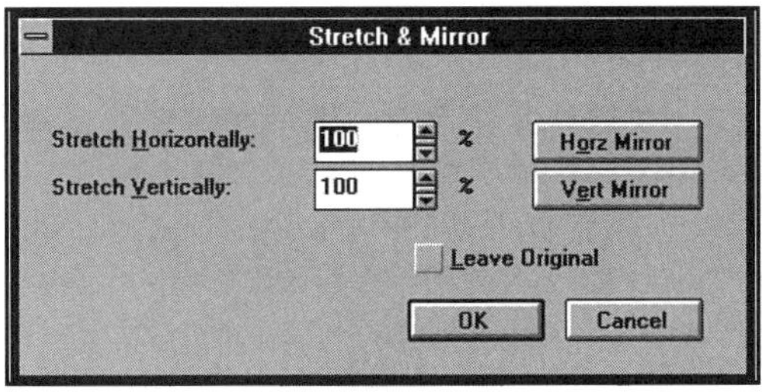

FIG. 7.3

The Stretch & Mirror dialog box.

3. Enter the percentage you want the object stretched in the Stretch **H**orizontally or Stretch **V**ertically box. There are three ways to enter stretch values: clicking in the box and typing, clicking the up- or down-arrow buttons next to the box, and placing the mouse cursor between the arrow buttons and dragging up or down.

TIP

Entering identical values in the two boxes proportionally scales the object.

4. Choose the H**o**rz Mirror and/or V**e**rt Mirror buttons to mirror the object horizontally or vertically. Clicking these buttons automatically places the correct numerical value for a true mirror image, -100, in the Stretch boxes.

5. If you want to leave the original object unchanged and apply the stretches to a copy, choose **L**eave Original.

6. Choose OK to apply the transformations.

The default stretch values are 100 percent of the object's current dimensions. Values higher than 100 percent increase the dimension; values lower than 100 percent decrease the dimension. Negative values create a reflection, or mirror image.

Rotating and Skewing Objects

Rotating an object turns it in a clockwise or counterclockwise direction around its center point, designated by a bull's-eye marker. The Skew transformation causes the object to lean or slant in one direction. When you select an object to skew horizontally (from side to side), the angle of the sides of the marquee box change, while the top and bottom remain in the same orientation on the page. Selecting an object to skew vertically (up and down) causes the angle of the top and bottom of the marquee box to change, while the sides remain in the same orientation on the page. When you release the mouse button, the object changes to the orientation defined by the marquee box.

To rotate an object or skew it with the mouse, activate the Rotate & Skew mode by clicking twice on the object with the Pick tool (or click-ing once on an already selected object). In the Rotate & Skew mode, the handles appear as double-pointed arrows, and a center point, repre-sented by a bull's-eye, appears in the middle of the object (see fig. 7.4). With the Pick tool, drag the corner handles (rounded arrows) to rotate the object clockwise or counterclockwise. Drag the side handles (double arrows) to skew the object from side to side or up or down.

As you rotate or skew an object, the status line shows the angle of deflection for this particular operation. Because this angle is not cumu-lative, it does not show the total deflection if you have changed the object multiple times.

To rotate or skew an object using menu commands, follow these steps:

1. Select the object. You can click or double-click on the object to select it because you can rotate and skew an object in either Stretch & Mirror or Rotate & Skew mode.

2. Pull down the Effects menu and choose the Rotate & Skew option; or press Alt+F8. The Rotate & Skew dialog box appears (fig. 7.5).

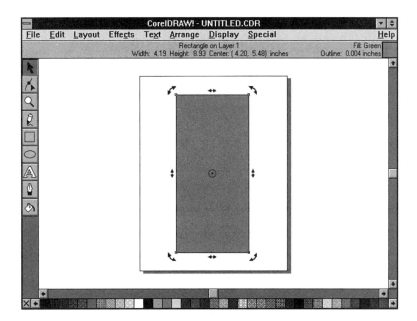

FIG. 7.4

The Rotate & Skew mode.

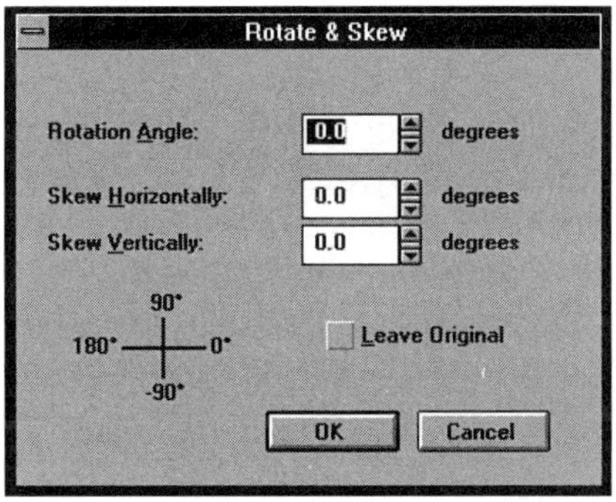

FIG. 7.5

The Rotate & Skew dialog box.

3. Enter (in degrees) the angle you want to rotate the object in the Rotation **A**ngle box.

or

Enter (in degrees) the angle you want to skew an object in the Skew **H**orizontally and/or the Skew **V**ertically boxes.

NOTE
You can skew an object both horizontally and vertically in one operation, but you cannot rotate and skew at the same time.

Enter the angles by typing them in, clicking the up- or down-arrow buttons next to the box, or placing the mouse cursor between the arrow buttons and dragging up or down.

TIP
Refer to the axes with degree markings in the dialog box to keep oriented to the angle of rotation or skew.

4. Choose **L**eave Original if you want the original unchanged and the transformations applied to a copy.

5. Choose OK to apply the transformations.

Using Additional Transformation Techniques

The effects introduced in the previous few sections are very useful and you will find that many of your drawings rely on them. If you find yourself using them often, you will want to find a faster way to make precise changes than by using the dialog boxes. In many drawings, you may want to make changes to a copy of an object but leave the original unchanged. Another useful feature is to repeat the same effects on several objects. And it is likely that you will occasionally make a mistake or change your mind and want to return the object to its original form. The following three sections discuss all of these operations, which CorelDRAW! makes easy.

Increasing Precision with the Mouse

Although the menu commands give you the most precise control over object transformations, you also can achieve a considerable amount of precision using the Pick tool and the mouse.

While you are transforming an object with the mouse, the center of the status line displays the percent change in object dimensions or the degree change in the angle of the object. By using the following methods to constrain these changes to specified increments, you can work more precisely with effects.

■ Hold down the Ctrl key as you drag the mouse in Stretch and Mirror transformations to constrain the percent change to increments of 100 percent.

■ Hold down the Ctrl key in Rotate and Skew transformations to constrain the angle to increments of 15 degrees.

TIP

To change these increments, pull down the **S**pecial menu and then choose Pr**e**ferences (Ctrl+J). In the dialog box that appears, make the appropriate changes.

NOTE

When constraining changes by holding down the Ctrl key, be sure to release the mouse button before you release the Ctrl key. Also, be aware that the percent or degree increment represents the change from the last transformation, not from when the object was created.

■ Hold down the Shift key before you begin dragging the mouse in Stretch and Mirror transformations to keep the transformed object centered around the center point of the original object.

You will notice that a dashed *marquee* outline, rather than the object itself, moves with the cursor until the mouse button is released. This feature enables you to keep the original object as a reference point when transforming it.

Leaving Copies of the Original Object

One of the most useful features of object transformations in CorelDRAW! is your ability to transform a copy of the object, rather than the object itself. When performing transformations with the mouse, click the secondary mouse button or the + key on the numeric keypad as you drag the mouse to transform a copy of the original object. `Leave Original` appears on the left side of the status line. When transforming objects from the Rotate & Skew and Stretch & Mirror dialog boxes, click the **Leave Original** button before clicking the OK button to transform a copy of the original object.

Repeating/Undoing Transformations

You can repeat the last transformation by using the **Edit R**epeat option (Ctrl+R). Repeating a transformation several times on copies of the original object can result in interesting patterns and images.

You can undo individual object transformations by selecting the **Edit Undo** option (Ctrl+Z). However, the Undo feature is limited to the number of levels specified in the Special Preferences dialog box. Regardless of the number of Undo layers, however, you can clear all transformations and return an object to its shape when it was originally created by selecting the **Clear Transformations** option from the Effects menu (Alt+C). This command resets all object dimensions to 100 percent and all angle changes to 0 degrees, and resets the center point to the middle of the object. It also clears the effects of any changes made in the Effects menu's Envelope and Perspective options.

TIP

Clear Transformations, when applied to a group of objects, clears only those transformations applied to the group. It does not clear transformations applied to the individual objects before they were grouped. You can, however, ungroup the objects and continue to clear transformations on individual objects in the group.

Practicing Using the Effects

Many of the effects are difficult to visualize without some practice. If you want to try your hand at a few examples, the rest of the chapter takes you through each of the five types of object transformations, using some concrete examples.

Scaling Objects

Use the following procedure to practice changing the scale of an object:

1. Create a large circle in the middle of the drawing area.

2. Change to the Pick tool by pressing the space bar or clicking the tool. The circle is selected.

3. Move the Pick tool to one of the corner handles. When the tool is over a handle, it changes from a cursor to cross hairs.

4. Press and hold the Shift key to keep the transformation centered, and then drag the handle toward the object until the object is about 80% of its original size, as shown on the status line. The object's dashed marquee box follows the handle to show you what the object's size will be.

5. Click the secondary mouse button. `Leave Original` appears on the status line.

6. Release the primary mouse button and then release the Shift key. Your drawing should now be two concentric circles.

TIP

If your circles aren't centered or if you only have one circle, you released the Shift key or clicked the secondary mouse button at the wrong time. Choose **E**dit and then **U**ndo (Ctrl+Z), and try again from step 4.

7. Repeat steps 4–6 three more times, using 60-, 40-, and 20-percent reductions of the original circle. You have created a bull's-eye (see fig. 7.6)!

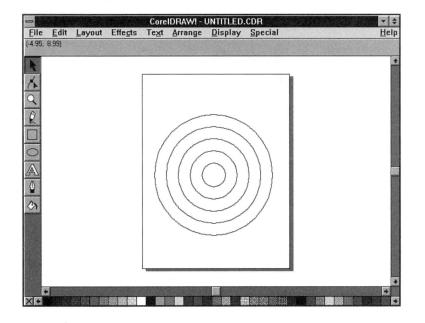

FIG. 7.6

An object created by scaling.

Stretching Objects

The basic procedure for stretching objects with the Pick tool and the mouse is the same as that used in scaling, except that you use the side handles. When you stretch an object with a mouse, you are constrained to dragging the side handle along a horizontal or vertical path toward or away from the center of the object.

Practice using the Stretch transformation by turning a circle into an ellipse by making its vertical dimension 50 percent longer than its horizontal dimension:

1. Create a small circle in the center of the drawing area.

2. Change to the Pick tool by pressing the space bar or clicking the tool. The circle is selected.

3. Move the Pick tool to the top side handle. The tool changes from a cursor to cross hairs.

4. Press and hold down the Shift key to stretch from the center of the object.

5. Press the mouse button and hold it down while you drag the handle upward until the status line shows approximately 150 percent. Your screen should look like figure 7.7.

FIG. 7.7

Stretching an object.

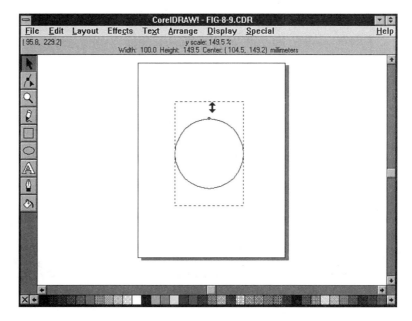

6. Release the mouse button before you release the Shift key, and CorelDRAW! redraws the circle as an ellipse (see fig. 7.8).

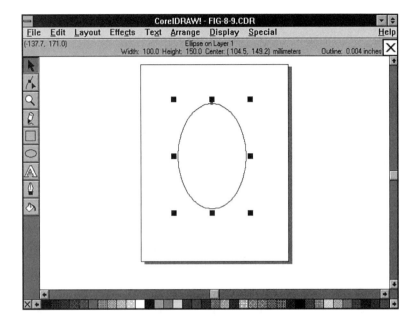

FIG. 7.8

An object created by stretching.

Creating Mirror Images

You create a mirror image with the Pick tool and the mouse by dragging one of the side handles all the way through the object to the other side. Try the following exercise to create a kite shape by mirroring a triangle with the Pick tool and the mouse.

1. Using the Pencil tool in Freehand mode, draw a vertical line and two connected line segments to make a triangle similar to the one shown on the left side of figure 7.9.

2. Change to the Pick tool by pressing the space bar or clicking the tool. The triangle is selected.

3. Move the Pick tool to the left side handle; then drag the handle across the object while pressing the Ctrl key. This action creates an accurate mirror image by making the new object -100 percent of the original, as shown in the middle of the status line. A dashed box similar to the one appearing on the left side of figure 7.9 indicates the object's destination.

FIG. 7.9

Creating a mirror image.

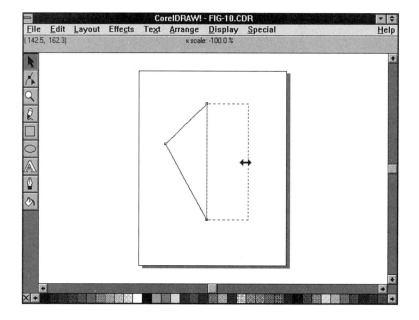

4. Click the secondary mouse button or, if you are very dexterous, press the + key on the numeric keypad as you drag to retain a copy of the original triangle.

5. Release the primary mouse button and observe the perfect symmetry of the kite shape you have created (see fig. 7.10).

FIG. 7.10

An object created by mirroring.

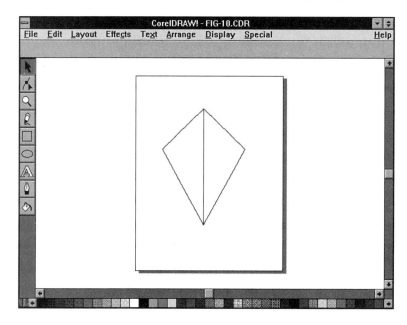

Rotating Objects

You may want to change an object's orientation on the page without changing the object's size or shape. For example, you might want to take a horizontal string of text and position it diagonally across the page.

You can change the angle of orientation of any object easily, and very precisely, using the mouse and the Pick tool in the Rotate & Skew mode. Practice this technique on the triangle you created for the last exercise:

1. Delete the mirror image of the triangle created during the last exercise, or draw a new triangle.

2. Activate the Rotate & Skew mode by clicking twice on the remaining triangle's outline with the Pick tool. The handles change to double-pointed arrows, and the center of rotation symbol (a bull's-eye) appears in the middle of the object.

3. Move the Pick tool to one of the corner handles. When the tool is over the handle, it changes from a cursor to cross hairs.

4. Press the mouse button and hold it down while dragging the corner handle in a clockwise or counterclockwise direction. Notice that the object's dashed marquee box moves with the mouse and rotates around the center point.

5. Hold down the Ctrl key as you drag the mouse to constrain the angle of rotation to increments of 15 degrees. Drag the mouse until the status line shows an angle of 45 degrees (see fig. 7.11).

6. Release the mouse button, and CorelDRAW! redraws the triangle at a 45-degree angle.

Rotating an Object Off-Center

In the preceding example, an object was rotated around its center. You can create unusual objects or special effects by rotating copies of an original object around some other selected point.

When you enter the Rotate & Skew mode, a center point symbol (a bull's-eye) appears in the middle of the selected object. CorelDRAW! rotates the object around this point. You can move the center point to a new location by dragging it with the mouse.

FIG. 7.11

Rotating an object.

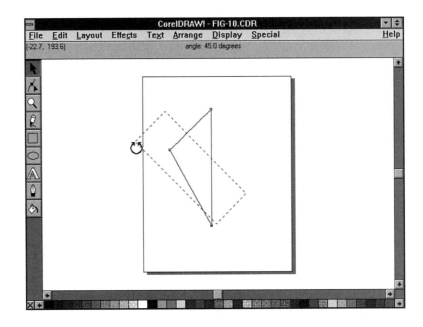

Holding down the Ctrl key while dragging the center point constrains it to the center of the object or one of the eight handles.

In the following exercise, create a pinwheel by rotating a triangle about its tip:

1. Select the triangle used in the last exercise, or create a new one that is similar to it.

2. Activate the Rotate & Skew mode by clicking the triangle's outline with the Pick tool.

3. Move the Pick tool over the bull's-eye and drag the bull's-eye toward the narrowest tip of the triangle. Hold down on the Ctrl key to constrain the bull's-eye to the corner and keep it pressed while you drag the bull's-eye. Release the mouse button and Ctrl key when the bull's-eye is over the tip.

4. Rotate the triangle 45 degrees, using either the mouse or the Rotate & Skew dialog box, accessed by pulling down the Effects menu and choosing **R**otate & Skew. Leave the original triangle by clicking the secondary mouse button while dragging.

5. Repeat the rotation (Ctrl+R) six times. You have created the pinwheel shown in figure 7.12!

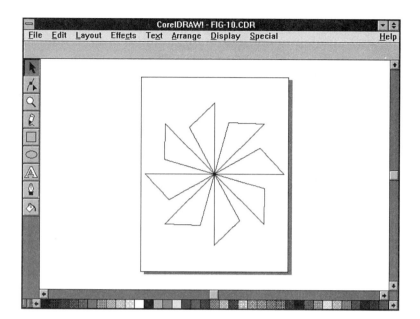

FIG. 7.12

Rotating an object off-center.

Skewing Objects

You can make interesting changes to the appearance of objects by slanting them at an angle. This transformation is called *Skew*. With the Skew transformation, you can slant text, transform a rectangle into a parallelogram, or change the shape of a curve.

As with the Rotate transformation, you can skew objects very precisely with the mouse by holding down the Ctrl key, which constrains the angle to 15-degree increments or whatever you specify as the constrain angle in the Special Preferences dialog box.

To skew an object using the mouse and the Pick tool, use the following procedure:

1. Create a square.

2. Activate the Rotate & Skew mode by clicking the outline of the square with the Pick tool until the skew and rotate handles appear.

3. Move the Pick tool to the top center handle. Notice that when the tool is over the handle, it changes from a cursor to cross hairs.

4. Press the mouse button and hold it down while dragging the handle to the left and then to the right. Notice that only the top and sides of the dashed marquee box move; the bottom remains in a fixed position.

5. Hold down the Ctrl key while dragging the handle to constrain the change in angle to 15-degree increments. Drag it until the status line shows a 30-degree angle (see fig. 7.13).

FIG. 7.13

Skewing an object.

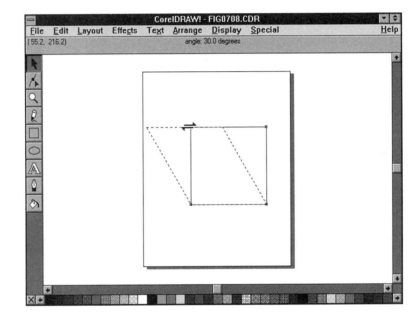

6. Release the mouse button. CorelDRAW! transforms the square into a parallelogram.

Creating an Object with Multiple Transformations

Now that you know how to do individual object transformations, you can perform successive transformations on a simple object to produce an interesting pattern. In the following example, you start with a square and transform it into an entirely different object:

1. Create a square.

2. Rotate it 45 degrees in any direction.

3. Stretch it 100 percent in either dimension.

4. Rotate it 45 degrees, this time leaving the original.

5. Repeat step 4 two times.

6. Pull down the **Edit** menu and choose Select **A**ll. Then pull down the **Arrange** menu and choose **W**eld. You have created an eight-pointed star (see fig. 7.14)!

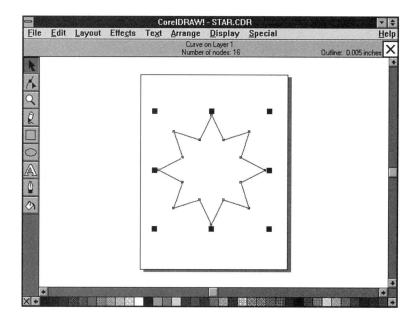

FIG. 7.14

An object created by transforming a square.

Summary

This chapter covers techniques for transforming the overall appearance of objects without altering their basic shape. The five types of object transformations are Scale, Stretch, Mirror, Rotate, and Skew.

You can transform objects with the mouse by using the Pick tool or by entering precise values in the Effects menu. The chapter describes the differences between mouse and menu transformations and their relative advantages and disadvantages. Included are tips on how to achieve considerable precision when transforming objects with the mouse.

The chapter then introduces you to the basic tools and techniques used in object transformation. Each of the five types of transformations is described, with concrete examples showing you how to use them effectively. The chapter concludes with exercises that allow you to use successive transformations to create complex images from a simple object.

The next chapter introduces you to the many interesting and powerful text selecting techniques provided with CorelDRAW!.

Adding Text to a Drawing

CorelDRAW! is unique because it enables you to manipulate text to achieve almost any design or layout. Not only can you edit text, you can color it, add a border, change the slant, and even arrange it on a curve or in a circle.

You can add text to your drawings in one of three ways: typing text directly into a drawing, importing it from other applications such as word processing or desktop publishing programs, or pasting it through the Windows Clipboard. After you place text within your drawing, you can edit and format it much as you do using traditional applications. You also can export text to a file, open it in a word processor, and later return it to the drawing.

This chapter covers basic text-related terminology, how to work with text columns, how to use the spell checker and thesaurus, and how to add artistic flair to text characters.

Understanding the Fundamentals of Text Design

Most text-design terms derive from those used by printers before the advent of computers. These terms remain with us today. Understanding these terms can help you make more informed decisions about the designs you create. The following sections explain typeface, point size, kerning, spacing, outline, and fill.

Typefaces

A collection of letters and symbols displaying common characteristics is called a *typeface* or *font*. Creating a particular type of text is an artistic endeavor with each letter and symbol regarded as a separate drawing. When an artist creates a typeface, he or she usually copyrights it; thus, you may see very similar typefaces with different names. Some of the more common typefaces are Times Roman, Helvetica, and Courier.

Although the terms font and typeface are often used interchangeably, a distinction exists. A typeface literally refers to the face, or design, of a type. A font is used in computer jargon to refer to a combination of the typeface design, the style (for example, bold or italic highlighting) and the size of the type (you learn more about this in the next section).

Point Size

The height of a character is its *point size*. Points are measured in *picas*. Six picas make an inch, and one pica equals 12 points. The higher the point size, the larger the type. Thus, 12-point type is half the size of 24 point.

TIP

A general rule of thumb is to use 9, 10, 11, or 12 point for body text; 12 or 14 for subheadings; 18, 24, 36, or 48 for headings; and 60 or 72 for headlines or displays.

Character and Line Spacing

When you deal with text, you must deal with the interline (leading) and intercharacter (kerning) spacing. The character height, or point size, determines interline spacing. Earlier versions of DRAW allowed you to set the interline spacing as a percentage of the character height, but release 4 deals with interline spacing as a point size. The interline spacing must be greater than the actual character height, or the lines will overlap each other. For example, an interline spacing of 8 points used with a 10-point type character makes the first line overlap the second.

Intercharacter spacing, or kerning, is used to different effect for different typefaces. *Proportional* typefaces have different spacing requirements for different characters. The letter M, for example, takes up more room on the line than the letter I. Proportional typefaces take this relative size difference into account when placing the characters on the line; nonproportional typefaces keep the intercharacter spacing constant. Most contemporary typefaces are proportional, but some old standards like Courier are nonproportional.

CorelDRAW! allows you to change the leading, the kerning, and the interword spacing using some simple mouse techniques.

Outline

The line that marks the edge of a letter (or any other CorelDRAW! object) is called the outline. You can display a letter with or without an outline and give the outline a custom thickness, style, and color, which creates a text character border.

Fill

The interior portion of a letter—whether the letter is outlined or not—is the fill. In CorelDRAW!, you specify the fill design and color independent of the outline specifications.

The text spacing, size, and font characteristics discussed in this chapter are generic to any text-processing application and are not necessarily unique to CorelDRAW!. However, the ability to modify the text display attributes, such as outlines and fills, in combination with the

artistic capabilities discussed later in this chapter distinguish
CorelDRAW! from the other drawing packages on the market.

Part of the reason for this distinction is CorelDRAW!'s effective use
of vector graphics as opposed to bitmapped images. Early graphics
packages used a series of dots to represent their objects, where
CorelDRAW! actually calculates an object's characteristics based
on a mathematical representation and then displays the results. This
method means that when you modify the DRAW objects, DRAW simply
recalculates the new orientation numbers and refreshes the display.
Bitmapped objects must recreate a facsimile of the original dot-
patterned design, but without an understanding of the underlying
objects. This difference in technology provides DRAW with a
superior ability to manipulate text and objects.

CorelDRAW! supports the industry type standards such as TrueType
(TTF), Adobe Type 1 (PFB), and the WFN font used by earlier versions
of DRAW. You will also find a wide variety of serif (text with small
marks at the ends of character stems) and san serif typefaces (which
do not have marks).

Differentiating between Paragraph and Artistic Text

CorelDRAW! divides text into two types: paragraph and artistic. In general, you use artistic text for accent and paragraph text for written
information. They have much in common, but keep their differences in
mind especially when you initially decide which one to use.

Paragraph text is like traditional text you use in a word processing
program, but you can manipulate it in many ways. In addition to standard text formatting and editing, you can rotate paragraph text and
even arrange it on a curve. Paragraph text's best use is for creating
longer stories that flow over multiple columns or pages. It also enables
you to add bullets, indents, tabs, and hyphenation.

Artistic text acts less like traditional text and more like a graphic object that you also can edit. You can apply many of the artistic capabilities described elsewhere in this book to artistic text (see fig. 8.1).

The type of text you choose depends upon what you want to do with it.
If you want to perform special artistic effects, choose artistic text. If
you don't expect to manipulate the text except for formatting (using
tabs, indenting, and setting columns), paragraph text is better suited to
your needs.

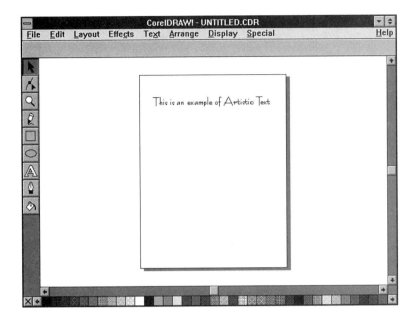

FIG. 8.1

A sample of artistic text.

Artistic text has a 250-character limit per artistic text string, but you may have an unlimited number of strings. Paragraph text has an 850-paragraph limit per document, and each paragraph can contain up to 4000 characters. A paragraph is a block of text that ends with a paragraph return mark.

You can edit artistic or paragraph text either directly on the DRAW screen or within the Edit Text dialog box.

Adding, Deleting, and Editing Artistic Text

Artistic text is the basis for many of DRAW's most striking artistic features. This section introduces the basic operations pertaining to artistic text such as entering, deleting, and editing artistic text.
To add artistic text to your drawing, follow these steps:

1. Choose the Artistic Text tool (the capital A) from the toolbar. If it is not showing, double-click the Text tool to display the fly-out menu and then click on the Artistic Text tool.

2. Place the cursor where you want text to appear in the document.

3. Type the text. When you finish typing, click elsewhere on the page.

You must click on-screen to end the previous block's editing procedure and move to the next text block.

DRAW always inserts text to the left of the current cursor position. If you click the text at a specific point, the existing text to the right moves over as CorelDRAW! adds the typed text to the drawing. If you select a section of text by using any of the standard selection techniques such as dragging the mouse over the text or double-clicking a word, text you type after that point replaces the highlighted text.

To delete all or a portion of the text, simply select the text portion you want to delete; then press the Delete key.

After adding text to your drawing, you can edit text from within the Artistic Text dialog box. Follow these steps to edit the text:

1. From the Text menu, choose the Edit Text option (Ctrl+T). The Artistic Text dialog box appears on-screen (see fig. 8.2).

FIG. 8.2

The Artistic Text dialog box.

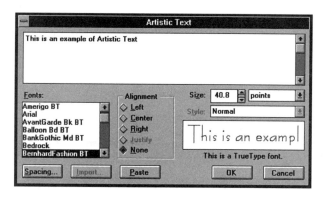

2. Click the cursor in the editing window where you want to edit.

3. Use the keyboard to make deletions or changes.

4. Choose OK when finished.

You also can change fonts, alignment, point size, and style by using the Artistic Text dialog box. Depending upon the font you select, you have access to different styles and sizes. Choose a font by selecting it from the scroll list at the bottom left of the screen.

Choose alignment type by selecting one of the five options in the Alignment box. The Left alignment option aligns text so the left side lines up where you click the cursor. Center aligns the text evenly, left to right, around where you click the cursor. Right aligns the text so the right side lines up where you click the cursor. Justify is used with paragraph text and forces the text to line evenly along the left and right sides. None keeps the current alignment, and does not automatically modify character spacing if the Shape tool is later used to modify individual character attributes.

The Size entry box in the dialog box enables you to specifically define the size of the text shown in the Text Entry box at the top of the dialog box. Text size is set in points with 10 or 12 points standard for paragraph text and 30 point and larger commonly used for drawings. The style selection determines whether the text is normal, bold, italic, or a combination. Different fonts support different style combinations. A sample of the text you create appears in the window at the right of the dialog box. A line at the bottom of the right file display tells the kind of type in use (TrueType, for example).

Changing Word and Line Spacing

You also can change spacing between characters, words, and lines for artistic text. Choose the Spacing button in the bottom-left corner of the Artistic Text dialog box. The Spacing dialog box, which enables you to select spacing options, appears (see fig. 8.3).

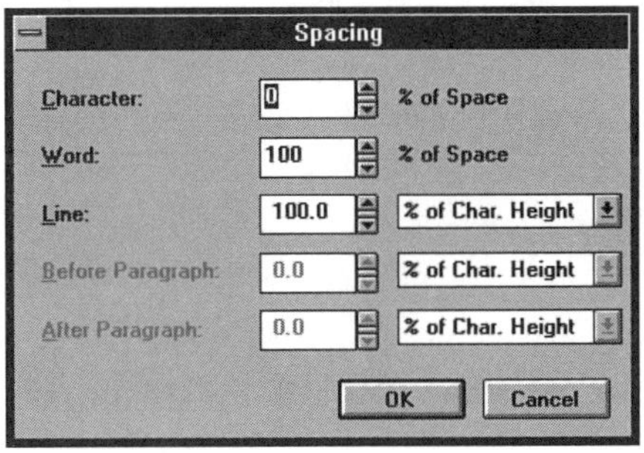

FIG. 8.3

The Spacing dialog box.

The Character option determines the amount of space between characters. Zero represents standard spacing. A positive percentage indicates more than standard spacing while a negative percent indicates less than standard spacing. The Word option enables you to set the percentage of a standard character space used between words; for example, 100% means an entire em space (a space the width of a capital letter M) appears between words.

Line defines the amount of space used for the height of each line of text. When set at 100%, the spacing appears at the height necessary to accommodate the current character height. Settings of more than 100% increase the line height, and those less than 100% decrease the line spacing. You also can set the line height in points instead of percent of character height by selecting points from the drop-down list to the far right of the option.

 You also can set the line, character, and word spacing by using the mouse in conjunction with the Shape tool. To change spacing with the mouse, click the Shape tool, and then click the text string. This displays small boxes near each letter and arrows on the ends of the text string that point to the right and down (see fig. 8.4). Then do any of the following procedures to change the spacing:

- Drag on the down arrow to set the line spacing.

- Drag on the right arrow to set the character spacing.

- Drag on the right arrow while pressing Ctrl to set the word spacing.

TIP

If your text is small, use the Zoom tool to zoom in and enlarge the text.

FIG. 8.4

Changing text spacing.

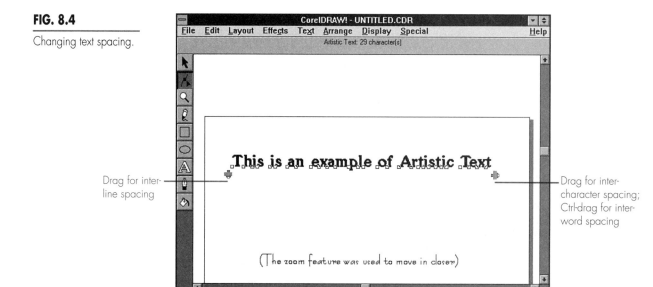

Drag for inter-line spacing

Drag for inter-character spacing; Ctrl-drag for inter-word spacing

Changing Fill and Outline Options

You can select the type and color of your text's fill and outline just as you can with any other CorelDRAW! object. You can achieve many interesting effects by using these two attributes in conjunction with each other. For more detailed information on setting the outline and fill colors and styles, review Chapter 6.

The procedure for changing the fill type is simple and requires the following steps:

1. Use the Pick tool to select the text. Handles appear to show the text you selected.

2. Choose the Fill tool from the toolbar.

3. Choose the fill type from the fly-out menu just as you choose fill for graphic elements. If you are working with monochrome printer devices, you can use the shading levels shown in the fly-out menu.

Selecting the text and then selecting a color with the left mouse button sets the text fill color. The procedure for setting the outline type and color is the same as with any other object. Select the text, click the Outline tool, and select the design and color. Selecting the text and color with the right mouse button sets the outline characteristics.

Adding, Deleting, and Editing Paragraph Text

Much of the information covered in the preceding section on artistic text also applies to paragraph text. Where artistic text is added using the Artistic Text tool, paragraph text is added using the Paragraph Text tool, which is stored under the Artistic Text tool as a piece of paper icon.

To add paragraph text to your drawing, follow these steps:

1. Place the cursor on the Artistic Text tool and hold down the mouse key until a fly-out menu appears.

2. Choose the symbol that resembles a piece of paper.

3. Place the cursor where you want to place the upper left-hand corner of the text.

4. Click and drag the cursor to the place where you want the lower right-hand corner of the text to be, and release the mouse button. A frame appears outlining the boundaries of the text box. The upper left-hand side of the frame blinks to indicate where your paragraph text begins.

5. Type the text.

6. Move the cursor outside the frame and click the mouse button. You have completed the paragraph text entry process, and the frame is no longer selected.

To delete a portion or all of the text, simply select the portion of text you want to delete, and press the Delete key. The text is highlighted when it is selected. You also can delete the entire paragraph by clicking the paragraph text with the Pick tool and pressing Delete.

TIP

Your text frame may not be large enough to display all the characters you entered. The characters are still entered but are not displayed. You can enlarge the frame by selecting the text frame with the Pick tool and then dragging the handles horizontally or vertically until the text frame is sized as needed.

Modifying Paragraph Text Attributes

You can change many of the attributes of paragraph text, such as spacing, fill, and outline, in much the same way you make changes to artistic text.

To interactively modify the word, character, and line spacing by using the mouse, first click the Shape tool and then click the paragraph text in question. Markers appear just as they did with artistic text and as shown in figure 8.5.

Drag the lower-left marker to adjust the character spacing, press Ctrl while dragging to adjust the word spacing, and drag the lower-left arrow to adjust the line spacing.

TIP

Mentally separating the paragraph text frame from the underlying text is an important point. You may have entered the text, but it must fit within the frame for CorelDRAW! to display it. If the view looks wrong, use the Pick tool to adjust the frame dimensions.

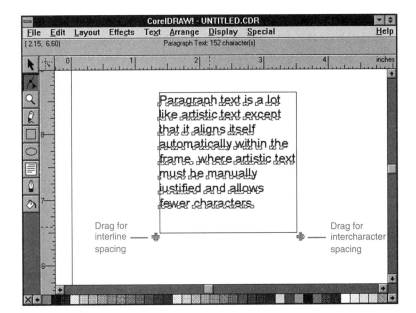

FIG. 8.5

Markers indicate
selected text.

You also can set the height of the line preceding and following a paragraph of text by using the Text Paragraph menu option to display the
Paragraph dialog box shown in figure 8.6.

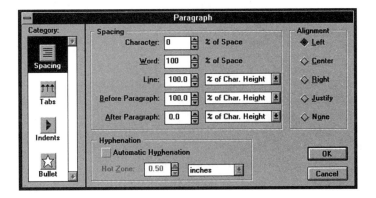

FIG. 8.6

The Paragraph text
attributes dialog box.

The Paragraph dialog box is used to set the line spacing, tab locations,
amount and type of indent, and bullet style depending upon which
object is selected from the list on the left. We will start with the line
spacing options shown in figure 8.6.

The Character, Word, and Line spacing options refer to the percentage of the letter M for the selected typeface that is to be used for spacing. The Character option default is set to 0%, which means that all character spaces butt up to each other. Word and Line are set at 100%, meaning one entire character space divides words and lines. At 0% character space, the spaces allocated for each characters may butt against each other but the characters themselves don't. Before Paragraph and After Paragraph options refer to the line height used before and after a paragraph, and they are both set as a percent of the M character height.

You can set the alignment by clicking the desired option in the Alignment box. Text aligns with the left, center, or right frame edges when you choose Left, Center, or Right. Justify aligns both left and right edges of text. You use None when you edit individual characters using the Shape tool and you do not want DRAW to rearrange spacing to accommodate alignment settings..

You also can select hyphenation options in the Paragraph dialog box. You can set hyphenation to automatic by choosing the Automatic Hyphenation option, and you can define the *hot zone* by clicking the Hot Zone option. The hot zone is the distance from the right margin within which DRAW looks to determine if hyphenation is required.

Many of these paragraph text related options are changeable under the Text Edit Text (Ctrl+T) option. This command displays the Edit Paragraph Text dialog box, which is identical to the Edit Artistic Text box seen earlier except that the paragraph text related options are now available for selection.

Changing the Fill and Outline Type

Paragraph text objects have interior fills and outline types just as any other CorelDRAW! object. You set these attributes exactly as you would with artistic text. Refer back to "Changing Fill and Outline Options" in this chapter or to Chapter 6 for details.

Changing Typeface, Style, and Size

CorelDRAW! applies the default font to any text you enter as paragraph text. After entering the text, you can change the typeface, style, and size from within the Text Edit Text (Ctrl+T) dialog box, which operates exactly as outlined in the artistic text sections in this chapter. Changes made to any portion of the paragraph text by using this approach affect the entire paragraph text object.

Setting Paragraph Text Tabs, Margins, and Indents

You can set formatting options such as margins, tabs, and indents by using the Paragraph dialog box (accessed by choosing **Paragraph** from the Text menu). Selecting the desired options in the list at the left of the box provides access to the appropriate window.

You can set tabs incrementally, spacing them as close together or as far apart as you like. You can align them at the left, right, or center, or you can use the decimal point to align a list of numbers. To set tabs, follow these steps:

1. Select the paragraph text for which you want to set tabs. Then choose **Paragraph** from the Text menu. The Paragraph dialog box appears.

2. Click the Tabs icon to display the Paragraph/Tabs dialog box shown in figure 8.7.

   The ruler at the top displays the tab settings indicated by the vertical arrows.

3. To set tabs at a given interval, such as every one-half inch, choose Apply Tabs Every and enter the interval in the box to the right (.5 equals one-half inch).

4. To add a tab at a specific location, type the location in the box to the right of **Set** and then choose **Set**. You also can choose a number from the drop-down list box, edit it, and then choose **Set**.

5. To clear a tab, select it from the location shown in the list; then choose Clear. To clear all tabs from the list, choose Clear **All**.

6. To interactively set the tab locations with the mouse, drag the tab indicators directly on the ruler. Set the tab type by clicking the tab marker and then clicking the desired tab alignment type. The tab marker changes shape to reflect the alignment selected.

7. The default alignment for tabs is Left. To change the alignment for any tab, select it in the list or on the ruler and then select the alignment type from the box. If you look carefully at the ruler, you will see that the tab position indicator is different for each type of tab.

8. When you have finished editing the tab settings, choose OK to return to the drawing screen or choose one of the other categories at the left to change other paragraph settings.

You can set the margin by clicking the Indents icon in the Paragraph dialog box to get the Paragraph/Indents dialog box shown in figure 8.8.

FIG. 8.7

The Paragraph/Tabs dialog box.

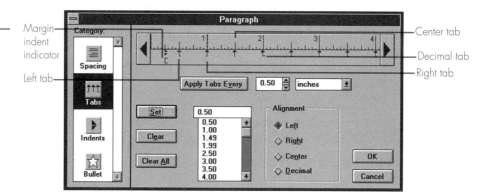

The margin setting is established from the left edge of the paragraph text frame, not the edge of the page unless the two just happen to be the same. A zero margin setting places the text precisely on the frame edge. CorelDRAW! measures indents from the margin location. So, first set the margins and then set the indents to provide consistency in paragraph text formatting.

Think of a paragraph as two separate parts: the first line and the rest of the paragraph. You set the two parts separately by using their respective setting boxes. The right margin setting determines how closely the text will track the right side of the text frame. In general, you will set the left and right margins to the same number to achieve symmetry in the paragraph box.

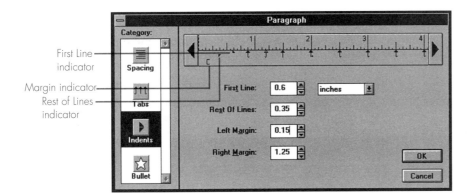

First Line indicator
Margin indicator
Rest of Lines indicator

FIG. 8.8

The Paragraph/Indents dialog box.

You can change the units of measure used for margins and indent by selecting a unit of measure from the drop-down list to the right of the First Line box.

You can set the indents and margins by dragging the indicators on the ruler. Dragging the margin indicator moves all of the indents along with it. Moving the rest of lines indicator also moves the first line indicator; moving the first line indicator only affects its settings. You cannot move the rest of lines or first line indicators to the left of the margin setting, although you can move the first line indicator to the left of the rest of lines indicator to create a hanging indent.

Creating Bulleted Lists

A bulleted list is a list of items (each usually no longer than one line) that's preceded by a single black symbol known as a bullet. A bullet can take a variety of shapes. Most commonly, it's a black dot; sometimes it is square. You can use almost any of the CorelDRAW! symbols as a bullet.

If you do not specify a size for the bullet, DRAW automatically sizes it to match the text point size. In addition, you can specify the amount of indent desired for the bullet and the associated text. Some manipulation of these two values is required if the bullet extends beyond the ruler setting for the first line indent. Insert a paragraph mark (Enter) at the beginning of paragraphs that contain bullets. The Bullet Indent setting replaces the left margin setting when the bullets are activated by choosing Bullet On from the Paragraph/Bullet dialog box.

Follow these steps to create a bulleted list:

1. Enter the paragraph text. Use a flush-left alignment and a paragraph return between each paragraph or line of text.

2. Choose **P**aragraph from the Te**x**t menu to display the Paragraph dialog box.

3. Click the Bullet icon in the left display box to display the dialog box shown in figure 8.9.

FIG. 8.9

The Paragraph/Bullet
dialog box.

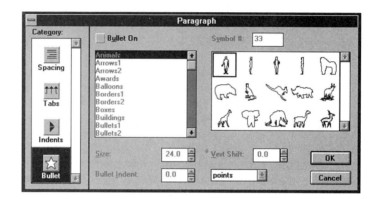

4. Click the box labeled B**u**llet On.

5. Select the desired bullet group (or directory) from the list box.

6. Select a bullet style from the symbol group displayed.

7. If necessary, make changes to the default values for point size, indentation, and vertical shift.

Size is determined in points and defaults to the text size currently active. Bullet Indent is set in whatever units are displayed in the drop-down list (for example, points or inches). This dimensional setting affects all of the settings made in the Paragraph/Bullets dialog box.

The Bullet Indent setting replaces the Left Margin setting in the Tabs dialog box, so you should set the drop-down list to points when you are setting the Size and set the list to page-relative units, such as inches, when setting the Bullet Indent. Either way, the setting always displays in page-related units on the Indents screen.

8. When finished, choose OK.

Working with Artistic and Paragraph Text

CorelDRAW! 4 provides you with several text tools that can be used on both paragraph and artistic text. These tools enable you to import text from other applications, find and replace text, spell check text, and use a thesaurus. These tools help create professional, polished CorelDRAW! documents.

Importing Text

You can bring text you have created elsewhere into any CorelDRAW! drawing. CorelDRAW! recognizes a number of text formats, including ASCII, WordPerfect, Microsoft Word, and Ami Pro. Text you import with these file formats retain their tabs, indents, and other formatting information. Note that if a paragraph frame is not already defined, the imported text assumes the entire page is the frame size and adjusts accordingly. This section covers two methods of importing text.

TIP

You also can paste text from the Clipboard. CorelDRAW! pastes any text with more than 250 characters as paragraph text and pastes any text with less than 250 characters as artistic text.

To import text using the Import command on the File menu, follow these steps:

1. Choose Import from the File menu. The Import dialog box appears, enabling you to select the file name and import format.

2. Choose the file format from the List Files of **Type** box and choose the file name from the list box.

3. Click OK. CorelDRAW! imports the text and displays it in a frame (see fig. 8.10). The size of the frame is determined by the size of the current CorelDRAW! page. If the text takes up more than one page, additional pages are automatically added to the drawing.

FIG. 8.10

A sample imported text file.

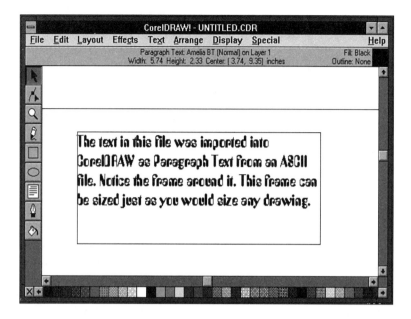

You also can initiate the import file text process from the Text Edit Text dialog box using the Import button. The imported data must be in ASCII TXT text format and cannot have a paragraph with more than 4,000 characters. Any paragraph with more than 4,000 characters is dropped from the import file. To import text from the Text Edit Text dialog box, follow this procedure:

1. Choose Text, Edit Text. The Text Edit Text dialog box appears.

2. Choose Import to open the Import Text dialog box.

3. Choose the TXT file you want to import.

4. Click OK. The text is brought into the editing area of the dialog box where you can edit it, or click OK to return to the CorelDRAW! image document where you again can edit the text.

TIP

Tabs and indents contained within imported ASCII files are converted to spaces, which may cause some unwanted large gaps in the text.

Finding and Replacing Text

You can locate and/or change words or phrases in a block of paragraph or artistic text using the Find and Replace commands on the Text menu. You must first activate the appropriate text tool before you have access to these commands. To find a word or phrase, follow these steps:

1. From the Text menu, choose Find. The Find dialog box appears.

2. Type the text you want to find in the Find What text box. (The maximum number of characters you can type is 100.)

3. If the case of the word or phrase is important, click the box labeled Match Case.

4. Choose Find Next and the search begins. When CorelDRAW! finds an occurrence of the word or phrase, it stops searching and highlights it.

5. To continue searching, choose Find Next again. To stop searching, choose Cancel.

> **TIP**
>
> If you want to find all occurrences of a word or phrase, regardless of whether all or some of it appears in upper- or lowercase letters, leave the Match **C**ase box blank. Otherwise, CorelDRAW! finds only those occurrences that match exactly.

It is often useful to have DRAW find a word and automatically replace it with a new one. To find and replace a word or phrase, follow these steps:

1. From the Text menu, choose Replace. The Replace dialog box appears (see fig. 8.11).

2. Type the text you want to replace into the Find What text box.

3. Type the text you want to replace it with in the Replace With text box. A maximum of 100 characters can by typed in the Find What or Replace With boxes.

4. If the case of the word or phrase is important, click the box labeled Match Case.

5. Choose **R**eplace to go to the first occurrence of the word or phrase, which is highlighted on-screen.

6. Choose either **R**eplace to change this one occurrence or Replace **A**ll to have DRAW automatically find each additional match and make the replacement. If you select Replace, CorelDRAW! stops at each occurrence and waits for you to confirm the replacement.

FIG. 8.11

The Replace dialog box.

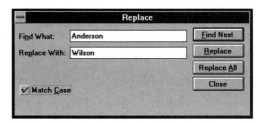

TIP

Use the Esc key to cancel the replacement operation at any time. Use the Undo command to reverse the replacement immediately after you complete it.

Using the Spelling Checker and Thesaurus

You can use the Spelling Checker to check a single word or a group of words in either paragraph or artistic text for spelling errors. The Thesaurus provides synonyms for individual words you select. Remember that a spelling checker checks only spelling and not grammar. The words too, to, and two, for example, all pass the spelling check even if you use them incorrectly (for example, if you type, **I want to buy too copies of Using CorelDRAW 4.0**).

The Spelling Checker finds spelling errors, suggests corrections, and enables you to manually correct the error, automatically correct the error, or add the word to a supplemental dictionary. You can use the supplemental dictionary to add words to the Spelling Checker not normally found in a standard dictionary. It is particularly useful when you frequently use technical or unusual terms such as those used in science or law or names of people you know.

Using the Spelling Checker

To check the spelling of a single word or a group of words, follow these steps:

1. Select the word or group of words you want to check with the Pick tool or the text cursor.

2. From the Text menu, choose Spell Checker. The Spelling Checker dialog box appears.

3. Click Check Text to begin the spell checking procedures. The Spelling Checker selects and displays any incorrectly spelled words in the Word not found box in the dialog box (see fig. 8.12).

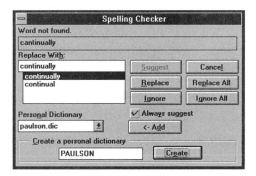

FIG. 8.12

The Spelling Checker dialog box.

4. Click Suggest to have DRAW make suggestions of properly spelled replacements for the work in question, or click Always Suggest to have the options automatically appear with each occurrence. If the word is not in the dictionary, the Spelling Checker displays the word in the Word not found box.

5. If you want the Spelling Checker to replace the word in question with the suggested word, choose **R**eplace or double-click the properly spelled word from the list shown.

6. If you want the Spelling Checker to replace every occurrence of the misspelled word, select the desired replacement word from the list or type in the proper spelling, and then choose Re**p**lace All.

7. If you don't want to replace a word (it may be spelled correctly and CorelDRAW! doesn't have it in its dictionary, or it may be incorrect and neither you nor CorelDRAW! have the correct spelling), choose **I**gnore. To ignore every occurrence of the same unknown or misspelled word, choose I**g**nore All.

8. If you often use special words that CorelDRAW! does not find (such as technical or medical terms or names of people or places) you probably do not want CorelDRAW! to flag them as misspelled at every occurrence. To create a personal dictionary to hold the spelling of people's names and other unusually spelled words, click Create and then type the desired name of the dictionary. In figure 8.13, the desired name is PAULSON. DRAW creates the paulson.dic file to hold the personal spelling dictionary.

9. To add a word to your personal dictionary, choose Add when the Spelling Checker lists it in the Word not found box.

10. When CorelDRAW! has completed the spell check, choose OK from the message box that appears. To stop the spell check before CorelDRAW! finishes, choose Cancel from the Spelling Checker dialog box at any time.

Finding a Synonym

The Thesaurus provides words with similar meanings to the word in question. To find a synonym for a word, follow these steps:

1. Select the word that you want to check with the appropriate text tool.

2. Choose the Text Thesaurus menu selection to display the Thesaurus dialog box (see fig. 8.13).

TIP

The Thesaurus also provides a brief dictionary, so if you are trying to determine the meaning of a word, simply type it in and use the thesaurus capability to find the definition.

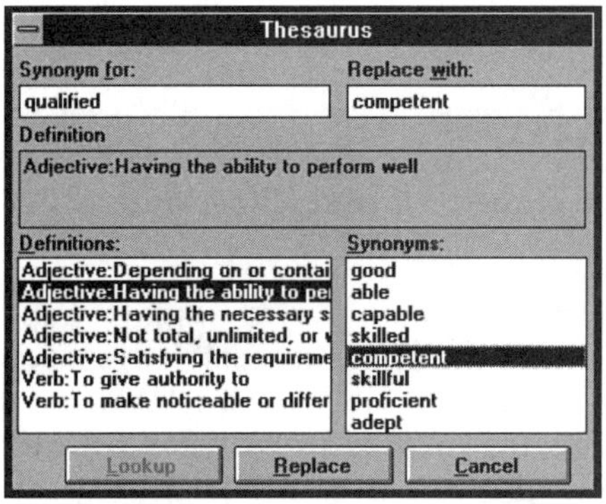

FIG. 8.13

The Thesaurus dialog box.

3. If CorelDRAW! does not display any information in the Definitions box, click **L**ookup. One or more definitions usually appear in the **D**efinitions list box. Synonyms for the highlighted definition of the word appear in the **S**ynonyms list box.

4. If you want to see synonyms for any of the other definitions, select the definition and check out its associated synonyms.

5. When you select one of the synonyms, it appears in the Replace with box.

6. To replace the word you searched for with the selected synonym, choose **R**eplace. If you don't find a word you want to use as a re- placement, choose **C**ancel.

Working with Columns and the Text Frame

You often want more than one column for your paragraph text, espe- cially when laying out newsletters and promotional literature. You also may want to define different styles for the frame outlining the text and for the way text aligns itself around objects that lie within the frame. These important desktop publishing capabilities are the topic of this section.

Setting Column Numbers and Gutter Width

DRAW allows you to define up to eight columns within a paragraph text box. You also can define the distance between columns, called the *gut- ter*, in the units most appropriate to your situation. You set these items within the Text Frame dialog box, which you can access by choosing **F**rame from the Text menu, or by choosing Frame from the Text roll-up window.

To set the number of columns and the gutter width, follow these steps:

1. Use the Pick tool to select the frame containing the text you want in columns.

2. From the Text menu, choose the **F**rame option to display the Frame Attributes dialog box shown in figure 8.14.

FIG. 8.14

The Frame Attributes
dialog box.

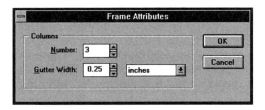

3. Choose the **N**umber box and enter the number of columns you want.

4. Choose a unit of measure from the drop-down list by clicking the down arrow if the current measure isn't the one you want to work in.

5. Choose **G**utter Width and enter the desired width.

6. Click OK. CorelDRAW! reformats the image text with the number of columns and the gutter width you selected.

TIP

Beware that the indents, margins, and tabs you set in the Text Paragraph dialog box apply to each column as though it is a separate document page. You probably need to set the margins, indents, and tabs to meet your layout needs after you define the desired column widths and gutters. If the display does not match what you expect, check these settings before becoming discouraged.

Making Text Wrap around Objects

You can use the Envelope feature to wrap paragraph text around an object. A text frame envelope is shaped to wrap around the object. Text does not naturally flow around an envelope surrounding the object. Refer to Chapter 13 for a detailed discussion of envelope shaping and use.

To frame text around an object, follow these steps:

1. Select the text frame.

2. Choose **E**nvelope Roll-Up from the Effects menu.

3. Choose Add New from within the roll-up.

4. Shape the envelope as needed. Notice that the envelope type selected is Text, which happens automatically when an envelope is applied to paragraph text.

5. Choose Apply. The text conforms to the new envelope shape which, in this case, flows around the object (see fig. 8.15).

Remember that you can make the envelope as complicated as needed to shape around the objects in question by adding nodes and Bézier control points.

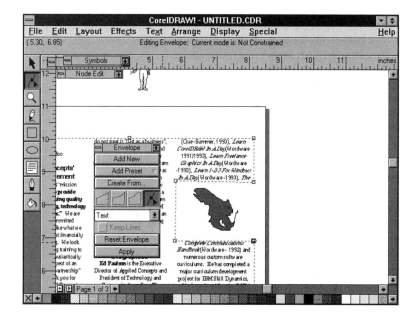

FIG. 8.15

An example of flowing text with modified envelope.

Flowing Paragraph Text between Frames

When you use desktop publishing, having a story begin in one column and end in another is common. Often the columns are on different pages, so you must have a way of linking the columns to make the text flow naturally from one frame to another. If the dimensions or characteristics of one frame change, the text automatically adjusts in the others to accommodate the change.

Documents are linked via the hollow box that appears at the top or bottom of the text frame. The hollow box often appears at the top of the frame, meaning that the frame is linked from the top to previous text in the document. You can link from top-to-bottom or bottom-to-top between text frames, as long as the box is hollow before linking. In general, you start the text in an initial frame and link from that frame's bottom hollow box to the top of the next frame to contain text. The subsequent frames can be on different pages of the document.

The + in the box indicates that the frame is linked from that point to another frame within the active document.

To create linked frames on the same or on different pages, follow these steps:

1. Create the first frame of paragraph text and select the text frame with the Pick tool.

2. Click the hollow box at the bottom (top) of the frame. The cursor changes to a paragraph text icon with an arrow.

3. Move the new cursor to the desired location of the second frame to which the text will be linked and drag another paragraph text frame.

When you finish, DRAW creates a link between the two text frames and continues to flow (display) the text to the top of the new frame. You can repeat this procedure as many times as needed until the entire story flows between text frames (or pages) the way you want.

If you change the size of the text, frame, or other components related to the text involved, the story will automatically adjust itself within the frames to accommodate the changes.

If you click anywhere on the page after selecting the hollow box on the first frame, DRAW creates a text box that takes up the whole page and inserts the paragraph text into that frame. You can now shape and size this frame as needed. If you click an existing text frame after selecting the hollow box, DRAW flows the text into that frame. It is best to link to new frames that are not linked to other frames, but you can link into a frame with existing linked text as long as you link-in from a direction containing a hollow box and a + isn't present.

The text may display in strange ways once linked to a prior frame. The text may not display at all. This situation is generally a result of the margin setting for the text frame being too large for the frame size itself so there is no room for the text. Use the Text Paragraph Indent dialog box to set the margins to reasonable sizes for the text frame in use. 0.25" as Right/Left Margins and Other Lines and 0.33" for First Line are good starting points.

In addition, you can change the text attributes for the entire story that flows between the frames by first selecting the text in the final frame and then applying the changes. These changes are applied to all preceding text in the story. If you change the text attributes in an intermediate frame, the changes only affect that frame and none of the others.

You can remove text from a frame, which causes the removed text to flow into the remaining frames. To remove the text, select the frame with the Pick tool, and then choose **Arrange Separate**. The text within the frame is removed, and the balance of the text flows into the remaining linked frames.

> To import text into a set of linked frames, make sure that it is formatted as ASCII text and then select the frame. From the Te**x**t menu, choose **P**aragraph and then Import. Then select the file from the dialog box to import it to the destination frame.

TIP

The procedure is the same for flowing text between pages except you move to the destination page before dragging the second frame.

Using Styles and Templates

Corel's Style option lets you save many of the formatting characteristics of text you have created as a style and apply them to other pieces of text. A style is a subdivision of a template; CorelDRAW! differentiates between them by regarding a template as a collection of styles. You can create a text style from paragraph or artistic text. Styles make working with objects and text much more efficient while providing a consistency between objects that make your drawings look more professionally done. This section explains how to create and apply styles and templates.

Saving a New Style

After you have created text with a set of attributes that you want to use again, follow these steps to save those attributes as a style:

1. Select the text whose characteristics you want to save as a style.

2. Choose the Style Roll-Up menu option from the Layout menu. The Styles roll-up window appears (see fig. 8.16).

FIG. 8.16

The Styles roll-up
window.

3. Click the black arrow to display the styles pull-down menu.

4. Choose Save Template to display the Save Template dialog box.

5. Accept the default file name or type in a different name. (The default extension for a template file is CDT, and the default DRAW template is CORELDRW.CDT. You are encouraged to create a new template instead of modifying the default template in case something goes wrong with your template modification process.)

TIP

Organize your styles within templates in a way that allows you to use only one template per document. If you have a style that you use in more than one type of document, save that style in all of the different templates you want to use it with.

6. Choose OK. The dialog box closes, but the roll-up window remains.

Saving Selected Characteristics of a Style

If you want to apply only certain characteristics from one piece of text to another, follow these steps:

1. Select the text with the characteristics you want to use.

2. Use the secondary mouse button to call up the Object menu. You must have **S**pecial **P**references Mouse Second button set to Object menu for this to work.

3. Choose Save As Style. A dialog box appears.

4. Select the characteristics you want to save from the selected text.

5. Type a name for the style.

6. Choose OK.

7. Follow the steps in the following section for applying a style.

Applying a Style to a Piece of Text

Now that you have saved a particular style, you need to know how to apply it to unformatted text. Follow these steps to apply a style from the library of available templates:

1. Select the text whose characteristics you want to change to those of a saved style.

2. From the **Layout** menu, choose the Style Roll-Up option. The Styles roll-up window appears.

3. Click the black arrow and choose Load Styles from the pull-down menu. The Load Styles from Template dialog box appears.

4. Select the file name, or type in a different name. The name should be the name of the template that contains the style you want to use.

5. Click OK. The dialog box closes, but the roll-up window remains.

6. Select the desired style name, and choose Apply to apply the new style to the selected text item.

Using Text Artistically

Text doesn't have to remain simply text. After created or imported, you can manipulate text in much the same way you create a drawing. Options include rotating or skewing both artistic and paragraph text and fitting artistic text to a path or baseline. You also can copy the attributes of one text string to another text string.

TIP

The application of various artistic effects may require some trial and error. Remember that you can use the Undo command to remove any unwanted effects up to the number of undo levels you define.

Scaling, Rotating, and Skewing Text

Paragraph and artistic text can be scaled, rotated, or skewed horizontally or vertically. You can perform these transformations by using the menu commands or the mouse. This section presents commands that use the mouse. The procedure for rotating and skewing text is identical to that used to rotate and skew objects. This topic is covered in great detail in Chapter 7.

To scale text objects, simply click the text object to reveal the small solid black scaling handles. Dragging the corner handles simultaneously scales the object evenly in both the horizontal and vertical directions. Dragging the handles along the sides of the object scales the text in the horizontal direction. Dragging the handles in the middle of the top and bottom scale the object vertically. Notice that the point size displayed on the status line changes with the scaling operation.

Clicking a text object twice reveals the rotation and skewing arrows. Dragging on the rounded arrows in the corners of the object rotates the object either clockwise or counter-clockwise (see fig. 8.17).

FIG. 8.17

An example of rotated text.

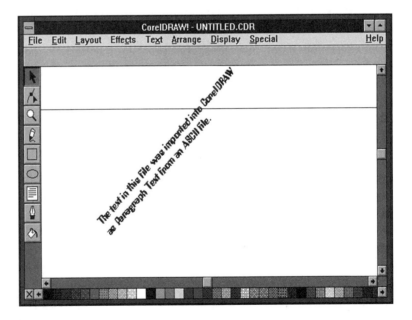

Dragging on the double arrows skews the object either horizontally or vertically (see fig. 8.18). Holding the Ctrl key while dragging constrains the rotation or skewing to a predefined angle increment. You also can move the bull's-eye to the desired rotation center point just as you can with any other DRAW object.

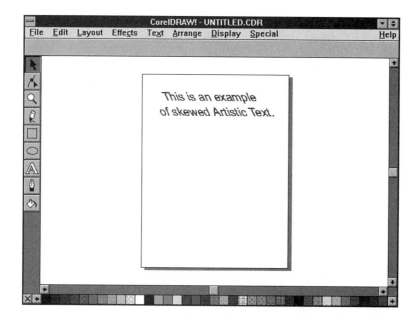

FIG. 8.18

An example of skewed text.

This method of scaling and rotating is best used when an object is drawn, and the text must be sized and rotated to match the object's boundaries. Move the text into the object, and then scale and rotate the text until it fits the object. If needed, open the Text Edit box to set the text size to an even number (for example, 30 points instead of a 30.7-point size).

You can also rotate text using the Effects **R**otate & Skew (Alt + F8) menu selection. Set the desired angles from within the Rotate & Skew dialog box and click OK to rotate the selected text. If you check the box labeled Leave Original, a duplicate of the text is created with the degree of rotation or skew you selected.

Fitting Text to a Path

A path is any line you select, define, or create in your drawing. The path even can be another object or letter that has been converted into curves. Paragraph text cannot be fit to a path.

To fit artistic text to a path, follow these steps:

1. Select the piece of text and the line you want it to follow. (Hold down the Shift key to select more than one item in the drawing.)

2. Choose the Text Fit to Path menu option. A roll-up window opens, showing you three fit alignment options (see fig. 8.19). The top option determines the arrangement of the letters while being aligned along the path (for example, rounded, straight, or skewed with the line slope); the vertical alignment of the text on the line (for example, above, centered, below, or interactively set by dragging with the mouse); and the alignment of the text on the path (for example, left, centered, or right justified).

FIG. 8.19

The Fit Text To Path roll-up window.

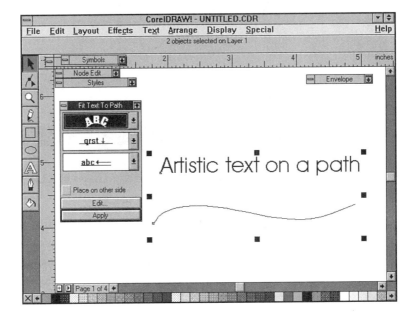

3. If you are fitting the text to a rectangle or an ellipse that has not be converted to curves, you will have a Quadrant option, which allows you to specify the quadrant in which you want the text to start its fitting process. The center point of the text aligns with the center point of the quadrant.

4. If you want more precise modifications of the horizontal offset of the text and its distance from the path, choose Edit to display the dialog box shown in figure 8.20. Choose OK to return to the Fit Text to Path roll-up after you have made the modifications.

FIG. 8.20

The Fit Text To Path Offsets dialog box.

5. Choose Apply to fit the text to the path.

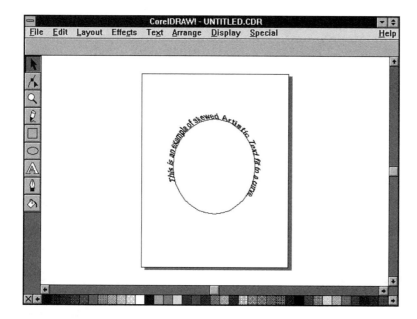

FIG. 8.21

An example of text that fits to a curve.

Press Ctrl while clicking the text to separate it from the path-text group and then press Ctrl+T or choose **Text Edit Text** to edit the contents of the text string. If you want to fit the text to a path that was previously a letter, you must first convert the letter to curves, and then fit the text to the path of the letters outline. You may want to remove the text character path's thickness or color to make it invisible.

Putting Text on the Opposite Side of the Line

If you want the text to appear on the opposite side of the line to which it has been attached, follow these steps:

1. Select the text.

2. Choose the **Text Fit to Path** menu option. The Fit Text to Path roll-up window appears.

3. Click the Place on other side box.

4. Choose Apply.

The Fit Text to Path roll-up window remains in place, and CorelDRAW! applies the choices you made to the selected text. To modify your choices, use the options in the roll-up window. To accept your choices, click Apply and then close the roll-up.

Separating Text from a Path

Before you can edit the text after it has been fit to path, you must separate the text from the path to which it is attached. To do so, follow these steps:

1. Select the text.

2. From the **A**rrange menu, choose **S**eparate.

3. To restore text to straight line, use Text Straighten Text.

The text has now been separated from the path. You may want to try Undo to see if it remembers the operation and corrects it for you.

Modifying an Individual Character's Attributes

You can modify almost every aspect of an individual character in a longer text string by using the Shape tool instead of the Pick or Text tools. After the text is selected with the Shape tool, small squares appear at the bottom left of each character (see fig. 8.22). You use these squares to select an individual character or to select a group of characters using either the marquee select or Shift-click selection procedures with the Shape tool.

Double-clicking any of the character boxes opens the Character Attributes dialog box, which is used to set the attributes associated with this particular character (see fig. 8.23). The character retains its text status but is modified in accordance with this screen's settings.

The font size and style of this particular character is set just as with prior screens. Placement options include normal, superscript, and subscript. The Horizontal Shift and Vertical Shift settings define a percentage of an ems (capital M for this typeface) shift you want for this particular character with respect to the others. The Character Angle option enables you to define a rotation for the character that does not affect the other characters in the text string. The *t* in text was modified using the setting shown in the dialog box to achieve the shift and type-face effect shown in figure 8.23. Notice that only the single letter was affected.

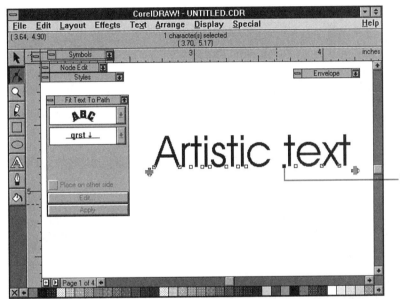

FIG. 8.22

Selecting text with the Shape tool.

Selected character

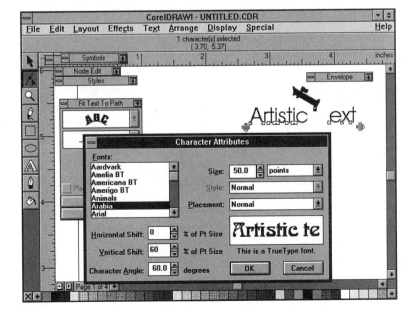

FIG. 8.23

The *t* in text flies to new heights.

Straightening Text and Aligning to a Baseline

After you modify text by using the Shape tool, you may need to straighten it back to how it was before you applied the modifications. This feat is accomplished by selecting the text with the Shape tool and then choosing Text Straighten Text. CorelDRAW! straightens the selected text and removes any horizontal, vertical, and angular changes. Selecting the text and then choosing Text Align to Baseline removes all vertical shifts applied to the characters but leaves all other transformations in place, which can lead to some strange results. This option is useful for lining characters along a common line from which they can be rotated or moved horizontally.

Copying Attributes from One Text String to Another

You can copy the attributes you have assigned to a selected string of text to another string. To copy the attributes, follow these steps:

1. Select the text to which you want to copy attributes.

2. Choose Copy Attributes From from the Edit menu. The Copy Style dialog box appears. Several options are available for copying: Outline Pen Type and Color, Fill Type, Text Attributes, and Power Line Attributes.

3. Select the attributes you want to copy.

4. Choose OK. The FROM? cursor appears on-screen.

5. Select the text from which you want to copy the attributes. CorelDRAW! applies the attributes you selected earlier to the target text.

Understanding Advanced Text Design

Now that DRAW has adequate paragraph text editing tools, you may find yourself creating original copy in DRAW that you want to transfer to another word processor for more extensive editing. After you edit the text in the word processor, you can bring the file back into DRAW. The procedure is simple, but it requires that you adhere to certain rules. This section introduces you to these rules and the basic text transfer procedures.

Extracting, Editing, and Retrieving Text

Text created in CorelDRAW! can be extracted, or removed from DRAW, into a separate ASCII text file, which you can access and edit by using a standard word processing application such as Word for Windows or the Windows Notepad. You can return the ASCII text file edited in Word for Windows to your drawing using the Special Merge Back menu option. Not erasing any of the coding inserted as part of the extraction process is important because DRAW does not know what to do with the file when it attempts to use Merge Back unless those codes are present.

Extracting Text

To extract a piece of text, follow these steps:

1. Select the text and then choose the **S**pecial **E**xtract menu option. If you have made modifications to the image since the last time you saved, CorelDRAW! prompts you to save your image before displaying the Extract dialog box.

2. After you save the image, CorelDRAW! displays the Extract dialog box.

3. If you want to extract the text to a file name other than the default, place your cursor in the File name box and enter a new name.

4. If you want to use a file path other than the default, select a new path.

5. Select OK.

TIP

Using the file name that CorelDRAW! suggests is a good idea because it is the same name as the drawing with a TXT extension instead of a CDR extension. This naming process will make it easier for you to determine which extracted text file goes with your drawings.

Editing Extracted Text

You can edit the extracted text with many ASCII capable word processing programs. You must be very careful not to alter any of the contents except for the text. Altering other characters in the file can have dire consequences that affect the Merge Back procedure. For example, the first line encodes the DRAW file from which the text was extracted, and the <CDR> at the end represents the end of the file (see fig. 8.24). Removing either of these will preclude the Merge Back operation.

FIG. 8.24

An example of extracted text for spell-checking.

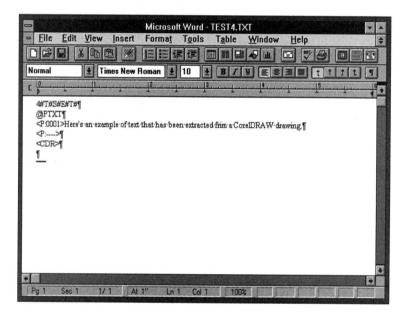

After you have finished editing the file, you can close it and merge the contents back into your drawing.

Restoring (Merging Back) Text

After the text has been edited, use the Special Merge Back command to insert the text back into its original file location. You can accomplish this procedure by choosing the Special Merge Back menu option, which displays the File Definition dialog box. Select or enter the name and path of the text file you want to bring back. The file is restored and any changes made to the file while in the word processor have been made to the text in the drawing.

Converting Text Characters to Curved Objects for Shaping

If you want to control the shape of the characters in a string of artistic text, you must convert artistic text to curves so that the object nodes can be modified. You cannot convert paragraph text to curves. Many of the dramatic effects achieved with CorelDRAW! are accomplished by first entering the artistic text, selecting a font that closely matches the final design, and then converting the text to curves for final design.

After CorelDRAW! converts text to curves, it loses its text attributes and becomes a series of combined objects. Make sure that the spelling and content of your text is accurate before converting to curve because you can't go back except by using Undo.

To convert the text, follow these steps:

1. Select the text.

2. Pull down the Arrange menu and choose the Convert To Curves option (Ctrl+Q). The text is no longer treated as text but as a combination of graphic objects.

3. If you want to work on individual letters in the string, select the Arrange Break Apart menu option.

You can now work on each letter with the Shape or Pick tool as if it were a separate object. Remember, the objects are no longer text characters even though they look the same as before. They are artistic objects that happen to look like text. You should have fun with this feature.

Adding a Graphic Symbol

DRAW comes with thousands of symbols that can be used as simple drawing accents or starting points for more complicated drawings. To add a symbol to an image, follow these steps:

1. Click and hold the mouse button on the Text tool until the fly-out menu appears.

2. Choose the star symbol to display the Symbols roll-up window (Ctrl+F11), as shown in figure 8.25. These symbols are not text characters but standard graphic objects.

FIG. 8.25

FIG. 8.25

The Symbols roll-up window.

The various symbol groups are selected using the list at the top of the dialog box. You can scroll through each symbol group using the arrows near the bottom. Click a symbol and drag it onto the drawing page to include it in your drawing. You can treat the symbol just as you do any other object.

The symbol number is shown at the bottom left of the dialog box along with the symbol's size. If you know the symbol number, enter it into this box, and DRAW finds it for you.

The Tile option is used to duplicate the symbol in both a horizontal and vertical direction across the screen. Clicking the Options button reveals the Tile dialog box in which you can set the size of the grid along which the tiles symbols are aligned. Set these values to the number of inches between each symbol grid line. Make sure that these numbers are larger than the symbol size, or you may get overlap between the symbols when they tile on the page. Selecting Proportional makes the horizontal and vertical number of tiles equal, meaning you only need to define one number and the other automatically tracks.

NOTE

You can make interesting wallpaper (desktop pattern) for Windows with this function. Export your drawing in a BMP file format to the Windows directory.

Adding a Special Character

You can add the special ASCII characters, such as the copyright and registered trademark symbols, to your text by following these steps:

1. Click the text string with the cursor where you want the special character to appear.

2. Press Alt and the ASCII code number for the special character, remembering to precede the number with a zero (for example, Alt+0169 is the copyright symbol).

3. Release Alt to insert the special character. A full listing of the extended character set is included in the appendix.

About TrueType Fonts

Microsoft Windows provides a built-in set of fonts known as TrueType. These are available to any Windows application. Using these TrueType fonts best ensures that the text will appear when printed as it does on-screen. In other words, you get WYSIWYG. In addition, TrueType fonts are scalable, meaning they can change size without any loss of text quality. This feature is particularly important when dealing with high-quality graphics and large text sizes as is often performed with CorelDRAW!.

A small selection of TrueType fonts are available with Windows, and CorelDRAW! installs a large additional set that is available to all other Windows applications running on your machine. CorelDRAW! also can create a custom typeface or font and then export it for later use.

The major benefit of creating a custom font is that you can then access the font characters just as you would any letter in the alphabet—except this character may be a graphic image such as your signature or a custom-designed text character. You can have a lot of fun with this feature and save yourself a lot of time if you set it up properly.

Creating Custom Typefaces (Exporting Text)

Though it's not likely that you'll create a totally new font, you can convert a portion of a drawn (or customized) text to a font. Keep in mind, however, that you should not attempt to change the existing typefaces or create new ones unless you feel comfortable with typesetting terminology and restrictions.

Here are a few restrictions placed upon you while making a custom font:

- The character must be a single object, so make it all at one time or use the combine feature.

- The object should contain no fill or outline color or thickness attributes.

- The overlapping objects that comprise the character should align to make a continuous outline as opposed to a jagged interior edge.

You create and save the typeface one character at a time using the following procedure:

1. Pull down the File menu and choose the Export option. The TrueType Export dialog box appears (see fig. 8.26).

FIG. 8.26

The TrueType Export dialog box.

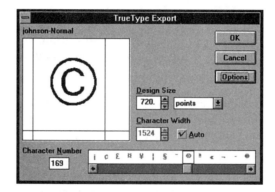

2. Select either Adobe Type 1 Font or TrueType Font depending upon your need. If you have created a new type face, type a name for the file in the File Name box. If you want to add a character to an existing typeface, select the typeface name from the listed files. (Be sure to select the proper path; for example, the TrueType fonts are usually in the Windows/System subdirectory.)

3. Choose OK.

The character number at the bottom of the dialog box determines which character is pressed to generate the type character being saved. The design size is the size of the object used for character creation, and you are encouraged to use a larger size to ensure better resolution during the translation process.

NOTE

The Options dialog box appears whenever you initially save a font. It allows for detailed definition of the of the style, grid size, and space width associated with the font in question. This topic is complicated and beyond the scope of this chapter. You are encouraged to review type creation procedures in a reference dedicated to this rigorous subject.

4. Type the family name for the typeface.

5. Set the style, grid size, and space width for the typeface and select OK. A font family export dialog box appears for either TrueType or Adobe, depending upon the type you choose.

6. Make the desired changes to the design size and character width.

7. Choose the appropriate character number.

8. Click OK.

The DRAW Typefaces

Adobe Type Manager, Bitstream's FaceLift (a popular set of fonts available separately for Windows applications), TrueType and the CorelDRAW! WFN fonts are all different from each other. For this reason, the CorelDRAW! font names do not match those of any other typeface. (A simpler reason for this is that typefaces are copyrighted and royalties must be paid for their use. CorelDRAW!, as well as others, is able to avoid this requirement by creating their own slightly different version of a popular typeface.)

The CD version of DRAW provides over 750 different fonts in both TrueType and Adobe Type I (PFB) designs. You are encouraged to work with the TrueType or WFN font designs until you are well acquainted with the font-related intricacies, at which time you may want to design your own. You may find that everything you want to do—at least until you become very advanced—can be accomplished with the standard fonts provided.

Summary

If you're familiar with the features found in most word processors these days, you shouldn't have much trouble with Corel's text functions. You may find that the desktop publishing capabilities of DRAW, combined with the easy access to a huge clip art library, make working in DRAW for layout and design a very attractive option.

With CorelDRAW!, you can select the text spacing, alignment, fill, outline characteristics, typeface, point size, and style. You can create a bulleted list, control the amount of spacing between words, characters, lines, and paragraphs, as well as impose standard word processing features like tabs, indentation, and automatic hyphenation.

A spell checker and thesaurus are useful features found in CorelDRAW!, as is the ability to generate your own fonts and typefaces. You can create columns of text, adjust the gutter width, and make the text wrap around objects.

The next chapter deals with file management techniques and using MOSAIC.

Working with Files

P A R T

III

O U T L I N E

File-Related Operations and MOSAIC

Much of CorelDRAW!'s value stems from its ability to import and export files in various formats. Some people buy the package simply for its graphic file conversion capability. This chapter introduces basic saving and retrieving processes, and then deals with file conversion and the use of MOSAIC, Corel's file manager.

Saving and Retrieving Files

The save and retrieve operations of CorelDRAW! follow Windows conventions, so if you are familiar with other Windows applications, you will have little problem with the CorelDRAW! operations. Save each file with a name that provides as much insight as possible into that file's contents. Unfortunately, you don't have much room for descriptive information in your file names because DOS accepts only up to 8 characters for file names and Corel tracks its files using the file name extension. You might not remember what you drew six months ago, so it is useful to add keywords to your files. They can provide a helpful way to sort your images later.

Saving Drawings

As you work on a drawing, save it regularly. If you don't save your drawing and the power to your computer is interrupted, you will lose your work. There's almost nothing more frustrating than losing several hours of work because you didn't take a few moments to save your file.

DRAW provides two methods of saving files—*Save* and *Save As*—which are both located on the File menu. Although they look similar, they serve very different functions except when you are saving a file for the first time.

If you want to save your current file in the currently active directory under its existing file name, choose **File Save** or press Ctrl+S. This action saves your file over the previously existing version of the same file. Depending on your backup settings, the earlier version is either saved in a backup file (with a BAK extension) or simply erased by the new save. See the later section of this chapter called "Making Backup Files and Autosaving" for more details concerning backup options. If you choose **File Save** before your file has been named, the Save Drawing dialog box shown in figure 9.1 appears and you are prompted to enter a name and directory location.

The extension shown in the List Files of Type box at the lower left of the dialog box determines which files from the current directory are displayed in the upper-left list box. The default value that appears is the extension used by the current Corel application. All CorelDRAW! files end with a CDR extension, so that is the default for the Save Drawing dialog box shown in figure 9.1.

To save the file, type the desired file name in the File Name text box and then choose OK. The file is saved in CDR format using the path designated in the Directories box.

You can include an *image header* with each file—a small image that can help you remember what the file contains. You don't have to include one, but you might find that these little pictures really are worth a thousand words. The various Image Header options can be accessed by clicking the arrow to the right of the Image Header drop-down list box. As usual, you must make trade-offs when choosing your image header strategy. The smaller the number associated with the image header, the less storage space your files require. But the space savings are counter-balanced by header images that are less clear and harder to recognize. You can eliminate the header image completely by choosing None, but doing so also eliminates much of the usefulness of MOSAIC (the handy visual file manager discussed later in this chapter). You should probably retain a header image of some sort for this reason.

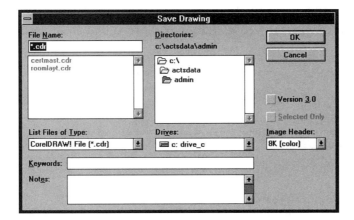

FIG. 9.1

The Save Drawing dialog box.

To save the current drawing in a DRAW 3-compatible format, select the Version **3**.0 option. You can use this option to provide files to service bureaus or persons who are still using DRAW 3. DRAW 4 can read version 3 and earlier files, but earlier versions of DRAW cannot read DRAW 4 files. The format differs from version to version; the only way to determine the file type is to open a file and see how DRAW reacts.

If you save using the Version 3 option, your existing file name is used and the active file is replaced with the version 3 file format. You can avoid this situation by saving the version 3 file under a different name or to a different drive/directory. In fact, if you are planning to transfer the file to another party you might want to save the version 3 file to a floppy disk to avoid later confusion.

Saving a Copy of an Open File

Use the Save As command to save the current file to another location or under another name. This procedure retains the original file on disk and enables you to save modifications of that file under other names without affecting the initial drawing design. Saving to the floppy drive is a simple but effective way to make a copy of an open file. To use the Save As command, follow these steps:

1. From the File menu, choose Save As.

2. Choose the desired floppy drive (A, B, and so on).

3. Choose the desired path as required.

4. Type the file name.

5. Choose the file type, and then click OK. A copy of the file is now saved to the floppy drive.

If you need to save the current drawing as a template or pattern file, use the Save As command and select either CorelDRAW! Template or Pattern File from the List Files of Type drop-down list.

NOTE

Using templates and patterns is discussed in Chapter 6.

Adding Keywords and Notes to Files

The Save Drawing and Open Drawing dialog boxes provide you with access to special sections for *Keywords* and *Notes*. These fields can help you keep track of the contents of your files. You can sort a group of files by their keywords, making it much easier to find specific files at a later date.

To add keywords to the current drawing, click the Keywords text box and enter words that describe the important aspects of that drawing. Keywords should be single words; if you want to add more than one, they should be separated by commas. You can add as many keywords as you like.

To enter a note, click the Notes box and type whatever text you want to enter. The information is saved as part of the file.

TIP

To view the notes and keywords while opening a file, choose **F**ile **O**pen **O**ptions to reveal the Keywords and Notes sections of the dialog box. You can edit the keywords and notes from within this screen.

Finding and Sorting Files

As you create numerous Corel drawings over an extended period of time you are bound to forget many of the names under which those drawings are saved. The Open Drawing dialog box provides several features that are useful for finding files that meet specific criteria. To investigate them, choose **O**ptions from the Open Drawing dialog box (see fig. 9.2).

> **NOTE**
>
> Choosing Options when the full dialog box with options is displayed returns you to the shorter dialog box.

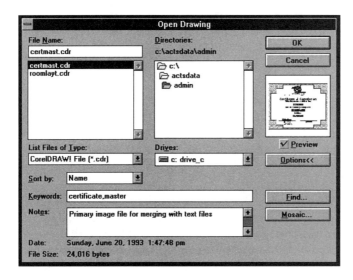

FIG. 9.2

The Open Drawing dialog box with Options selected.

After a file is selected, information concerning that file—including its size and the day, date, and time of the last save—is shown at the bottom of the dialog box. Any notes and keywords attached to the highlighted file are shown in their respective fields.

If you want to see a preview of each file as you select it, be sure that the Preview box in the Open Drawing dialog box is checked. If it is not checked, simply click the box to select it. If a diagonal line appears in the Preview window, no file is selected, the file is an earlier DRAW 2 release file, or else there is no Preview information available for the selected file.

The Sort By field is used to sort the files contained in this directory by either Name or Date last saved.

Click **F**ind to open the Keyword Search dialog box (see fig. 9.3).

FIG. 9.3

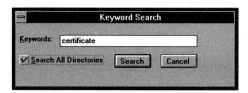

Enter the keywords for which you want DRAW to search. It searches either the currently active directory or all directories on the drive (if the Search All Directories option is checked). Click Search to perform the search and display a listing of the chosen files.

After you have selected a file to open and looked at the preview to be sure it is the file you want, you are ready to open the drawing. Double-click the desired file (or select it and click OK) to load that file into DRAW for editing.

Saving and Retrieving DRAW 3 Formatted Files

CorelDRAW! 4 can save and retrieve drawings in CorelDRAW! 3 format. This can be a useful feature if you need to open files that you drew in CorelDRAW! 3 or if you want to save a file for someone who is still using CorelDRAW! 3.

When you open a file that is in CorelDRAW! 3 format, the image of that file appears in the Preview box (if an image was attached to the file). DRAW 4 prompts you to convert the text in the image to DRAW 4 format. You should accept this option unless you plan to do more work with the file in DRAW 3.

When you save a file in version 3 format you may be queried about the text contained in the drawing. Because some of the typefaces used in version 4 were not provided with 3, problems can occur when drawings are converted back to 3 format. DRAW 3 has no way of interpreting these characters, and strange things, such as weird text spacing, can happen.

You can avoid this situation by selecting typefaces common to both versions, or by converting all text to curves before saving in version 3 format. If you convert the text to curves, letters are treated as objects instead of text and the problem is resolved (at the expense of a more complicated drawing). You may want to try the save and verify the results before trying any fancy workaround procedures.

Making Backup Files and Autosaving

CorelDRAW! is capable of automatically creating a backup file each time you save a new version of an existing file; it can also back up your work every few minutes. Unfortunately, no method for setting up or altering these backup options is built into the standard user interface. The good news is that an automatic timed backup every 10 minutes and a backup when you save are both options that are automatically installed when you load CorelDRAW! and should not need changing. To customize them, you must modify the CORELDRW.INI file.

This section outlines the procedure for setting your backup options. You should not take on this task, however, unless you are familiar enough with Windows and INI file editing to avoid trouble. As a safeguard, use the Windows File Manager to make a backup copy of the CORELDRW.INI file before you edit it. That way you can restore the old INI file if things don't work out as you plan.

To change CorelDRAW! backup and autosave criteria, follow these steps:

1. Exit CorelDRAW!.

2. Open the Windows File Manager and find the CORELDRW.INI file (probably located in the C:\COREL40\CONFIG subdirectory).

3. From the File menu, choose Copy, type **CORELDRW.BAK** as the new file name, and then press Enter.

4. Close the File Manager.

TIP

Make sure that you type in the DOS path information *exactly* as you want it. If there is a mistake in the path, your data could end up somewhere else in your system.

5. Open the Windows Notepad (or any other ASCII editor). Notepad is usually located in the Accessories Group. If you use another editor, such as Word for Windows, make sure that you save the file in ASCII format, or it won't work.

6. Choose **File Open**, and open the CORELDRW.INI file.

7. Find the [Config] section of the CORELDRW.INI file and locate the options shown in table 9.1. Set the option parameters to those desired by typing the necessary information after each equal sign (=), and then save the file. Restart CorelDRAW! to activate the new parameters.

Figure 9.4 displays the probable default settings for your CORELDRW.INI file. Once again, *do not change these values unless you are sure what you are doing.* In most cases, the default values are the best ones to use.

Table 9.1 Backup-Related CORELDRW.INI Settings

CORELDRW.INI Config Option	Setting Options and Defaults
AutoBackupDir	Type the disk drive and path to the directory in which you want to store the currently active version of a file that has not been saved. The default setting is *\COREL40\AUTOBACK*. These backup files have a BAK extension.
AutoBackupMins	A setting of 0 turns off Automatic Backup. Any other positive value sets the number of minutes between each automatic backup of the currently active file. The default setting is *10*.
MakeBackupWhenSave	When this option is turned on, DRAW creates a backup of the previous version of a file every time a new version of the file is saved. DRAW gives these files a BAK extension. The default setting is *1* (on).

You should have DRAW automatically set up as part of the install procedure to save backup files to the C:\COREL40\AUTOBACK directory, to create a backup each time an existing file is saved, and to save the currently active file automatically every 10 minutes.

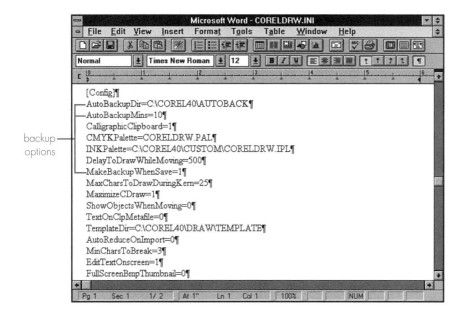

backup options

FIG. 9.4

A typical default CORELDRW.INI file.

Exporting and Importing Drawings

At times, you might want to use a DRAW image in another application (employing a DRAW-created logo design in a page layout package, for example), to use selected objects from the active drawing in another CorelDRAW! image file, or to use an image created in another application in your active DRAW image. You can accomplish these tasks using the Windows Clipboard, or the Export and Import options on the File menu. This section deals with the file-related Import and Export functions that enable you to share image information. The next section deals with using the Clipboard to accomplish the same things.

You generally import and export when you are dealing only with a small portion of the currently active file. You save and open when you are dealing with the total file.

Exporting versus Saving

If you use the File Save option on an image, you save the entire file in a
Corel format (as a drawing, template, or pattern). If you use the File
Export option, on the other hand, you send the current image through
a *filter* that converts it to a file format compatible with other industry
standard applications. In most cases, you should save the currently
active file in Corel standard CDR format before exporting. By doing so,
you make it easier to modify the drawing at a later date and you protect
yourself in case the computer hangs up and you lose your file during
the export.

To export a file, follow these steps:

1. Choose File Export to display the Export dialog box.

2. Select the destination file type from the List Files of **T**ype pull-
down list; make sure that the proper directory and path are selected (see fig. 9.5). All files of the selected type are displayed
under the File Name text box.

FIG. 9.5

The Export dialog box.

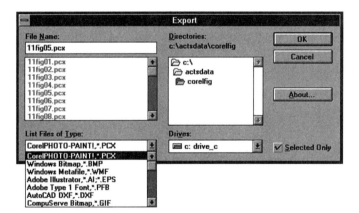

3. Type the desired file name for the exported file, and then click OK.
Depending upon the file type selected, DRAW may present another dialog box to gather additional information. After completing this process, DRAW translates the current file into the desired
file type and stores the results in the selected directory. DRAW
automatically adds the proper extension for the file type selected.

DRAW supports a wide variety of file types. Some people purchase it
simply for its file conversion capabilities.

Exporting Portions of a Drawing

You can export a selected section of a drawing. To do so, select the desired objects and then follow the preceding export procedure, checking the Selected Only option of the Export dialog box. This technique comes in handy when you are working with individual DRAW objects that you want to use multiple times. After selecting the desired objects and exporting them in CDR format, you can import them (following the import procedure for CDR format files) whenever you want to use them again.

Exporting only a portion of the file is also useful for bitmaps because the fewer the number of objects and the smaller the image dimension, the smaller the bitmap image. Once again, select the objects and then follow the export procedure with Selected Only active and the proper bitmap format for your needs highlighted.

Exporting in Encapsulated PostScript (EPS) Format

Encapsulated PostScript (EPS) is an industry standard file format that can support the complete complexity of CorelDRAW! images. However, CorelDRAW! cannot read its own EPS exports even though it can export in both EPS and Adobe Illustrator (AI) formats. The AI-EPS format does not support all of DRAW's capabilities, but it is readable by DRAW. EPS files created by DRAW are usable in Ventura Publisher and Page-Maker, but these files keep the bitmap images at low resolution. You should always save your images as CDR files before exporting to EPS format so that you can edit the images later if necessary.

When you choose File Export and select the EPS file type, choosing OK opens the Export EPS dialog box shown in figure 9.6.

The Text section of this dialog box determines whether the text embedded in the image is exported as text or converted to curves before being exported. Choosing the As Curves option makes the object more complex and might cause your printer to hang up due to unacceptable complexity. If you choose the As Text option without checking All Fonts Resident, the CorelDRAW! fonts are used for printing. If you check All Fonts Resident, DRAW assumes that all text fonts are already resident in the printer and that the Adobe versions of typefaces should be used rather than the DRAW fonts. If a font is not resident when printing the file, the text either prints in Courier or doesn't print at all.

FIG. 9.6

The Export EPS dialog
box.

If you are wondering which fonts are resident, refer to the
CORELFNT.INI file which shows a listing of the CorelDRAW! fonts on the
left and the equivalent PostScript font on the right followed by either 0,
1, or 3. These fonts are listed in the [PSResidentFonts] section. A trailing 0 means that the typeface is not resident in the printer; a 1 means
that the typeface is resident in all PostScript printers; and a 3 means
that the typeface is resident in printers that support the 3J standard
PostScript typefaces.

EPS files containing color bitmaps do not print on black-and-white
PostScript level 1 printers. To resolve this issue, check the **C**onvert
Color Bitmaps To Grayscale option.

The Fountain Steps setting determines the quality of fountain fill
printing. Keep this number low when printing proofs to speed up the
printing process, but set it to the desired level when printing your final
output. Settings below 20 are considered low; settings over 40 are considered high. As you increase the number of steps, you will reach a
point of diminishing returns at which you can no longer tell much of a
difference. Play with the settings to determine the levels that suit your
equipment and drawings.

The EPS file format allows the incorporation of a low resolution bitmap
image header. CorelDRAW! adds an image header in TIFF 5.0 format.
The low resolution header adds around 2K to the file size, the medium
adds around 8K and the high resolution adds 32K, assuming the bitmap
is square. If the image header is not square it can grow to sizes larger
than 64K which is the maximum acceptable import limit for some applications. Select the resolution you want to use from the Header Resolution drop down list. Selecting 0 exports the file without a TIFF header.

Some applications do not read TIFF 5.0 file formats, which means that the image is not adopted by the importing applications. You can set the TIFF format for the image header to TIFF 4.2 (an older standard) by setting ExportToTIFF42=1 in the [CorelTIFFExport] section of the CORELFLT.INI file located in the C:\COREL40\CONFIG subdirectory. Corel claims, in the on-line help under EPS technical notes, that this situation is required to use Corel created EPS files with WordPerfect, including version 5.2.

> You can change settings in the CORELFLT.INI file following a procedure very similar to the one used earlier in this chapter to change the CORELDRW.INI file.

NOTE

Exporting Bitmap Formats

If you select a bitmap format from the Export dialog box, the Bitmap Export dialog box appears (see fig. 9.7).

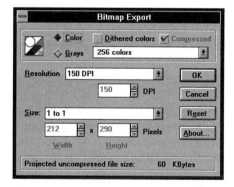

FIG. 9.7

The Bitmap Export dialog box.

This dialog box allows you to set the resolution, the type of coloring, and the aspect ratio (width to height of the image depending upon the type of computer display used) of your output image. It also estimates the size of the final file.

You can set your colors to include the full 16 million provided with DRAW, or a smaller subset created through a process called *dithering*. A later chapter of this book deals with dithering in detail. When you are faced with the decision—"to dither, or not to dither"—you should generally use dithering with 16-level grayscale or 16- to 256-color images (or with images that you will not rescale or touch up in the final application). If you are using 16 million colors or plan to rescale the image in the final application, do not use dithering.

TIP

To maintain maximum image clarity, set your image to the desired size using the DRAW vector graphics format *before* exporting. The process of sizing bitmapped images should be avoided if possible because it usually degrades image quality.

Table 9.2 shows a listing of the Export file filters provided by CorelDRAW!.

Table 9.2 CorelDRAW! Export Filters

Format	File Names	Format	File Names
Illustrator 88, 3	*.AI, *.EPS	TIFF Four Color	*.TIF
OS/2 Bitmaps	*.BMP	Computer Graphics Metafile	*.CGM
Adobe Type 1 Font	*.PFB	TrueType Fonts	*.TTF
Matrix/Imapro SCODL	*.SCD	HP Plotter HPGL	*.PLT
AutoCAD DXF	*.DXF	Windows 3 Bitmaps	*.BMP
PostScript (EPS)	*.EPS	IBM PIF	*.PIF
CompuServe Bitmaps	*.GIF	Windows Metafile	*.WMF
Targa Bitmaps	*.TGA	JPEG Bitmaps	*.JPG
CorelPHOTO-PAINT	*.PCX, *.PCC	WordPerfect Graphic	*.WPG
TIFF 5.0 Bitmaps	*.TIF	Mac PICT	*.PCT
GEM Files	*.GEM		

In this dialog box, you can choose from a number of Resolution values and Sizes. Whatever choices you make, CorelDRAW! will attempt to maintain the same aspect ratio (width to height) for the image selected. As you change the Resolution and Size values, the Width and Height values automatically calibrate themselves. Choosing any size other than 1-to-1 fixes the resolution. Choosing 1-to-1 provides access to several resolution settings such as FAX (Fine and Normal) and between 75 and 300 dpi. You can also set custom values between 60 and 600 dpi. To minimize bitmap storage size, use a 1-to-1 size ratio, lower bitmap resolutions, and set the image to the desired size within DRAW before exporting.

Importing versus Opening a Drawing

The File Open option is used to open a new file that has been saved in a DRAW format (as a drawing, a template, or a pattern). Using File Open simply replaces whatever image was on-screen with the one chosen during the open process. File Import, on the other hand, allows you to bring images and information into the current drawing without losing the currently active image. A set of Import filters translates the selected image from an external format (such as PCX, TIF, or WPG) into a format that DRAW can use in the current drawing. You usually import pieces that comprise smaller subsections of the currently active larger drawing, but you open an entire drawing. Import is also used to bring a complete drawing in a non-Corel format into CorelDraw!.

DRAW Format Compatibilities

DRAW supports numerous image and text file formats that can be directly imported into a drawing without intermediate steps. Table 9.3 shows a listing of these import filters.

Table 9.3 CorelDRAW! Import Filters

Format	File Names	Format	File Names
Adobe Illustrator 1.1, 88, 3	*.AI	CorelPHOTO-PAINT	*.PCX, *.PCC
MacWrite II 1.0, 1.1	*.*	Microsoft Word for Windows 2.x	*.*
Ami Professional 2.0, 3	*.SAM	CorelTRACE	*.EPS
Micrographx Draw 2.x, 3.x	*.DRW	Microsoft Word for Mac 4.0	*.*
AutoCAD DXF	*.DXF	Computer Graphics Metafile	*.CGM
Microsoft Rich Text Format	*.RTF	Microsoft Word for Mac 5.0	*.*
CompuServe Bitmaps	*.GIF	EPS Thumbnail	*.EPS, *.PS, *.AI
Microsoft Word 5.0, 5.5	*.*	OS/2 Bitmap	*.BMP
CorelDRAW!	*.CDR	Excel for Windows 3, 4.0	*.XLS
Microsoft Word for Windows 1.x	*.*	TARGA Bitmaps	*.TGA

(continues)

Table 9.3 Continued

Format	File Names	Format	File Names
GEM files	*.GEM	Windows Metafile	*.WMF
Text	*.TXT	Lotus PIC	*.PIC
HP Plotter HPGL	*.PLT	WordPerfect Graphic	*.WPG
TIFF 5.0 Bitmaps	*.TIF	Lotus 1-2-3 1A, 2.0	*.WK?
IBM PIF	*.PIF	WordPerfect 5.0	*.*
TIFF Four Color	*.TIF	Lotus 1-2-3 3 for Windows	*.WK?
JPEG Bitmap	*.JPG	WordPerfect 5.1 for Windows	*.*
Windows Bitmaps	*.BMP	MAC PICT	*.PCT
Kodak Photo-CD	*.PCD		

You should be able to find a file format that is supported by the receiving application in this list of filters. As an alternate approach, you can try copying the file to the Clipboard and then pasting it into the destination applications file.

Importing a CorelTRACE File

CorelDRAW! cannot import an EPS file that it created, except for Adobe Illustrator (AI) EPS files, but it can import a CorelTRACE-generated EPS file. You can select image portions or objects from the currently active CorelTRACE EPS file and export them in the desired format, including CDR. In this way, a scanned image can be converted into a vector graphic using TRACE which can then be exported and scaled within DRAW for use in other applications. CorelTRACE is covered in Chapter 17.

Using the Clipboard instead of File Transfers

Windows provides a memory area called the Clipboard which can be used as a temporary storage area for text and image information.

The Clipboard is one of the most useful features of Windows; you are encouraged to learn its operation and limitations. Using the Clipboard allows you to transfer images and text between applications without using the Export and Import operations.

If an image gets too large or complex, the Clipboard may not be able to transfer it, and you should use the Import and Export commands. Import and Export also provide more detailed control of the transfer process.

Using Copy, Cut, and Paste

You can remove the information you want to transfer from the active file by using either Edit Copy or Edit Cut. Edit Copy duplicates the selected objects and stores them on the Clipboard. Edit Cut removes the selected objects from the currently active image and stores them on the Clipboard. The difference might sound trivial, but the practical implications can be substantial.

Edit Copy does not interfere with the original image; Edit Cut actually removes the selected portions of the original image and places them on the Clipboard. If you use Edit Cut to remove objects and then forget to paste them into another file before copying something else to the Clipboard, those initially cut objects are replaced by new ones and lost forever.

TIP

When cutting and placing information on the Clipboard, always complete the paste operation as soon as possible to avoid copying new information to the Clipboard and erasing the initially cut images.

Edit Paste is used to insert information from the Clipboard into an image. You can size and move the object after it is pasted into the file. If the pasted object is in a vector format, such as Metafile, then the sizing and moving can be accomplished with no loss in object image quality.

NOTE

CorelDRAW! does not support these Windows Metafile features: background commands, pattern fills, clipping regions, flood fills, individual pixel manipulations, WINDING polygon fill mode (ALTERNATE mode is supported) and ROP2 modes other than R2_COPYPEN.

When text is pasted from the Clipboard, CorelDRAW! applies several rules to determine its spacing and text type:

- Pasted text of 250 characters or less is included as artistic text.

- Pasted text over 250 characters is included as paragraph text.

- RTF file formatted text is always included as paragraph text.

- The fill, outline, typeface, and point size of the text are set to the currently active CorelDRAW! default values.

- Artistic text spacing defaults to 0% of intercharacter space width, 0% of interword space width, and 100% of character point size interline width.

- Paragraph text defaults to the same values as artistic text.

TIP

Copying fountain fills via the Clipboard is often a slow process. You can speed things up and achieve a similar result by blending two objects together with the same relative size, location, and color as the radial fills. Remove the object outlines and then blend the two objects together. The final result looks a lot like a fountain fill with a radial offset, and it does not create the Clipboard copying problems associated with fountain fills.

CorelDRAW! supports Windows Metafile and CorelMetafile (CMF) formats when cutting or copying information to the Clipboard. Objects containing pattern fills, PostScript textures, and bitmap fills cannot be copied or cut to the Clipboard. Windows Metafile, ASCII text, Rich Text Format (RTF) text, and Windows Bitmaps can be pasted from the Clipboard into a Corel image.

As you become an advanced CorelDRAW! user, you may need to customize the way the Clipboard handles Fountain Fills, PostScript calligraphic outlines, and text (whether it is converted to curves or retains its text attributes). These settings are established in the CORELDRW.INI file found in the COREL40\CONFIG directory; you can edit this file using a text editing program such as the Windows Notepad. Table 9.4 shows the parameters to use, the possible settings, and the effects of those settings. Stay with the defaults until you are at an advanced level with CorelDRAW!.

Table 9.4 Custom CORELDRW.INI Settings

CORELDRW.INI File Attribute ([Config])	Settings and Effect
ClipboardFountains	0 = Enable high-quality cutting/clipping
	1 = Disable high-quality cutting/clipping
CalligraphicClipboard	0 = Keep calligraphic outlines
	1 = Ignore calligraphic outlines
TextOnClpMetafile	0 = Paste text as curve objects
	1 = Paste text as text

Any changes you make will take effect the next time you start CorelDRAW!.

Using MOSAIC

Most text-based applications contain some type of file management tool. CorelDRAW! contains a visual file manager called MOSAIC which allows you to view the image file just as other applications allow you to view the text file. You can use MOSAIC to automate many of DRAW's file-related activities (such as printing). MOSAIC also provides file-related operations specific to text files and supports drag-and-drop moves and copies (thumbnails and text-displayed files can be moved and copied between directories by simply selecting the desired files and performing the correct mouse operations). Finally, you can create your own *libraries* (actual files in compressed form) and *catalogs* (thumbnails with pointers to real data files) within which you can group your files for easier access.

Accessing MOSAIC and Setting Preferences

MOSAIC is a stand-alone application that can be started by double-clicking the MOSAIC icon located in the Corel application group, or by choosing **F**ile **O**pen **O**ptions **M**OSAIC from within CorelDRAW!. Figure 9.8 shows a typical MOSAIC screen in which a directory is displayed in both text mode and thumbnail image mode. Notice that the same file is selected in both the left and right directory windows. The screen was set up this way by selecting **W**indow Tile **V**ertically (Shift +F4).

FIG. 9.8

The MOSAIC display screen.

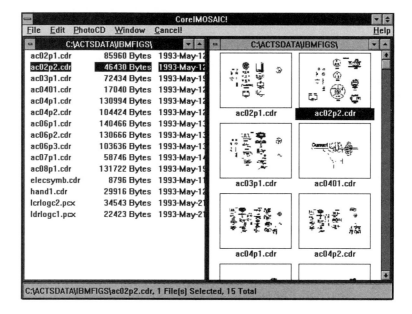

To set how MOSAIC displays directories, choose **F**ile **P**references. The Preferences dialog shown in figure 9.9 appears.

Four thumbnail sizes are available: *Portrait, Landscape, Square,* and *Custom.* Setting the Width of the file thumbnail image (in pixels) automatically sets the Height (except in the case of Custom, which allows you to set all dimensioning options). The Pad Width setting determines the left/right distance between thumbnails, and the Pad Height setting determines the over/under distance between thumbnails. These settings are valuable when you want to display a lot of file information in the window. Making the thumbnails and pad distances smaller allows more images to be placed in a given screen space. The Page Color option displays a dialog box that allows you to define the color of the directory window background. If you click the Font button, the Font dialog box appears that allows you to set the fonts used for the file names placed under the thumbnails and in the text-only directory displays (see fig. 9.10).

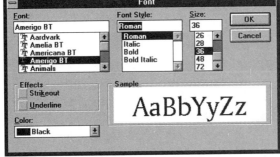

FIG. 9.9

The Preferences dialog box.

FIG. 9.10

The Font dialog box.

If you activate the Text Mode Display option, the text information on a file displays whenever you choose a directory to view. If this option isn't selected, the image information displays.

To view a directory using the preferences you've chosen, choose File View **D**irectory, or press Ctrl+D, to open the View Directory dialog box shown in figure 9.11.

This dialog box should be familiar by now. The file names are displayed in the left box, the directories in the center box, and the thumbnail preview in the right box (if Preview is checked). Options is selected in the example shown in figure 9.11, so keyword, note, and font information appears at the bottom of the dialog box. The Sort By option allows you to sort the files by file name or by last date saved. Double-clicking a file name (or selecting a file name and choosing OK) opens the directory in either text or image mode, depending on whether the Text Mode Display option is selected in the Preferences dialog box.

TIP

The status of the Text Mode Display option when the directory is first opened remains unchanged for the entire time that the directory remains open. To change the display mode, you must close and reopen the directory.

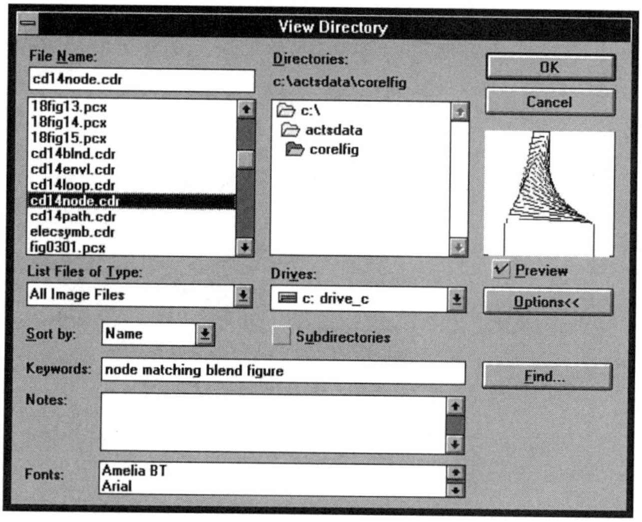

FIG. 9.11

The View Directory dialog box.

Selecting, Moving, and Copying Files

The processes of copying and moving files in MOSAIC are similar to those used in the Windows File Manager. You simply select a file or files and then copy or move them to the new directory. But selecting files can be a somewhat tricky maneuver. Clicking a file name or image works like a toggle switch: clicking once selects it, clicking again deselects it. The file's name is highlighted when the file is selected. Pressing the Ctrl key while selecting allows you to simultaneously select files that are not next to each other. Selecting one file and then pressing Shift while you select another file in the directory selects both of these files and all the files in between.

After the files are selected, you can copy from one directory to another by dragging the selected files to the new location. You can move them by pressing Shift+Alt while dragging the files. Moving a file removes it from the initial directory and copies it to the new one. Copying leaves the initial files where they were and makes a copy of the data in the destination directory.

Searching for Files

You can search directories for specific file types and names by opening a directory and then typing the desired file name or wild card parameters in the File Name box (or selecting the desired file type from the List Files of Type pull-down list). Only those files corresponding with the set criteria are displayed. You can also do keyword searches by opening a directory and then choosing Options Find to display the Keyword Search dialog box (see fig. 9.12).

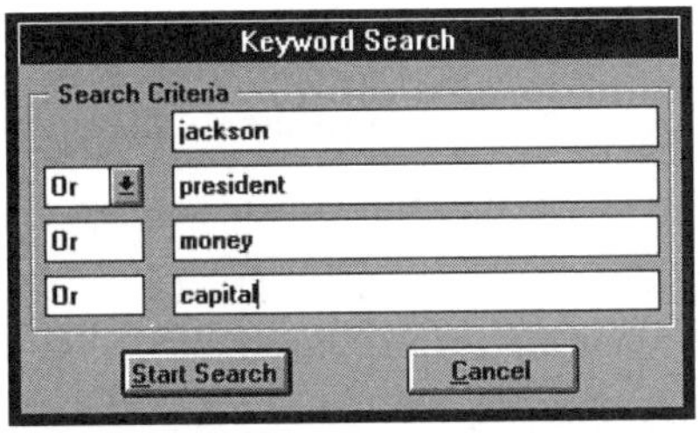

FIG. 9.12

The Keyword Search dialog box.

Enter the primary keyword for your search on the top line in this dialog box. Use the other lines to further refine the keyword sifting process. A logical operator (AND or OR) relates the keywords entered for the search. Setting the first operator to either AND or OR sets the remaining keyword operators. If AND is chosen, the files selected must have both or all keywords entered. If OR is chosen, the files selected must have at least one of the set of keywords entered. After the search is completed, all files matching the keyword search criteria display in the window.

Using MOSAIC Libraries and Catalogs

MOSAIC uses both libraries and catalogs for storage and coordination of image file information. The two perform similar functions in different ways; they have different effects on your data files.

A *catalog* is used to group file images without affecting data files. Just as an icon in the Windows Program Manager points to a data file's disk location, the image in a catalog points to the image data file. Catalogs are useful when you want to break your files into separate groups by subject, for example, or by project title. You might want to include a picture of the president, for example, in catalogs called POLITIC and LEADERS. By creating these two catalogs and dragging the image header (thumbnail) into them, you are functionally grouping the images without making duplicates of their associated data files. This method serves your purposes without taking up unnecessary disk space.

TIP

> Moving a data file after including its image header in a catalog will invalidate the image pointer and cause you problems when you attempt to find the file at a later date.

A *library*, on the other hand, actually contains the image data as well as the image header. The data is compressed, if possible, to minimize the library storage size. Previously compressed file formats such as Compressed TIFF are not compressed any further. After the library is opened, you can access and decompress its files by way of thumbnails.

To create a library or a catalog, follow these steps:

1. Choose File New Catalog/Library. The Create New Catalog/Library dialog box shown in figure 9.13 appears.

2. Type the desired name for the catalog or library in the File Name box, choose Library or Catalog from the List Files of Type pulldown list, and then choose OK.

   An empty window opens for the new library or catalog, indicating that MOSAIC is ready to accept files.

3. Move or copy files into your library, or copy image headers into your catalog as required for your needs. (Remember that there is no file storage capability provided with catalogs; only the thumbnails are stored.) Dragging a file from a directory into a library makes a copy of the file, and holding the Shift key while dragging moves the file from the directory into the library. Moving or copying a file into a library automatically compresses the file. Moving or copying a file from a library automatically decompresses (expands) the file.

TIP

Library files have a CLB extension and catalog files have a CLC extension.

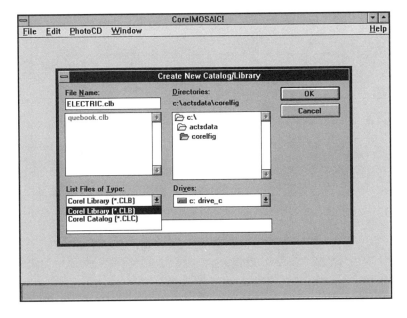

FIG. 9.13

The Create New Catalog/Library dialog box.

Printing File Summaries (Thumbnails) in MOSAIC

You can print single or multiple thumbnails in MOSAIC. This feature allows you to keep a handy visual record of files contained within a directory. To print directory thumbnails, follow these steps:

1. Open the directory, catalog, or library.

2. Select the thumbnails to be printed using any of the selection techniques (click, Ctrl-click, or Shift-click).

3. Choose File Page Setup, and set the desired dialog box printing options; then choose OK. See Chapter 10 for additional information on printing.

4. Choose File Print Thumbnails to display the Print dialog box (see fig. 9.14). Set up your desired parameters such as thumbnail size

and padding as explained in the beginning of this section, and then choose OK to have the thumbnails print in your specified "picture album" format.

FIG. 9.14

The Print dialog box for printing thumbnails.

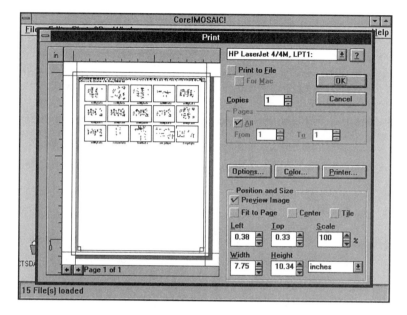

Printing Multiple Files in MOSAIC

One wonderful feature of MOSAIC is its capability for printing multiple DRAW documents at once. You select the files to be printed and define the print criteria, then MOSAIC handles the printing procedures. This capability makes it easier and less burdensome to work with many files in situations like the completion of a project when a client needs copies of all work done to date. To print multiple files, follow these steps:

1. Open the directory, catalog, or library.

2. Select the thumbnails for the files you want to print using any of the selection techniques (click, Ctrl-click, or Shift-click).

3. Choose File Print Files. MOSAIC opens DRAW and loads each of the files you selected. Set the print criteria desired just as you would with any DRAW image, and then choose OK. MOSAIC handles the rest, automatically loading and printing each of the selected images.

NOTE

All files printed must be the same orientation, landscape or portrait.

Using Photo CD Images

If you have photos saved in the new Photo CD format, you can import them through MOSAIC into DRAW and use them as images. This may greatly expand your flexibility with respect to how images are captured and used. Photo CD commands are accessed under the PhotoCD menu selection, which offers Convert Images and View Kodak Photo CD commands.

View Kodak Photo CD instructs MOSAIC to access the CD-ROM drive and look for Photo CD files. After they display, you can select files, convert files to other formats, and print files or thumbnails just as you would with DRAW directories and files. But before the Photo CD files can be used in DRAW, they must be converted to a compatible format.

Choose Convert Images to display the Convert Images dialog box. Select the directory and file type from the List of File **T**ype box, the specific file name from the File **N**ame box, and the drive from the Drives pull-down list. The Color Depth option allows for conversion of the image to grayscale, black and white, 8-bit, or 24-bit color. File Resolution sets the number of pixels desired for the converted file. The sizes are wallet (128 x 192 pixels), snapshot (256 x 384 pixels), standard (512 x 768 pixels), large (1024 x 1536 pixels), and poster (2048 x 3072 pixels). Remember that the higher the resolution and the greater the number of colors, the larger the file storage size and the longer the conversion time required. The native Photo CD format is 2048 x 3072, and selecting a size smaller than that decreases image quality.

TIP

Double-clicking an image opens CorelPHOTO-PAINT and loads that image in a Windows BMP format at 768 x 512 pixels.

Summary

The first portion of this chapter covered the various file-related activities used in DRAW, such as the standard Open, Close, Save, and Save As processes. It then covered importing and exporting as they relate to using various file formats in Corel or with other applications.

CorelMOSAIC provides some excellent tools for automating routine tasks such as printing. It also allows you to use image-based file management instead of having to work with image files using their text name formats. CorelDRAW! is an image-based application, so it makes sense to deal with the files based on their image content rather than their names. Catalogs and libraries can make file management simpler and less risky when working with many clients and multiple projects. Create catalogs that contain a header record of the file contents, and then deal with the text listing of the files as needed on an exception basis.

The next chapter deals with creating the actual output of your images and merging images and text.

Printing and Merging Files

Eventually all files are routed to an output device such as a laser printer, 35mm slide developer, color printer, or linotype. In some cases, as with CorelSHOW, the output device may be the computer screen itself. This final category is discussed in Chapter 19, "Making Presentations with CorelSHOW"; the others are discussed here.

This chapter investigates the printing methods provided by CorelDRAW! and suggests ways in which you can capitalize on DRAW's automated features to speed up the final steps of drawing creation. CorelDRAW! enables you to scale your output from 1/10th of its original size up to 10 times that size. You can even print your drawing in *tiles* (sections on multiple pages which form the final output when assembled). This chapter covers printing procedures in general. Chapter 11 covers many of the details, including color printing.

This chapter also contains a section covering file merging procedures. This new release 4 feature merges information contained in a text document into an existing Corel drawing. A classic application for this feature is the creation of certificates or awards. The Corel document serves as the certificate shell, and the merged text can include information such as student names and class dates. The basic concept is the same as with any word-processing merge procedure, such as the creation of mailing labels, except that a Corel image is merged with text to create a final, combined document.

Corel, Windows, and the Printer

The communication between Corel and the final output device is handled by the Windows output device *drivers* or command interpreters. These drivers interpret Corel output instructions and pass translated instructions to the output device (with the aim of making the output a close match to the screen representation). This interface makes it possible for a Corel drawing to be output easily, via Windows, to different devices such as printers or slide developers. But even though the technology makes the procedure easy, you must always be aware that the final product is only as good as its design (which must take the limitations of the final output device into account).

To design in color when the output device is monochrome (black and white), for example, is to set yourself up for disappointment. The conversion from color to monochrome is unpredictable; you might be better off working with shades of gray when creating your drawings to ensure that "What You See Is What You (Really) Get." If you plan to print to a slide developer, you should set the page size of your drawing (accessed as Layout Page Setup) to the Slide Page Size. That way the dimensions, along with the relative horizontal and vertical size ratios seen on-screen, match those of the final slide format. If you start with Letter size and later convert to Slide, on the other hand, the drawing will probably need modification because it will not have its original appearance in the new format.

The general printing procedure is as follows:

1. Create the drawing, and then highlight the objects you want to print. If you don't select any objects, the printing procedure defaults to the entire drawing.

2. Choose File **Print** (Ctrl+P) to display the Print dialog box and the related print options.

3. If needed, select the desired print device and its associated options by using the top-left list box, or by clicking on the Print command button and following the dialog box instructions.

4. Define the desired number of copies.

5. Size and scale the image as needed for your desired output using either the Position and Size dialog box options or the mouse.

6. Choose OK from within the Print dialog box to begin the print process.

The following sections cover these basic steps in more detail, but the general procedure remains relatively consistent.

Previewing before Printing

You can get a pretty good idea of what your final output will look like by viewing the standard Editable View display. Or you can get a more detailed preview by choosing Display Show Preview (F9), which uses the entire screen for the display. You also have the option of getting a customized close up preview of selected objects. To preview selected objects, follow these steps:

1. Choose **D**isplay Selected Objects **O**nly.

2. Select the objects for previewing.

3. Choose Show **P**review. Only the selected objects display.

4. Press Esc to cancel the full-screen Show Preview and return to the Wireframe or Editable Preview mode.

Finally, you can use the Print dialog box to get a preview that shows the actual page location of the drawing during printing. This topic is covered in the next section.

Printing a File or Selected Objects

Choose **F**ile **P**rint, or press Ctrl+P, to access the Print dialog box (see fig. 10.1). This dialog box provides you with access to the major printing features and settings of CorelDRAW!.

The large box at the left shows a preview of the graphic as it will print on the page with the current settings. The lines near the edge of the preview page represent the cutoff points beyond which the selected output device will not print. For many laser printers, this cutoff point is .25 inches from each edge of the page. As long as you have not selected Center in the Position and Size box, you can drag the image to any desired section of the screen just as you would any DRAW object. Preview Image is enabled/disabled by clicking the Preview Image check box located under Position and Size.

FIG. 10.1

The Print dialog box.

Sizing handles

Page selector for
multipage documents

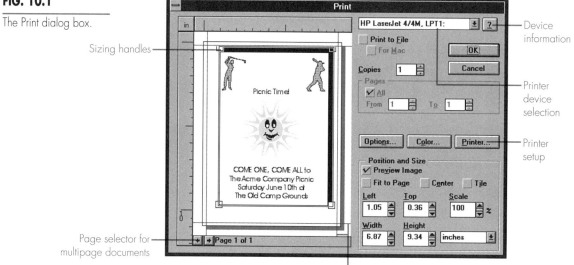

Device
information

Printer
device
selection

Printer
setup

Printer cutoff lines

A pull-down list of the available output devices appears in the upper-right corner of the dialog box. To choose an output device, click the down arrow to display a listing of devices and then choose the device from the list. The list of available devices reflects those drivers you have loaded on your computer. To display information about the selected device, click the question mark button to the right of the printer selection list. This procedure displays relevant information including the current resolution level, the printer driver release level, the printer port, and the expected image size when printing (see fig. 10.2). You can fax an image from within CorelDRAW!, for example, by selecting the desired fax output device from the pull-down list and following the printing procedures provided with your fax software (such as WinFax Pro). This procedure is useful as a time saver when working with remote clients.

You can also define a specific image size using the Width and Height boxes included in the Position and Size section of the dialog box. Setting one value automatically sets the other based upon the established initial image size. When you change the image size using the Width and Height boxes, the Scale value changes accordingly. To choose the units used for image measurement, click the down arrow of the units pull-down list at the lower-right corner of the dialog box and make your selection.

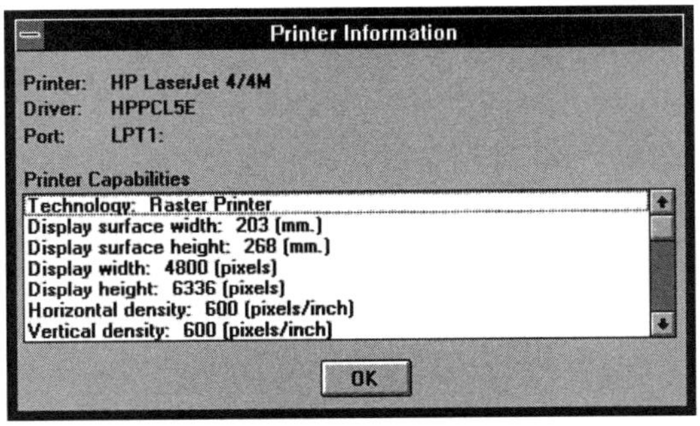

FIG. 10.2

The Printer Information
dialog box.

TIP

If you are sending drawings to a commercial printer, the value that appears in the Scale box can be used to determine scaling requirements. This information is often necessary when dealing with printers who are making final plates for printing. They might need to reduce the image to a certain size; your ability to provide them with a percentage scaling factor makes the process easier.

You can set the scale of the image directly using the Scale box. Or you can interactively scale the image using the mouse by dragging the corner control handles just as you would any DRAW object. If you know the size for your final image, the Scale box can also be used to determine what scaling is required. Scaling and positioning the image in the print preview window changes only the printed output size, not the object itself.

The settings in the Left and Top boxes enable you to manipulate the page location of the printed image. The Left setting determines the distance from the left edge of the page at which the left side of the image begins printing. The Top setting determines the distance from the top of the page at which the top of the image begins printing. If Center has been selected, these options are unavailable because they have no meaning when the image location is already set.

The Fit to Page option is generally used to reduce an existing image to the currently active page size for proofing purposes. It also allows for hard copy verification of the image's appearance when actually printed. Center aligns the center of the printed image with the center of the page. All dimensions and scaling are then done around this centering point.

Tile is used to print an image that is larger than the currently selected printed page. Any portions of the image that extend beyond the edges of the page are printed on additional pages, which can then be manually aligned and assembled to create a larger finished image. Notice that Fit to Page and Tile cannot be active at the same time because they perform mutually exclusive operations. Tile is also used when Scale is set to a value that makes the printed image larger than the actual page size.

Print to File instructs DRAW to store the output information on disk instead of printing it directly to an output device. A default extension (PRN) is automatically added to files created with this option. You can then send this file to a printer directly from DOS without CorelDRAW! running or give it to a service bureau for special printing needs. Because you can print these files from DOS without DRAW, this option can be particularly valuable when you must print at a remote location where a copy of DRAW is not available. The printing screen frequency (the number of printed dots per inch) used is that set within the CorelDRAW! Print Option dialog box. If you select color separations while printing to a file, a four-color print file is produced and the separations print when the DOS COPY command is used.

TIP

Make sure that you match your PostScript output device dpi setting to that intended for the final output. In essence, print to file creates a final image of the document just as though it went to the intended printer; it is just saved to disk instead of being sent to the printer. If these settings do not match those of the final print devices, the output results may be unpredictable. The dpi value is set under the Printer Setup Options dialog box.

The For Mac option sends output in a file format compatible with the Apple Macintosh computer which is commonly used by service bureaus. During the save process, this option removes codes such as $^\wedge D$ that stop the Mac from printing a PostScript file properly. Notice that you still need to convert the disk to Mac format before you can print the resulting file on the Mac. The service bureau should be able to help you handle this task; be aware that the disk formatting issue will stop transfer to the Mac unless you have the right disk conversion software on either the Mac or PC.

The value entered in the Copies box determines the number of copies of the image that DRAW prints. This number overrides the number set in the Windows Control Panel Printer Setup and any Printer Setup values set in other dialog boxes. If the image is a multipage document, you can specify the desired range of pages for printing by setting the From and To values as desired. For a single-page document, these settings are not available. Clicking the Page Selector arrows at the bottom left of the dialog box moves the image from one page to the next of a multipage document.

If you need to make multiple copies of a drawing and your printer does not provide a multiple copy option, you can use the Print to File option and then copy the file to the printer using the DOS procedure outlined in the following section. This eliminates the DRAW portion of the printing cycle and only involves transfer of the data to the printer.

Clicking the Printer button displays a Windows Printer Setup dialog box like the one shown in figure 10.3. This dialog box is the same one that you reach by selecting the Printers icon in the Windows Control Panel application group. The form of this dialog box will vary based on the type of output device chosen and its associated options. In general, you can select the quality of output, the number of copies, and the output orientation (portrait or landscape) from this dialog box. Choosing Options allows access to the various other features associated with your particular output device.

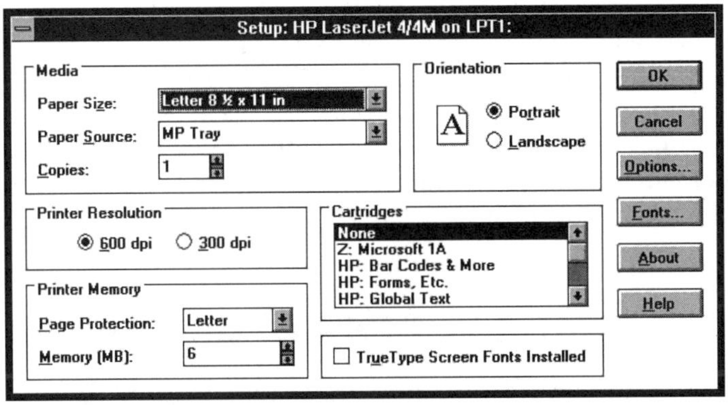

FIG. 10.3

A typical printer Setup dialog box.

The Options and Color buttons in the Print window open further dialog boxes which deal with color separations and selections. These topics are covered in detail in Chapter 11.

Using the Print Setup Dialog Box

Choosing the File Print Setup option from the main CorelDRAW! menu bar displays the Print Setup dialog box shown in figure 10.4. You can use this dialog box to select the output device as an alternative to entering the Print dialog box. Notice that this dialog box allows ready access to two output devices: the Default Printer (as established by the Windows Printer Setup dialog box) and a Specific Printer (which can be specified here). You must install these printer drivers using Windows before they are accessible here. Refer to your Windows manual for the proper procedure for installing a printer driver.

FIG. 10.4

The Print Setup dialog box.

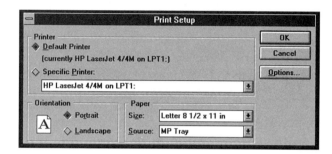

To choose an output device, click the Specific Printer diamond to make the pull-down list available and then make your choice (WinFax on COM4, for example). After you make a choice, the output routes to the chosen device until you return to the Default Printer. This procedure is more convenient than working through the other dialog boxes when you need special access to specific output devices, such as fax modems, slide developers, and so on. The Options command button provides access to a dialog box that allows you to set the print options provided for that specific printer.

Printing Specific Layers of a Drawing

You might want to print different layers of a drawing on different pages. This can be easily accomplished by first opening the Layers roll-up window (Ctrl+F3), and then double-clicking any of the layer names in the roll-up window to access the Layer Options dialog box (see fig. 10.5). For detailed information on DRAW layers, refer to Chapter 5.

Printable is initially selected for each layer. To disable its printing ability, deselect **P**rintable from the Layer Options dialog box. Only those layers with Printable selected print. You can make color separations in this way if you restrict certain colors to specific layers, but it is easier and more accurate to use the Color Separations feature included with the Print functions. See Chapter 11 for more information on creating and using color separations.

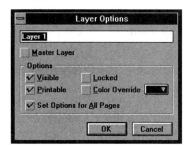

FIG. 10.5

The Layer Options dialog box.

Printing without Starting CorelDRAW!

There are three ways to print drawings without starting CorelDRAW!: using the drag-and-drop feature of Windows 3.1, using MOSAIC as the print manager (see Chapter 9 for details), and printing a PRN file from the DOS prompt.

Windows 3.1 has a wonderful feature called drag-and-drop that allows you to print files from within the Program Manager and File Manager without having to open the source application. This feature works with any Windows application that Windows can identify by way of a file extension (CRD files are associated with CorelDRAW!, XLS files are associated with Excel, DOC files are associated with Word for Windows, and so on). You simply open the File Manager and then drag the file from its directory location to the minimized, but running, Print Manager icon. Windows references the extension, opens the proper application, and initiates the Corel print operation. You are presented with the standard DRAW screens, and the print process starts when you click OK. You must close the application after the printing operation is completed. Unfortunately, this feature does not allow you to print multiple files at once. Use CorelMOSAIC for this operation.

TIP

An even easier way to print a file from the File Manager is to select the file, and then choose **F**ile **P**rint. You don't have to start the Print Manager and then iconize it using this method.

The CorelMOSAIC application, which is included with CorelDRAW!, is a multipurpose file and image management application that, among other things, allows you to print multiple files at once. See Chapter 9 for a detailed discussion of MOSAIC and file management operations. You are encouraged to review this chapter because the procedures outlined there streamline many of DRAW's routine and time-consuming operations.

Finally, you can print a file from the DOS prompt as long as it was initially printed within DRAW using the Print to File option. This procedure is useful when you must transfer files to people who do not have CorelDRAW! and still need to print a drawing on their own printer. After saving the file in the PRN format, simply type the following command string at the DOS prompt to initiate the print process:

Copy *filename.PRN* [/b] LPT*x*:

The string *filename.PRN* should be replaced, of course, with the name of the CorelDRAW! image in PRN format that you want to print. The **/b** parameter must be included when printing to non-PostScript printers, and **LPT*x*:** represents the system port designation for the printer device (*x* usually equals a number from 1 to 4 for stand-alone systems). Make sure that the output device type you specify while printing matches that used by the person ultimately doing the actual printing.

Printing Color Files

Creating color output used to be very expensive. The per page cost was very high if done by a service bureau, and only the most dedicated companies bought expensive color output devices. But now things are different. Color laser printers are becoming more common; 35mm slide-producing machines are becoming inexpensive enough for companies to justify creating customer presentations using the Corel family of products and then creating their own slides.

Corel provides a test file that can be used to verify color fidelity. When printed, this file should closely match the CMYK Color Chart card included with your copy of CorelDRAW!. This color card was printed by a commercial printer, so it provides you with an excellent reference as to what colors you can expect when actually printing. To verify your device's output, simply load the COLORBAR.CDR file (included as one of the CorelDRAW! sample files), print it on your color device, and compare the output with the color card. They should match closely.

TIP

Printing COLORBAR.CDR on a monochrome printer gives you a rough idea of how the screen colors will translate into grayscale. Use these shades of gray to determine the color that provides the best grayscale output on your monochrome printer.

To best ensure that the colors received from your commercial printer match those that you expect, use industry standard color-matching systems such as Pantone and TRUMATCH. Color-matching charts for these systems can be easily acquired.

Halftone Patterns, Screen Frequency, and Angle Considerations

Halftone screens are applied to drawings to meet specific commercial printing requirements or for special artistic effect. If you are using a PostScript printer, you can define a halftone screen that is applied when the image is printed. The screens are defined by the user at the time of object creation in the form of an outline, fill, or patterned fill type. You cannot view the effect of a halftone screen on the display. You must print it to see the effect. When an object has one of the PostScript fills, the object is displayed with PS. The status line shows the selected pattern.

PostScript and Non-PostScript Printing

Most PostScript printers have their own internal processor that performs many of the calculations needed to create the final output. Consequently, they tend to print faster because the computer's processor does not have to perform those functions. *PostScript emulators*, which are generally software-based, allow for PostScript printing where it may not be allowed otherwise. But they also increase the processing load of the computer and generally slow the printing process. If you are using a non-PostScript printer such as a non-PostScript LaserJet, your processing time increases because your computer must perform printing-related calculations. When using PostScript printers, be sure to use the Windows PostScript driver, *PSCRIPT.DRV*. If you don't, CorelDRAW! may not operate properly. You can verify the printer driver being used by opening the Print Manager and choosing **O**ptions **P**rinter Setup. Then select your PostScript printer, click **S**etup, and click **A**bout to display driver information.

Printers have their own resident fonts that can be printed directly from the printer with a minimum of computer interaction. PostScript printers provide an All Fonts Resident option in the Print Options dialog box that informs DRAW that all required fonts are resident in the printer. Using resident fonts speeds up the text printing process, but may limit your flexibility of font selection during design (many printers do not support a full complement of fonts). If CorelDRAW! attempts to print a font that is not resident, it either defaults to Courier or interrupts the print process (depending upon the printer type). If text has been modified by an envelope, an extrusion, or another operation, it prints as curves instead of text.

Non-PostScript LaserJet printers essentially print the information provided directly to them by the computer. As the information is received, it is stored in memory until a printed page is complete; then it is printed. Some LaserJet printers come with limited memory (500K, for example); they cannot store very much information before the printer memory is full and the page must print. In this case, drawings that extend over multiple printer-determined pages are printed in bands which correspond to pages. Limited memory can limit image size and reduce resolution, or it can require you to split images over multiple pages and combine them by hand.

TIP

Printers that print one line at a time, such as the DeskJet 500C and dot-matrix printers, do not have these problems because they have enough memory to retain one line of information at a time. They also have their downside, however. They print more slowly and offer lower quality output than that obtained with LaserJet-type printers.

To speed up the printing of draft images, you might want to set the output resolution of the printer device to 75 dpi. If you have trouble printing the entire image on a single page, you might want to try reducing the resolution from 300 dpi to 150 dpi, or even 75 dpi. The lower the resolution, the less printer memory is required for printing. Unfortunately, the lower resolutions also provide a lower print quality. If you want your drawings to look their best and you plan to print on a regular basis, you should seriously consider increasing the printer memory.

Bitmapped images tend to take up a lot of memory space, especially at higher resolutions. To minimize printing problems when using bitmapped images, try to keep them as small as possible and use the lowest acceptable resolution. If you know that a bitmapped image will shrink between the time you scan it and the time it is used, you should scan it at a lower resolution, crop it, and modify its attributes using CorelPHOTO-PAINT. Chapter 16 discusses CorelPHOTO-PAINT operations.

The more complex the drawing, the larger its file size and the greater the printer resources required to create the output. If you are using a PostScript printer, you can modify the amount of curve *flatness* which reduces the complexity of the drawing and decreases the printer memory required for printing. Flatness is set either manually or automatically using the Options dialog box, which you access by choosing **File Print Options** (see fig. 10.6). Increasing the flatness smooths down the curve and reduces its complexity.

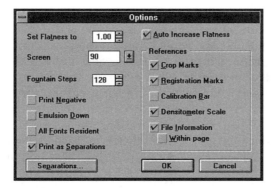

FIG. 10.6

The Options dialog box.

The Set Flatness To option defaults to 1.00; you can manually set it to a maximum value of 100. If you have trouble printing due to *limitcheck error* or other memory-related issues, try incrementing the Flatness value by 4 or 5 and printing again. To minimize your involvement with this process, DRAW provides the Auto Increase Flatness option which automatically increases the flatness until the value exceeds the original Set Flatness To value by 10 points. The printer then skips the object creating problems and moves on to print the next object.

If the flatness gets too high to accommodate the printing function, the curves may lose a lot of their character. You can take several steps to print your drawing as you created it without crashing the printer. Try to break the complex object causing problems into several smaller objects by using the Shape tool and the Node Edit features. Remove all unnecessary nodes and objects because they take up memory space and add complexity. The AutoReduce feature may help you to reduce the number of required nodes without compromising drawing quality. Try not to convert large text strings to curves unless absolutely necessary, or at least break curved text objects into smaller objects that are treated individually when printing. These steps slow down the printing process, but they can help you to avoid overreaching the complexity limit of your printer. See Chapter 12 for a detailed discussion on node selecting; refer to Chapter 8 for information on converting text to curves.

To test images being prepared for high-resolution output devices, Corel recommends printing them on a PostScript printer at 300 dpi with a flatness of 0.20. This combination simulates printing at 1270 dpi. If your image prints, you should not run into any problems printing to a higher resolution device. If problems occur, try to decrease the image complexity using some of the previously mentioned techniques, and then try printing again.

The Screen option contained within the Options dialog box pertains to the screen frequency used while printing. Non-PostScript printers generally use the printer's default screen because individual control is not provided. PostScript printers allow access to this setting. Check with your printer or service bureau about their preferred screen frequencies to ensure that the drawing is printed without annoying blotches or Moiré patterns. When printing separations, the screen frequencies set in the Separations dialog box override those set in the Options dialog box. See Chapter 11 for more details on using these options.

Merging Text into a Corel Drawing

Now you can use DRAW to merge text information from a word processing file into a DRAW graphic image file. The text stored in the word processing file is converted into artistic text in the image; the process allows you to create multiple copies of an image, each of which has a different text entry. One classic application of this procedure, for example, is to create certificates of completion for a computer software training center. For this application, student, class type, date, and instructor information is stored in an ASCII text file, and the certificate image shell are stored in standard DRAW file format. Using the Print Merge feature, the information from the text file is inserted into the DRAW image file, and each student receives a customized certificate.

An Overview of the Merge Process

Two files are required to perform a merge in CorelDRAW!: a DRAW image file and an ASCII text file. To work correctly, the ASCII file name must have a TXT extension. In this explanation, the text contained in the image file (text that will be replaced during the merge) will be referred to as *primary text,* and the text contained in the ASCII file (text to be inserted during the merge) will be called *secondary text.* You cannot use the merge process to replace paragraph text in an image file; only artistic text can be replaced.

The ASCII secondary text file contains information which guides the replacement of artistic text strings in the image file with the text contained in the secondary file. It contains *records*, each of which corresponds to a complete set of information for a single certificate in the example case. And each record contains *fields*, each of which corresponds to a particular text entry to be inserted in the certificate (student name, course name, date of completion, and so on). The structure of the secondary file is critical to performing a Print Merge successfully, so be sure to follow the instructions carefully.

Creating Merge Files

It takes some time to set up the merge process, but the time that you save by automating what would otherwise be a routine procedure more than pays for the initial time invested to make it work. The following sections outline the basic steps for creating the files involved in the merge process.

Preparing an Image File for a Merge

To prepare an image file for a Merge, follow these steps:

1. Create or open an image file.

2. Give the image locations at which you want to insert secondary text unique names that are not duplicated anywhere else in the image file. This artistic text information is not meant to be printed. It simply acts as placeholders for DRAW during the merge process, so you can make the names distinctive yet simple—NAME1, ADDRESS1, FIELD3, and so on. The image can contain any image designs that you want. It can be treated as a standard DRAW file and can contain any features you would normally include.

3. Assign text attributes (type style, typeface, and point size) to the artistic text in the image file. These attributes will be applied to the secondary text that is merged into these field locations. If you want the printed text to be centered and bold, for example, then create the initial artistic text with those attributes.

When you run the merge, DRAW inserts the secondary text and applies the attributes to the new text. If you shift individual text characters with the Shape tool during image creation, those shifts may make the final output unpredictable. You are encouraged to work with simplified text strings and effects until you have the merge process under control. Then you can experiment with other designs using your more thorough understanding of DRAW's implementation of this time-saving feature.

Assume that the artistic text entries to be replaced in the example are STUDENT, CLASSNAME, CLASSDATE, and TEACHER (see fig. 10.7).

4. Set up the desired attributes and alignment features within the image file, taking care to ensure that merged information from one field does not overrun the information inserted into another field.

Creating the Secondary Text File

Next, create the secondary text file that contains the information to be inserted into the image file artistic text locations. This file must meet strict format standards to function correctly:

■ It must be in ASCII format.

■ The file name must end with the TXT extension.

■ The secondary file must have the same name as the primary image file, substituting the TXT extension for the standard image CDR extension.

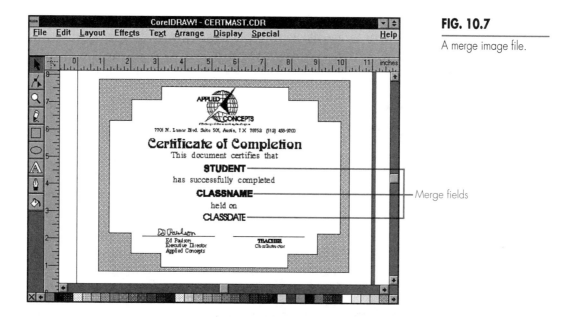

FIG. 10.7

A merge image file.

The content of the file must also be formatted in a particular way to function correctly:

1. The first line of the file must indicate the number of fields within the image file that you plan to replace.

In our example, the number is 4 because we are going to replace information in the STUDENT, CLASSNAME, CLASSDATE, and TEACHER fields.

2. The next line must start with a backslash (\), supply the name of the first artistic text field to be replaced, and then end with another backslash (\).

In this example, the first field name is STUDENT, so the second line entry in the merge file would be **\STUDENT**.

3. The remaining lines should contain the names of the other fields to be replaced during the merge. You can place each entry on a line of its own, between two backslashes, or you can enter all of them on the second line. (In our example, line 2 would read **\STUDENT\CLASSNAME\CLASSDATE\INSTRUCTOR**.) Remember that if you enter each field name on its own line, each entry must have a backslash at both the beginning and the end. This information informs DRAW that it should seek out the four fields in the image file with the names provided.

CAUTION

The names in the image fields must match exactly with the names entered in the secondary file. This rule includes spaces, punctuation, and capitalization. If they do not match exactly, the merge will not work correctly. You also cannot leave a secondary file data field blank. DRAW expects information and uses what it gets. If there is a blank field without backslashes to make it clear that it has been left intentionally blank, DRAW replaces the artistic text with the next available field of information (this throws off the whole merge process, of course). You also cannot have two artistic image fields with the same name.

TIP

When you have the merge procedure working properly, you can reuse the files with their respective names. Enter the new merge data (i.e., new teacher or student names) into the secondary file and save it. When you perform the merge, the new data contained in the secondary file is used in conjunction with the existing image file.

4. Enter the actual text information that will be merged into the image file, separating the fields with backslashes. Lines need to begin and end with backslashes as well. This information does not have to appear on separate lines for each document, but you will find it easier to keep track of things if you make a separate line for each single record, as shown in figure 10.8. In this example, each line represents an individual student record.

5. Save the file in an ASCII text format. You should use the same file name as that used for the image file so that you can easily correlate the two files.

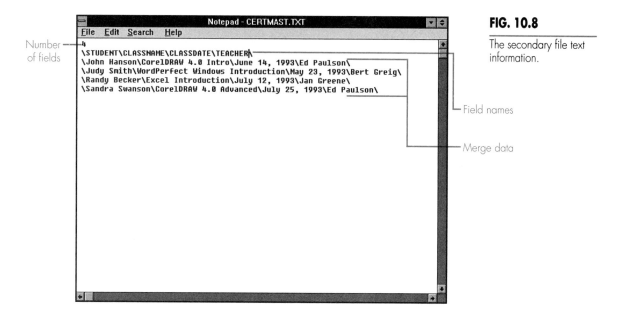

Number of fields

FIG. 10.8

The secondary file text information.

Field names

Merge data

Performing the Merge

The merge itself is a simple procedure after the image and secondary files are set up properly. To perform the merge, follow these steps:

1. Open the image file containing the artistic text to be replaced.

2. Choose File Print **M**erge. A standard Windows-oriented Open dialog box appears. Select the TXT file containing the merge information and choose OK.

3. Select the desired options from the Print Options dialog box and click OK. DRAW replaces the information in the image file with that contained in the secondary file and then routes the merged image to the printer (see fig. 10.9).

Each document is individually created, so the printing itself can be time-consuming for a large number of complex image documents. Remember that the initial image file is not permanently changed during this process. Its information is modified for printing purposes only.

FIG. 10.9

Certificate after merge.

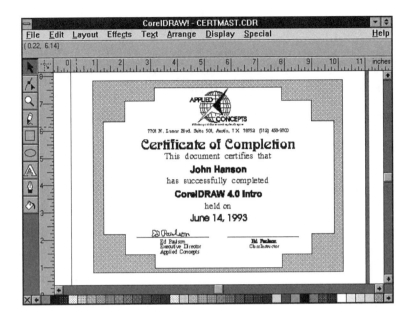

Summary

This chapter covered the basic procedures for printing with CorelDRAW!. It dealt with the many options available to get the most out of printing, covered issues involved with printing to PostScript and non-PostScript printers, discussed the ways you can print without starting DRAW, and explained how to merge text into image files.

A drawing is only as good as the final output. You should consider where you eventually want to end up before spending a lot of time creating your drawing. If you don't, there's a good chance that some of your initial work will need modification to accommodate the restrictions associated with the final output device.

The next chapter deals with the information pertaining to printing color file information in a form useful to commercial printers. Reviewing it best ensures that what you create can be printed at a price you can afford.

PART IV

Becoming an Expert

OUTLINE

Using Color for Commercial Success

The difference between black-and-white illustrations and those created in color goes beyond an appealing appearance. Using color well can be part of your signature, the way you communicate. Color can direct the viewer's attention, add emphasis, simplify a complex illustration, or create an emotional reaction. The design aspects of color have been covered in previous chapters; this chapter discusses color in the context of the commercial graphics industry, especially commercial printing.

This chapter is particularly important because your drawings must ultimately be printed. If you do not pay attention to the standards of good reproducible design, your drawings may be prohibitively expensive to reproduce.

Every object in CorelDRAW! has an outline and a fill—even letters and words of text. You set the width, color, and pattern of object outlines, as well as the color and pattern of an object's fill. You can stay with the user-defined default values for these characteristics or you can exercise sophisticated control over color choice through the color palettes and the myriad of additional colors and texture patterns you create.

In previous chapters, you learned about object creation and attribute definition. In this chapter, you learn how to use color professionally to communicate to your advantage and why every choice should be based on the final use of the illustration and its method of reproduction. Also, keep in mind that the color displayed on your computer monitor is only a rough approximation of final, or printed, color. Once you create a few drawings of the type you need, you will discover a format that works for you and is cost-effective.

Commercial Printing Process Primer

The many powerful features of CorelDRAW! enable you to produce full-color artwork of professional quality. Understanding the basics of the commercial printing process can help you to use these features to your best advantage. This section gives you some direction, but you might want to discuss the plans and intentions of your project with your printer even before you present him or her with the final art. An understanding of the steps it takes to transform your original illustration into several thousand or more color reproductions can help you make cost-effective design decisions.

The commercial printing process has come a long way since the Guttenberg press, and the capabilities of commercial printers continue to grow. In the past few years, commercial printing has become an electromechanical process of great sophistication. Commercial printing, which includes letterpress, mimeograph, silk screen, and offset lithography, uses a master from which many copies are produced. (Photocopying and photography, in comparison, take one shot or exposure of the original art to make each copy.) The printing method used by most quick print services is *offset lithography,* also called *photo offset.* Lithography uses a flat plate with an image chemically etched or burned onto it. Ink sticks to the etched portions of the plate and is repelled by the nonetched portions. Paper, or other stock, becomes imprinted with the ink when it contacts the plate.

It is important to remember that printing, unlike photography, does not duplicate the original art exactly, but creates an illusion of the original with tiny dots of overlapping ink. The human eye blends these dots of the four process colors (abbreviated CMYK)—the three primary colors plus black—into the full spectrum of color. Because these process inks are transparent, blue overlaid on red, for example, creates purple. When offset printing in spot or PMS color, blends and screens of the specific PMS inks, usually black and one or two other colors, are also printed in these tiny dots. See the spot and process colors section in this chapter for more details.

In the usual commercial printing method, the original artwork has to be transferred into several printer's plates. Offset lithography uses a special camera and light-sensitive plates to transfer the original image. You need a plate for each of the colors (four if the project is a process-color job). This procedure is called *prepress,* and includes such procedures as making negatives, assembling and aligning the negatives, positioning the image, creating special effects, and making the plates.

After you've done the prepress work, the physical printing begins. If a multiple color job runs on a one-color press, each color requires a separate trip through the press, increasing the cost of printing. A basic one-color printing job, like black, only has to go through the presses once. Many larger printers have presses that run two, four, or even more colors on the same press. In any case, the more plates required, the higher the cost, the harder it is to align all the different colors, and the harder it is to produce consistent color.

The most advanced printing technology uses no printer's plates at all. An image digitizer turns the original art into data that can be read by a computer which then controls a bank of ink jets to print the image. Sometimes the graphic artist completes the prepress process electronically and delivers to the printer the data needed to create the image on the printing presses already on a computer disk or tape. CorelDRAW! supports this type of electronic prepress as well as color separations from disk (so you don't need any original artwork from which to shoot transparencies). This method is very expensive and has limited availability.

Selecting Fill and Outline Colors from the Palette

CorelDRAW! gives you so many sophisticated options on color, fill, texture, and outline that some procedures might require opening a series of dialog boxes to set many different parameters. Keep in mind there are also simple ways to accomplish the basic commands.

- Clicking one of the colors in the palette with the left mouse button fills the selected object with that color.

- Clicking one of the colors in the palette with the right mouse button changes the outline of the selected object to that color.

- Clicking the X button at the left of the color palette with the left mouse button removes an object's fill.

- Clicking the X with the right mouse button removes an object's outline.

Chapter 6 already covered many of the fine points of setting fill and outline colors.

Selecting Fill Colors

An object's fill is the area inside its outline. CorelDRAW! gives you many ways to fill an object; previous chapters covered these in detail. In general, the status line tells you the fill of the currently selected object. An X in the fill box means the object has no fill. A quirk in CorelDRAW! is that an object's fill technically covers its entire highlight box, even though only the fill inside the object is visible. Because the highlight box is always a rectangle or square, an irregularly shaped or rotated object, like a circle or ellipse, can have some "lost" fountain fill. You can set the Edge Pad amount—up to 45 percent—to adjust for this lost fill.

At the most basic level, you can fill an object with one color. This is called a Uniform Fill, and can consist of any solid color, including black and white and shades of gray. You can also select a screen of the Uniform fill color, if it is from the PANTONE Spot Color Palette, in whatever percentage you choose by setting a value in the %Tint box.

TIP

To open the Uniform Fill dialog box, select the object to fill and press Shift+F11.

Or you can use two colors to fill one object in a fountain fill (see fig. 11.1). You choose how the colors blend and change: a linear fountain changes color in a straight line and a radial fountain changes color in concentric circles. Use a linear fountain when shading a background from dark to light, for example. Carefully choosing the colors and placement of a radial fountain can give your object the illusion of three dimensions.

With CorelDRAW! 4, you can also choose a conical fountain. A conical fountain changes colors in rays from the center of the object (like a sun).

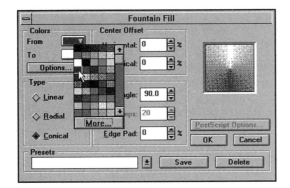

FIG. 11.1

The Fountain Fill dialog box.

> **TIP**
>
> To open the Fountain Fill dialog box, select the object to fill and press F11.

> **TIP**
>
> If you plan to print color separations with your drawing and are using spot color, you should use two tints of the same spot color when you create fountain fills.

You can also fill one object with many colors—even create a rainbow effect—by creating custom fountain fills using one of three options: Direct, Rainbow, and Custom. The Direct option enables you to choose a start color and an end color on the displayed color wheel; then CorelDRAW! fills in each of the intermediate colors between these two in a straight line. The Rainbow option enables you to draw an arc through the color wheel to specify the color choices in either a clockwise or counterclockwise direction, and then CorelDRAW! fills in the start, end, and intermediate colors. The Custom option enables you to specify up to 99 intermediate colors by clicking them in any order from the Custom Palette at the bottom of the dialog box. To access these custom fills, choose Options, Custom in the Fountain Fill dialog box.

Bitmap fills are patterns made from bitmap tiles, either from CorelDRAW! or from TIFF and PCX files imported into CorelDRAW!. Because a bitmap is just an arrangement of dots forming a pattern and has a fixed resolution, even when you rotate the object, the bitmap fill inside it stays oriented the same way. You can select the height and width of the pattern and how the bitmap tiles line up. You can also select the foreground and background colors in a bitmap pattern. Vector patterns, however, are fill patterns that you can resize without losing any of the sharpness of the pattern. These also stay in a fixed orientation and size inside the object they fill, but you can edit the vector pattern file to make changes. You can create vector and bitmap fills as patterns in CorelDRAW! that you can then save and use.

TIP

You cannot fill color and gray-scale bitmaps, because they are not closed-path objects.

TIP

To view the actual effects of a fill, choose Preview or print the drawing. Wireframe view shows no fill information at all, and the appearance of fills in Editable Preview does not always match the final drawing.

Selecting Outline Colors

All objects in CorelDRAW! have an outline, although it may be hard to see—or even invisible. If you click an object, the status line tells you the width of the outline. Adding color to an outline is like using Uniform Fill under the Fill tool. Though you can't create fountain fills or textures for the outline of an object, you can add colors in several different ways. One way to add outline color is by accessing the colors on the predefined color palettes. The quick and simple way covered earlier is

1. Click the Pick tool.

2. Select the object.

3. Select a color on the color palette at the bottom of the screen by clicking it with the right mouse button.

After the object is selected, you can also choose the Outline tool and open the Pen roll-up window, in which you can access the current color palette either by clicking the colored fill bar (see fig. 11.2), or by choosing Edit and clicking the Color button.

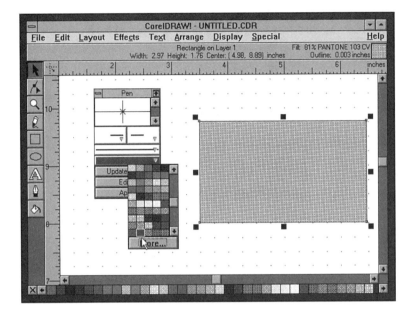

FIG. 11.2

Selecting outline colors from the Pen roll-up window.

The color palette that displays from both of these last two options includes a More button. Clicking this button displays the Outline Color dialog box which enables you to create your own process colors or to specify tints of PMS colors. Again, when creating new process colors, you use the same three models: CMYK, RGB, and HSB. These methods were covered in great detail earlier. If you plan to commercially print your drawing, it is less confusing for the printer if the same model for creating new colors is used throughout the drawing, but you can change from one to the other at any time. If you do not plan to commercially print your drawing, use whatever colors and color combinations you want on the outline colors.

TIP

If you know right away that you want to create a new color, a quicker way to get to the Outline Color dialog box is to simply click the Outline tool and then click the color wheel button.

TIP

F12 is the shortcut to selecting the Outline Pen dialog box. Shift+F12 is the shortcut to the Outline Color dialog box.

Using CorelDRAW!'s Color Capabilities

Open a CorelDRAW! document, and you see a wealth of color options laid out for you at the bottom of your screen. In Chapter 6, you learned that these groups of colors are called color palettes, but these colors represent only a fraction of the colors you can specify. You have over a hundred colors preprogrammed into these color palettes, plus you can create millions of new ones. CorelDRAW! enables you to organize this abundance of color choices into arrangements that work for you.

After you create a document, you have three basic methods of reproducing it in color:

- Printing it on a color PostScript or non-PostScript printer (on either paper stock or film stock for transparencies) and then making color photocopies

- Displaying it on a color computer monitor

- Commercially printing it, using spot or process color

The method you use plays an important role in color choice.

The first method, printing the drawing to a color PostScript or non-PostScript printer, such as a Hewlett-Packard inkjet or a color thermography printer, takes time for each copy and causes wear on the printer. It works best when you need only limited copies.

The second method is displaying the document on a computer monitor, as in presentation packages. The CMYK model for creating new colors in CorelDRAW! uses a color-specifying system that emulates computer monitor color production and gives more consistent colors when the document is transferred to new systems.

The last method, commercial printing, is an industry with a long history and a vocabulary all its own. Commercial printing is the best choice for hundreds, even thousands, of copies of a drawing even though it is often an expensive process. This is true especially if the drawing has many colors or if you want to use the full spectrum of colors found in nature.

Defining the Color Palettes

CorelDRAW! provides you with one spot color palette and four process color palettes. The CorelDRAW! window displays only one of these palettes at a time (though the others can be accessed from other dialog windows). You can revise these palettes or create custom palettes of your own. The process color palettes differ in the range of colors they display, and whether the on-screen colors display as dithered or pure. The default color process palette contains about 100 colors, but you can create many more process colors using the three process color models provided with CorelDRAW!. Once you create a color, you have the option of adding it to the active palette or creating a new palette containing several new colors. It is usually easier to revise an existing palette. The next few sections deal with creating and editing color palettes.

You can create up to 16-million colors with CorelDRAW!, but only if your computer has enough memory. Systems that support 16–256 colors use dithering to emulate the wide array of color possible with color output devices. *Dithering* is a process that intersperses on-screen pixels of different colors in a gradual pattern to form the best rendition possible of the desired output color.

Spot versus Process Colors

Commercially printing in spot color is usually substantially cheaper than printing in process color. Still, when a drawing contains more than three different colors (a tint or screen of a color is not considered a different color), it's usually best to go to four-color process printing. That way, you have access to the full range of colors found in nature for the price of only four colors of ink. CorelDRAW! contains color palettes in both spot and process color to make it easier later when you take the project to a printer. The simple procedure for converting a spot color to a process color is covered in the next section. However, you cannot convert a process color to a spot color. If you are going to display your final work on a computer screen, use process colors because they provide the widest variety of colors. If, however, you eventually plan to print your file, make the process or spot color decision up-front, or you may be surprised by unexpected expenses and radically changed output.

Spot Color

Spot color is generally used when a drawing contains black and one or two other colors for decoration or emphasis. Because there are fewer inks and fewer press runs required, spot color can be commercially printed comparatively inexpensively. Almost all commercial printers are familiar with the system used to specify spot colors, or you can reproduce the work on a color PostScript printer using the PostScript halftone screen patterns. If a drawing has four or more colors and is to be commercially printed, it is usually more cost effective to create it in process color.

Spot colors use the PANTONE Matching System and are called PMS colors. The spot color palette provided in CorelDRAW! contains over 700 PMS colors, each with its own unique number (for example, PMS 131 is a brownish yellow). The colors you see on your computer screen are only approximations of the actual PMS colors, however. You can view the true PMS colors by looking at a PMS book—available at most art supply stores—which has swatches of each PMS color. A PMS book is a basic tool for anyone doing graphics and illustrations for reproduction. Some printers even suggest that you buy a new PMS book yearly because the inks tend to fade with age.

Process Color

Process colors, on the other hand, are best used when your drawing has four or more colors, or when you want the full range of colors found in life. Reproduction of process colors, as in full-color magazines, usually requires a commercial printer with sophisticated equipment, but you can also output your illustration to a color PostScript or non-PostScript printer. Process color is based on the theory that over 16-million colors can be specified as some mixture of the inks used in four-color printing: CMYK, for cyan (or bluish), magenta (or reddish), yellow, and K (for black). In effect, these are the three primary colors, plus black. These four inks, in various percentages, combine to make up literally millions of colors.

You can save time and money when commercially printing your full-color drawing because CorelDRAW! separates process colors into their CMYK components, provided you use a PostScript printer and choose Process Color Separations when printing. You can match your on-screen process colors to the process colors achieved in commercial printing by selecting colors according to the TRUMATCH Swatching System, which is another book you can buy at an art supply store. CorelDRAW! even gives you a TRUMATCH color palette with the unique numbers noted.

Converting Spot Colors to Process Colors

Though you can send an illustration that combines both spot and process colors to a commercial printer, you will save money on the final printed piece by converting any spot colors to their process color equivalents. You do lose a little of your control over the color of the final piece because the printed results can show a slight variation between the process and spot color. To do this conversion, follow these steps:

1. Select the Pick tool and click the object with the spot color to select it.

2. Click the Fill or Outline tool, depending on the attribute to be changed, and then click the Color Wheel icon on the fly-out menu.

3. Click the spot color to select it.

4. Click the Show drop-down list to choose one of the process color models, and click it (see fig. 11.3).

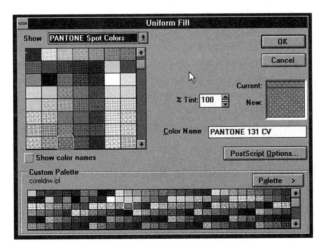

FIG. 11.3

Selecting a spot color.

The menu now tells you what percentages of the four CMYK inks simulate the spot color (see fig. 11.4).

FIG. 11.4

The same color converted to a process color equivalent.

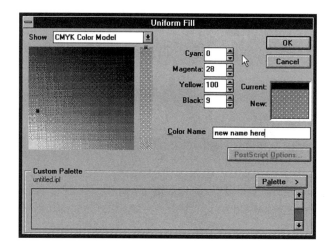

5. Give the newly created process color a name and click OK.

6. To store the converted color in a palette so you can use it later, click the Palette button, then choose Add Color. CorelDRAW! adds the new color to the end of the active palette. Click the Palette button again and choose Save or Save As to save the changes to the palette.

Creating Custom Colors

The 700 or so industry-standard PMS or spot colors are given, but you can select a screened-back version of any PMS color by specifying a percentage tint in the %Tint box (see fig. 11.5). The effect of screening or tinting a PMS color is the same as screening black to make gray—you get a paler version of the color. You can then include this new tint in the PANTONE Spot Colors palette for later use.

To add a tint of spot color to the palette, follow these steps:

1. Select the Pick tool and click the object with the spot color to select it.

2. Click the Fill or Outline tool, depending on the location of the spot color to be changed.

3. Click the color wheel icon. In the window that comes up, the spot color is already selected (or select a new spot color if you want to change it at this time).

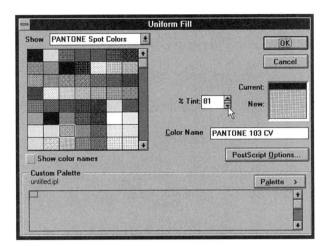

FIG. 11.5

Specifying a screened (tinted) version of a spot color.

4. Reset the %Tint figure. (The changes might be too subtle to change your on-screen display.)

5. Click the P**a**lette button, and then choose Add Color. The new tint will be added to the end of the active palette. Click OK.

You can also create your own new colors from process colors using one of the three process color models. Of these three process color creation models, only the CMYK model enables you to specify TRUMATCH colors that your commercial printer can more easily match. The new process color's name is added to the list of Named colors; if you switch models after creating a color, CorelDRAW! converts the new color into the new format for you. Once in the dialog box that enables you to create new process colors, you have a choice of methods: typing in the percentages of CMYK or using the visual selector (see fig. 11.6). The visual selector enables you to drag two markers to indicate the amount of cyan and magenta (using the marker on the large box), and to indicate the amount of yellow (using the marker in the narrow box).

TIP

TRUMATCH colors are industry-standard process colors. Many printers have TRUMATCH color swatch books, which you can also buy at your local art supply store. CorelDRAW! also gives you a TRUMATCH process color palette with the unique number of each color included to make it easier to achieve the printed colors you want. Small print shops still use PMS.

FIG. 11.6

Using the visual selector to create a new process color.

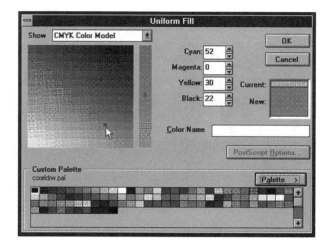

If you want to add to the 100 premixed colors in your process color palette, CorelDRAW! gives you three color models for creating process colors:

- *CMYK.* This uses the four colors from commercial printing (cyan, magenta, yellow, and black).

- *RGB.* This uses various intensities (from 0 to 100) of the colors red, green, and blue.

- *HSB.* This varies three parameters to create colors—hue, saturation, and brightness.

With the CMYK you specify the percentages of the inks, or use the visual selector color wheel to specify the color, and CorelDRAW! creates a screen approximation of it. The Gray Component Replacement (GCR) is an option that will give you better contrast, better color fidelity, and improved sharpness on your color separations, and will ensure better consistency during the press run. The GCR process is done automatically by CorelDRAW! when you use the visual selector. See "Using CorelDRAW! for Maximum Color-Related Benefit" later in this chapter for details on GCR.

The RGB model emulates color reproduction by the RGB pixels on your computer screen, so it is often the best choice when creating color illustrations that are transferred to new computer systems, as in presentation software (see fig. 11.7). You produce white by setting all three intensities to 100; you produce black by setting them all to 0.

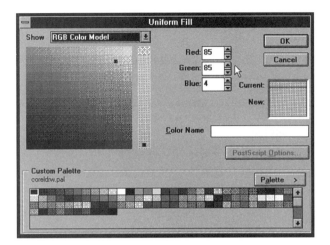

FIG. 11.7

The RGB model of creating process colors.

The HSB model varies three parameters to create colors—hue (the color itself such as red or green), saturation (the purity or intensity of the hue), and brightness (the percentage of black in the color where 0% is black and 100% is white). Hue is set by defining a number that corresponds to rotational degrees on a circle. For example, 0 equals red, and 180 equals cyan. Create the HSD color you want and then save it as a color for later use (see fig. 11.8).

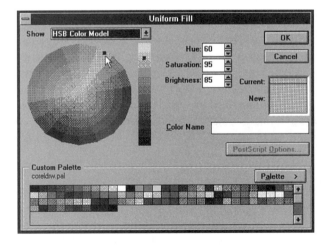

FIG. 11.8

The HSB model of creating process colors.

To create a custom process color, follow these steps:

1. Select the Pick tool and click the object you want to fill or outline with the new color.

2. Click the Fill or Outline tool, depending on the location of the color, and then click the color wheel icon.

3. Choose one of the three models for creating process colors that you want from the Show box. Your choices are CMYK, RGB, or HSB.

4. Define the new color by moving the color-adjustment markers in the visual selector box, or by entering exact percentages in the text boxes.

5. To save the color in the palette to use later, give it a name in the Color Name box.

TIP

For quick recall, name new colors according to their percentage mix. 66B22R0Y10K, for example, is 66-percent cyan/blue, 22-percent magenta/red, 0-percent yellow, and 10-percent black.

6. Click the Palette button, choose Add Color, and then click OK.

Converting from One Color Scheme to Another

As you have seen, CorelDRAW!'s default palettes relate to how your document will ultimately be reproduced. You may decide to change from spot to process color later, and CorelDRAW! supports that. It is also a good idea to use different palettes, or color schemes, for certain projects for consistency and to prevent confusion. You can also create a specific color scheme and use it for all drawings related to specific projects by revising an existing palette and renaming it or creating a whole new palette for the project. Keep in mind that the PANTONE spot color palette is for a different commercial printing process than any of the process color palettes.

CorelDRAW! shows only one of the many color palettes at the bottom of your screen. More color options in the displayed palette can be accessed by using the scroll arrow. There are two ways to reset the color palette. A quick way to reset to one of the basic palettes is to access the Display pull-down menu and choose the Color Palette option; a window comes up with several choices, including No Palette. Make your choice by clicking it, and the palette at the bottom of the screen changes.

To choose one of the other preprogrammed palettes, or a palette you have created yourself, follow these steps:

1. Select an object, then click the Outline or Fill tool, then on the color wheel icon to get a color dialog box called Uniform Fill (for the Fill tool) or Outline Color (for the Outline tool).

2. At the bottom of this dialog box is a Palette button. Click this button, and then click Open. The Open Palette dialog box displays (see fig. 11.9).

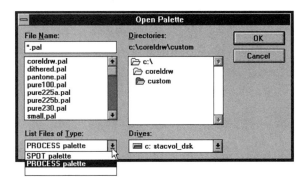

FIG. 11.9

The Open Palette dialog box.

3. Select either Spot Palette or Process Palette from the List Files of Type option. You then get a list of process color palette files, indicated by the extension PAL, or a single spot color palette file, indicated by the extension IPL.

4. Make a selection from either list, to replace the current palette, and then click OK.

5. Click OK again to return to the drawing.

The default CorelDRAW! palette is a process color palette called CORELDRW.PAL. If you modify this palette and then want to return to the default colors, choose the backup palette PURE100.PAL, also provided, because these two palettes were identical when you first installed CorelDRAW!.

TIP

Never save changes to the PURE100.PAL palette. This way, you always have a true copy of the original CorelDRAW! default palette. Always save your modified palettes using the Custom Palette Save As option provided in the dialog box. Either save the palette under a new name or save it as CORELDRW.PAL default if you are sure that the old palette is no longer useful and should be reset to the active palette.

Adding and Removing the Color Palette

The color palette displayed along the bottom of your CorelDRAW! window can be toggled on or off by activating the Display pull-down menu and then choosing the Show Color Palette command and No Palette. The window that appears also enables you to change the color palette to one of the other defaults. CorelDRAW! also enables you to rearrange the colors on a given palette by clicking the color and dragging it to a new location. You might want to put the four most-used colors in a drawing grouped at the beginning of the palette, for example. You can also create totally new arrangements of colors that are specific for a certain job or project. Save this special arrangement by using the Palette Save As option, and CorelDRAW! will load the new palette automatically on startup.

Printing Process Color Drawings

CorelDRAW! gives you a wealth of options for having your drawing commercially printed; using these in an educated way can save you time and printing costs. Of course, if you plan to print just one or a few copies of your color drawing on your office printer, CorelDRAW! enables you to print your process color drawings on a variety of PostScript and even non-PostScript color printers. (Release 4 feature: This option is available on PCL and other non-PostScript printers.) Hopefully, you knew you meant to print using commercial process color or PMS color while you were creating your drawing, so you choose the best palettes and color specification models to cause the least amount of confusion for your printer. It is a good rule to visit your commercial printer before beginning your design. The printer can offer you production tips that will help you avoid problems. Find out what your printer's requirements are.

Commercial spot/PMS color and four-color process printing both require many steps between the original art and the full-color final result. Because spot color usually involves fewer inks and requires fewer press runs, commercially printing PMS color is often substantially cheaper than four-color process printing. The process of getting the original art to the printing press is called prepress and can involve shooting the image with a special camera, digitizing the colors into the four process color basics, creating a negative for each of the four colors, and assembling these negatives to expose the printer's plates. Many of these manual prepress steps can be replaced by computer technology, which CorelDRAW! supports.

Commercial Printing Options in CorelDRAW!

Printing a file as color separations creates a page for each of the process colors (Cyan/blue, Yellow, Magenta/red, K/black) and/or a page for each of the spot (PMS) colors. Your black-and-white printer can produce the separations. Your commercial printer combines these separations to produce full-color output. If you combine process and spot colors, a page is printed for each one. In the Print Options dialog box, covered in an earlier chapter, you have other choices that can be of benefit when you go to a commercial printer (see fig. 11.10).

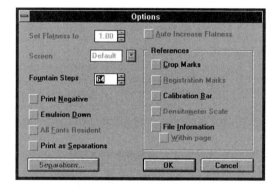

FIG. 11.10

The Options dialog box with prepress options.

The Print as Separations option enables the Separations button. Click on the Separations button to display a Separations dialog box. Printing as color separations means that each process color and each spot color in your drawing are printed on a separate page. Your printer can use these images to create the plates needed for color printing. Clicking OK from within the Separations dialog box returns you to the Options dialog box, where you can select Crop Marks (used for page trimming), Print Negative (used to reduce prepress degradation by one generation), and File Information (used to put file and related information on the same page as the output).

Sometimes the CorelDRAW! illustration uses only a portion of the page, or a drawing may have what is called a *bleed*, which means the color extends to the edge of the page. To get the bleed effect, the printer must print a little past the edges of the drawing and then trim the paper back. The Crop Marks option prints crop marks to indicate four corners of the image. For this to print out, your CorelDRAW! document must be smaller than the paper on which you are printing.

TIP

If you plan to print color separations with your drawing and are using spot color, you should use two tints of the same spot color when you create fountain fills, and not fills of two different colors.

The Registration Marks option prints registration marks on the four corners of a color separation. The printer uses these marks later to align the printer's plates and precisely place the four ink colors to achieve the desired color mix.

The Densitometer Scale option creates a grid showing the levels of intensity of each of the four CMYK, from 0 to 100, on color separations. This enables you and your printer to check the consistency and accuracy of ink coverage for the printed output.

TIP

Choosing screens of process colors for type can give your text a ragged look. Use 100-percent cyan, magenta, or black (not yellow) in the mix to fix this.

The Print Negative option specifies a type of printing onto film that a printer can then use to make printer's plates. The drawing is usually relayed as a datafile to a service bureau for printing out on its photo-typesetter. Emulsion Up, which specifies an image facing up, is the default setting here, and Emulsion Down is the option. Tell your service bureau if you select Film Negative, because most service bureaus set their equipment to print negatives. Two negatives results in a film positive image.

If you are printing to a PostScript printer, the Use Custom Halftone option is enabled. This option allows you to reset from the default half-tone screen frequency. The halftone screen frequency refers to the number of dots, lines, or circles printed per inch. The screen angle and frequency settings affect the number of grays, the sharpness, and the intensity of the printed image.

Manually adjusting these areas in your drawing to overlap is a process called *trapping*. Trapping is done to prevent the color of the paper showing through when the alignment on two adjacent colors is off a fraction. CorelDRAW! offers two options that aid the program in autotrapping. The first option, Always Overprint Black, should be selected if you want all objects containing 95 percent or more black to be trapped. The second option, Auto-Spreading, when selected, automatically adds trap to objects meeting these three conditions:

- They are filled with a uniform fill

- They have no outline

- They have not been selected to overprint from the Object menu

Auto-Spreading has a related value, Maximum Points, that is used to set the maximum outline width for the object. This outline color that is added for trap matches the fill color of the object.

Many commercial printers request no trap on digital separations, and charge fees to do trapping prepress by hand. Understanding trap and applying it judiciously can save you unnecessary expense.

Trapping should be done as a final step if the drawing will be commercially printed. You can do this manually if you understand the process, or the autotrapping feature does this preventative step for you.

Auto Trapping performs automatic trapping of colors (see fig. 11.11).

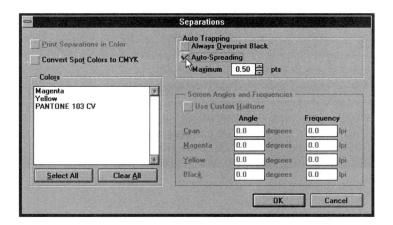

FIG. 11.11

The Auto Trapping option.

Some other suggestions when printing in full color:

- Printers need a registration mark on each different sheet of your final illustration if it has process or spot colors. If you are not using the Color Separation options when printing which automatically print registration marks, use the circle with cross hairs found in the Geographic font, and make sure each symbol prints at 100-percent of all the colors (CMYK or PMS) in the drawing so that the marks appear on each sheet.

■ In the Fountain Fill dialog box, the PostScript Options dialog box enables you to specify halftone screens and frequency and angles.

■ If you are sending your final illustration to a printer, add a percentage of the three other process colors for a richer black (ask your printer for the best ratios).

■ Stick with the same method (CMYK, RGB, or HSB) of creating new process colors throughout your drawing to make it easier to later match printed colors.

Avoiding Fountain Fill Banding

Fountain fills can sometimes have a problem with banding, or visible stair-stepping of the colors, if offset printed in process color. The illustration may look fine on a laser printer or color printer, whereas the banding appears only when the illustration is professionally printed. This is because office PostScript printers have a relatively low resolution (a few hundred dots per inch) and can only produce a maximum of 256 shades of each of the four process colors. Professional printing equipment has a much higher resolution (a few thousand dots per inch). The number of shades available in fountain fills is a factor of this resolution and the halftone screen frequency used, which is measured in lines per inch.

To create smooth fountains, you can calculate the number of shades:

1. Divide the number of dots per inch in the equipment by the number of lines per inch of the halftone resolution, as in dpi/lpi.

2. Multiply the resulting number by itself to get its square, which gives you the number of shades, as in: $(dpi/lpi)^2$.

3. If the fountain used does not contain the full range of shades from 1 percent to 100 percent, figure what fraction it does use. Example: a gradation going from 20 percent to 80 percent uses 60 percent (or a factor of .6) of the shades available.

4. Multiply the number in step 2 by the factor, if any, in step 3, as in $(dpi/lpi)^2 \times .6$.

5. Measure the distance between the end points of the blend in points.

6. Divide this distance by the number of shades from step 4 (or step 2 if the full range of shades is used). This gives you the size of each step in the fountain fill.

If the result is greater than 1, banding is likely. You can prevent banding by changing one or more factors: increase the percentage of the gradation, decrease the distance, raise the output resolution, or lower the frequency of the screen.

The Cost of Printing in Color

You can commercially print just about anything you create in CorelDRAW!, if you are willing to pay the price. Printing in color, especially four color, may be more than your budget can allow. The cost of commercial printing is related to the materials and services used. Effective use of CorelDRAW! can eliminate or reduce some of the printer's work, saving you money on your print job. A printer might charge extra for film and plates, doing a press proof, shooting and assembling the negatives, and more. Special effects, like dropouts, reverses, special screen, retouching, all can add extra costs. Bleeds (in which the ink goes to the edge of the paper) and trapping are also additional.

Color printing costs more than black-and-white (or single color) printing because it requires more negatives, extra printer's plates, and more impressions. It takes more time from the strippers, who shoot and assemble the negatives, and the press operators to get the job right. And it usually requires more expensive paper stock. Setup costs related to commercial printing are fixed, no matter how many units you choose to print.

Using some of CorelDRAW!'s advanced features can also save you money on commercial color printing. You can create a CorelDRAW! illustration as a file to be read by an imagesetter—usually available at a service bureau or your printer may have one on-site. By specifying Print as Negative under the Printing dialog box and changing the setting of the output device to the imagesetter or other equipment your service bureau uses, you can eliminate many of the manual prepress steps. By understanding and correctly using CorelDRAW!'s auto-trap feature, you can save a considerable amount of money. Trapping by hand is a time-consuming, tedious job that the printer must charge to the client, often at more than $50 per hour. You can also save money by limiting the number of process colors to two. If you are printing photos or illustrations where accurate color is critical, try not to use color for text objects; your photos will be less likely to have uneven color due to using more ink on the screens. Ask your printer to tell you the settings and data she or he needs for effective electronic prepress.

Using CorelDRAW! for Maximum Color-Related Benefit

The reality of printing in more than one color is that registration, aligning the paper stock correctly for each press run, can often be a problem. Usually only large commercial printers with sophisticated offset printing equipment can handle many colors and tight registration. Ask your printer what type of equipment she or he uses, what she or he needs from you to do the job more efficiently, and what design elements can create added printing costs. If you have a budget for only two colors at what is called a "Quick Print" shop, you may be better off designing an illustration that has no large areas of abutting colors.

CorelDRAW! makes matching commercially printed colors easy if you use the provided PANTONE or TRUMATCH color palettes with the TRUMATCH (for process color) and PMS (for spot color) color reference books.

The PANTONE palette contains spot colors that match the PANTONE Match System used by many printers and service bureaus. Comparing your on-screen colors to the PANTONE color reference book can give you a better idea of how your colors will look when commercially printed.

The Gray Component Replacement (GCR) is a technique that reduces the three primary process colors and replaces them with varying amounts of black. Using GCR will give you better contrast, better color fidelity, and improved sharpness on your color separations, and will ensure better consistency during the press run. The GCR process is done automatically by CorelDRAW! when you use the visual selector. If you use another method, you must enter the appropriate percentage of black yourself. Alternatively, you can follow these steps:

1. Choose **File** and then choose **Print**.

2. Click the Color button.

3. Select Prepress Tools. The Prepress Tools dialog box appears.

   Use the GCR control and replace the K/black value for the entire drawing in one step (see fig. 11.12).

4. Use the mouse to move the control boxes on the GCR scale to specify GCR values.

5. Click on the OK button.

6. Rename the Circuit file name to avoid overwriting the default circuit file, DEFAULT.SMT.

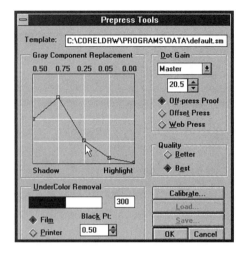

FIG. 11.12

The GCR control in the Prepress Tools dialog box.

The file COLORBAR.CDR included with your CorelDRAW! samples enables you to test the color fidelity of your color printer. To do this, follow these steps:

1. Load and print the file by going to the **F**ile menu, choosing **O**pen and selecting COLORBAR.CDR. A disk file of the CMYK Color Chart card appears on-screen.

2. Choose **P**rint from the **F**ile menu.

3. Compare this printed illustration with the CMYK in a ClipArt manual, for example, to see how the process colors on-screen appear when commercially printed.

Drawing Some Simple Color Illustrations

Some illustrations are created for no other purpose than for the artist's enjoyment. CorelDRAW! gives you more than enough tools if this is your goal. If, however, you plan to create a drawing that will be used later in a proposal, or copied and disseminated in a PC "slide show," or even commercially printed in mass quantities in a 16 x 20 poster, CorelDRAW! has many features that make it easy to get the effect you want. As an example the following steps demonstrate some of the vivid colors available in CorelDRAW! in an eye-catching illustration that can be printed on a Hewlett-Packard color PostScript printer:

1. Use the various CorelDRAW! tools to draw an artist's palette on a background with six blobs of "paint" (see fig. 11.13). Before you select the color fills for the various paint blobs, reflect on how the illustration will be reproduced. Because you will be printing on your color office printer, the PANTONE Spot Color palette or any of the process color palettes are all suitable.

FIG. 11.13

Sample Illustration— drawing a palette.

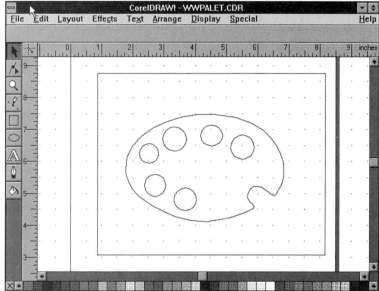

2. From the **D**isplay menu, choose the **C**olor Palette, and then choose PANTONE **S**pot Colors.

3. Click a paint blob shape to make it active, and then click one of the color choices in the palette at the bottom of the screen with the left mouse button. The color fills the interior of the paint blob shape (see fig. 11.14).

4. Continue to fill the other paint blob shapes with other colors from the PANTONE Spot Color palette. Fill the palette shape itself with one of the PMS brown shades.

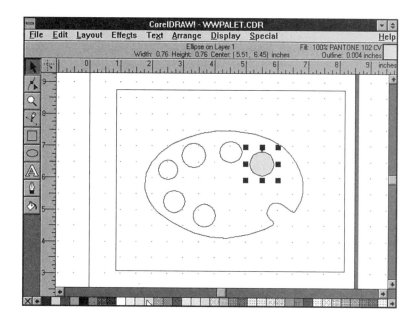

FIG. 11.14

Choosing color fills.

5. Choose a two-color pattern to fill the rectangle forming the backdrop (see fig. 11.15) by selecting the Fill tool and using the two-color pattern icon. Click in the two-color Fill Tool Colors boxes to set the background and foreground colors from the PANTONE Spot Color palette.

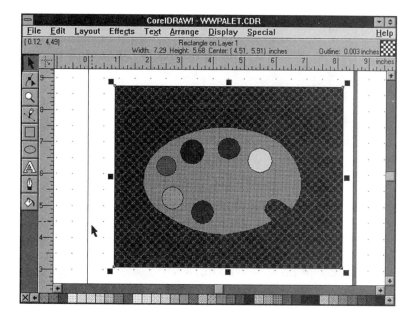

FIG. 11.15

Choosing Color pattern fills.

6. Choose the Text tool in Paragraph format, and type the words:

CorelDRAW! features a rainbow of ways to communicate using color!

7. Use Center Alignment on this sentence.

8. Set the typeface at 24-point Times New Roman.

9. Choose the Pick tool and click the text to select it.

10. Click the Fill tool and choose the color wheel icon, or press Shift+F11. This opens the Uniform Fill dialog box. (You used the mouse button to fill objects before; this is just another way to set the fill of an object, even text.)

11. Select a red color of your choice or type **Pantone 498 CV** in the Color **N**ame box (see fig. 11.16).

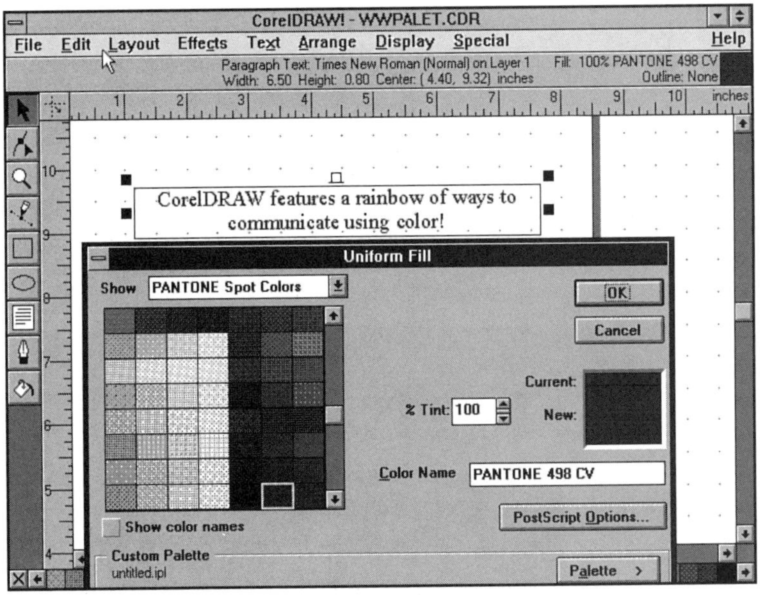

FIG. 11.16

Adding color fill to text.

![Uniform Fill dialog in CorelDRAW]

12. Click OK, and the text is given a red-colored fill.

13. At this point the illustration is ready to print. Under the **F**ile menu, choose **P**rint; or press Ctrl+P. If you want more than one copy so you can show it off to your colleagues, change the number in the copies box. Because you are not preparing your illustration for commercial printing, you do not have to select any other options.

14. Click OK to print the document (or Cancel if you are not attached to a color printer and you are just practicing).

What if you wanted 1000 copies of this illustration, on a 16-by-20-inch poster, to be printed by a commercial offset printer? You remember that you used six PMS colors for the six paint blobs, another PMS color for the brown palette, two PMS colors in the backdrop rectangle, and another PMS color for the text. Printing these 10 different PMS colors requires 10 different inks and up to 10 press runs. Going to four-color process is cheaper and probably will look better. Using CorelDRAW!'s prepress features, you can save the cost of intermediate steps with your printer and/or service bureau.

To convert your illustration and get it ready for four-color process printing, follow these steps:

1. Click the Pick tool to activate it, and then select the text.

2. Click the Fill tool to get the fly-out menu, and then choose the color wheel icon. You see the PANTONE Warm Red in the visual calibrator and the color name or number in the Color Name box.

3. Choose the CMYK Color Model from the Show drop-down list, and the PANTONE color is assigned a process color—you may or may not get a name in the Color Name box; you can create your own name if not (see fig. 11.17).

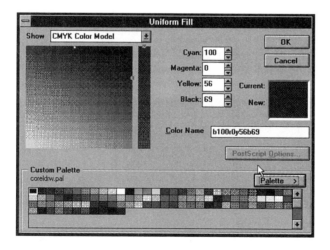

FIG. 11.17

Converting PANTONE spot color fills to process colors.

4. Click OK, converting the PANTONE color to a process color.

5. Continue to select and convert fills for each element in the illustration.

You want to provide the illustration already separated into its four CMYK color components so the printer will not have to have color separations done manually (usually by shooting a slide photo to get a transparency, then running the transparency through an electronic color scanner). Steps 6 through 8 describe how to do this.

6. Go to the **File** menu, choose the **P**rint command; or press Ctrl+P. Then click the Opti**on**s button. Now you see the Options dialog box (see fig. 11.18).

FIG. 11.18

Selecting the Print as Separations Option.

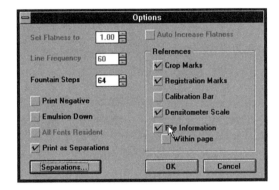

7. Select Print as Separations, but do not choose Print Negative. Now you notice all the information that gets automatically checked in the References boxes. These are all okay.

8. Click the Separations button, and you see the Separations dialog box (see fig. 11.19).

FIG. 11.19

Selecting Auto Trapping to fix tight registration problems.

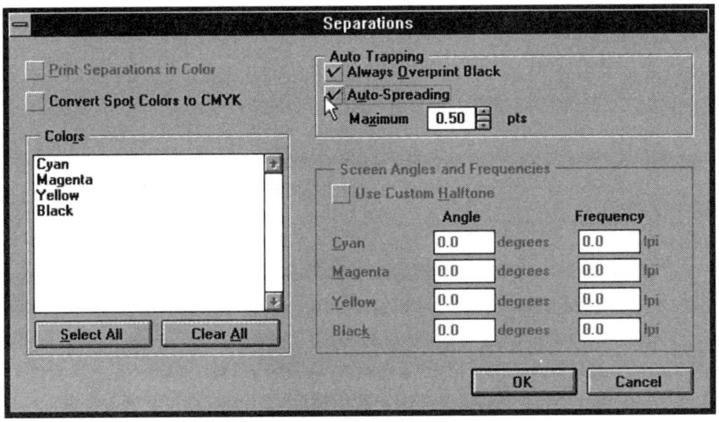

9. Click both the Auto Trapping options because your illustration has several places in which colors abut other colors and you want to be sure registration is no problem. This will create enough spread and overprinting to prevent the color of the paper stock from showing through along these critical color edges.

10. If you have PMS colors showing in the list of colors, click on the Convert Spot Colors to CMYK option to remove them.

11. Click OK, and OK again to return to the main Printer window.

12. If you have chosen to print multiple copies previously, change this in the Print dialog box to avoid multiple separation print copies.

13. If you want to print to your office printer now, choose OK. You will get four different versions of this same illustration, one for each of the CMYK process ink colors. The cyan separation, for example, will show everywhere that blue ink prints, and in what percent screens. If these office printouts were at a high enough resolution, a printer could conceivably make film and plates directly from them.

or

Choose the Print to **F**ile option then choose OK. This way you can give your printer this information electronically, on a disk or tape. CorelDRAW! asks you to name the printer file and specify a path for it.

Again, talk to your service bureau and your printer before you finalize your project to learn the best formats and how to transfer the information. You may also want to specify TRUMATCH process color numbers so the final printed piece will more accurately reflect your vision. You can write this information on one of the printouts you made on your HP color laser printer above and give it to your printer along with the tape or disk.

Summary

In this chapter, you took the knowledge and skills from previous chapters—specifying colors and fills for an object's interior and outline—and learned how to make effective color choices that reflected how your drawing would be used and reproduced (if indeed it would). You also learned how to create new colors and add those colors to existing palettes or create new ones. This chapter gave you an overview of the commercial printing process, and how CorelDRAW! can replace some of the manual prepress procedures with electronic procedures. You also learned about some of the realities of printing in color, and why the ultimate use and method of reproduction of your illustration should affect your design decisions.

Now that you have covered the basics of creating a drawing in a way that is commercially feasible to print, you can move on to the more sophisticated methods of creating drawings. Chapter 12 explains advanced line and curve techniques that can help you improve your drawing efficiency.

Using Advanced Line and Curve Techniques

In Chapter 4, you learned how to draw line segments, curve segments, rectangles, and ellipses. Most of your drawings will start out with these kinds of simple objects. To develop your drawings fully, however, you need to be able to change objects from basic shapes having a few nodes into complicated shapes having multiple layers and hundreds of nodes. The first part of this chapter covers changing the shapes of objects, using the Shape tool and the Node Edit roll-up window.

Chapter 6 dealt with the basics of modifying the thickness and color of object outlines. In the second part of this chapter, you learn about more advanced outline features, including line style (dashed lines, dotted lines), calligraphy, arrowheads, and aligning the outlines of several objects.

With these advanced line and curve techniques, you can more fully exploit CorelDRAW! and increase your efficiency when creating your pictures.

Changing Object Shapes

Drawing objects with CorelDRAW! involves creating objects such as rectangles, circles, lines, and multisided objects and then changing their shapes to meet your particular needs. This section covers techniques for using the object nodes, the Shape tool, and the Node Edit roll-up window to change the shapes of objects.

CorelDRAW! thinks of most objects as being composed of line and curve segments. A line has two end points and a slope. You have no way to change the angle of the line entering or leaving an end point. A curve, on the other hand, has end points, but the line enters and leaves the end points at a different angle depending on the amount of curvature present. Understanding how curves work is extremely important in using CorelDRAW! effectively.

Introducing the Shape Tool and the Node Edit Roll-Up Window

The Shape tool, as its name suggests, enables you to change the shape of an object. You use the Shape tool to move and alter the nodes of an object, which in turn affects the object's shape. To select the Shape tool, click the Shape tool icon in the toolbox, or press F10.

The power of the Shape tool is expanded when you use it in conjunction with the Node Edit roll-up window shown in figure 12.1. To open this roll-up window, select an object with the Shape tool and double-click an object node. With the Node Edit roll-up window, you can add and delete nodes, fuse nodes together, break nodes apart, or change the line segment type (straight line or curve) or node type characteristics (cusp, smooth, or symmetrical). These tasks are discussed in the following sections.

Understanding Line Segments and Nodes

Before you start reshaping objects, you should have a basic understanding of how CorelDRAW! draws objects. It thinks of an object as nodes connected by a path. The path can be a line or a curve. The node type and control point angle control the shape of the curve on either side of the node. You change the shape of an object by moving nodes, adding and deleting nodes, and modifying the types and line angle characteristics of nodes.

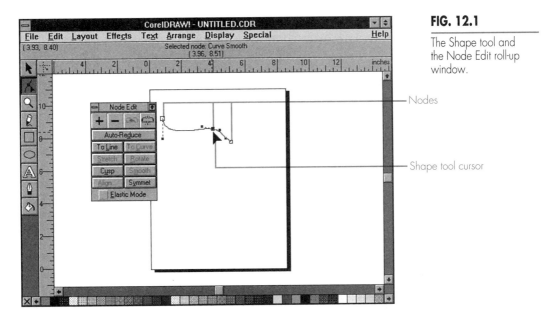

FIG. 12.1

The Shape tool and the Node Edit roll-up window.

Many of your drawings will start out with lines, rectangles, and ellipses. As your drawing proceeds, you often want to change the shapes of these objects, but soon discover that CorelDRAW! does not let you do so. The program assumes that an object is of a certain size and cannot be modified from that basic characteristic (for example, a circle cannot easily become a square). You can, however, convert these objects to curves so that you can edit the nodes and modify the object's shape at will.

Converting Objects to Curves

In CorelDRAW!, basically two kinds of objects exist: curve objects and non-curve objects. You can change the shape of curve objects freely by moving or modifying the nodes with the Shape tool. With non-curve objects, you are much more limited in what you can do with the nodes.

Two of the basic types of objects you create with CorelDRAW!—rectangles and ellipses—are non-curve objects and cannot be reshaped with the Shape tool, except for the special corner-rounding and arc/pie techniques described in Chapter 4. But you can convert one of these objects to a curve object by selecting it and choosing the Convert to Curves command from the Arrange menu (or pressing Ctrl+Q). Although the object looks the same after being converted, CorelDRAW! no longer constrains its shape, and you can move the nodes with the Shape tool. Be aware that the only way to convert a curve object back to a rectangle or an ellipse is with the Undo command from the Edit menu; also, only the number of operations covered by the defined levels of Undo are covered by this safeguard.

You also can convert artistic text to curves, which enables you to reshape individual characters with the Shape tool. You might use this technique, for example, to create a company logo. You cannot, however, convert nonartistic text to curves.

Objects have specific node point locations. A circle or ellipse, for example, has a node point at each 90 degree point. When a circle is still a circle (rather than a curve), it has only one point that you drag to create the arc and pie shapes you saw previously. After being converted to a curve, an ellipse has four nodes, and text letters have many nodes (see fig. 12.2).

FIG. 12.2

Objects converted to curves.

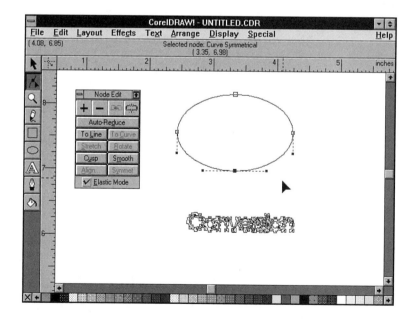

After you convert an object to a curve, you can modify the nodes just as with any object to achieve many of the dramatic effects that CorelDRAW! is renowned for creating.

Converting Lines to Curves

Curve objects can be composed of any number of connected line and curve segments. Every segment has a beginning node and an end node. The end node determines whether the segment is a line or a curve. If it is a line node, the path connecting it to the previous node is constrained to be linear; you cannot alter its shape and can change only the line's angle. You can convert the segment from a line to a curve, however, and then modify its shape as you can any other curve. The basic procedure is as follows:

1. Create a line with the Pencil tool in either Freehand or Bézier mode.

2. Select the line by clicking it with the Shape tool. Notice that the line has a node on each end, represented by an unfilled box, and that one of the boxes is larger than the other. The larger box is the origin or *first node* of the line.

3. Select the end node of the line, represented by the smaller box, by clicking it with the Shape tool. Notice that the status line identifies the selected node as a *line cusp*.

4. Double-click the node to open the Node Edit roll-up window, and click the To **C**urve button. The status line identifies the selected node as a *curve cusp*.

5. Click the segment between the nodes with the Shape tool. Notice that you now can change the shape of the segment by using either the Elastic mode or Bézier editing.

You change a curve into a line by following the same procedure, except you start with a curve and choose To **L**ine rather than To **C**urve.

In general, CorelDRAW! chooses the proper line segment type for a given drawing. Illustrations tend to use more complicated curved segments, and technical drawings tend to use more lines and simple curved objects. Making a curved segment look like a straight line is time-consuming and often frustrating, and making a line act like a curve is impossible. Careful choice on your part early in the drawing process can greatly assist your drawing efficiency.

Examining Characteristics of Nodes

As mentioned previously, the characteristics of nodes control the shape of the curve, and you can change the shape by altering these characteristics. A node can be cusp, smooth, or symmetrical.

A *cusp node* represents a sharp change in the shape of the curve when passing through the node. The angles of the line entering and leaving the node are independently controlled by the Bézier control points on either side. Changes to one side do not affect the other. Figure 12.3 shows examples of cusp nodes.

FIG. 12.3

Cusp nodes.

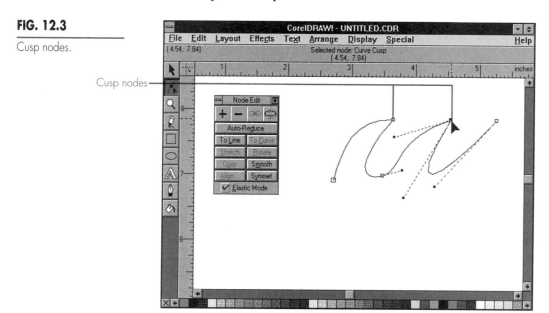

A *smooth node* constrains the curve to a gradual change in shape and requires that the line passing through the node enter and leave at the same angle. Moving the control point on one side of a smooth node changes the angle of the line on the other. Changing the length of the control arm on one side of the node does not affect the size of the control arm on the other. The curve angle is the same on both sides, but the amount of curve deflection varies based on the size of the control arms. If one side of a smooth node is a line segment and the other is a curve segment, the angle of the curve segment is constrained by the line because the line's curve is fixed by the other end's node. No angle changes are possible with this situation, and you should convert the line to a curve so that you can alter the line's curvature. Figure 12.4 shows an example of a smooth node.

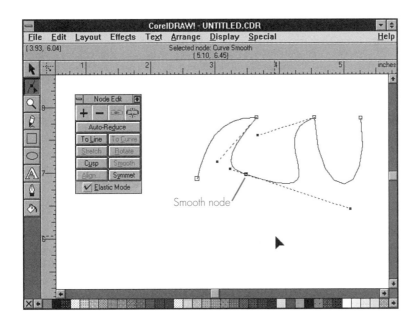

FIG. 12.4

A smooth node.

A *symmetrical node* further constrains the shape of the curve so that the curve on one side is symmetrical (or equal) to the other. The control points are always equally distant from the node and are always connected by a straight line. Changing one side of a symmetrical node makes the exact same change occur to the other side. Figure 12.5 shows an example of a symmetrical node.

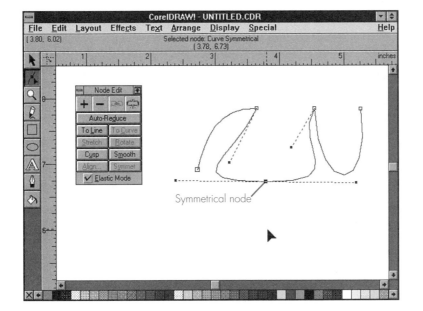

FIG. 12.5

A symmetrical node.

Curve nodes have control points that control the shape of the curve segments on either side of the node. Line nodes also have a control point if the next segment is a curve segment, but the angle of the curve is constrained to the angle of the line segment. You can change the shape of curve segments by dragging the nodes and their respective control points with the Shape tool. How much flexibility you have in moving the control points depends on whether the node is cusp, smooth, or symmetrical. You can change dramatically the overall look of a line by simply changing a series of nodes from one type to another.

Understanding Open and Closed Curve Objects

Objects can also be either open path or closed path (see fig. 12.6). An *open-path object* has two unconnected end points and does not completely enclose a space. *Closed-path objects* do not have end points, and the path or curve between the nodes returns to the point of origin. A freestanding line or curve segment is an example of an open-path object.

FIG. 12.6

Open- and closed-path objects.

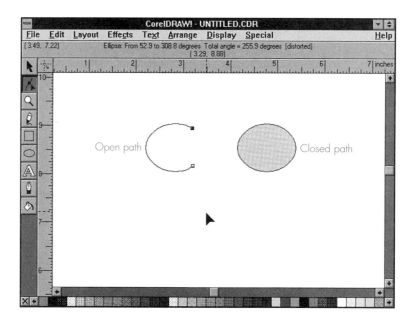

Because open-path objects do not enclose space, they cannot contain fill. In some cases, you may want to put a tiny break in a closed-path object to keep it from adopting a fill.

One special characteristic of open-path objects is that you can apply special treatments, called *arrowheads*, to the end points. (For more information, see this chapter's section on "Adding and Creating Arrowheads.") You also can join the end points of an open-path object, or multiple open-path objects, to create a closed-path object that can then be filled. (For more information, see this chapter's section on "Joining and Breaking Nodes.")

Using the Shape Tool To Move Nodes

This section covers the basic techniques of using the Shape tool to modify object shapes by moving individual nodes and their control points. Using the Node Edit roll-up window in conjunction with the Shape tool is covered in the following section.

> **NOTE**
>
> Object modifications made with the Shape tool differ from those made with the Pick tool in that the Pick tool changes the overall object characteristics such as size and rotation, and the Shape tool deals with the nodes that comprise the object.

Selecting Objects and Nodes

You must select an object before you can view, move, or modify its nodes with the Shape tool. To select an object, click its outline with the Shape tool if you are in Wireframe mode, or click anywhere in the object interior if it has a fill and you are in the Editable Preview mode. If an object is already selected when you select the Shape tool, the object remains selected as shown by the node display. When you are manipulating node points, the Wireframe mode allows you to work faster and it is cleaner.

You can work on only one object at a time with the Shape tool. If more than one object is selected when you select the Shape tool, they all are deselected. You generally modify one node at a time, but you can marquee select several nodes and simultaneously modify them.

Unselected nodes appear as open squares on the object and become solid black squares when selected. When you select a single node, information about the segment and node type (such as Curve Cusp or Line Smooth) is displayed in the center of the status line. In addition, the control points affecting the two adjacent segments are displayed (see fig. 12.7).

FIG. 12.7

Selecting a single node on an object.

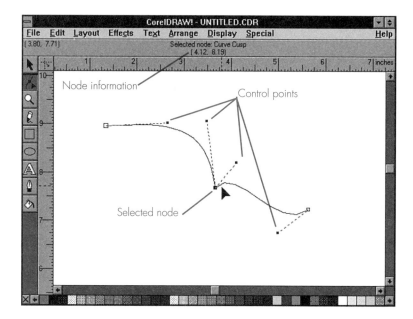

If you have already selected a node and you click a second node, the first node is deselected. Pressing the Tab key deselects the current node and selects the next node on the object's path. Pressing Shift+Tab cycles the node selection in the opposite direction.

You may want to select more than one node so that you can move them together, change their characteristics simultaneously, or join two nodes together. To select multiple nodes, press the Shift key while clicking each additional node. You also can marquee select a group of nodes by dragging a rectangular box around the nodes with the Shape tool. A dashed marquee box appears around the nodes while you drag, and the nodes are selected when you release the mouse button. Clicking white space with the Shape tool or pressing the Esc key deselects all nodes.

Changing Object Shape by Moving Nodes

You can change the shape of an object in amazing ways by moving its nodes with the Shape tool. To move a selected node, click and drag it to its new position, and release the mouse button. The other nodes remain where they were, and the line or curve segments that are connected to the node stretch as you move the node. The object remains a closed or an open path but adopts the new shape.

You can nudge a node just as you nudge an object by first selecting the node, or group of nodes, and then pressing the arrow keys that correspond to the direction you want to move the node. You establish the nudge distance in the Preferences dialog box, which you access by choosing Preferences from the Special menu (or by pressing Ctrl+J).

TIP

When multiple nodes are selected, they all move together. You can move all the selected nodes by dragging one of the nodes with the Shape tool.

You can scale a segment of a curve by first selecting the nodes that correspond to the segment and then selecting Stretch from the Node Edit roll-up window. The Stretch function provides the same sizing boxes that are used in conjunction with the Pick tool and overall object sizing, except they now apply only to the selected line segments. When the small black boxes (handles) appear, you can drag them to new locations, which scales the selected line segments while leaving the other nodes and their related segment in their prior positions.

TIP

Dragging a handle while pressing the Ctrl key changes the selected segments in 100-percent increments. Dragging while pressing the Shift key scales the selected segments from the center of the line, and pressing Ctrl+Shift while dragging scales from the center in 100-percent increments. You can increase in only 100-percent increments. CorelDRAW! does not decrease in 50-percent increments, but provides 100-percent scaling that corresponds to a mirror.

NOTE

A simple exercise with an object composed of line segments illustrates the range of possibilities for modifying object shapes by moving nodes with the Shape tool. Follow these steps:

1. Create a rectangle with the Rectangle tool and convert the rectangle to a curve object by selecting it and then choosing the Convert to Curves command from the **A**rrange menu (or pressing Ctrl+Q).

2. Click one of the nodes with the Shape tool, and drag the node around. Notice that you can move the node in any direction and for any distance, and that the two line segments attached to the node stretch and change their angle of orientation in response to the movements of the node.

(continues)

(continued)

3. Select an additional node, holding down the Shift key and clicking, or using marquee select. Then click one of the nodes with the Shape tool, and drag the node around. Notice that, this time, both of the nodes move together.

Changing the Curvature

Although you cannot change the shape of a line segment, you can change the shape of a curve segment by using the Bézier control points attached to the nodes or by dragging the curved line itself. Typically, you make the curve the basic shape you want by dragging the curve segment itself, and then fine-tune the shape by moving the control points associated with the nodes. The Elastic mode of operation is valuable when working with multiple nodes because the nodes move proportionally, rather than independently, at exactly the same time.

The control points have a different effect on each curved segment depending on the type of node attached to its end point. Cusp nodes affect only one side or the other of the node, smooth nodes affect both sides from an angle in/out of the node standpoint but leave the amount of line curvature on the opposite side alone, and the symmetrical node changes both sides of the node equally. The amount of line curvature is related to the length of the control arm. Tremendous flexibility is provided with the CorelDRAW! Bézier-curve editing, and you are encouraged to work with the curves before trying to draw something exactly right the first time around.

TIP

You can change the curves you draw at a later date to match any type of curve you need. Don't worry too much about getting it right the first time.

All nodes have two control points. You may occasionally click a node and find only one control point. The second control point is probably hiding under the node. Press the Shift key while you drag the node, and the control point should appear, but the node stays in the same place.

The easiest way to change a line's curvature is to drag the line itself with the Shape tool. If the control points are visible while you drag the line, you see them update themselves based on the new line design. If the control points are not present, you can still drag the line and change its shape.

You can have nodes and multiple segments move in concert with each other in a proportional type of relationship with respect to the segment point upon which you drag. This means that the curves move like a rubber band as opposed to separate segments. Follow these steps:

1. Open the Node Edit roll-up window.

2. Select **Elastic Mode**. A check mark should appear in the box to the left of the option label.

3. Select two or more nodes you want to move together. You must select multiple nodes.

4. Drag any of the selected nodes. Notice that the other nodes move a distance that is proportional to the selected node's movement.

In summary, you can drag the node itself, the control points associated with the node, or the line itself to change the shape of a curved line. You can change a line's appearance dramatically by changing the segments from lines to curves (and vice versa) and choosing different node types such as cusp, smooth, and symmetrical. The Elastic mode of operation makes selected nodes move in proportion to the movement of the dragged node, which gives the line's rate of deformation a more realistic appearance and shapes the object segments as a total entity instead of as separate segments.

Adding and Deleting Nodes

The more complicated the curve you want, the larger the number of nodes you need. In general, the number of nodes corresponds to the number of times the line changes directions (called an *inflection point*) or every 120 degrees if the line moves in one direction.

> **TIP**
>
> If you are having trouble fitting a curve the way you want it, you may have too few or too many nodes. The more nodes included, the closer the line fits. Too many nodes cause the curve to become complicated to work with. Try the Auto-Reduce feature to get the number of nodes into the right neighborhood. For more information, see "Using the Auto-Reduce Feature" in this chapter.

In this section, you learn how to add nodes, delete nodes, and use the Auto-Reduce option to eliminate unnecessary nodes.

Adding Nodes

 To add a node, first click the curve where you want the new node, and then click the + symbol in the Node Edit roll-up window. You then can change the node to the type you need.

Deleting Nodes

 Deleting a node is just as easy. Click the node, and click the - symbol in the Node Edit roll-up window. The curve shape may change dramatically when a node is deleted because CorelDRAW! no longer can curve around the deleted node. Deleting a node also deletes a line segment.

TIP

You can select several nodes and delete them all at once by choosing the - symbol in the Node Edit roll-up window.

Using the Auto-Reduce Feature

When you freehand draw a line, CorelDRAW! does the best it can to approximate your drawing. Many of the little variations added by your hand movement may be unnecessary to the drawing but sensed by CorelDRAW!. These variations may require nodes to match accurately, which means that simple-looking lines sometimes end up with an exceptional number of nodes. You can delete the nodes, but you should first try the Auto-Reduce option provided in the Node Edit roll-up window. This option deletes unneeded nodes within a curve segment and reduces the number of nodes used to fit the curve. Traced images or scanned objects can have large numbers of nodes, and Auto-Reduce helps simplify these images.

The Auto-Reduce procedure is straightforward. Select the nodes included in the segments you want affected, and choose Auto-Reduce from the Node Edit roll-up window. CorelDRAW! looks to the Auto-Reduce (min-max) setting in the Preferences-Curves dialog box (see fig. 12.8) and determines which nodes are required to meet expectations, and deletes the rest for those segments you selected.

The Auto-Reduce (min-max) option has a maximum setting of 10 and a default setting of 5. The lower the number, the less the line changes with Auto-Reduce. You probably need to experiment with this setting until you find the correct level for your applications.

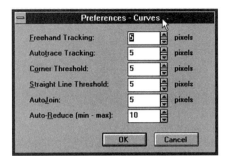

FIG. 12.8

The Preferences-Curves dialog box.

Using the Preferences-Curves Dialog Box

The other items contained in the Preferences-Curves dialog box affect whether a segment is treated as a line or a curve, whether a node is treated as smooth or a cusp, how closely CorelDRAW! should track hand movements when drawing, and when two nodes should be automatically joined.

The Freehand Tracking setting specifies a threshold for the number of display pixels within which CorelDRAW! should ignore the line variations and not insert a node. If this number is low (1 to 3 pixels), Corel-DRAW! attempts to match the complexities of the curve precisely and create the number of nodes required to make that happen. The result is often a large number of unnecessary nodes and a jagged-looking line. A high setting (6 to 10 pixels) gives a wider margin and creates fewer nodes and a smoother curve. For most drawings, a setting of 6 to 8 is adequate, but you need to experiment for yourself to determine the level that matches your needs.

Autotrace Tracking has to do with the level of accuracy you want when tracing a bitmap. This topic is covered in Chapter 17.

Corner Threshold sets the level at which a cusp node turns into a smooth node. A low setting (1 to 3 pixels) creates many cusp nodes because the sharp line-direction changes are required to match the smaller hand movements. A higher number (7 to 10 pixels) causes more smooth nodes rather than cusp nodes and creates a smoother curve that may not exactly match the curve drawn. Once again, you need to experiment to determine the proper level setting for your needs.

Straight Line Threshold sets the number of pixel variations allowed before CorelDRAW! treats a straight line as a curve. This feature simplifies a drawing by ignoring small variations and making the drawing as elementary as possible. On the other hand, you may want a complicated drawing that exactly matches your hand movements. You would then set this level between 1 and 3 pixels and deal with the curves rather than lines. If you want more lines than curves, set the threshold level between 7 and 10 pixels.

AutoJoin determines the number of pixels within which CorelDRAW! naturally assumes that two nodes are the same point and does not create separate objects. This feature generally comes into play with the double-clicking involved in multisegment objects. If the second click is within the pixel radius, the two nodes are joined. If the click is outside the pixel boundary, a new segment is started, and the two nodes are treated as distinct and not joined.

Joining and Breaking Nodes

  You can always join or break nodes by using the join and break icons located in the Node Edit roll-up window. Use join to combine objects and to create a closed path that can be filled. Break divides one node into two which opens a path and can create multiple objects after separation.

Before you can join two nodes, you must combine them into a single object. You combine two separate objects by selecting them, opening the **Arrange** menu, and choosing **Combine**. Then when you click one object, the nodes on both objects appear because they are combined. To join the nodes, select them, and then select the join icon from the Node Edit roll-up window.

TIP

Joining nodes is a good way to change an open-path object into a closed-path object that can accept a fill. Join the beginning and ending nodes to complete the path, and define the fill type. Be aware that the object's shape will change.

To break two joined nodes, simply click the nodes, and then select the break icon from the Node Edit roll-up window. You can drag either of the newly unjoined nodes to a new location.

A sine wave like the one shown in figure 12.9 is a common object used in technical drawings. It is difficult to draw freehand, but easy to draw if you use the automated features of CorelDRAW!. This application note leads you through the design of a sine wave. The procedures apply many of the topics discussed in this chapter and provide a good summary of curve modification techniques.

TIP

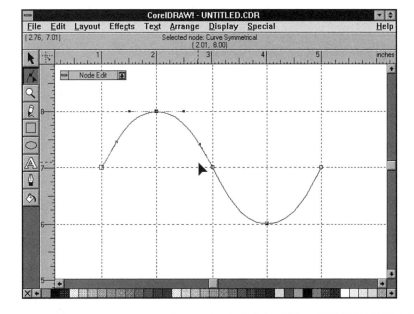

FIG. 12.9

A sine wave drawing.

Follow these steps to draw the sine wave:

1. Set up a working grid that corresponds to the beginning, middle, end, top, and bottom of the sine wave (0, 180, 360 degrees, positive and negative amplitude, respectively).

2. Drag a horizontal guideline (from the top ruler) to an even ruler marker location (such as the 5-inch mark). This ruler represents the neutral axis of the sine wave.

3. Drag another horizontal guideline to a location 1 inch above and another to 1 inch below the neutral axis.

4. Drag a vertical guideline from the left ruler to an even ruler marker. This ruler corresponds to the 0-degree point.

5. Drag guidelines to each 1-inch marker to the right of the initial guideline until you have four more guidelines. These guidelines indicate the 90-, 180-, 270-, and 360-degree locations.

(continues)

(continued)

 6. Select the Pencil tool.

7. Click at the 0-degree point; double-click at the guideline intersection points that correspond to the 90-, 180-, and 270-degree points; and click at the 360-degree point.

8. The lines connecting the nodes are straight lines and not curves, so you need to change them to curves. Select the first line segment, and click To **C**urve in the Node Edit roll-up window. Repeat this procedure for each of the other line segments.

9. You need to change the maximum and minimum node points to the symmetrical type to make the alignment of the curve on each side of the node match the symmetrical nature of the sine wave. Click the maximum node, and select the S**y**mmet option from the Node Edit roll-up window. Do the same for the minimum node. Finally, repeat the same procedure for the 180-degree (center neutral axis) node, but select S**m**ooth rather than Symmet. The nodes and segments are now set up for the final step of adjusting the curvature.

10. Click the maximum node, and move one of the control points to around the 1/2-inch point. Notice that the other side moves in concert. Repeat this procedure for the minimum node location. Click the 180-degree node, and move the control point until it lies on the curve. Repeat this procedure for 0- and 360-degree points, and admire your replica of nature's wonder.

You can now size, rotate, expand, contract, and combine this basic shape into many various forms that you may need for technical drawings. You can create a series of sine waves, for example, and then apply an envelope to the series and replicate an amplitude modulation signal, or you can scale the signals and attach them to each other to create a frequency modulation signal as shown in figure 12.10

Aligning Nodes between Objects

Often you may have two objects that you created separately but that need to share the same interobject boundary. Trying to perform this operation by hand is difficult and usually time consuming. You can, however, use the Align option in the Node Edit roll-up window to align the nodes and control points associated with the nodes. Each object then shares the same shape along the interface (boundary) between the objects.

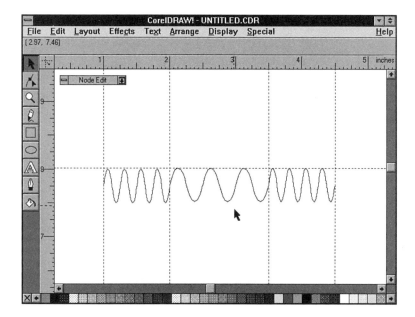

FIG. 12.10

A frequency modulation signal using the sine wave.

To align nodes between two objects, follow these steps:

1. Select both objects.

2. Combine them by choosing the **Combine** option from the **Arrange** menu.

3. Make sure that the interface lines along both objects have the same number of nodes. If they do not, use the Node Edit roll-up window's + and - options to adjust the number of nodes, keeping them preferably in the same relative positions on their respective lines. Figure 12.11 shows two objects before alignment.

4. Using the Shape tool, select the node that you want to move during the alignment process.

5. While holding down the Shift key, select the node that is to remain stationary. In essence, the first selected node moves to align to the second, or reference, selected node.

6. Choose Align from the roll-up window, or double-click either of the nodes to open the Node Edit roll-up window. The Node Align dialog box appears, as shown in figure 12.12.

FIG. 12.11

The objects and nodes
before alignment.

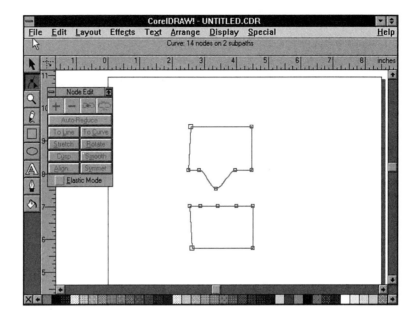

FIG. 12.12

The Node Align dialog
box.

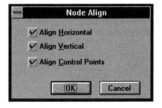

7. Select the appropriate alignment options. The default setting is for all three options to be selected.

Align Horizontal moves the first selected node so that it rests on the same horizontal line as the reference (second) node. Align Vertical moves the first selected node so that it rests on the same vertical line as the reference (second) node. Selecting only one of these two dims the Align Control Points option because you must have both vertical and horizontal alignment before the control points can align. Selecting Align Control Points in combination with the other two options aligns the node location and the slope of the line entering and leaving that node, because the control points exactly overlay each other.

8. Click OK, and watch the nodes align in accordance with your settings, as shown in figure 12.13.

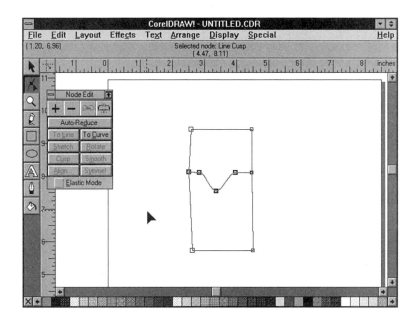

FIG. 12.13

Object nodes after alignment.

You will probably get more consistent results if you start aligning nodes from one end of the overall line segments and then sequentially align each of the nodes to the other end. After you have aligned the object nodes, you can divide the combination into two objects, as shown in figure 12.14, by first selecting the combined objects and then choosing **Break** Apart from the **A**rrange menu.

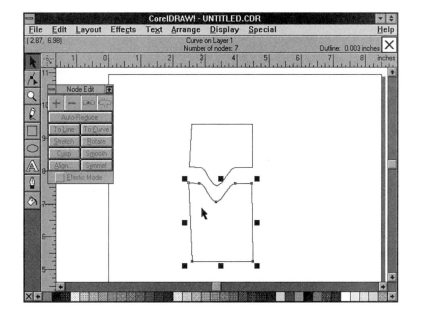

FIG. 12.14

Breaking apart two aligned objects.

Adding and Creating Arrowheads

CorelDRAW! comes with a wide variety of standard arrow designs. You can place these designs at a line's beginning, end, or both. The design for each end does not have to be the same type. To add an arrowhead, you use the Pen roll-up window. To add arrowheads to a line, follow these steps:

1. Choose the Outline tool. The Outline fly-out menu appears.

2. Choose the roll-up icon (second icon from the left in the top row). The Pen roll-up window shown in figure 12.15 appears.

FIG. 12.15

The Pen roll-up window.

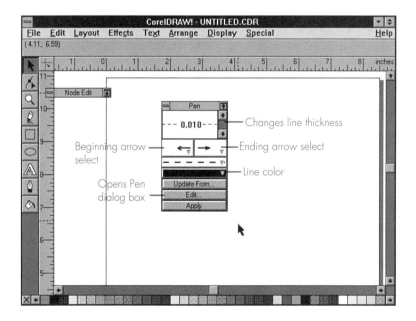

3. To display the available standard arrow selections, click the small triangle in the bottom-right corner of the Beginning Arrow Select box. Figure 12.16 shows the arrowhead types displayed.

4. Scroll through the various designs, using the scroll bar located at the right.

5. Click the design of your choice to add it to the dialog box display, selecting it for the beginning arrow.

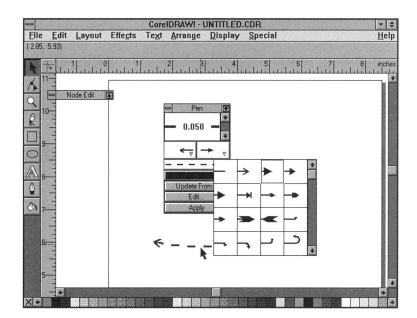

FIG. 12.16

The arrowhead selections.

6. To add an arrowhead to the end of the line, repeat steps 3 through 5 but use the Ending Arrow Select box. Remember, your two arrowheads do not have to be the same.

7. Click Apply to add the arrowheads to the selected line.

You also can add an arrowhead to the line by using the Outline Pen dialog box shown in figure 12.17. To access this dialog box, select the pen icon in the upper-left corner of the Outline fly-out menu.

> **TIP**
>
> Selecting a line with the Shape tool and then pressing the Home key highlights the beginning node. Pressing End highlights the series of the segment's ending node. In this way, you can determine which arrowhead will appear at the ends of the selected segments.

The Arrows box in the upper-right corner of this dialog box includes two arrow selection buttons that give you access to the beginning and ending arrow designs. You select your designs in the same way you do in the Pen roll-up window, using the left button to select the beginning arrowhead and the right button to select the ending arrowhead. Click OK to apply the arrow designs to the selected line.

Although CorelDRAW! gives you many designs from which to choose, you may have something else in mind for your arrowhead. You can customize the standard arrowheads to meet your specific needs. The procedure for accessing the Arrowhead Editor is straightforward, and editing the arrowheads follows many of the standard CorelDRAW! object-editing conventions.

FIG. 12.17

The Outline Pen dialog box.

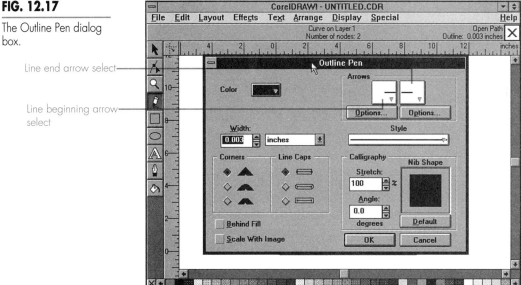

To edit an arrowhead, follow these steps:

1. Select the arrow you want to edit from the Outline Pen dialog box's arrow selection boxes.

2. Click the **O**ptions button under the arrow selection box.

3. Choose Edit from the menu. The Arrowhead Editor dialog box appears, as shown in figure 12.18.

FIG. 12.18

The Arrowhead Editor dialog box.

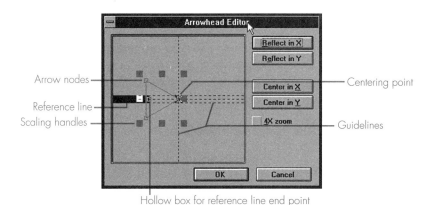

This dialog box shows a detail of the selected arrowhead design. Many of the components, such as the scaling handles, guidelines, and nodes, should now look familiar to you.

4. Use the scaling handles to change the size of the arrowhead, following the same conventions you use to scale objects. The corner handles scale simultaneously in both X and Y directions, and the other handles scale in X or Y only, based on their location.

5. Use the guidelines to align the arrowhead object within the editing screen. The arrowhead object nodes "stick" to the guidelines, just as when you align any other object. The three horizontal guidelines enable you to align with the top, center, and bottom of the reference line. The vertical guideline enables you to align in the horizontal direction with respect to the reference line. If you want the arrowhead applied to the end of the reference line, drag the hollow box that represents the end of the reference line to the vertical guideline, and then drag the back nodes of the arrowhead to the vertical guideline. They line up perfectly because of the guideline magnetism effect.

6. Use the **R**eflect in X and **R**eflect in Y options if you want to make a mirror image of the arrowhead around the X and Y axes, respectively. The initial arrowhead is erased, and the new, reflected arrowhead takes its place. The reflections occur around the X-marker centering point in the middle of the editing screen.

7. Use the Center in **X** and Center in **Y** options if you want to position the arrowhead center with the X-marker centering point in the middle of the editing screen.

8. Use the **4**X Zoom option to view a close-up of the arrowhead, centered on the X-marker centering point.

9. Click OK when you're finished in the Arrowhead Editor dialog box.

You can also apply the complete power of CorelDRAW! to creating your own custom arrowheads, which you then can access from the standard arrowhead lists. Up to 100 arrows are allowed in the arrowhead file.

To create your own arrow, follow these steps:

1. Create the arrowhead design just as you would any CorelDRAW! object.

2. Make sure that the object is selected, and choose Create **A**rrow from the **S**pecial menu.

3. Answer Yes to the dialog box question about saving the arrowhead.

Look in the arrowhead library, and notice that the new design is there. Remember that an arrowhead adopts the attributes of the reference line, so fill and outline colors are irrelevant in arrowhead creation. Also remember that you can edit the new arrowhead by using the Arrowhead Editor, so don't be too concerned about getting the arrowhead design perfect the first time.

Modifying Line Thickness, Color, and Style

CorelDRAW! provides three ways to modify line thicknesses and colors once the line is drawn. One is through the Outline fly-out menu, another is through the Pen roll-up window, and the third is through the Outline Pen dialog box. The roll-up window is by far the fastest way to modify lines while working on a drawing.

In addition, after you create a line style within a roll-up or as a template style, you can apply it to multiple lines by following the styles application procedure.

Using the Outline Fly-Out Menu

Draw a line object and then click the Outline tool to display the fly-out menu shown in figure 12.19.

FIG. 12.19

The Outline fly-out menu.

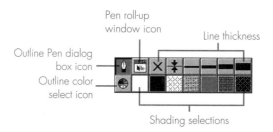

Pen roll-up window icon

Line thickness

Outline Pen dialog box icon

Outline color select icon

Shading selections

Click the pen icon in the upper-left corner of the Outline fly-out menu to reveal the Outline Pen dialog box. Next to the pen icon is the roll-up icon, which you click to activate the Pen roll-up window.

The rest of the icons in the top row of the fly-out menu represent various line thicknesses you can select. The icon next to the roll-up icon, the one marked with an x, represents a line of no thickness. This setting is often used for alignment purposes. The next few icons represent various line thicknesses from hairline (0.003 inches) to thick (0.333 inches). Simply select a thickness, and CorelDRAW! applies it to the line.

The first icon on the bottom row of the fly-out menu is the color wheel icon. Click this icon to display the Outline Color dialog box shown in figure 12.20. This dialog box is discussed in detail in Chapter 11.

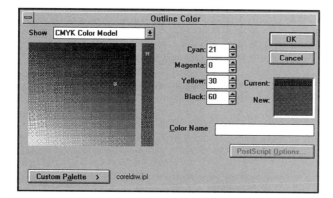

FIG. 12.20

The Outline Color dialog box.

The other buttons on the lower level of the Outline fly-out menu represent various outline shading levels from white to dark gray.

After you have selected a line thickness, you must select the Outline tool again and then select a color from the Outline fly-out menu. Continually having to select the Outline tool is cumbersome, and unnecessary if you use the Pen roll-up window.

Using the Pen Roll-Up Window

Choose the roll-up icon from the Outline fly-out menu to activate the Pen roll-up window, which contains many options you can use to modify the appearance of your lines (see fig. 12.21).

Use the top portion of the window to select a line thickness. First select the line you want to modify. Then scroll through the line thickness options until you reach the thickness you want to use, and click Apply to apply it to the selected line. The no thickness option is represented by a large x that extends completely across the display window. The hairline thickness is represented by a small x intersecting in the center of the window. The other thicknesses are shown numerically in inches.

FIG. 12.21

The Pen roll-up window.

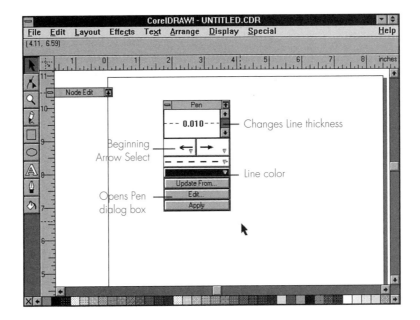

As you learned in this chapter's section on "Adding and Creating Arrowheads," you use the two buttons labeled with arrows to select arrowhead designs.

To set the line design, select your line and click the small triangle in the thin horizontal space below the arrowhead selection buttons. A listing of various line designs, including dashed, dotted, and mixed, appears (see fig. 12.22). The top of the list shows the currently active design, and you change this design to another by scrolling to a design and selecting it. Click Apply to apply the design to the currently selected line.

Click the horizontal bar below the Line Design button to display an array of colors that you can apply to the selected line (see fig. 12.23). Click More to display the Color dialog box, which is discussed in more detail in Chapter 11.

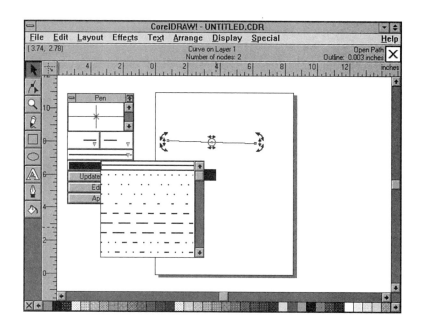

FIG. 12.22

Viewing the various line styles.

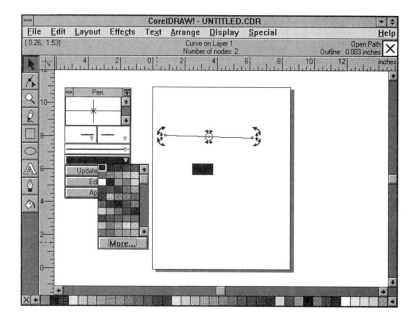

FIG. 12.23

The color palette.

Using the Outline Pen Dialog Box

Click the pen icon in the upper-left corner of the Outline fly-out menu to reveal the Outline Pen dialog box (see fig. 12.24).

Select an object and press F12 to open the Outline Pen dialog box.

FIG. 12.24

The Outline Pen dialog box.

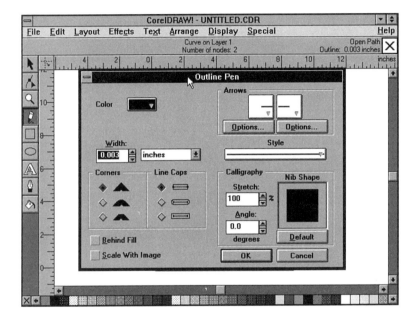

To change the color of the line, click the Color box located in the upper-left corner to display your color choices and choose one.

Adjust the thickness of your line by entering a number in the **W**idth box.

The Line Caps determine the design added to the end points of each line. The rectangular design gives the drawing a technical, sharp feel. The rounded line caps soften the drawing.

Select **B**ehind Fill from the Outline Pen dialog box to move the outline behind the fill when displaying the object. Otherwise, the outline is displayed in front of the fill. Use the **S**cale With Image option to ensure that the outline of the object increases and decreases in thickness proportionally to any scaling done on the base object. Otherwise, the line thickness remains constant as the image is scaled, which gradually looks unacceptable.

After you select a line, you can set the line style by clicking the Style box. A listing of various line designs, including dashed, dotted, and mixed, appears. The top of the list shows the currently active design, and you change this design to another by scrolling to a design and selecting it.

In the lower-right corner of the Outline Pen dialog box is a set of Calligraphy options, which you use to control the nib shape. The *nib* is the imaginary brush tip used to draw the lines. The nib shape is determined by a combination of the corner style, the angle of the imaginary paintbrush, and the stretch (the thickness of the nib). The second corner design shown in the Outline Pen dialog box provides a round nib, and the other two produce rectangular nibs. You can change the stretch and angle of the nib by dragging the nib shape with the mouse. If you get lost and want to return to the original design, click the **De-fault** button.

The effect of the pen tip is to provide a less harsh look to the lines and give them a more pen-and-ink quality. By changing features such as the line thickness, nib design, and attributes, you can take an ordinary-looking design and make it into something unique. An important thing to remember is that changing the line width resets the Angle and Stretch values to 0 degrees and 100 percent, respectively. Decide on a line thickness first, and then play with the nib design.

Using Dimension Lines

CorelDRAW! provides a convenient way for you to label object dimensions: dimension lines. This feature is particularly useful for technical drawings in which the measurements of objects are a critical part of the drawing. The dimension lines are located in the Pencil fly-out menu as the vertical, horizontal, and diagonal lines with the double arrows.

The procedure for using dimension lines is relatively simple after you understand the overall concept. CorelDRAW! senses where you click to begin the dimension line and where you click to end the line. The program then calculates the distance based on the currently active measurement (as set in the Preferences dialog box) and waits for you to define where to print the dimension value. You specify the spot where you want the dimensions to print when you click the next time.

CorelDRAW! not only draws the dimension line, but also calculates the dimensional values based on the dimension line drawn.

Three dimension line tools are contained in the Pencil fly-out menu: vertical, horizontal, and diagonal. To access these tools, click the Pencil tool and click the desired tool on the fly-out menu. You use the vertical dimension line tool for defining dimensions along a vertical axis (even if the object itself is not vertical). You use the horizontal dimension line tool to draw lines and measurements along the horizontal axis. The diagonal dimension line creates a dimension line that extends along the side of the object at the angle you prescribe.

TIP

Dimension lines are useful for determining the size of grouped objects because the status line provides information only on the number of objects within the group, and no dimensional information.

TIP

You should activate the **S**nap To **O**bjects feature by choosing that option from the **L**ayout menu before drawing dimension lines. The lines then snap to the nodes of the underlying object and give you an easy and accurate measurement of the object dimensions.

Figure 12.25 shows an example of a wedged object. To get some practice drawing dimension lines, follow these steps to add dimension lines to this object:

1. Make sure that the **S**nap To **O**bjects option, accessed from the **L**ayout menu, is selected, and draw the simple wedge-shaped object shown in figure 12.25.

2. Click the Pencil tool, and hold the mouse button until the Pencil fly-out menu appears.

3. Choose the horizontal dimension line tool. You use this tool to create the bottom (4.13") dimension line.

4. Click at the left node of the object bottom; then move the cursor to the right side of the object bottom and click again. This step defines the overall dimensions. You must next tell CorelDRAW! where you want it to print the dimensions.

5. Move the cursor to the center of the bottom and just below the object. Notice that the extension lines follow the cursor. When you are in the appropriate position, click. The dimension line and its numeric measurement are added to the object.

6. To begin drawing the vertical dimension lines on the right side of the object, click the horizontal dimension line tool and hold the mouse button until the fly-out menu appears; then select the vertical dimension tool.

7. Move the cursor to the top of the object and click; then move to the center right node and click again. This step adds the dimension of the 1.61" segment.

8. To insert the dimension number, move the cursor to the same relative position as the number shown in figure 12.25, and click again. CorelDRAW! inserts the dimensions where you designated.

9. Repeat the procedure for the 1.01" segment by clicking the center node, then the bottom node, and finally where you want the dimensions printed.

10. Create the overall 2.61" dimension line by clicking at the top of the object, then at the bottom, and finally at the 2.61" text dimension location.

11. To draw the diagonal dimension line, select the diagonal dimension line tool from the toolbox, and click at the top and then at the bottom-left corner of the object. The angled dimensions are defined; you need only click the location where you want the text printed.

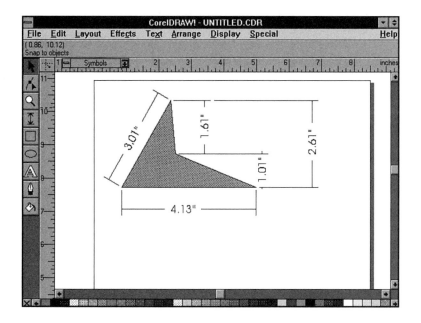

FIG. 12.25

Dimensioning a wedged object.

Selecting and deleting a dimension line not only deletes the line but also the associated dimensioning text. You also can choose Undo from the Edit menu to correct recently inserted dimension lines.

You set the color of dimension lines just as you do with any other line, by clicking the right mouse button on the color palette at the bottom of the screen or by using the Pen roll-up window.

You can apply all CorelDRAW! effects and transformations to dimension lines. Dimension line text is automatically given the default font and point size. You can change these attributes just as you can normal text by using the Text roll-up window or by dragging with the mouse (see Chapter 8).

To set the default preferences for dimension line characteristics, choose Preferences from the Special menu. Choose Dimension from the Preferences dialog box. The Preferences-Dimension dialog box appears (see fig. 12.26). Then choose the Format option, which displays the Format Definition dialog box (see fig. 12.27). Choose Linear as the format type and the dimension format you want, and click OK to use this setting as the new default. Choose Horizontal Label and Center Label from the Preferences-Dimension dialog box to define the dimension text location as always centered along the dimension line, as long as the final click of the mouse occurs between the two end points. In addition, the text will always be printed horizontally for all dimension line types.

FIG. 12.26

The Preferences-Dimension dialog box.

TIP

The Create text entry box in the Format Definition dialog box enables you to create a custom dimension line text format (see fig. 12.27).

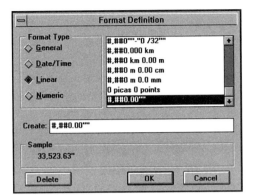

FIG. 12.27

The Format Definition dialog box.

Summary

Much of the work performed within DRAW is accomplished with simple line and curve shapes. The power of DRAW lies in its ability to easily modify shapes using the advanced line and curve techniques provided as standard features. This chapter covered the differences between lines, curved objects and curves, adding and deleting nodes, modifying nodal characteristics, changing object shapes using the node edit tools, defining default line approximation techniques, adding and breaking nodes, and aligning nodes with each other to create perfect object boundaries. Adding and customizing arrowheads and the use of line and node roll-up windows were also covered. The final sections covered the use of styles and introduced the useful dimension lines feature that is new to release 4.

At this point, you should have a good understanding of lines, curves, and objects. You are now ready to apply your skills with the wonderful special effects provided with DRAW. Chapter 13 covers these effects in great detail.

Using the Special Effects

CorelDRAW! includes powerful graphic effects that can give a sense of depth and style to your graphic and text objects. In essence, CorelDRAW! automates many of the standard features such as duplicating, rotating, and cloning, and combines the created objects in special ways for optimal graphic impact.

Simplicity is often the mark of artistic quality, but sometimes making a bold statement is desirable. CorelDRAW!'s special effects are useful for advertising illustrations and become particularly valuable when used in conjunction with the program's many other features.

Table 13.1 summarizes the various special effect options.

Table 13.1 Special Effects

Special Effect	Function
Perspective	Makes an object appear as though it is far away from the viewer through the use of vanishing points.
Extrude	Gives an object a three-dimensional impression by forming a group of duplicates behind the original object.

(continues)

Table 13.1 Continued

Special Effect	Function
Blend	Starts with one object and blends it into another over a series of steps. Rotation and a path can be included in the blend process.
Envelope	Provides a rubbery type of surface to an object that allows for dramatic deformation of the object.
Contouring	Similar but opposite to extrude in that a series of duplicated and reduced shapes are created inside (or outside) the object to give an illusion of depth. Useful for contour, or topographical, maps.
PowerLine	A computer-generated representation of a real pen's operation. Allows for dynamic creation of thin to thick lines with various pen points depending on the "pressure" applied.

You apply most of the effects, except for perspective, through the roll-up windows. This approach gives you an easy and fast method of trying new effects until you get just the right combination.

Unfortunately, however, overall system performance degrades with each special effect you use. You may consider placing the different special effects on separate layers and displaying only one layer at a time to decrease the wait time associated with each change. See Chapter 5 for information about using layers in CorelDRAW!.

Experimenting with special effects is an exciting and fun part of CorelDRAW!. Express your creativity while enhancing your skills by playing with the various special effects.

Adding Perspective to an Object

An easy yet effective special effect is *perspective*. This technique takes an ordinary object and gives it the illusion of length, as though it is vanishing into the distance. To add perspective to a drawing, follow these steps:

1. Create the base drawing without trying to add any perspective. Figure 13.1, for example, shows a simple drawing of a road, without perspective added.

2. Group the objects together before adding the perspective to ensure that all objects are affected simultaneously.

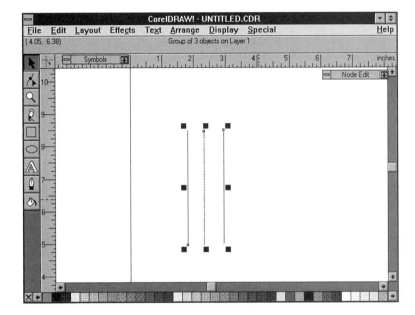

FIG. 13.1

A road without perspective.

3. Select the objects, open the Effects menu, and choose **A**dd Perspective. A colored dashed line representing the perspective bounding box encloses the selected objects.

4. Drag any of the four small handles in the corners of the bounding box to move the vanishing point of the perspective. The *vanishing point* is an imaginary location in the distance toward which all object lines converge. The convergence gives the object a feeling of depth or perspective. The vanishing point in both a vertical and horizontal direction is represented by an x that appears somewhere on-screen (see fig. 13.2).

Drag the x itself to change the perspective vanishing point. (You may have to drag the corners first to get the x to appear on-screen.) You also may want to use the Zoom Out tool (F3) to get a bigger picture and closer view of the vanishing points.

5. Deselect the objects to add the perspective.

FIG. 13.2

The road with perspec-
tive and vanishing point
(zoomed out view).

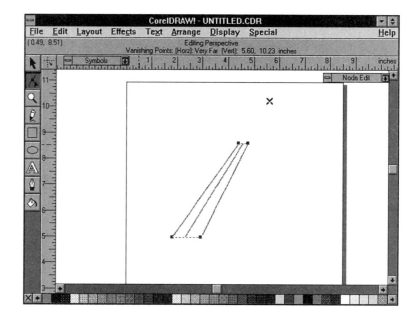

From the **Edit** menu, choose **Undo** to remove the perspective you just
added. Choose **Clear Transformations** from the **Effects** menu to return
the object to its original state, including the removal of perspective and
bounding boxes.

TIP

Adding perspective in two dimensions adds a combined depth that can
make the object appear as though it is twisting into the horizon.

You can ensure that all objects on a page vanish to the same point by
first determining the appropriate vanishing point location and marking
it with a pair of crossing guidelines. Select each object to which the
perspective is to be applied, and drag its respective vanishing point x
to the guideline cross hairs location. This technique makes the vanishing point for each object the same page location. Guideline use is
covered in Chapter 5.

Using Extrude on an Object

Extruding an object gives it the same effect as pressing a putty substance through a hole of a particular shape. The base object is retained,

but the trailing objects are extended, or extruded, behind. This process gives the object an illusion of depth.

Figure 13.3, for example, shows a drawing with no extrusion added. Figure 13.4 shows the same object after the extrude special effect has been applied.

FIG. 13.3

An object that has not been extruded.

FIG. 13.4

The same object after extruding has been added.

The basic extrude process involves the following steps:

1. Create the base object, which can be a text string, an open path, or a closed path object.

2. Open the Effects menu, and choose Extrude Roll-Up (Ctrl+E). The Extrude roll-up window shown in figure 13.5 appears. The four icons along the left side of the roll-up window control the extrusion's depth and type, rotation specifications, direction of the light source for shading effects, and colors.

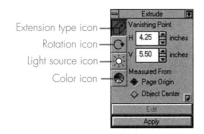

FIG. 13.5

The Extrude roll-up window.

3. Click one of the four icons to set the extrude effects you want, such as type of extrusion, rotation, location of light source for shading purposes, and extruded colors. (When you click an icon, another roll-up window appears corresponding to that icon. These windows are discussed in the following paragraphs.)

4. Click Apply to implement the extrusion attributes selected, and watch the fun start.

Setting the Extrusion Type

When you click the upper-left extrusion effect icon to choose the depth and type, a list of options appears in the text list in the roll-up window. You can select the type of extrusion (such as Small Back Perspective) and the distance over which you want to extrude the object (such as 20) directly from the Extrude roll-up window. You can extrude to the back or front of the selected object, and three extrusion types are provided for both directions. You can extrude with all lines parallel (no perspective), with the extruded objects smaller than the original objects, or with the extruded objects bigger than the original objects. The depth accepts values between 1 and 99, with 1 equal to the original object (no depth) and 99 being the maximum allowable depth.

TIP

An extrusion is a series of dynamically linked objects with the initial object being the master of the other objects that make up the extrusion. This means that changes to the initial object are automatically added to the objects that make up the extrusion effect.

TIP

The vanishing point for the perspective extrusion is represented by an **x** just as with the original perspective discussion. Dragging the **x** moves the vanishing point and varies the degree of perspective included with the object.

Setting the Vanishing Point

The small page icon located in the lower right of the roll-up window switches the display between a graphical interface display and a menu box setting of perspective parameters. You determine the vanishing point selection by entering a number in the menu screen or by dragging in the graphical screen. As you work with DRAW extrusion, switch between the two views to determine the operational mode you prefer.

You set the horizontal (H) and vertical (V) measurements for the vanishing point in the standard Windows manner by first highlighting the numbers to be changed and then typing in the new values (see fig. 13.6). Choose Page Origin or Object Center to determine whether these numbers set the vanishing point location relative to the page origin or the center of the object. Click Edit to view the effect of moving the vanishing point, and click Apply to create the extrusion.

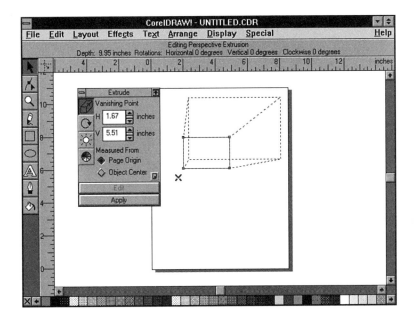

FIG. 13.6

Numerically setting the vanishing point.

Remember that you are moving the extrusion vanishing point, not the back side of the extrusion. Thus the rear projection of some extrusions moves in the opposite direction of the numbers set in this roll-up window. For example, the vanishing point of a Big Back would be in front of the objects; moving the vanishing point (located in the front of the object) to the left would move the Big Back (which is behind the object) to the right.

Rotating the Extrusion

The second icon on the left side of the Extrude roll-up window is the rotation icon, which controls the amount of rotation added to the extrusion. When you click the rotation icon, the extrude rotator shown in figure 13.7 appears. You use this rotator to change the orientation of the object. DRAW provides both parallel and perspective extrusions.

A parallel extrusion essentially creates a multisided cube without a vanishing point; a perspective extrusion has a vanishing point that causes a series of objects to be drawn to create the illusion of depth. These objects can each be rotated by a set amount; the parallel extrusion, however, is a fixed object and cannot be rotated.

FIG. 13.7

The Extrude rotation roll-up window.

Each time you click an arrow, the extrusion (and initial object) rotates 5 degrees in the direction of that arrow, but around the center of the object. Click the left horizontal arrow once, for example, to rotate the extrusion 5 degrees to the left, which appears to rotate the object to the right. Click the down vertical arrow to rotate the extrusion down, which appears to rotate the object up.

The upper-right arrow rotates the object and extrusion 5 degrees in a clockwise direction for each click. The bottom-left arrow rotates the object in the counterclockwise direction.

Click the x located in the center of the object to eliminate all rotations and return the object and extrusion to their original orientation.

Controlling the Shading

Specifying the location of the assumed light source for an object determines the shading that appears on the object. To turn on the light source and thus control the shading for your extrusion, click the third icon on the left side of the Extrude roll-up window. The roll-up window shown in figure 13.8 appears. You can turn off the light source by clicking the light switch a second time.

The object contained within the grid represents your extruded object, and the x shows the current light source location with respect to the object. You move the light source location by clicking at any junction between two lines on the grid that surrounds the object. The display changes to show the expected shading associated with the selected options and settings.

FIG. 13.8

The Extrude light source
roll-up window.

The light source Intensity setting affects the darkness of the shaded areas. The intensity range is from 0 (dim) to 200 (bright), with the default intensity set at 100. Adjusting the intensity affects the coloring shadows seen on the extruded object. You can enter the intensity value directly, or drag the slide to the appropriate value.

When the settings are the way you want them, click Apply to add the current light source settings to the selected object.

Choosing Extrusion Colors

You can set the color characteristics of the extrusion by clicking the color icon, the bottom icon in the Extrude roll-up window. The roll-up window shown in figure 13.9 then appears.

FIG. 13.9

The Extrude color roll-up
window.

The Use Object Fill option is selected by default, which means that the extrusion surfaces adopt the fill characteristics of the initial object. Choose Solid Fill if you want to define a solid fill type for the extruded surfaces different from those for the initial object. Clicking the down arrow just below Solid Fill displays a palette of fill color options. Clicking the More option below the palette displays the standard Corel spot and process color choice windows.

The Shade From and To options enable you to specify a starting and ending color for the extrusion. The color range starts close to the object and ends farthest away. You can create some artistic effects by simply modifying this criteria. The extrusion takes much more time to draw with shading applied, but the effect is appealing. Figure 13.10 shows an example of an extruded object with a shaded fill.

FIG. 13.10

An extruded object with shaded fill.

NOTE

Extrude can also provide some interesting special effects when you use the feature in conjunction with open-path objects. The following steps lead you through the creation of a "warp" wave that might appear in a science fiction document. You use a similar procedure to create a rolling landscape effect.

1. Draw an open-path curve, as shown at the top of figure 13.11.

2. Select the object, and open the Extrude roll-up window.

3. Select the Small Back type, and move the vanishing point to the far upper-left corner of the screen.

4. Click Shade From, and select white; click Shade To, and select dark gray.

5. Click the light source icon, and move the light source to the upper left by clicking that corner of the display box. Notice that the x moves to that location and the display changes to reflect the new location.

6. Click Apply to create the lower object shown in figure 13.11.

7. Select several other light source locations and notice the dramatic effect that this simple adjustment makes to the object's appearance.

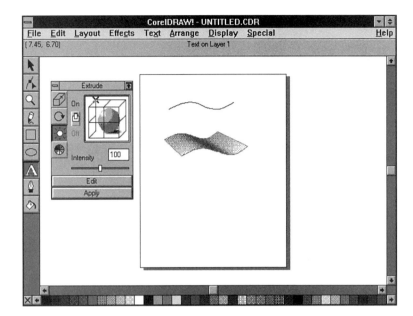

FIG. 13.11

An open-path curve
and the same object
"warped."

Blending from One Object to Another

Blending objects is a lot of fun and enables you to create wonderful artistic impressions. In essence, blending transitions one object into another over a user-specified number of steps. You can specify the object portions to blend into each other by designating their nodal relationship, you can rotate the objects as they blend into each other, and you can even blend them along a curve.

CorelDRAW! treats a blend as a group that includes the beginning object, the end object, and the blended objects in between. The blend is itself a group of objects that you can ungroup for individual manipulation and then regroup when done.

Understanding the Basic Blend Procedure

The blend procedure involves four basic steps:

1. Select the two objects (or group of objects) that you want to blend.

2. Choose **B**lend Roll-Up from the Effects menu (or press Ctrl+B). The Blend roll-up window shown in figure 13.12 appears.

FIG. 13.12

The Blend roll-up window.

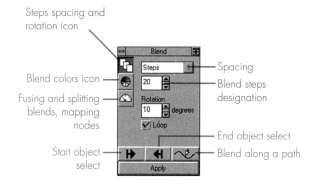

Steps spacing and rotation icon

Blend colors icon

Fusing and splitting blends, mapping nodes

Start object select

Spacing

Blend steps designation

End object select

Blend along a path

3. Set the blend options.

4. Click Apply to modify the drawing accordingly.

Arranging Objects in a Blend

Blend automatically places the top object as the original blend object with the bottom object as the blend's endpoint. You should move blend objects to the proper orientation, front-to-back, to ensure that the blend occurs in the way you intend.

When you have completed a blend, you can find the blend's starting or ending object by using the selection arrows located in the bottom-left corner of the Blend roll-up window. Click the start object select icon (the arrow pointing right), and choose Show start from the drop-down menu to display the starting object. Click the end object select icon (the arrow pointing left), and choose Show End from the drop-down menu to show the ending object.

You also can set the starting and ending objects of a new blend by separating the objects, ungrouping the blend objects, using the start and end object select icons, choosing New Start and New End from the appropriate drop-down menus to set the beginning and end points of the new blend, and applying the new blend. This procedure provides some interesting effects. Make sure to regroup the objects when you're finished so that the orientation is preserved. See Chapter 5 for details on object arranging and grouping.

Controlling Blend Steps and Spacing

Use the icon in the upper-left corner of the Blend roll-up window to set the number of blend steps, the space between each step, and the amount of rotation used when blending between objects. Clicking this icon displays the roll-up window shown in figure 13.12, if it is not already displayed.

The Steps list box is accessible only when you're blending along a path. With this box, you can set the interblend object spacing along the path or simply accept the number of steps defined in the Steps box just below the list box. The number shown in the Steps box determines the number of intermediate objects included in the blend. The larger this number, the closer the intermediate blend objects will be spaced. When blending along a path, this box enables you to set explicit intermediate interobject distances.

TIP

The first and last objects often lose their emphasis after blending, as shown in figure 13.13. You can break the objects into their separate pieces by choosing Separate from the Arrange menu (see fig. 13.14). You then can individually control the objects for coloring and top-to-bottom orientation. Group the objects after you orient and fill them as you want.

TIP

You can edit text after blending by selecting the text and choosing Edit Text from the Text menu (or pressing Ctrl+T). The artistic text editing box shown in the Text Edit dialog box enables you to change the text itself. The blend then reflects the new text. This feature gives you a handy way to use a previously completed blend as a template for future blends. Create the initial blend, duplicate it, and then edit the text to reflect the new text. The overall blend characteristics remain the same but revolve around the new text.

FIG. 13.13

Two objects after
blending.

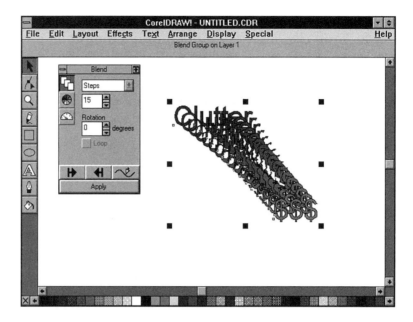

FIG. 13.14

Separated blend
objects.

Rotating the Blend

The Rotation and Loop options are selected separately, but are related. Use the Rotation option to determine the amount of rotation included with the entire blend, with negative numbers producing a counterclockwise rotation and positive numbers a clockwise rotation. Setting the rotation to 90 degrees causes the final blended object to rest at a 90-degree angle to the ending blend object. A setting of 180 degrees causes the blend to flip over while blending from the start to end object.

Selecting the Loop option rotates the intermediate objects around the halfway point of the blend. The effect is dramatic and very different from a nonlooped blend. Figure 13.15 shows a rotated blend without a loop; figure 13.16 shows the same blend when Loop is selected.

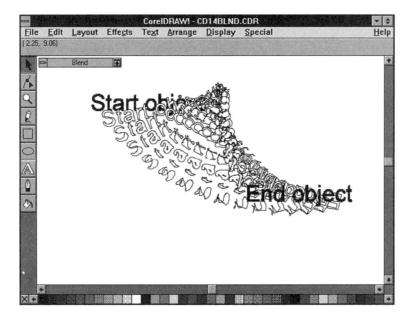

FIG. 13.15

A rotated blend without Loop selected.

Mapping Nodes in a Blend

The node mapping blend option enables you to specify a node on both the start and end objects that CorelDRAW! uses for alignment while blending. CorelDRAW! creates the blend so that the selected node on the first object blends into the selected node on the second. This feature allows for the creation of some interesting effects.

FIG. 13.16

A rotated blend with Loop selected.

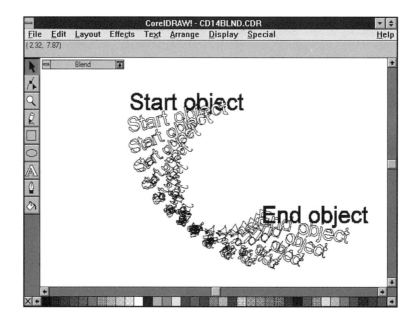

The following steps outline various effects provided with node mapping. Ensure that the Blend roll-up window is visible before beginning these procedures.

1. Select both objects.

2. Click the node mapping icon located at the bottom of the icon column to display the Blend roll-up window shown in figure 13.17.

3. Click Map Nodes, and move the cursor to the editing window. Notice that the cursor turns into a curved arrow and that the nodes are displayed on one of the objects, indicating that you are in node mapping mode.

4. Click the node of the first object and then the node of the second object as shown in figure 13.17. This step tells CorelDRAW! to map these nodes while performing the blend and ensure that they align upon completion.

5. Click Apply to perform the blend.

Figure 13.18 shows the results of node mapping on a blend.

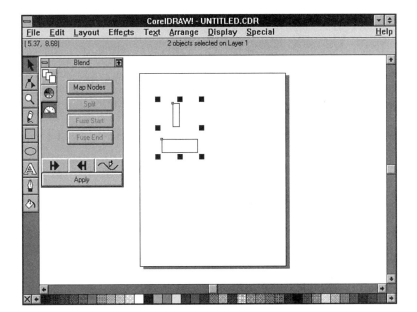

FIG. 13.17

The Blend node mapping roll-up window.

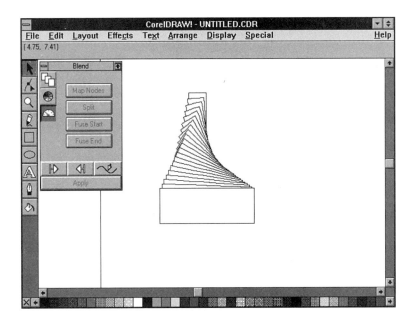

FIG. 13.18

Blending with node mapping.

Blending along a Path

When a blend is completed, you can apply the blended group of objects to a path for additional effect. The center of rotation (the bull's-eye) for each object created during the blend is placed along the curved path. The start and end objects are called the control objects, and they define their respective orientations using the designated path. If one of the control objects' center of rotation is placed on the path away from the object's interior, the blended objects drift away from the line because they are blending to the control object's center of rotation, not the center of each intermediate blend object itself.

The following procedure assumes that the Blend roll-up window is open and applies an existing blend to a curved path:

1. Draw a curved line on the same page as the blended objects.

2. Select the blended group and then click the blend along a path button shown at the bottom-right corner of the Blend roll-up window (the arrow pointing to the line). The Blend along a path roll-up window appears, as shown in figure 13.19.

FIG. 13.19

The Blend along a path roll-up window.

3. Select the New Path option, move the cursor to the editing page, and click the curved line to be used for the blend path.

4. Set the Full Path and Rotate All options to your preferences.

   The Full Path option specifies that the beginning and ending objects' centers of rotation should fall on the beginning and end points of the path. If this option is not selected, the blend aligns along the path starting at the closest path endpoint and continuing until the number of steps is exhausted.

   The Rotate All option rotates each object as it aligns along the path. The degree of rotation is defined by the slope of the line.

Horizontal line segments apply no rotation, and vertical line segments apply a 90-degree rotation. Other slopes are interpolated between these two values.

5. Click Apply, and watch the blend align itself along the path.

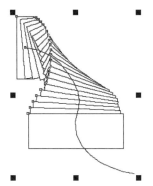

FIG. 13.20

Blending along a path.

TIP

If you do not want the path line to show, give it no thickness (X) or the same color as the paper.

You can also blend an object into two separate objects. However, you must perform some steps on the first blend before you can create the second blend. Figure 13.21 is the result of blending three symbols. The disk drive and monitor are blended along an angled path, separated, and moved to the top of the blend objects. The blend itself is then ungrouped, and the apex blend object is then blended into the currency symbol. Then everything is grouped together.

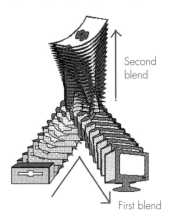

Second blend

First blend

FIG. 13.21

An image created using two blends.

Using a blended group as the control group for another blend is possible, but you have to eliminate the blended relationship before CorelDRAW! allows the second blend. You cannot blend an established blend group along a path because a blend group cannot be a starting or ending control object. You can get around this situation by first creating the blend and then separating and ungrouping the objects until they are treated as unrelated objects. Either select an object as a start for a new blend as was done in the figure, or group these objects into a simple, now nonblended, group that can be used as a control object for a blend. The orientation of the objects and their attributes remains the same, but they are no longer dynamically linked as they were in the blend.

Changing Object Shapes by Using the Envelope

Applying an *envelope* to an object enables you to shape the object's outline in virtually any imaginable way. Think of an envelope as an imaginary boundary to which the object conforms. Changing the envelope changes the object shape. Follow this basic procedure to apply an envelope:

1. Choose Envelope Roll-Up from the Effects menu (or press Ctrl+F7) to open the Envelope roll-up window shown in figure 13.22.

2. Select the object.

3. Choose Add New from the roll-up window to add an envelope to the object.

4. Select one of the four envelope types from the Envelope roll-up window.

5. Use the Shape tool to modify the envelope shape to suit your preferences.

6. Click Apply to make the object conform to the envelope outline. You can add multiple envelopes to an object.

Selecting the Keep Lines option from the Envelope roll-up window keeps all object segments defined as straight lines while the envelope is applied. Otherwise, the lines curve as the envelope is applied. This topic is explored further in the following sections.

Straight line envelope

Double arc envelope
Unconstrained envelope

Envelope

Single arc envelope

FIG. 13.22

The Envelope roll-up window.

Using Existing Envelope Designs

To use a preset envelope shape, you must first select the object, and then choose Envelope Roll-Up from the Effects menu to open the Envelope roll-up window. Next, choose Add New. Choose the Add Preset option from the Envelope roll-up window to display a group of pre-defined object shapes that you can use as envelope shapes (see fig. 13.23). Click a shape to add its envelope outline to the object shown in the drawing. Keep in mind that this envelope shape is not applied until you choose Apply.

You use the Envelope roll-up window's Create From option to copy an existing envelope shape from one object onto another object. Follow these steps:

1. Create a source object, and give it an envelope shape you want to duplicate to other objects.

2. Create the destination object onto which you want to copy the envelope.

3. Make sure that the destination object is selected, and choose Create From. The cursor changes shape, and the arrow reads From?.

FIG. 13.23

Various preset envelope
shapes.

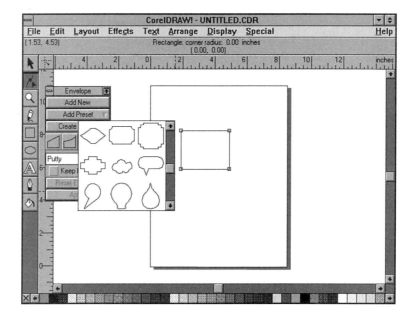

4. Click the source object to copy the source envelope to the
destination object.

5. Click Apply to define the second object's shape in accordance
with the copied envelope outline.

Create From is particularly useful when you want to match the outlines
of two objects exactly. Suppose, for example, that you have artistic text
that is to fit within an object such as a rectangle. To set up this type of
drawing, follow these steps:

1. Create the rectangle, and apply the envelope of the shape you
want.

2. Type the text, and then select it.

3. Use Create From and Apply to make the text's outline match that
of the box.

4. Choose Align from the **Arrange** menu. Choose the center-center
options from the Align dialog box to align the two objects inside
one another for an easy and interesting effect.

Figure 13.24 shows an example of how the text *Flag Day* can be aligned
within the shape of a blowing flag.

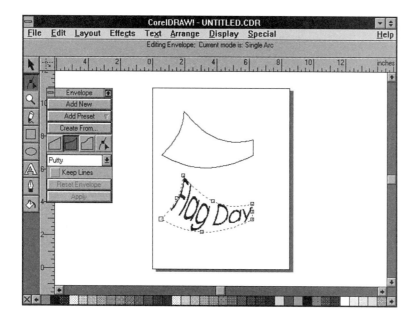

FIG. 13.24

Using Create From on
text and objects.

Creating a New Envelope Design

Below the Create From option in the Envelope roll-up window are the
icons representing the four different envelope types you can create.
From left to right, they are single line, single arc, double arc, and
unconstrained. The potential complexity of the envelope's design
increases with each envelope type.

The *single line* design keeps the envelope outline as a series of straight
lines and is best used to show end-to-end ramp type of effects such
as that shown in figure 13.25. In this case, the upper-right node was
dragged up and the upper-left node was dragged down. (Notice that
Vertical node mapping is on for this effect. This feature is covered in
the next section.)

You can use the *single arc* envelope to create a uniform curved effect to
the sides of the underlying object, as shown in figure 13.26. In this case,
the upper- and lower-right objects were dragged down, with the lower
node dragged farther than the upper node.

FIG. 13.25

The single line envelope effect.

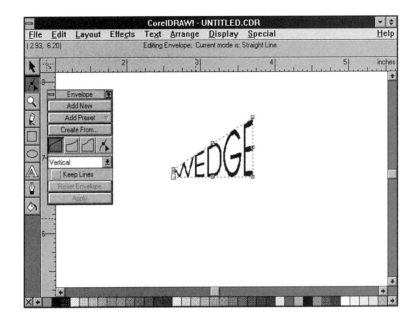

FIG. 13.26

The single arc envelope effect.

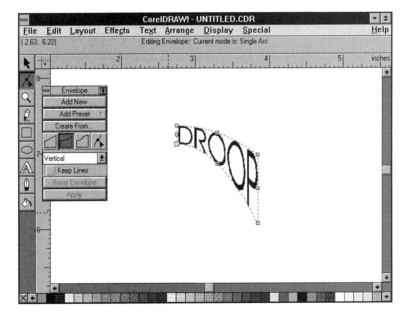

Use the *double arc* envelope to create more complicated curved outlines to the underlying object, as shown in figure 13.27. In this case, the upper-left node was dragged up a significant amount, the center node was dragged down a little, and the upper-right node was dragged up a little.

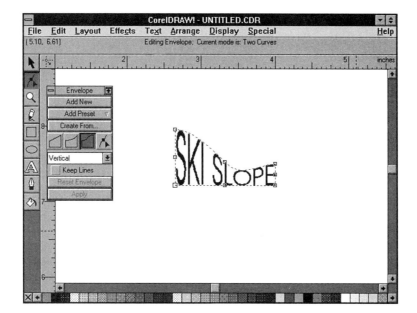

FIG. 13.27

The double arc envelope effect.

The *unconstrained* effect allows the most flexibility and complexity to the envelope design. You essentially can drag each node in any direction without concern for the other node locations or characteristics. The drawing shown in figure 13.28 was created by dragging the upper- and lower-center nodes up and down, respectively, and then using the Bézier control points to accentuate the curve from each of the corner nodes.

You can use the Ctrl and Shift keys while shaping the envelope to move multiple envelope nodes at the same time. These features work in either a horizontal or vertical direction, but not both at the same time.

FIG. 13.28

The unconstrained
envelope effect.

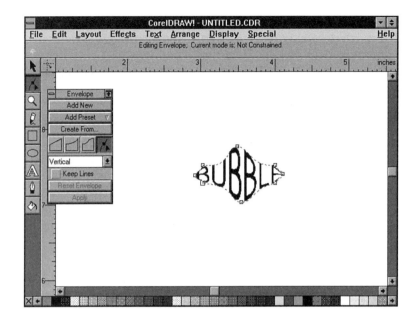

Table 13.2. Using the Ctrl and Shift Keys with Envelopes

Key	Effect
Ctrl	Moves the selected node and its opposite node in the same direction
Shift	Moves the selected node and its opposite node in opposite directions
Shift+Ctrl	Moves all four corners or sides in opposite directions

Object Node Mapping to Envelope Design

The node mapping options provided with CorelDRAW! are Original
(used by DRAW 3), Putty (default mode), Vertical, Horizontal, and Text.

Table 13.3 Node Mapping Options

Option	Effect on Underlying Object	
Original	Aligns the corner nodes of the envelope with the corner nodes of the underlying object's bounding box. Intermediate nodes along each side align themselves along a line or fit between the nodes. The fit for simple objects is adequate, but the fit is inadequate for more complicated objects that require a nonlinear outline. This style is named original because it was first used in CorelDRAW! 3.	
Putty (default mode)	Bases the underlying object's final design on the corner node locations and the envelope itself, so it tends to cause less distortion. On relatively simple envelopes, Putty and Original should look similar, but more complicated envelopes show a difference.	
Vertical	Allows only up-and-down movement of the object and constrains horizontal movement. The corner nodes are aligned, and then the object's interior is moved vertically to match the defined envelope outline. Vertical works well with text.	
Horizontal	Performs the same way as vertical, except in the opposite direction. Useful for objects containing horizontal lines that you want to keep linear and still align along the edge of the envelope.	
Text	Used in conjunction with paragraph text. This mode is allowed only when a block of paragraph text is selected for envelope addition. All other mapping options are unavailable when you're using Text mapping.	

TIP

When you select an object with an envelope, the roll-up window displays the current envelope setting for that object.

Resetting and Clearing an Envelope

You can reset an envelope before it is applied to an object. As long as the modified envelope is still in its dotted-line form, simply click the

Reset Envelope button in the Envelope roll-up window to return the envelope to its state after the last Apply usage. If you want to delete the latest envelope application, choose Clear Envelope from the Effects menu. You may have to repeat this procedure a few times to remove all envelopes if several have been applied to the same object.

4 Using the Contour Feature

The *contour* special effect is a sort of blend in that one object's attributes transition to another object's attributes over a user-specified number of steps. Where a blend transitions from one distinct object to another, however, contour works with smaller or larger versions of a single object. Only a single object can be contoured, but multiple objects or groups of objects can be blended. In addition, you cannot contour along a path as you can with a blend.

You can contour text but not groups of objects, blended objects, bitmaps, or Windows OLE objects. You can edit a specific contour object by holding the Ctrl key while clicking the object. It is essentially a child curve of the contour group of objects.

Contouring an object gives it a three-dimensional look similar to that seen on topographical, or contour, maps. You can contour objects in three ways:

- From the perimeter to the center of the object (To Center)
- From the outside to the inside of the object, but not necessarily the object's center (Inside)
- Outward from the object's perimeter (Outside)

You can specify the distance between contour steps (the offset) and the number of contour steps as long as the dimensions are consistent with the dimensions of the object. You can specify up to 50 steps in a contour.

TIP

Displaying the rulers is helpful when working with contours because the offsets are measured in display units (such as inches), and you can get the relative measurements easily from the display.

Learning Contour Fundamentals

To add a contour special effect, follow these basic steps:

1. Draw and select the object to which you want to apply a contour.

2. From the Effects menu, choose Contour Roll-Up (or press Ctrl+F9). The Contour roll-up window appears, as shown in figure 13.29.

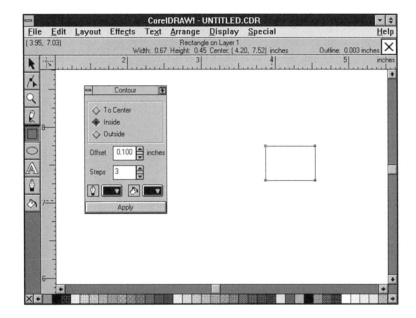

FIG. 13.29

The Contour roll-up window.

3. Select the contour type (To Center, Inside, or Outside).

4. Enter the offset and the number of steps.

5. Choose the outline and interior fill characteristics you want to use.

6. Click Apply, and watch the contours draw from the object's perimeter to your designated ending location.

Figure 13.30 shows a rectangle with a To Center contour added.

To remove a contour, open the Edit menu and choose Undo immediately after performing the contour operation, or just choose Clear Effect from the Effects menu.

FIG. 13.30

Adding a To Center
contour to a rectangle.

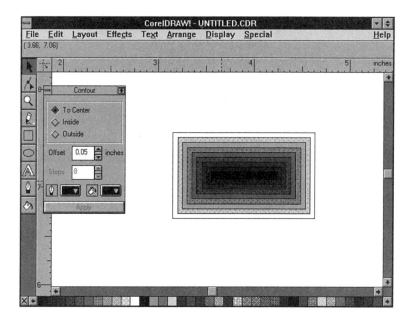

The To Center and Inside options appear similar, but they perform very differently. To Center literally takes the contour to the center of the object. CorelDRAW! determines the number of contoured objects required to cover the distance between the object perimeter and its center, based on the offset value you establish, and creates that number of contour objects. You must set the offset value when using the To Center option.

Inside, on the other hand, draws the contoured objects inside each other, but not necessarily to the object's center unless you specifically designate that. CorelDRAW! begins moving inward on the object to the first offset point and draws a new object. The program repeats this procedure until exhausting the designated number of steps or reaching the object's center, whichever comes first. If you designate only a few steps, and those steps in combination with the offset do not reach the center, CorelDRAW! simply draws the designated number of contoured objects and stops.

Outside accomplishes the opposite effect of Inside. CorelDRAW! creates a number of contoured objects in an outward direction from the original object and in a quantity defined by the Steps value. Each contoured object is placed at the defined offset location from the preceding object. Figure 13.31 shows an example of a rectangle with an Outside contour.

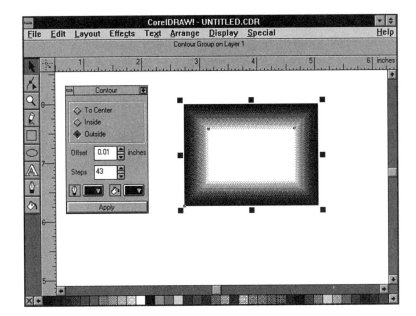

FIG. 13.31

Applying an Outside contour.

Setting Contour Attributes

When you create a contour, CorelDRAW! uses the original object's outline and fill type for the beginning of the contour. The original object must have a fill color defined, or the contoured objects will not contain a color even if you define one and the contour operation creates a series of contour objects with no fill. You do not have to define an outline color for contour to function properly.

You can set the interior and outline colors of the original object directly from the standard color palette shown at the bottom of the window. To change the outline and fill attributes of the final objects of the created contour, click the proper tool (Outline or Fill) on the Contour roll-up window and then select the colors you want from the displayed palette (see fig. 13.32).

TIP

Eliminate the lines around each contour by choosing the No Outline (X) option from the toolbox's Outline fly-out menu. Make sure that the contoured group of objects is selected before you change the value. This technique provides a smoother blending of colors between the initial object and the final contour point. Adding more steps also enhances the smoothness of the contour.

FIG. 13.32

Setting contour colors.

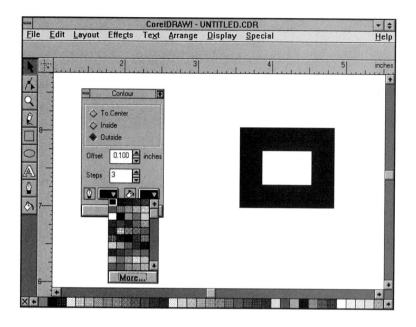

NOTE

You can create many similarly shaped objects in one step by using the contour feature with no fill on the initial object. Specify the number of steps, and apply the contour. CorelDRAW! now treats the objects as a contour group. Click the group and separate/ungroup as needed to get each object on its own so that you can individually assign attributes. Many interesting effects are possible when you use the contour feature in this way. You also can access each individual contour object by pressing Ctrl while clicking the object. It is treated as a child group until deselected.

14 Using PowerLines

PowerLines help you get away from the technical feel of standard computer-based drawings and approach a standard brush type of drawing capability. When an artist draws with a brush, the flow of paint is not always consistent, and the brush flattens or thins based upon the amount of pressure applied by the artist. PowerLines enable you, the CorelDRAW! user, to achieve similar effects through the use of several settings that ultimately combine to make an artistic effect.

If you have access to a pressure-sensitive stylus and digitizer, you can use the Pressure Preset contained under the PowerLines Preset list to instruct CorelDRAW! to translate your hand and pressure movements into PowerLines. This special equipment makes using PowerLines easier, but it is not necessary to fully use the PowerLines feature.

Comparing PowerLines to Regular Lines

Although you draw both standard lines and PowerLines with the Pencil tool, the end results are very different. When you define a path for a conventional line, CorelDRAW! defines the start node, the end node, and the intermediate nodes required to create the drawn curves, and then applies a uniform line thickness to the line. The procedure is similar for a PowerLine except that the drawn line becomes a path along which the PowerLine is drawn, but line shape is determined by several factors (see fig. 13.33). Each of these factors combine to determine the overall line outline shape, the density of the applied color, and the variations in line thickness over the length of the line. Similar effects were possible with the nib shapes provided with earlier versions of DRAW, but the PowerLines take this concept to another level.

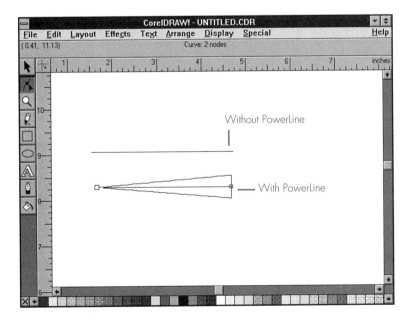

FIG. 13.33

A line drawn without PowerLines and a line drawn with PowerLines.

To access the PowerLine features, you use the PowerLine roll-up window shown in figure 13.34. To display this window, choose **P**owerLine Roll-Up from the **Effects** menu (or press Ctrl+F8).

FIG. 13.34

The PowerLine roll-up window.

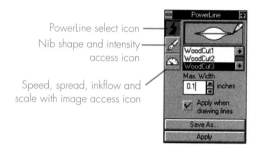

PowerLine select icon

Nib shape and intensity access icon

Speed, spread, inkflow and scale with image access icon

NOTE

The examples in this chapter assume that you are not using a pressure-sensitive stylus and that the lines and attributes are created using the standard DRAW tools and menu options.

Analyzing the Components of the PowerLine Roll-Up Window

The PowerLine roll-up window activates and deactivates the PowerLine feature. When the roll-up is open and the Apply when drawing lines option is active, the drawn lines adopt the currently active PowerLine outline. Closing the PowerLine roll-up deactivates the PowerLine feature.

The general procedure for applying a PowerLine is as follows:

1. Open the PowerLine roll-up by choosing the **P**owerLine Roll-Up option from the **Effects** menu (Ctrl+F8).

2. Click the Apply when drawing lines option within the roll-up window.

3. Choose the desired PowerLine design and related features.

4. Choose the Pencil tool and draw the desired line path, and CorelDRAW! applies your designated PowerLine features to that line.

If you do not like the drawn effect, choose **U**ndo from the **E**dit menu to remove the line, or choose a new effect from within the roll-up window and then click on Apply to overlay the newly selected PowerLine design to the drawn line.

The following sections explain the details associated with the use of PowerLines, such as modifying the overall PowerLine shape and width, creating and saving a custom PowerLine design, and using more sophisticated features.

Using the Provided Preset PowerLines

CorelDRAW! comes with 24 preset PowerLine designs, which are displayed in the PowerLines select list near the top of the PowerLine roll-up window (see fig. 13.34). You can scroll through the list to reveal the various designs after you click a specific name. (The design is not applied to a line until you choose Apply with a line selected.) Think of these designs as the outline shape that surrounds your drawn line when you apply the PowerLine. The WoodCut3 PowerLine design, for example, is thin at the beginning of the line, thick in the middle, and thin again at the end of the line. Applying this preset to any drawn line causes the WoodCut3 overall line thickness variations to appear relative to the selected line's beginning, middle, and end.

Notice that the PowerLine Design Display box at the top of the PowerLine roll-up window shows a thin line surrounded by the overall PowerLine outline. Think of the thin line as the line you draw and the outline as the effect of the PowerLines. Scrolling through the list of designs gives you a good overview of the standard PowerLine designs.

Setting PowerLine Width

To set the width of a PowerLine at its thickest part, use the Max. Width option in the PowerLine roll-up window. This setting corresponds to the amount of pressure an artist would apply with a brush. The more pressure applied by the artist with a paintbrush, the thicker the line becomes. The higher the PowerLine Max. Width setting, the thicker the PowerLine becomes. The default value is 0.5 inches, and the overall allowable range is from 0.01 inches to 16 inches.

You can also change this Max. Width setting for a selected line by using the Shape tool and the Node Edit roll-up window's Pressure Edit option. Choose the Shape tool and then select the PowerLine object. The nodes that correspond to the PowerLine pressure outline points appear. You can drag the pressure-related node points to the thickness you want (see fig. 13.35). When you modify the nodes using the Shape tool, the PowerLine design becomes a custom design, and you should save it under a new name to prevent it from being lost.

FIG. 13.35

Editing pressure with the Shape tool.

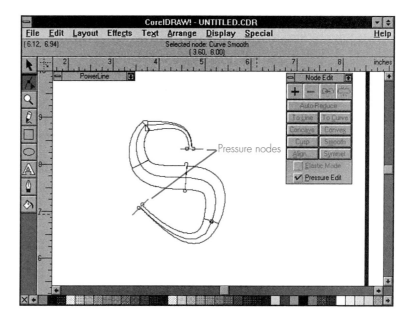

Applying PowerLine Selections to Multiple Lines

Choose the Apply when drawing lines option if you want to apply the current PowerLine selection to every subsequently drawn line. This feature is valuable when you are sketching something and want the applied effect on each line to be consistent.

Saving PowerLines

To save a modified PowerLine under another name that you can access later, use the PowerLine roll-up window's Save As button. Make the necessary changes to a particular PowerLine and then choose Save As to reveal the Save PowerLine As dialog box shown in figure 13.36. In the Powerline Name box, type the name you want to use; click OK to save the new design.

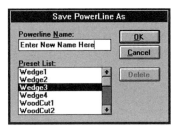

FIG. 13.36

The Save PowerLine As dialog box.

Controlling Nib Shape

The second icon along the left side of the PowerLine roll-up window is the nib shape and intensity access icon. Click this icon to display the PowerLine roll-up and currently active nib design as shown in figure 13.37. The nib is like the tip of a pen, and different nib shapes provide different drawing effects.

FIG. 13.37

The PowerLine roll-up for controlling nib shape.

Change the nib shape in one of two ways: by dragging the nib shape itself until you reach the orientation and size you want or by clicking the small page icon in the lower-right corner of the roll-up window to display another roll-up window in which you can set the nib characteristics directly (see fig. 13.38).

FIG. 13.38

Directly setting the nib shape.

You use this second roll-up window to control three aspects of the nib shape: the angle, the size, and the intensity. The Angle option in this second roll-up window sets the angle of the pen point relative to a vertical reference line, with a positive angle rotating the nib counterclockwise. The Nib Ratio option determines a rough ratio of the thickest part of the nib to the thinnest. The lower the ratio number, the thinner the nib; the larger the number, the more like a circle the nib shape becomes. The Intensity setting has a maximum value of 100. At the maximum level, the line drawn is at its maximum width when the PowerLine is at a 90-degree angle. You can set intensity from the Nib Display window or directly from the numeric entry field.

To change the nib ratio and angle by dragging with the mouse, click the small page icon until the actual nib design appears in the roll-up window. You can then change the ratio and angle of the nib by dragging it with the mouse until the nib meets your needs. Modifications done in the two nib modification views update each other so the graphical and numeric displays always match.

Controlling the PowerLine's Overall Appearance

Click the third icon in the PowerLine roll-up window to display the roll-up window shown in figure 13.39. Here you can set the speed, spread, and ink flow, interrelated attributes that determine the overall line appearance.

FIG. 13.39

Using the Speed, Spread, and Ink Flow PowerLine settings.

Think of the Speed setting as the level at which CorelDRAW! tracks the mouse movements. If the speed is set high, the tracking follows just as a car with inertia coming around a curve in the road. The higher the speed, the more the car skids from the designated path. In the same way, the higher the PowerLine speed setting, the larger the amount of "skidding" that occurs from the designated line path. You can set a speed from 1 to 100.

You can set the Spread value only when the Speed option has a non-zero setting. As the Spread value increases, more ink is available to apply to the curve, and the curve color continuity is high. The lower the Spread setting, the less ink is applied to a given segment, and the line may have a bumpy color continuity. Spread can have a value between 1 and 100.

Ink Flow determines the total amount of ink available for a given line. Even though the line may be drawn as long, if not enough ink is available to create the line, it eventually fades away before its drawn end. Unless you have a specific reason otherwise, leave the Ink Flow option set at 100, which represents a full pen of ink.

In general, you should select the Scale with Image option to ensure that the overall PowerLine characteristics are scaled accordingly if the PowerLine itself is resized.

Exploring Some Examples

You can use the blend feature to highlight an object effectively. The pinwheel shown in figure 13.40 was created from symbol #34 of the Stars1 symbol group. The symbol was brought into the drawing and then duplicated and scaled to 10 percent of the original size, leaving the original object in place. The larger star was given a black fill and no outline thickness, and the inner star was given a gray fill with no outline thickness. The two were then blended over 75 steps with a 45-degree rotation to give the shown effect.

Figure 13.41 could be a flier for a local library and was created from the clip art, a blend of two artistic text objects, and the addition of perspective. The "Reading leads to..." text was added first with a black fill and outline in Arabia 50 point. The "Life" text was also added in Arabia, but with a white fill and at 70-point size. The two objects were then blended together over 45 steps with a 180-degree rotation. The entire group was separated, the text objects were moved to the top, and the "Reading..." text was given a white fill for accent and made a little larger. The boy and girl are from the People symbols group, and the building is from the Building symbol group. The line at the bottom of the building was added and then combined with the other lines comprising the building object. The entire building object had a perspective added to it with the vanishing point moved up and to the right.

FIG. 13.40

Highlighting with the blend feature.

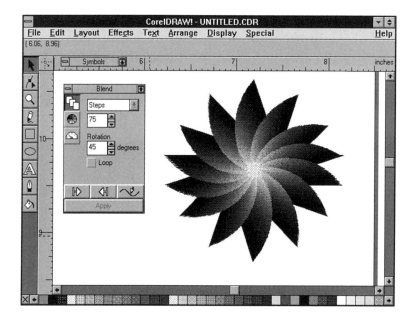

FIG. 13.41

Giving movement with an artistic text blend.

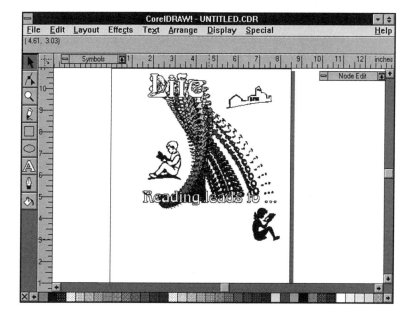

Summary

This chapter looked at the many special effects contained as standard features with CorelDRAW! 4. The contour and PowerLines features are new to release 4, and the others, such as blend, perspective, and envelope, have been improved to provide more effectiveness. Learning the benefits associated with using special effects can greatly improve the quality of your drawings while speeding up your creation process.

The next chapter covers the use of multipage documents, a new feature of release 4. It also covers the useful Object Data Manager, another new feature, that associates database information with an image's objects. Completing Chapters 14 and 15 will round out your DRAW expertise and prepare you for your drawing projects. It will also lay the groundwork for the later chapters that deal with the additional Corel applications.

Multipage Documents and the Object Data Manager

A welcome addition to CorelDRAW! is its capability to edit images that cover more than one page. Many people use DRAW to create newsletters, and the previous versions required that each page of the newsletter be treated as a separate document. Now, with the addition of multipage editing capability, up to 999 pages of a newsletter or other document can be edited as a single image. Using this single-file approach offers a major benefit: it frees you from the task of keeping track of the point at which text ends in one file and begins in another. Text automatically flows across multiple pages, making document editing substantially easier.

The Object Data Manager is a useful addition for people who need to correlate database information (weight, size, price, and so on) with an image of some kind. Examples of this sort of application include catalogs that use product descriptions and pictures, and personnel rosters that associate a person's picture with his or her personal information. The Object Data Manager makes this type of integration possible. Most Windows OLE-based data managers can link an image with a text source (that is, select a person's name and the person's picture appears). DRAW reverses this process by displaying text information when the image is verified.

Multipage Document Fundamentals

In general, the basic CorelDRAW! operating principles apply equally well to multipage documents. The one exception, perhaps, is that you must make more efficient use of the page layout and layering options, or your screen refresh times may become unbearable. To create and work with a multipage document, follow these steps:

1. Choose File New to create a document from scratch; choose File New From Template to use a Corel supplied template; or choose File Open to use a previously created document with the desired formatting information already embedded.

2. Choose Layout Page Setup and define a page layout style that includes decisions about the assumed page size and the way in which you plan to use it for paste-up layout purposes.

3. Set up the master layer of the document, which includes all the information that is to appear on each page.

4. Add the desired text and image information to the document.

TIP

You can use any document template as a starting point for a multipage document.

The steps in this process are explained in detail in the next few sections.

There's good news and bad news about the CorelDRAW! multipage document feature. The good news is that it allows you to import DRAW graphic images directly into your document and to spread document stories over multiple pages. The bad news, however, is that it currently does not include a utility for importing PageMaker documents. Many of your current multipage documents may have to be re-created using the DRAW formats. And text must be imported in a supported format such as ASCII text, RTF, Microsoft Word, Ami Pro, or WordPerfect. Text formatting is preserved, but the associated graphic images in the original document will probably be lost.

Choosing a Page Layout and Display Style

DRAW provides numerous page layout styles which are used to automate the actual *paste-up* procedures necessary to optimize the printing process. The best page layout style for a particular job depends on the size of the paper upon which the images will be printed, the method of folding and binding to be used, and the page numbering scheme. The items used to determine the relationship between the actual page size and the layout of the designed pages are located under the Layout Page Setup menu selection. When you choose this menu option, the dialog box shown in figure 14.1 appears.

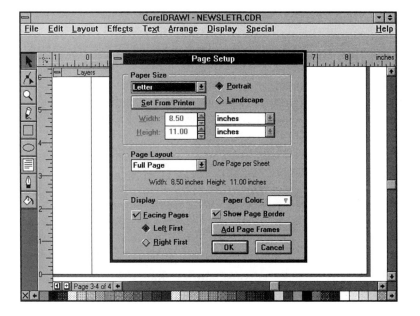

FIG. 14.1

The Page Setup dialog box.

Choose the correct paper size for your page layout design using the Paper Size option at the top of the dialog box. Click the arrow to display the pull-down list, then choose the desired size from the choices provided (tabloid, letter, legal, and other sizes). The Width and Height settings reflect your paper size choice in the specified units (*inches* in the figure provided). The Portrait and Landscape options determine whether the paper is to be printed long-side vertically oriented (portrait) or turned on its side (landscape). Choosing Set From Printer adopts a paper size with dimensions equal to that currently set as the currently active printer paper size.

The Page Layout options define the orientation and size of the pages that will contain the information. The basic layout styles are Full Page, Book, Booklet, Tent Card, Side-Fold Card, and Top-Fold Card. Each one has a different effect on how the paper size is subdivided into the smaller page layout areas.

If you are planning to create a document with folds, make certain the pages are upside down with respect to the others because of the folding and cutting (trimming) operations required to create the final document. Those operations will align them correctly. Under certain circumstances, pages that follow each other may not even print on the same piece of paper because the actual printing, folding, and trimming processes require that they print on opposing pieces of paper. But whatever the paper dimensions, the layout design divides the physical page into the sections required to meet these folding needs.

The Paper Color is used to set a background color for the editable preview display area. You might want to set this color to the paper color on which you plan to print; doing so helps you to determine whether your choice of colors is appropriate.

The Show Page Border option should always be selected before printing because it represents the actual page border, not the expected image area which is dependent upon the output device. Most output devices require some type of outer edge, which moves the print area in somewhat from the actual page edge. Selecting Show Page Border allows you to determine the actual orientation of your image on the page with respect to the printer mandated border requirements.

Add Page Frames places a drop-shadow behind the page; this feature facilitates viewing of the displayed image.

Choosing Facing Pages simultaneously displays two pages on-screen. The choice of Left First or Right First depends on whether you plan to start your document on the left or right page. This feature is typically used for book layouts.

Changing, Adding, and Deleting Pages

You can move around in your document and add pages by using the icons located in the lower-left corner of the window. The triangle moves you either forward or backward through the document depending upon the triangle's direction. You can also press the PageUp or PageDown keys on the keyboard. If you want to move to a specific page, choose **L**ayout **G**o To Page from the menu bar to display a dialog box in which you can enter the desired page number. Pressing Ctrl while clicking the Page Forward/Back icons moves you to the first or last page of the document, respectively. Clicking the Page Forward/ Back icons with the right mouse button moves you in the respective direction by 5 pages for each click. If the Facing Pages option is active, each right mouse button click moves you 10 pages.

Clicking the small + icon opens the Layout Insert Page dialog box which allows you to insert a specified number of pages either before or after the current page, depending upon the location of the + when selected. The plus appears on the left side when you are on the first page of the document and appears on the right side when you are on the last page. You delete a page by choosing **L**ayout **D**elete Page, selecting the page range for deletion, and then clicking OK.

Designing a Master Layer

The *master layer* contains all the information that will appear on each page of the document (unless you specifically turn off the display for that particular page as outlined later in this section). Any created layer can be designated as a master layer. You can also have multiple master layers by naming them differently when designating them as master layers in the Layer Options dialog box. Follow these steps to establish your master layer(s):

1. From the **L**ayout menu, choose **L**ayers Roll-Up (Ctrl+F3) to open the Layers roll-up window.

2. Click the solid triangle to open the menu, and select New to add a new layer to the drawing. The Layer Options dialog box appears (see fig. 14.2).

FIG. 14.2

The Layer Options
dialog box.

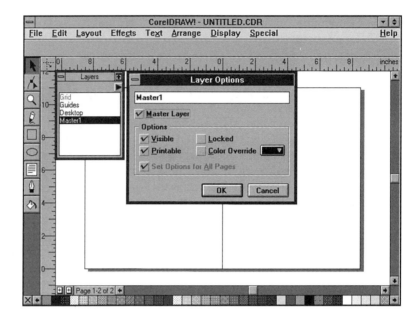

3. Type the desired layer name in the top rectangular area, select **M**aster Layer, and then click OK. A master layer with the designated name is added to the drawing. Notice that after the Master Layer option has been selected, the Set Options For All Pages option dims because it is automatically applicable for a master layer.

TIP

If you display the document with facing pages, the information displayed on the left-hand page is repeated on all left pages, and the right-hand page information is repeated on all right pages. Each must be set up separately.

You can hide Master Layer information on specific pages by following this procedure:

1. Go to the page for which you want to hide the Master Layer information by choosing **L**ayout **G**o To Page and giving the page number; then open the Layers roll-up window.

2. Double-click the master layer containing the information you want to hide. The Layer Options dialog box appears.

3. Click Set Options For **A**ll Pages to disable it. This keeps your selections from being applied to all pages.

4. Click the **Visible** check box to disable it. This makes the master layer invisible on this page. Click OK. The currently selected page(s) will not display the information contained on the disabled master layer. You cannot selectively delete master layer information from individual pages; the entire master layer is either used or hidden.

Additional information on using CorelDRAW! layers is presented in Chapter 5, so it is not covered in detail in this section.

Printing and the Page Layout Styles

Determining the proper layout of pages to accommodate specific printing situations is tricky business, and you can easily get confused if you do not clearly understand the process. Luckily, DRAW does a lot of the work for you when it prints the final documents. It determines the proper sequencing of pages so that they print on their respective sheets and line up properly when finally printed.

In a 12-page document printed in the booklet style, for example, pages 1 and 2 would not appear on the same sheet of paper. Instead, pages 1 and 12 would be printed on one sheet, pages 2 and 11 on another sheet (or the back of the first sheet), and so on. When the pages are printed this way, they align perfectly and give the desired page numbering in the bound booklet. This process is tricky, so you are encouraged to let DRAW make the decisions for you. Just don't be alarmed if you see non-sequential page numbers coming out of your printer. Check with your printer before finalizing your output. The printer works with the final product and can tell you exactly what he needs.

Object Data Manager Basic Concepts

The Object Data Manager is a device that allows you to access database information by way of images (instead of accessing images by way of textual information). Most databases present a text representation of some type (name, location, and so on) and then present the image if requested. DRAW turns this process around by presenting the image first and recovering the database information as a secondary action.

Assume that you are an interior designer, for example, and you are working with a house floor plan. You are using various symbols in your drawing to represent the pieces of furniture to be placed (as well as their dimensions, costs and purchase locations). With the Object Data Manager, the database information for each object in the drawing can be retrieved by clicking the object itself. The Object Data Manager also provides some simple mathematical operations to sum columns of information for objects formed into groups using the DRAW Arrange Group command.

Remember that in this case, you start with the objects and create the database around them, not the other way around. To group database information, group the objects. To separate database information, separate the objects. This procedure is contrary to most conventional database operations, and you are encouraged to shift your thinking so that you can take full advantage of the benefits associated with image- or object-oriented database operations.

Designing the Object Database

Begin with a DRAW object to which you want to attach data. Let's assume that you are working with a floor plan for a conference room, and want to create a database of information related to the interior design project (see fig. 14.3).

FIG. 14.3

A conference room floor plan.

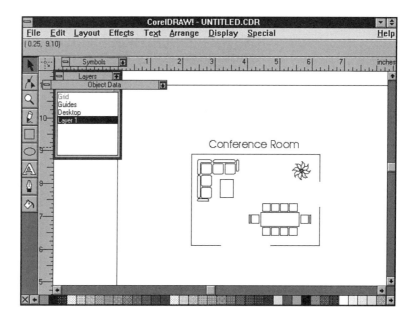

Follow these steps:

1. Create the floor plan and incorporate the objects from the Furniture symbol library. As shown in the figure, the sample project consists of four basic objects: a sofa, a coffee table, a plant (in the corner), and a conference table. This project could just as easily include a large number of objects, but these four are enough to illustrate the use of the Object Data Manager.

2. Decide what types of information you want to track. For the purposes of this example, track each object's Name, Purchase Price, Purchase Location, and Color. These categories of information are called *field names*. Each field name is a general category of information that pertains to each object in an image. Once again, you could make this list of field names as detailed as necessary to meet your needs.

3. Position the mouse pointer on an object, and then click and hold down the right mouse button until the Object Data menu appears. Establish, edit, and rearrange your field names using the Object Data Field Editor, which is accessed via the Data roll-up window.

4. Choose Data Roll-Up, and the Object Data roll-up window appears (see fig. 14.4).

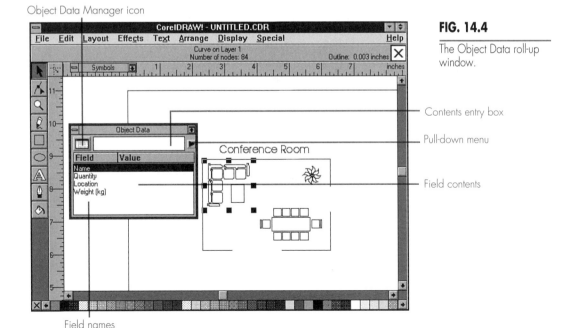

Object Data Manager icon

Contents entry box

Pull-down menu

Field contents

Field names

FIG. 14.4

The Object Data roll-up window.

5. Notice that the field names listed in the figure do not match the desired field categories of Name, Purchase Price, Purchase Location, and Color. They can be edited, however, by clicking the small, black triangle to reveal a pull-down menu. Choose Field Editor from the resulting list, and the Object Data Field Editor dialog box appears (see fig. 14.5).

FIG. 14.5

The Object Data Field Editor dialog box.

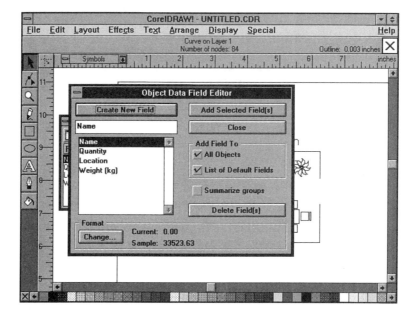

TIP

Double-clicking any of the field names opens the Field Editor dialog box.

6. Edit a field name by clicking the appropriate name in the left window and editing the name in the edit box located at the top of the window. It takes little effort to change the listed names to Name (remains unchanged), Purchase Price, Purchase Location, and Color. Remember that you are not dealing with the actual data associated with an object at this point; you are simply setting up the general fields under which the data will be stored.

To add any additional fields needed to meet your needs, choose Create New Field. If you don't give new fields names, they are created with the names Field0, Field1, and so on.

The Add Field To All Objects option adds the fields that you have selected at the left side of this dialog box to each of the objects contained within the currently active image. You can select all the fields by pressing Shift while clicking at the beginning and end of the listing of field names, or you can select a group of fields that appear randomly in the list by pressing Ctrl while clicking the group of field names. Add Field To List of Default Fields adds the selected field names to an overall listing of field names that appear each time you create a new document and use the Object Data Manager. To remove fields from the database for the currently active image, select the appropriate field names and then choose the Delete Field(s) option.

If the All Objects option is not selected, you can use the Add Selected Fields option to add individual fields to the image objects currently selected. Until you are familiar with the Object Data Manager's operation, you are encouraged to leave All Objects selected.

The Summarize Groups option instructs DRAW to total the numbers contained in any set of objects grouped by the Arrange Group menu command. You can occasionally get strange results with this option selected because DRAW simply adds whatever numbers appear in the columns, and places the total in a cell at the end of the list. Remember that DRAW lists the objects as they are grouped, and summarizes the column listing for that group. Make sure that the Show Crop Details option is activated from within the Object Data Manager Preferences dialog box.

Format Change is used to present data in a desired format such as currency, comma separated, percent, and so on. You can also change data and distance formats using the Change option and the Format Definition dialog box shown in figure 14.6.

You can see DRAW's numerous Date, Time, Linear dimensional unit, and Numeric display formats by clicking the appropriate box in the Format Type section of this dialog box. You can also create a custom format by entering the proper symbols in the Create text box. See table 14.1 for a listing of the most frequently used formatting characters.

FIG. 14.6

The Format Definition
dialog box.

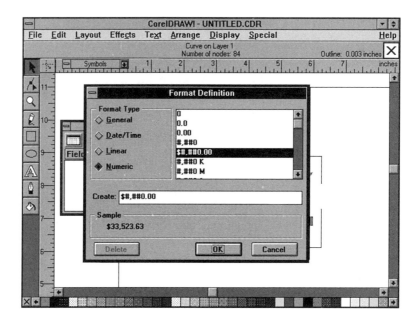

Table 14.1 Formats and Their Uses

Type of Format	Format	Use
General		Adds text just as you enter it, except all leading and trailing zeroes are dropped and commas separating thousands are not recognized
Date/Time	M	Month in numeric form
	MMMM	Month in full text form
	d	Day of the month as a number
	dddd	Day of the week in full text form
	yy	Year in two digits
	yyyy	Year in four digits
	h	Hour as a number
	mm	Minutes with a leading zero as required
	am/AM	Shows AM or PM, as required

Type of Format	Format	Use
Number	0	Keeps a place for this number of digits to display
	#	Designates comma separator location
	,	Used with # to determine comma separator location
	$	Currency (Use $$"x" to show another currency symbol where x represents the symbol)
	.	Decimal separator
	K	Thousands abbreviation
Linear	Feet	Single quotes or ft
	Inches	Double quotes or in
	Miles	MI
	Kilometers	KM

NOTE

You can mix formats, but you must enter the minor format or units of smallest measure. For example, to display 1 ft 6 in, you must enter 18 (inches) as the value in the Object Data roll-up window with a 00ft00-in formatting definition.

If you choose the two decimal point currency option, for example, you can then edit it to remove the two decimal places. Simply enter **$#,###** over the format displayed in the Create entry box to do so. Detailed explanations of the symbols used in these formats and the way they are used can be obtained using the Help Search for Help On Formats: for object data. Choosing OK returns you to the Object Data Field Editor, and clicking Close returns you to the DRAW image and the Object Data roll-up.

You can reorder the field names by dragging a selected field to a new location and dropping it there. A double arrow appears to indicate that DRAW is ready to move the field to a new location.

Now that the fields have been defined, it is time to enter some object database information.

Adding, Editing, and Printing Object Data

Selecting any of the image objects displays a listing of its associated field names and their contents. At this point in the process, no data has been entered for the image objects, so the Object Data roll-up window, displays the field names without any value entries. If no object is selected, the window comes up empty.

To enter data associated with an object, first select the object. Then select the appropriate field name from the Object Data roll-up window, and type the desired field contents in the entry box at the top of the window. The data shown in figure 14.7, for example, was entered by clicking the Name field and entering **Sofa**, clicking the Purchase Price field and typing **1100**, clicking the Purchase Location field and typing **Jacobson's**, and then clicking the Color field and typing **Blue**.

FIG. 14.7

The Sofa Object Data.

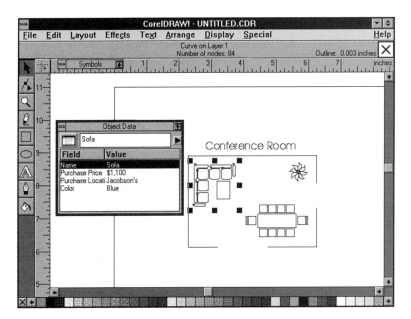

The data associated with the other objects could be entered in the same manner, but DRAW provides an easier method using the Object Data Manager. First select the Sofa, Coffee Table, Conference Table, and Plant objects using the Shift-click or marquee techniques. Then click the Object Data Manager icon located just to the left of the entry box in the Object Data roll-up window. The Object Data Manager data entry screen appears (see fig. 14.8).

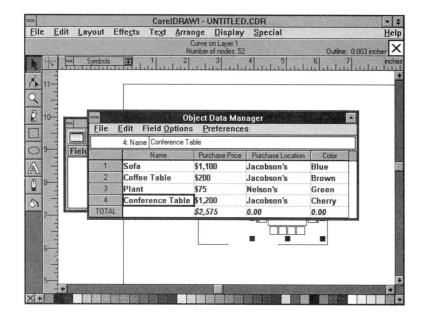

FIG. 14.8

The Object Data Manager data entry screen.

The data is stored in a spreadsheet format with the object number and name shown on the left side. Notice that each of the columns represents one of the field names that you defined earlier. The listing order of the objects depends on their order of creation and any Front/Back reordering you might have applied after initial creation. To determine which image object corresponds to each database row number, click the row of interest to highlight the associated image object.

You can enter data by clicking the cell of interest and typing in the desired information. If the columns are not wide enough for the information you enter, drag the dividing line between the field names on the top row until the width meets your needs.

TIP

Make sure you select the objects of interest before entering the Object Data Manager screen, or you might not have access to the objects you need.

You can turn the column totals on or off by using the Field Options Show Totals menu option. To turn on column totals, select a column by clicking its field name, and then select Field Options Show Totals. If you do not want the field totals shown, as in the case of the color column in the example, repeat the procedure for the color column to turn off the

Show Totals option. If your column totals are erratic, you may want to total the columns before summarizing the group to avoid adding the summary numbers to the column total.

Edit Cut, Copy, Paste, and Delete work just as they do in other Corel applications; they can be used to copy and move data within the data manager screen.

The object data can be printed by choosing File Page Setup to determine how the data will print. You can determine whether grid lines, row and column headers, page numbers, and file names will print and whether the data will be centered on the page based upon your selections from this dialog box. Margins are also set from within this dialog box.

Choosing File Print opens the Print Options dialog box which is used to determine the number of copies printed, scaling of the data on the printed page, whether DRAW should size the output to fit the selected cells on one page, and whether the entire database should be printed or just the selected cells.

Refer to Chapter 10 for more information on printing. You can also print the database to a disk file for use with other spreadsheet products such as 1-2-3 or Excel. The database will automatically be given a PRN extension that is readable by most spreadsheet products.

Grouping and Data Hierarchy

Object data is grouped in the Object Data Manager in accordance with the image grouping defined in the DRAW image using the Arrange Group functions. For example, if we group all of the objects to be purchased at Jacobson's into one DRAW group (the sofa, coffee table, and conference table), they appear together with their own subtotal within the Object Data Manager. You can also define a name for any group of objects (*Jacobson's Purchases*, for example) and create up to 10 hierarchical group levels. The number of hierarchy levels displayed in the data manager is determined by the Preferences Show Group Details menu selection of the Data Manager.

The basic procedure for creating a group is as follows:

1. Make sure all data is correct for the objects to be grouped.

2. Select the objects to be grouped.

3. Group the objects by choosing **Arrange Group** (Ctrl+G).

4. Type the desired group name into the text entry box of the Object Data roll-up window.

5. Open the Object Data Manager and verify that the new group was created (see fig. 14.9).

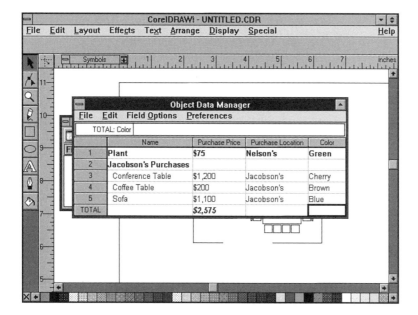

FIG. 14.9

Data Manager information using a hierarchy.

You can still change Object Data from within the Object Data Manager if required. You can also create groups of groups (just as with DRAW objects). Selecting an object or group from the Object Data Manger selects the object on the image screen and shows the circles as handles, which is characteristic of a child object or group.

Objects placed in a group are indented two spaces to set them off from the others in the database. In addition, a space is left at the top of the group for a group name definition. You can set all Top Level (or first level) group titles or objects to have a boldface text appearance, once again for easy recognition. This is done using the Preferences Highlight Top-level Objects menu selection. Preferences Italicize Read-Only Cells displays all noneditable cells (such as calculated totals) in italic form.

The Data Manager information shown in figure 14.9 shows the Jacobson's purchases formed into a group using the standard DRAW Arrange Group command, Highlight Top-level Objects, and Italicize Read-Only Cells. The Jacobson's Purchases text in Row 2 was typed in as a group name. Field Options Show Totals was enabled for Purchase Price and disabled for Purchase Location and Color.

Summary

The multipage document feature of CorelDRAW! 4 is a welcome addition, and one you will probably use quite often. After you have a retinue of various document designs, you will find it much easier to edit documents than to create them from scratch. Unfortunately, the transition from your present desktop publishing system to DRAW may require some redundant work.

The Object Database Manager is a clever tool that has a multitude of uses. You are encouraged to review its capabilities and experiment with some simple applications, like those outlined in this chapter. The ability to link database information to a graphical image is becoming more important in today's computer environment, and Corel is leading the way with this interesting new version 4 feature.

Now that you have a solid understanding of the various DRAW features, move on to Chapter 15 to look at techniques for customizing DRAW to meet your specific needs.

Customizing CorelDRAW! To Fit Your Needs

The power of CorelDRAW! would be a potential curse if you constantly needed to define *all* a new object's attributes. The length of time involved in creating new objects would increase substantially, and the enjoyment derived from image creation would decrease. Fortunately, CorelDRAW! comes with a number of customization options that make the display appear more to your liking while also speeding up the drawing process. This chapter leads you through the customization characteristics that keep you from having to "reinvent the wheel" each time you work and also help you increase your drawing productivity. A section is included on templates because Corel provides several standard page layout designs, and you may want to use some of your own to leverage the time spent on prior projects.

Knowing Which Characteristics You Can Customize

CorelDRAW! enables you to customize the following characteristics:

- Display characteristics
- The location of the toolbox and roll-up windows
- The mode of screen refresh
- Object outline and fill attributes
- Secondary mouse button functions
- Certain printing functions
- Screen alignment grids

A few things apply every time you start CorelDRAW!. The page setup always appears as the last design used in your most recent CorelDRAW! session. If you last edited in Tabloid-Landscape page layout mode, for example, that page setup mode is adopted by CorelDRAW! for the next session. In addition, CorelDRAW! always starts a session in the Editable Preview mode.

To change many of the attributes, you need to modify the INI file associated with that particular application. You are encouraged to stay away from these modifications unless you are familiar with text editing and computers in general. In addition, make a copy of the initial INI file before editing it so that you can always return to the prior file if something unwanted occurs in your edited file.

Customizing Screen Characteristics

The screen display is integral to effective CorelDRAW! operation. If the display is not set up properly, you can be frustrated by small screens, insufficient area to accommodate your images, poorly aligned objects and text, and time-consuming refresh of the screen after any major change. This section deals with those screen-related options that are stored in the Preferences dialog box.

Defining Display Preferences

Choose the Preferences option from the **S**pecial menu (or pressing Ctrl+J) to display the Preferences dialog box shown in figure 15.1. You use this dialog box to set many of CorelDRAW!'s parameters, but in this section you look at only the display-related items, which are located along the bottom of the dialog box.

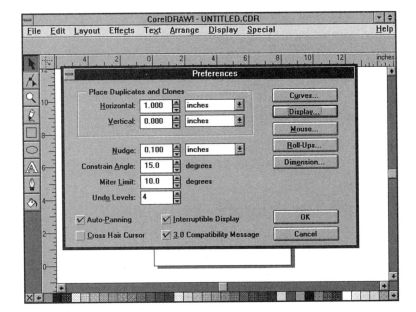

FIG. 15.1

The Preferences dialog box.

Choose Auto-Panning to instruct CorelDRAW! to move the underlying image one direction or the other, as required, while you drag with the mouse, thus enabling the cursor to stay on the image page. This feature is particularly handy when you're working in Zoom mode because the image and objects are often larger than the display area.

Choose Cross Hair Cursor to replace the standard CorelDRAW! cursor with a set of lines that extend from top to bottom and left to right across the screen. These lines are occasionally handy for alignment purposes when you begin drawing an object.

Choose Interruptible Display to instruct CorelDRAW! to stop the screen refresh when you click either mouse button or press a key. You should wait for the object before clicking because the object cannot be seen. You can still click an object, even though its refresh has not completed.

If you take no actions, the refresh starts again in a few seconds. When working in Wireframe mode, you can initiate the redraw of a specific object—one that is not part of a group—in advance of the others by first selecting the object.

The 3.0 Compatibility Message option gives you the option of either changing the type of interline spacing from version 3 to version 4, or leaving the type as 3 spacing. If you do not select the option, the type is automatically converted from 3 to 4 spacing. In general, you will not notice the difference unless more than one typeface or size is included in the text string, in which case the conversion may fail.

It is suggested that you work with Auto-Panning, Interruptible Display, and 3.0 Compatibility Message activated.

Click the **Display** button to open the Preferences-Display dialog box shown in figure 15.2. These options determine the quality of the displayed image, which has a direct effect on the screen redraw time.

FIG. 15.2

The Preferences-Display dialog box.

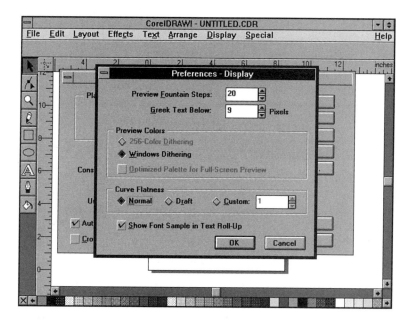

Choose Preview Fountain Steps to specify the number of steps used to display a fountain fill. This setting has no effect on the printed version of the fountain fill but affects how the fill appears on-screen.

(You access the printed fountain fill options in the Print Options dialog box.) While creating the initial drawing, you may want to set this option to a number under 15 and later change it to 20 for the final drawing stages.

Choose Greek Text Below to specify the character-size threshold, in pixels, under which text is displayed as small gray boxes rather than text. If a great deal of paragraph text is involved with an image, and you do not need to see the text itself (such as during page layout), you can set this option to a high value (such as 30 or more) so that the screen refreshes substantially faster. Any text under the specified number of pixels is drawn as gray boxes but is viewable as text if you zoom in on it with the Zoom tool. After you are in the final editing mode, set this option to a smaller number (such as 9 pixels), and view the final document. The maximum Greek value is 500.

The Preview Colors options determine the quality of color used to display the image. These settings have nothing to do with the final printed output. Windows Dithering is the only option provided for display devices that do not support 256 colors. 256-Color Dithering is automatically selected if your display does support the full 16-bit color range. The screen refreshes quicker if you set it to Windows Dithering, even if you have a 256-color display device. Optimized Palette for Full-Screen Preview instructs CorelDRAW! to make its best estimate of the ideal colors to use for a full-screen image preview. 256-Color Dithering is used if the hardware supports it.

Choose one of the Curve Flatness settings to specify how many nodes you want CorelDRAW! to use to re-create a drawn object. The Normal setting has a value of 1, and the Draft setting has a value of 10. You can set Custom anywhere in between. The higher the number, the fewer nodes CorelDRAW! uses for the objects, which means that they draw faster but track the originally drawn object less accurately. In essence, the lines become flatter, and the curves become smoother. This setting affects both the display and the printed output.

The Show Font Sample in Text Roll-Up option is in a strange place—strange because it doesn't affect any of the other options in the Preferences-Display dialog box. But here it is. Choose this option to have CorelDRAW! display, to the side of the Text roll-up window, a small fly-out window that contains a sample display of the selected typeface. By dragging the mouse across these listed typefaces, you can survey the various designs until you find the one you want. Deselecting this option removes the typeface display box from the Text roll-up window.

Establishing Grid-Related and Display Dimension Defaults

You use the grid to align objects along predefined intersecting divisions. It helps tremendously when you want to ensure a regular pattern and alignment for image objects. Detailed grid usage is covered elsewhere in the book, but the basic grid concepts are covered here.

Choose Grid Setup from the Layout menu to display the Grid Setup dialog box shown in figure 15.3. You use this dialog box to establish the grid-related defaults.

FIG. 15.3

The Grid Setup dialog box.

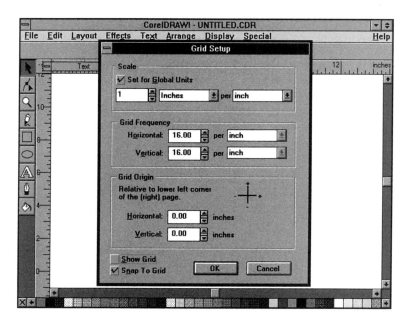

The Vertical and Horizontal Grid Frequency settings determine the number of grid lines per dimension unit in each direction. 16.00 per inch causes 16 grid lines to be inserted for every inch of image distance. The horizontal and vertical frequencies do not have to be the same number. Various dimensional units are provided.

The grid origin is always assumed as the lower-left corner of the image page. You are encouraged to leave it there unless you have a specific reason to change it and really know what you are doing. Refer to the detailed grid section for additional information and suggestions on use of the Grid Origin settings.

Show Grid and Snap To Grid determine whether a representation of the grid lines displays on-screen and whether objects snap to, or magnetically attract to, the grid lines.

> Another way to access Snap To Grid is by choosing Layout, Snap To Grid (or by pressing Ctrl+Y).

TIP

At the top of the dialog box are the dimensions used for distance measurement on the image display. You can set the values to represent a wide variety of combinations, but you must choose Set for Global Units first. Choosing Set for Global Units and then setting the left box to 1 kilometer and leaving the right box at inch, for example, means that the display dimensions appear as kilometers per inch of image distance. You use this type of setting for drawing large-scale maps. Deselect Set for Global Units to reset the display dimensions to the standard page setup units.

Modifying the Rulers and the Status Line

You can add and remove the screen rulers by choosing the Show Rulers option from the Display menu. You add and remove the status line by choosing the Show Status Line option from the Display menu. You can reset the grid origin by dragging the intersection point between the horizontal and vertical rulers to the new grid origin location.

In addition, you can relocate the ruler to another part of the page by pressing and holding Shift while dragging the ruler itself. After the ruler is where you want it, release the Shift key and the mouse button to lock the ruler into place. Double-click the ruler to return it to its normal spot.

Relocating the Toolbox

You also can relocate the toolbox from its normal position at the left side of the screen. Choose the Floating Toolbox option from the Display menu, and drag the toolbox to any location of your choice. You return it to the standard position by double-clicking the toolbox's control menu, or by once again choosing Floating Toolbox from the Display menu.

Customizing the Mouse

The right mouse button can greatly increase your drawing efficiency. You can set it to perform specific menu-related functions automatically with a simple click. This short section introduces you to the provided mouse-related options.

Using the Right Mouse Button

From the **S**pecial menu, choose Pref**e**rences and then choose **M**ouse to access the mouse setup options located in the Preferences-Mouse dialog box shown in figure 15.4. This dialog box enables you to associate various actions with a click of the right mouse button.

FIG. 15.4

The Preferences - Mouse dialog box.

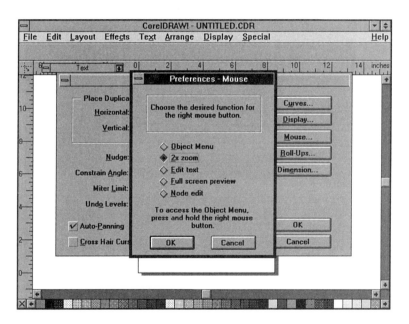

When you select the first option, Object Menu, clicking an object displays the Object Menu shown in figure 15.5 for that particular object. With this menu, you can apply a particular object style, determine whether the outline prints on top or under the interior fill, or display the Data roll-up window, which you use in conjunction with the Data Manager functions. This menu is available with all other right mouse button selections, but you must place the cursor on the object and hold the button for a longer period of time before the menu displays.

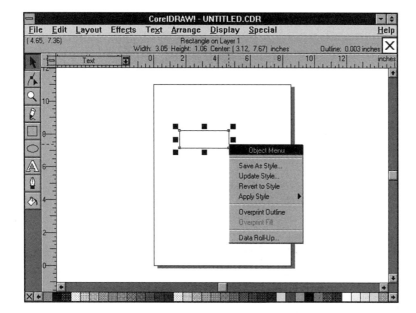

FIG. 15.5

The Object Menu.

The 2x Zoom option in the Preferences-Mouse dialog box instructs CorelDRAW! to apply a two-times zoom to the image at the click location. You can repeat this action as many times as needed.

With Edit Text selected, CorelDRAW! displays the Artistic Text dialog box shown in figure 15.6 when you select text before clicking the right mouse button.

Select Full Screen Preview if you want CorelDRAW! to display the image in Full Screen mode (F9) when you click the right mouse button. Pressing Esc returns you to the previous editing screen.

The Node Edit option is a shortcut to the Shape tool for node editing purposes. Node editing using the Shape tool is covered in detail elsewhere in the book.

FIG. 15.6

The Artistic Text dialog box.

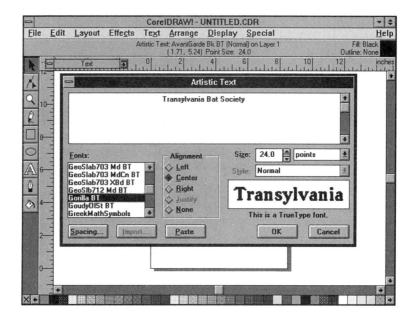

Calibrating Mouse Speeds

You set the mouse double-click speed and level of tracking sensitivity not within CorelDRAW!, but by using the Windows Main application group's Control Panel Mouse option. After you select that option, the Mouse dialog box shown in figure 15.7 appears. You should play with these settings until you find the right combination for you. If you're left-handed, you may want to try the Swap Left/Right Buttons option to be more comfortable while using the mouse.

Defining CorelDRAW!'s Appearance at Startup

You can define a set of CorelDRAW! related characteristics that define how the program appears when you start it up. These characteristics automate the standard step-by-step procedures that you might follow to set up your display in a way best suited to your needs. Finally, including CorelDRAW! in your Windows StartUp application group automatically starts CorelDRAW! whenever you start Windows.

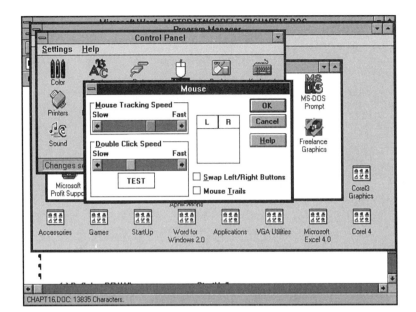

FIG. 15.7

The Mouse dialog box.

Positioning the Roll-Up Windows

You have some flexibility in how the roll-up windows display when you initially start CorelDRAW!. These selections are particularly valuable if you typically perform the same type of operations and use the same roll-up windows. You set the roll-ups in the Preferences-Roll-Ups dialog box shown in figure 15.8. To access this dialog box, open the Special menu, and choose Preferences. Then, from the Preferences dialog box, click the Roll-Ups button.

Choose No Roll-Ups to tell CorelDRAW! to close all roll-up windows whenever you exit and to make sure that all are closed whenever you start the program again. Choose All Roll-Ups Arranged to open all roll-up windows automatically and stack them, in closed form, in the upper right and left corners of the window. Choose Appearance of Roll-Ups on Exit to tell CorelDRAW! to retain the roll-up information at the time of exiting and to reestablish that roll-up configuration whenever you start the program again. Choose Current Appearance of Roll-Ups to save the roll-up windows as they currently look and to have CorelDRAW! reestablish this arrangement the next time you start the program.

FIG. 15.8

The Preferences -
Roll-Ups dialog box.

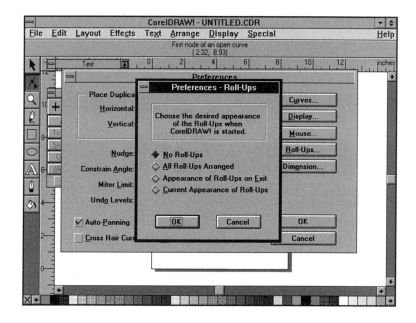

Automatically Starting CorelDRAW! Minimized

You can start CorelDRAW! automatically whenever you start Windows 3.1 by including the CorelDRAW! icon in the Windows StartUp application group. This feature is a Windows function, but you may find it useful if you start CorelDRAW! every time you use your computer. To copy the CorelDRAW! icon from the Corel application group to the StartUp group, press the Ctrl key while dragging and dropping the icon from the Corel group window into the StartUp window or over the StartUp icon.

To start the program minimized, follow these steps:

1. Open the StartUp group.

2. Select, without opening, the CorelDRAW! icon.

3. With no fly-out menu present, open the **F**ile menu and choose **Properties**.

4. Click **R**un Minimized, and then OK. The next time you start Windows, CorelDRAW! starts up automatically and runs as an icon at the bottom of the screen.

Defining Image Defaults

Setting the object and dimension line defaults early in the drawing process saves you a great deal of time and aggravation. In addition, it better ensures a consistent look to your drawings. Setting the image defaults is an easy procedure that you can accomplish by following these steps:

1. Make sure that no objects are selected. CorelDRAW! then knows that you are planning to define a default attribute.

2. Open the Pen roll-up window, set the outline default attributes, and click Apply. Because no object is selected, CorelDRAW! opens the Outline Pen dialog box shown in figure 15.9.

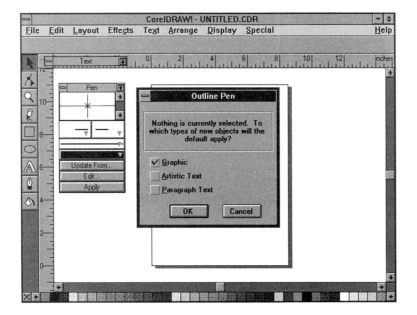

FIG. 15.9

The Outline Pen dialog box for setting defaults.

3. Select the type of objects to which you want to apply the specified outline attributes (**G**raphic, **A**rtistic Text, or **P**aragraph Text), and click OK.

You probably want different defaults for graphic objects and text because an outline appropriate for an object may make text characters illegible.

4. Repeat the procedure for each type of object.

5. Make sure that no objects are selected, and select a fill type to perform the same exact procedure, except this time for the interior fill attribute. Define the fill for graphic, artistic, and paragraph text objects.

Now watch how your new default attributes are applied to all new objects you create.

Setting Dimension Line Attributes

Dimension lines are used primarily in technical drawings, and they can save you a tremendous amount of time if you set them up properly. The following procedure is a synopsis of another section of the book that deals with them in more detail.

You set the dimension line defaults by choosing Preferences from the Special menu and then clicking the Dimension button in the Preferences dialog box to display the Preferences-Dimension dialog box. You set the location and orientation of the labels in this dialog box. Choose Horizontal Label to tell CorelDRAW! to print the label always in a horizontal direction, independent of the underlying line type. Choose Center Label to tell CorelDRAW! that you want the dimensions to appear in the center of the line segment but at a stand-off that you define when drawing the line. Click Format to define how the dimensions should be displayed. Format provides access to numerous numbering formats that you can use when creating dimension lines. After you set them, these defaults apply to all subsequently created dimension lines.

Using CorelDRAW! Templates

CorelDRAW! comes with a set of standard templates that represent a combination of page layout design and text styles. After a template is created, it can make updating a file a trivial task and greatly increase your efficiency. In addition, you may be able to start with the template, make the modifications necessary for your needs, and still greatly increase the speed of drawing creation. Finally, you can save a custom drawing as a template for later use. Why reinvent the wheel, when you can use a template instead?

You load template-related files by following these steps:

1. Choose New From Template from the File menu to display the standard directory dialog box. Notice that all files have the CDT extension and are stored in the DRAW\TEMPLATE subdirectory.

2. Scroll through the various designs with Preview selected until you reach the template design you want.

3. Click OK. CorelDRAW! loads the drawing into the editing area for your use.

Save a currently active image as a template by following these steps:

1. Choose Save As from the File menu.

2. Choose the Template (CDT) option in the List Files of Type pull-down list.

3. Select the DRAW\TEMPLATE subdirectory.

4. Give the file a name.

5. Click OK to save the file as a template.

Customizing the CORELDRW.INI File

Whenever CorelDRAW! starts, it first looks to the CORELDRW.INI file to determine the preset parameters that it should install. Many of the parameters you set while running CorelDRAW! are updated to the CORELDRW.INI file, but others you can set only by modifying the file. *You should not perform these operations unless you are sure of what you are doing and have a backup of the original file.* If you damage the data in the CORELDRW.INI file, CorelDRAW! may not run as expected, if at all.

You edit the CORELDRW.INI file with any ASCII text editor such as the Windows Notepad. At the beginning of the file is a listing of many file parameters and their settings to achieve specific results. Some of the definable parameters are enabling automatic backup and defining how often to back up, where to store backup (ABK) files, whether to back up the existing file when saving one with the same name, whether CorelDRAW! should start as a maximized window or not (MaximizeCDRAW?), and whether objects should be shown when you're moving them on-screen (ShowObjectWhenMoving?).

If you need additional information, choose Reference from the Help menu to find the most current definable commands and their parameters.

Summary

You can improve your drawing efficiency substantially when you use CorelDRAW!'s automated functions to perform routine tasks that don't require your expertise. The defaults are there for this purpose, and you are encouraged to make good use of them. If you do not learn the default characteristics, you may think that CorelDRAW! is a frustrating program with quirks. If you understand the defaults, you will find CorelDRAW! a pleasure to use and that those so-called quirks make perfect sense.

The templates were introduced in the interest of having you take advantage of your prior work, and the work of others, while creating your future drawings.

PART

V

OUTLINE

Using the Other Corel Applications

hIEROGRAPhIX ™

PRODUCTIONS

ANNACIS ISLAND   520-6663

Terry Henkel
Heirographix Productions
New Westminster, British Columbia, Canada

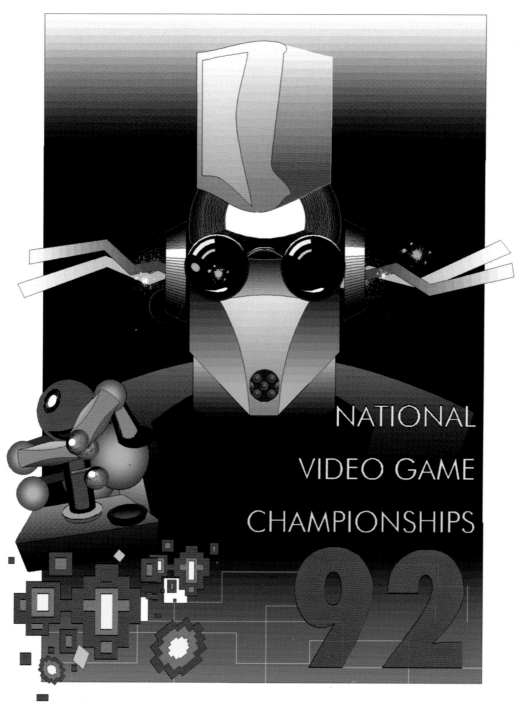

NATIONAL

VIDEO GAME

CHAMPIONSHIPS

92

10ᵗʰ–12ᵗʰ March 1992 at the London Games Centre, Covent Garden

Stephen Green
Highworth, Swindon Wiltshire, UK

MEXICANA

Steve Green 1992

Stephen Green
Highworth, Swindon Wiltshire, UK

Mike Giles
Jasper, Alabama

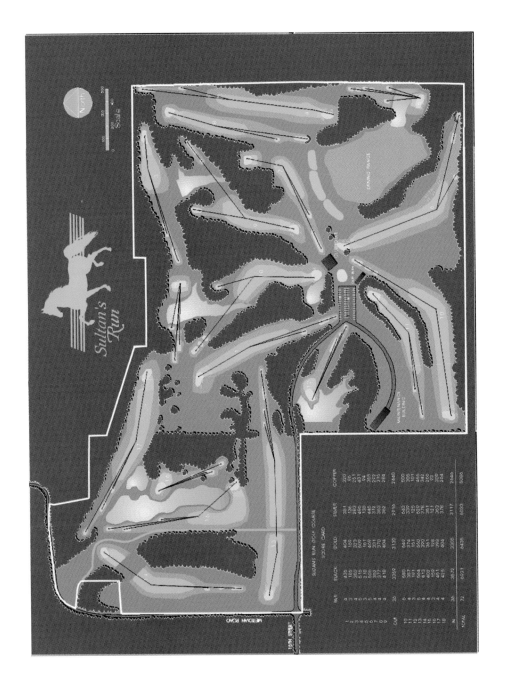

Robert Pursley
Indianapolis, Indiana

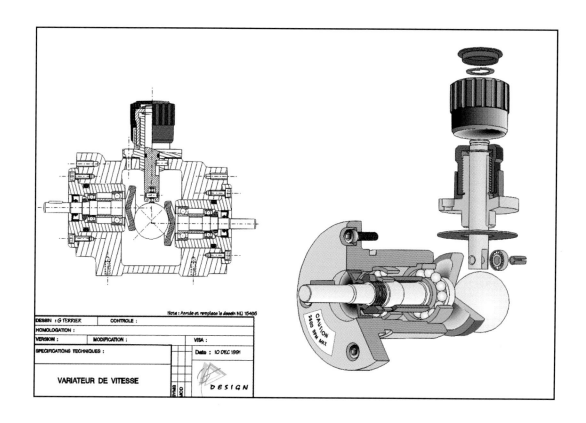

DESSIN : *G TERRIER* CONTROLE :
HOMOLOGATION :
VERSION : MODIFICATION : VISA :
SPECIFICATIONS TECHNIQUES : Date : IO DEC 1991

VARIATEUR DE VITESSE

DESIGN

Nota : Annule et remplace le dessin NO 15406

CAUTION
2400 RPM MAX.

Guy Terrier
GF Creations
Herbly, France

Glen Rashak
Woodlands, Texas

Bill Frymire
ShowMakers
Vancouver, British Columbia, Canada

PRESENTING A WORLD OF IDEAS

Bill Frymire
ShowMakers
Vancouver, British Columbia, Canada

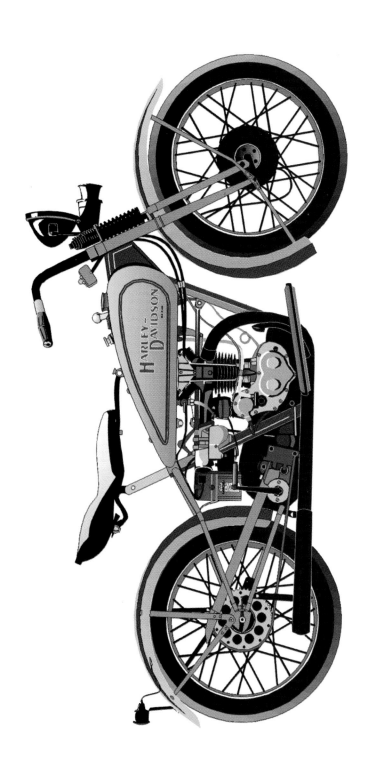

Robert Fletcher
Prolog
Monterey, California

Matti Kaarala
Helsinki, Finland

HAPPY HOLIDAYS!

William Schneider
Athens, Ohio

Mohamed Idmessaoud
Eastbourne, East Sussex, England

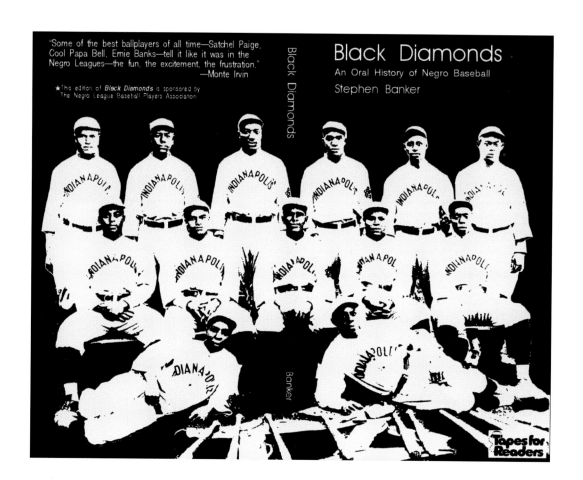

"Some of the best ballplayers of all time—Satchel Paige, Cool Papa Bell, Ernie Banks—tell it like it was in the Negro Leagues—the fun, the excitement, the frustration."
—Monte Irvin

★This edition of *Black Diamonds* is sponsored by The Negro League Baseball Players Association

Black Diamonds

Banker

Black Diamonds
An Oral History of Negro Baseball
Stephen Banker

Tapes for Readers

Stephen Banker
Tapes for Readers
Washington, D.C.

FROM BOTH SIDES

THE IMAGES CODE

HEMISPHERES

Keith Wm. Donally
Ottawa, Canada

(c.1500 – c. 1575)
Jan Sanders van Hemmessen
The Madonna and Child (detail)
Prado, Madrid

Shelley Hatt
Hull, Quebec, Canada

Photograph Touch-Up with CorelPHOTO-PAINT

Included with the CorelDRAW! package is CorelPHOTO-PAINT, a painting and photo-retouching utility that enables you to create new bitmap images with tools that emulate paint brushes, airbrushes, and drawing tools. PHOTO-PAINT also allows you to manipulate and compile bitmap images—especially photographs—which have been captured using a monochrome or color scanner. This separate software utility from CorelDRAW! works very much like other PC paint programs, but it provides a variety of sophisticated effects that those programs don't. You can use the images you create or rework in PHOTO-PAINT directly, or you can export them for use as bitmap images in CorelDRAW! documents. You can also export PHOTO-PAINT images to CorelTRACE, another utility program included in this package, to convert the bitmap image to a vector image (this topic is covered in the following chapter).

Understanding Memory Limitations

PHOTO-PAINT is a memory-intensive program; the usefulness of some of its features depends on how much random-access memory (RAM) and virtual memory your computer has at its disposal. The more memory you have, the larger the picture you can handle and the more colors you have to work with. Available memory is reduced when you display a single document multiple times or open multiple PHOTO-PAINT documents at the same time. If your available memory is low when you open a new document in PHOTO-PAINT and attempt to set its dimensions, choosing a large image may limit the number of colors available to you in the program. Start with 4M and move to 8M or more if necessary.

In the best possible scenario, you would have enough memory to support *24-bit color*, the PHOTO-PAINT setting which gives you the most options and effects (and uses all the 16.7 million colors available in the CMYK commercial printing model). Realistically, however, you might be better off choosing the 256-color mode. The average PC monitor displays only about 256 colors accurately, so you won't miss much on-screen. But if you plan to have your PHOTO-PAINT picture commercially printed in a four-color process and want to use the electronic prepress functions of PHOTO-PAINT and/or CorelDRAW!, 24-bit color gives you a great deal of control over the final printed piece because what you see on the display will match the output. (See Chapter 11 for the details of color use.)

TIP

> Because PHOTO-PAINT uses so much memory, you should quit all your other Windows applications, including CorelDRAW!, before launching it.

Basic PHOTO-PAINT Operation

You should be acquainted with several basic features before attempting any advanced editing with your drawings. You need to know how to start PHOTO-PAINT and how to open an image to edit before you can do anything else. You should also know how to save and print your images.

Starting PHOTO-PAINT

When you installed CorelDRAW!, an icon for CorelPHOTO-PAINT was also placed in your Program Manager group. To start PHOTO-PAINT from Windows, double-click this icon. The screen shown in figure 16.1 appears.

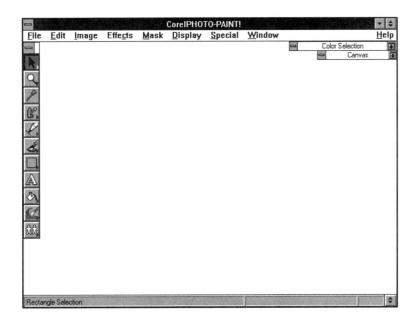

FIG. 16.1

The initial PHOTO-PAINT screen.

Notice that this screen does not contain an open file for editing or an image area in which to work. Before proceeding, you must open a new or existing file. To open a new file, follow these steps:

1. Choose **File New**. This opens the Create a New Picture dialog box shown in figure 16.2.

FIG. 16.2

The Create a New Picture dialog box.

2. Enter the desired dimensions, resolution in dpi (dots per inch), and units of measure.

3. Choose the type of image (black and white, gray scale, 256 color, or 24-bit color) by clicking one of the options in the **M**ode list.

NOTE

Remember that dimensions, resolution, and image type are limited by the amount of RAM in your computer. PHOTO-PAINT monitors the memory available and the memory required by your choices. If your choices require more memory than is currently available, you will be required to reduce some of the settings.

4. After making your choices, choose OK to create the new image area (see fig. 16.3), or choose Cancel to leave the dialog box without opening a new file. The actual appearance of your screen depends on your size and image type choices; it may look different from the one shown in the figure.

FIG. 16.3

The PHOTO-PAINT screen with a new image area.

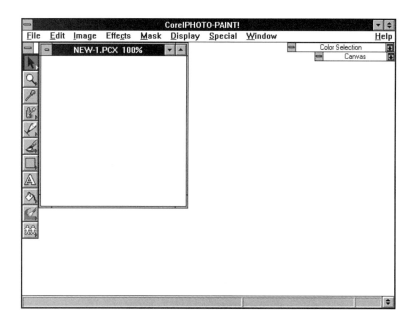

To access an existing file (one that has been previously saved), choose the Open command to access the Load a Picture from Disk dialog box. You can view on-screen bitmap representations of the available files and/or display textual information about them.

Saving an Image

Whether you are saving a scanned-in photograph, a piece of line art, or a picture created within PHOTO-PAINT, the process is the same. You can also save a selected portion of a PHOTO-PAINT picture. All images created or reworked within PHOTO-PAINT are saved as bitmap images. To save an entire PHOTO-PAINT picture, follow these steps:

1. Choose File **S**ave. If the image has been saved before, that's all you have to do. If the image has not been saved previously, the Save A Picture To Disk dialog box appears.

> If you choose **F**ile Save **A**s, the same dialog box appears.   **NOTE**

2. Choose a file type from the List Files of **T**ype box within this dialog box.

3. Specify a new drive and directory to which you want to save the file.

4. If you desire, click the backup box to tell PHOTO-PAINT to save a backup copy of the file in BM$ or EP$ format.

> This action puts another copy of your file on disk. If the file is very large, you may want to skip this option.   **CAUTION**

5. Name the new file, and then choose OK.

Printing an Image

At some point, you are going to want to print your image. The basic steps are the same no matter what type of image you are printing or what type of printer you use. To print your image, follow these steps:

1. Choose File **P**rint **P**rint. The Print dialog box appears (see fig. 16.4).

> Many of the features and options in this dialog box are the same as the ones provided in the CorelDRAW! Print dialog box. Please see Chapter 10 for a complete discussion of this dialog box.   **NOTE**

FIG. 16.4

The PHOTO-PAINT Print
dialog box.

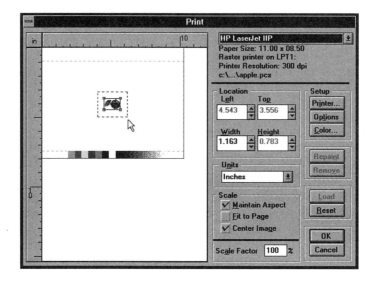

2. Choose the appropriate printer for the current print job from the drop down list at the top of the dialog box.

3. Change the location, size, and units of measurement for the image if necessary.

4. Choose Printer, Options, or Color if you need to make any changes to the printer setup, printing options, or use of color.

NOTE

Options and Color are covered in a later section of this chapter entitled "Advanced PHOTO-PAINT Operations." The Printer option is covered in Chapter 10.

5. After setting all the options the way you want them, choose OK to print.

Getting To Know the PHOTO-PAINT Screen

The PHOTO-PAINT screen is not the same as the DRAW! screen. If you have worked with other painting programs before, some of the screen elements might be familiar to you. But even if you have never worked with paint software, getting to know the PHOTO-PAINT screen only takes a few minutes. Understanding the PHOTO-PAINT screen and knowing how to navigate from one area or option to another are the keys to producing quality art and retouched photos (see fig. 16.5).

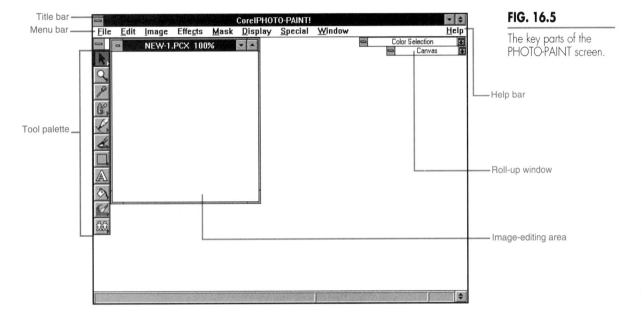

FIG. 16.5

The key parts of the PHOTO-PAINT screen.

The PHOTO-PAINT screen has many of the same features as the CorelDRAW! screen (and both screens have features similar to those provided in many other Windows-based graphics programs). These shared features include the title bar, the tool palette, the pull-down menus on the menu bar, and the roll-up windows.

NOTE

See Chapter 2 if you need to refresh your memory on the mechanics of using these parts of the screen.

The PHOTO-PAINT *image-editing area* is different from the one provided in CorelDRAW! in a few key ways. First, as covered in the previous section, no image area opens automatically when you start PHOTO-PAINT. Second, you can open more than one image area at a time and work on different images at the same time in different windows or on different parts of the same image in different windows.

The *Help bar* at the bottom of the window works like the status line in CorelDRAW!; it gives you information about the *x* (horizontal) and *y* (vertical) coordinates of the pointer position, using pixels as measurement units (these units can be changed by choosing the Special dialog box from the Preferences menu). The 0,0 position indicates the upper-left corner of the screen. The Help bar also gives you information about the currently selected tool, including its name.

For information concerning the current image, choose Image Info. The information box shown in figure 16.6 appears. This box provides you with the name of the image, its width and height, its dimensions in dpi, and its type and size. It also shows whether the image has been altered since the last save and provides the image's format and subformat (if any).

FIG. 16.6

The Image Info box.

Like CorelDRAW!, PHOTO-PAINT also uses *roll-up windows*. Choose the **D**isplay menu to see the list of available roll-up windows: Tool Box, Tool Settings, Fill Settings, Color Selection, Canvas Settings, and Tile Fill. These windows provide most of the command buttons, list boxes, and options found in regular dialog boxes, but they remain open after you choose an option.

Sizing and Rearranging Windows

CorelPHOTO-PAINT offers you some flexibility when you are choosing how you want to display information and graphics. To provide more work area on your monitor for a large picture, pull down the **D**isplay menu and choose the Ma**x**imize Work Area command. This command enables you to use the space normally reserved for the PHOTO-PAINT title bar and menu bar. In this mode, you can still access menu commands by holding down the Alt key and selecting each command's underlined letter (use Alt+F to open the File menu, for example). To return to the regular PHOTO-PAINT screen, press Ctrl+F, or click the double arrows on the right side of the Help bar.

To remove everything from your screen but the active PHOTO-PAINT picture, choose **D**isplay Full **S**creen Preview (F9). This mode, unlike the maximized work area mode just described, does not allow you to edit your image. To return to the regular PHOTO-PAINT screen, press the Esc key.

If you plan to work on more than one image at once or to work with parts of an image in several windows, you need to be able to switch between and rearrange your windows. To change your active picture, click any part of the desired image window or choose the desired window from the list offered at the bottom of the Window menu. The separate numbered items in the Window menu are the various displayed and minimized pictures and copies currently available. The active picture is indicated with a check mark.

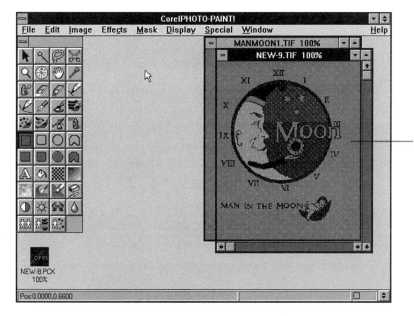

FIG. 16.7

The active picture among other PHOTO-PAINT windows.

Active window

PHOTO-PAINT can arrange image windows in three ways designed to make your work area neater and your images easier to find. To arrange your windows, simply choose **W**indow and then make your choice of the following three menu options:

Cascade. Layers the PHOTO-PAINT picture windows so that each Title bar is visible.

Tile. Arranges the PHOTO-PAINT picture windows side by side across the screen.

Arrange Icons. Arranges minimized pictures (now shown as icons) across the bottom of the PHOTO-PAINT desktop.

Magnifying and Reducing the Image View

When you are editing an image, it is often useful to be able to *zoom in* or *zoom out* so that you can see more detail or get a better view of the big picture. These techniques are particularly useful if you want to draw large shapes or to cut and paste large cutouts while viewing the entire picture on screen.

NOTE

When you open a picture, it is at 100%, even if that is larger than the display area. Zoom outs are at 25%, 33%, and 50%. PHOTO-PAINT chooses whichever one gives you the full picture.

To zoom in or out on the active picture, choose **Display Zoom**. A submenu appears offering zoom percentages from 25% to 50% (smaller than actual size; used to shrink the picture or zoom out) and from 200% to 1600% (larger than actual size; used to magnify the picture or zoom in). PHOTO-PAINT provides the 1600% setting so you can distinguish one pixel from another in your image. Each time you zoom, the title bar of the active window and the PHOTO-PAINT Help bar indicate the current zoom percentage.

TIP

You can also use Ctrl+1 to zoom out.

TIP

To get more control over the precise area that you zoom in on, choose the Zoom tool, move the cursor to the area you want to see, then click the left mouse button (to zoom in) or the right mouse button (to zoom out). The Help bar indicates what zoom percentage the buttons will provide. The cursor looks like a magnifying glass when the Zoom tool is selected. Clicking the right mouse button while you are using the Zoom tool reverses Zoom.

To show the actual size of the picture, choose **D**isplay **1**00% (No Zoom), or press Ctrl+1. You can accomplish the same result by double-clicking the Zoom tool.

To magnify or shrink the image to fit your desktop, choose **D**isplay Zoom to Fit.

To view other portions of a picture larger than the PHOTO-PAINT window, you can use the scroll bars at the side and bottom of your screen. You can also choose the Hand tool and hold down the left mouse button to drag the pointer toward the area of the image that you want to view.

Working with Duplicate Windows

You might often find it useful to work with more than one view of an object in PHOTO-PAINT. You might want to do some detailed retouching work on someone's eyes, for example, while still viewing their entire face in another window. To facilitate this sort of work, PHOTO-PAINT provides the option of using *duplicate windows*.

To copy a specified picture so that you can see changes at different magnifications, choose **W**indow **D**uplicate, or press Ctrl+D. A second window opens, showing the original image at the same magnification. The title bar of the second window indicates that it shows view 2 of the image (see fig. 16.8). You can then change the magnification, move around in the second window, or apply special effects and editing to the second image. If you don't want changes on your original image, however, use Save As to save the second image with a new name. You can open up to 20 views of the same image.

Because it would be easy to get lost in one view of a complex image and not know where that part of the image was in another view, Corel has provided the Locator tool. This tool helps you to navigate among duplicate images without getting lost.

Simply choose the Locator tool and click the area you want to work with in the window where you can see the area. All other windows with the same image then highlight that area. You can then select the window showing the view that you want to use for editing purposes.

FIG. 16.8

A duplicated window.

Original window —

Duplicated window —

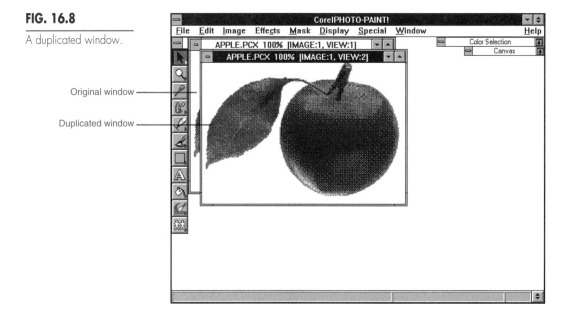

PHOTO-PAINT Tools

The CorelPHOTO-PAINT toolbox has over forty tools that perform various tasks related to drawing, painting, editing, and choosing colors and patterns. The toolbox itself can be turned on or off, and can be rearranged to display the tool icons in different ways. You have options on how to display the toolbox; click the toolbox control bar to access the toolbox layout options. Buttons with a small triangle in the corner (in the default toolbox layout) have more tools that you can view and select by holding down the mouse button as you select so that the fly-out menu for that group of tools comes up. Also, the various roll-up windows, which can be shown or hidden by going to the Display menu, control how each of these tools work to let you create different effects. Deselect Group to display all icons at once. The four-column format is a good compromise between screen space and ready icon availability.

Display tools:

Tool	Icon	Tool	Icon
Zoom		Hand	
Locator			

Selection tools:

Tool	Icon	Tool	Icon
Rectangle Selection		Lasso	
Scissors		Magic Wand	

Painting tools:

Tool	Icon	Tool	Icon
Freehand Brush		Airbrush	
Impressionism Brush		Pointillism Brush	
Spraycan		Flood Fill	
Tile Fill		Gradient Fill	
Clone		Pointillism Clone	
Impressionism Clone			

Drawing tools:

Tool	Icon	Tool	Icon
Line		Curve	
Pen		Text	
Hollow Box		Hollow Rounded Box	
Hollow Ellipse/Circle		Hollow Polygon	
Filled Box		Filled Rounded Box	
Filled Ellipse/Circle		Filled Polygon	

Retouch Tools are specific for types of paintbrushes, so the name of an icon may change (i.e., Freehand Contrast, Pointillism Contrast, etc.). These tools are in the following table:

Tool	Icon	Tool	Icon
Freehand Contrast		Freehand Brighten	
Tint		Freehand Blend	
Smear Paintbrush		Freehand Smudge	
Sharpen		Eyedropper	
Local Undo		Eraser	
Color Replacer			

Editing Images in PHOTO-PAINT

Painting and photo-retouching are done in PHOTO-PAINT by way of a combination of menu commands and tool functions. The basic editing commands—Copy, Cut, Undo, and Paste—are similar to those used in CorelDRAW! and other Windows applications. They are covered briefly here; if you need more information about these basic commands, see Chapter 3 for a complete discussion of the CorelDRAW! commands.

After covering the basic tools briefly, this section discusses the commands and tools used to edit color, transform parts of images, and touch up images in PHOTO-PAINT.

But before you can use any of these commands or tools, you need to know how to select objects in PHOTO-PAINT.

Selecting Image Areas

PHOTO-PAINT provides four basic selection tools which can be used to define the areas of an image to be included in a cutout:

> **Rectangle Selection.** Defines a rectangular or square area.

> **Lasso.** Defines irregular areas.

> **Scissors.** Defines multisided geometric areas (polygons). The shape can have three or more sides of any length, but must be an enclosed figure. The sides must be straight—no curved lines are allowed.

> **Magic Wand.** Defines areas with similar colors.

The most basic of these tools is the Rectangle Selection tool, which looks like the CorelDRAW! Pick tool. To select an image area using the Rectangle Selection tool, follow these steps:

1. Select the Rectangle Selection tool.

2. Click at one corner of the area to be defined, then hold the mouse button down while dragging to the opposite corner. Using the left mouse button gives you an opaque cutout; using the right mouse button gives you a cutout with a transparent background color.

3. When you get to the opposite corner, release the mouse button. A marquee appears around the selected area.

TIP

Hold down the Shift key during this operation to constrain the cutout to a square shape.

To select an area using the Lasso, follow these steps:

1. Click once to start defining the area to be selected, and then drag the pointer while holding down the mouse button to create any shape you want.

2. When the shape has been defined, release the cursor and the area is selected.

To select an area using the Scissors, follow these steps:

1. Click once at one of the corners or turning points of the area you want to select.

2. Click the next corner or turning point; the two points you have defined are connected with cut-out lines. Repeat this step until you have only one more turning point or corner to go.

3. Double-click the last corner and it connects to the first; the area is selected.

If you want to select an area based on color, the Magic Wand is the tool you need. Simply choose the tool and click the desired color with the Wand's point. Be warned, however, that this is a tricky tool to master. It selects all adjacent pixels of a similar color. A good idea is to use this tool only when you are zoomed in close enough to the image to see individual pixels.

To refine the color selections of the Magic Wand, you must adjust its color tolerance. Simply choose **S**pecial **C**olor Tolerance to open the Color Comparison Tolerance dialog box (see fig. 16.9).

FIG. 16.9

The Color Comparison Tolerance dialog box.

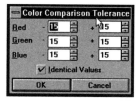

Enter or select a +/- percent color tolerance range for red, green, and blue. Click Identical Values to set all the ranges to the same values. Set the values to zero to fill, replace, or select a single, narrowly defined color. These values tell PHOTO-PAINT what color ranges to accept as red, green, and blue.

> Even the shapes of the cursors of these irregular tools are irregular. The bottom tip of the Lasso indicates its position, the top of the Scissors is the cursor point, and the furthest tip of the Wand indicates its position.

Manipulating Image Cutouts

After a portion of a PHOTO-PAINT picture has been selected using one of the means discussed previously, it becomes a *cutout*. Cutouts can be manipulated in many ways:

- To move the cutout to another location, place the mouse pointer inside its boundaries, and then click and drag it to the desired location.

- To move the cutout to another location, leaving a single copy behind, hold down the Shift key while you click and drag it.

- To move the cutout to another location, leaving a trail of copies behind, hold down the Ctrl key while you click and drag it.

- To resize the cutout horizontally and/or vertically, click and drag one of its corner handles.

- To resize the cutout proportionally in all directions, hold down the Shift key while you click and drag one of its corner handles.

- To make the cutout opaque, drag holding down the left mouse button.

- To make the cutout's background color transparent, drag holding down the right mouse button.

- To move the cutout one pixel at a time, use the arrow keys.

Of course you can also manipulate the cutout in a variety of other ways using the Edit, Image, and Effects menus.

Cutting, Copying, and Pasting Parts of an Image

PHOTO-PAINT, like CorelDRAW!, allows you to alter images by cutting, copying, and pasting parts of them. These are the most basic image editing skills; they are used frequently.

Like many other applications, PHOTO-PAINT uses a *clipboard* as a temporary storage area to hold text and graphics. From the Edit menu, use Copy to duplicate or Cut to remove the contents of the selected area and place them on the clipboard. Then use Paste to copy the contents of the clipboard into the current PHOTO-PAINT picture.

To cut or copy an image, follow these steps:

1. Select the desired portion of the image using any of the available image selection techniques and tools (Rectangle, Lasso, Scissors, or Magic Wand).

2. Choose **Edit Copy** to make a copy of the selection and leave the original in place.

   or

   Choose **Edit Cut** to cut the selection from its original place.

In either case, you have now placed the selected image area on the clipboard. If you want to paste it somewhere else, simply move the cursor to the desired location (another part of the same image, another image, or another Windows application) and choose Edit Paste. You are given two options at this point. Choose As New Selection to place the image in the upper-left corner of a picture, surrounded by the marquee. This way you can then drag the image to any area in the picture. Or choose As New Image to place the image into its own window and treat it as a new file.

If you change your mind immediately after cutting, copying, or pasting something, you can reverse your most recent editing action by choosing Edit Undo. Only one undo level is available.

TIP

Edit Undo can also be used to reverse the transformations covered in any of the following sections on editing.

To save a defined area of a PHOTO-PAINT picture, follow these steps:

1. Define the portion of the picture to be saved using one of the selection tools. A marquee appears around the selected portion.

2. Under the **Edit** menu, choose Copy to File. The Copy a Picture to Disk dialog box appears.

3. Select a file type from the List Files of Type box. If applicable, select other options from the File Sub-Format drop-down list.

4. Set the Drive and Directory to which the file should be saved.

5. Give the picture a file name.

6. If you want PHOTO-PAINT to save a backup copy of the file in either EP$ or BM$ format, check the Backup box.

7. Click OK.

Editing Image Color

To adjust the way that colors are displayed, choose Image Color. This menu offers four options, and the dialog box associated with each option provides a Preview choice which enables you to see the effect of that option on your image before actually applying it. The four options are in the following list:

Brightness and Contrast. Lightens or darkens a picture (the brightness control) and changes the distinction between light and dark areas (the contrast control). The Intensity control affects the brighter parts of the picture more than the darker parts by increasing the overall intensity level.

Threshold. Changes an image to solid colors with no gradual shadings. You specify the threshold in pixels; values lower than this threshold become white, and values higher than this threshold become solid colors of the appropriate hue.

Gamma. Enhances detail by adjusting the midtones without affecting the shadows and highlights.

Hue and Saturation. Adjusts colors without affecting brightness. Hue is the particular color (red, blue, orange); saturation is the amount of the color. You can adjust this using sliding controls or by entering values for the colors. A negative color value usually gives a grayscale image.

> **NOTE**
>
> All of these options are only available when working with 24-bit color or gray-scale images. Some effects do not apply to black-and-white or 256-color images.

You can also replace colors one at a time with another color by using the Color Replacer tool. Follow these steps:

1. Select an outline color, which is really the color you want to change.

2. Select a fill color, which is really the new color you want to use as the replacement.

3. Adjust the shape and width of the Color Replacer's tool in the Tool Settings roll-up menu.

NOTE

> If the Tool Settings roll-up window isn't open, choose **D**isplay Tool Settings Roll-Up (F8) to display it.

4. Adjust the range of colors to replace in the Special Color Tolerance dialog box.

5. Finally, drag over the areas in which you want to automatically replace the color. By holding down the Shift key, you constrain the tool to vertical or horizontal. By pressing the space bar, you can change the direction of the constraint.

Working with Detail and Sharpness

To add more definite edges to boundaries and additional detail choose Image Sharpen.

NOTE

> All of the detail and sharpness options are available only when working with 24-bit color or gray scale images. Some do not apply to black-and-white or 256-color images.

This command gives you the following options:

Sharpen. Enhances edges and brings out detail; the higher the number, the greater the sharpness. Choosing Wide Aperture enlarges the affected area.

Enhance Detail. Analyzes the values of the pixels in different directions to determine where to apply the most sharpening. Control by setting percentage with the slide control.

Unsharp Mask. (Usually more apparent in high-resolution color images.) Accentuates edge details as well as sharpening the smooth areas. This command works by blurring the contrast zones, then eliminating them from the original. You control this by setting a percentage on the slide control.

Adaptive Unsharp Mask. (Usually more apparent in high-resolution color images.) Accentuates edge detail without affecting the rest of the image.

When pixels change radically from one color or level of darkness to another, they create a harsh transition that shows up in the image. To change the appearance of the pixels in the image, choose from the following Image Smooth options:

Smooth. Tones down differences in adjacent pixels, so there is only a slight loss of overall detail.

Soften. Tones down transition harshness without losing detail.

Diffuse. Scatters the colors and makes the image fuzzier. The higher the percentage, the greater the scatter or fuzziness.

Blend. Smooths and softens colors and makes more gradual color changes in light-to-dark areas. A Wide aperture creates a smoother blend and enlarges the area to which the blending is applied. This option makes the image blend into an overall whole instead of individual pixels and areas. Many of the smoothing functions do not have a noticeable effect on the computer display unless you are in a zoom mode. The output changes, however, so experimentation is necessary.

> **NOTE**
>
> The Blend tool is related to the Freehand Blend toll located in the toolbox. This tool also performs the same function as the Image Smooth Blend command, but on a freehand basis over the area on which it is dragged.

To adjust for lighting and the light/dark of the colors in the picture choose Image Tone. You have two settings in this command:

Color/Gray Map. Adjusts for lighting inaccuracies in the picture. You can adjust your picture automatically by choosing Darken Midtones or one of the other options in the Color/Gray Map dialog box (see fig. 16.10). You can use several different styles to get the effect you want, or set the Curve command to create a style that enhances the image. You can specify changes in one color or in all the colors (you only have one color to adjust when in Grayscale mode). To return to the original response curve values, click Restore.

FIG. 16.10

The Color/Gray Map dialog box.

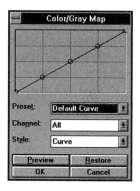

Equalize. Makes the darkest colors black and the lightest colors white, then distributes the other colors in between. If you choose this filter, a dialog box containing a histogram that represents the shades in the picture appears (see fig. 16.11). You simply drag the arrows or enter numbers to adjust the colors. You cannot, however, improve an overexposed photograph where the histogram shows most of the shades at or near full white. You can drag the lower and upper limits to define the desired shading range to include in the image.

FIG. 16.11

The Histogram Equalization dialog box.

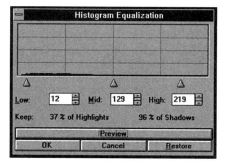

Changing Overall Photo Contrast Characteristics

Often a photograph looks less than perfect as a graphic image, so some of the most useful features of PHOTO-PAINT help you improve a medio-cre photograph. You can add contrast and change the highlights and shadows in the photograph to enhance detail or emphasize certain images. To do this to selected areas of the picture, follow these steps:

1. Select the area(s) to be changed.

2. Choose the Contrast tool.

3. Adjust the size and shape of the tool using the Tool Settings roll-up window.

4. Drag the arrow in the palette to adjust the tool's effect (the amount of contrast).

5. Finally, click and drag over the area you want to change.

If you want to adjust overall brightness, contrast, and intensity, on the other hand, go to the Image menu and select the Color Brightness and Contrast option. In the Brightness and Contrast dialog box that appears, there are controls for brightness, intensity, and contrast. The higher the number, the greater the effect. You should usually increase contrast about one tenth the amount you increase brightness. Check the effects using Preview and then click OK.

Sometimes portions of a photograph appear to have too much contrast (overexposed) or to be too dark (underexposed). To fix these conditions, follow these steps:

1. Choose Image Tone Equalize filter. This filter works on either selected areas (be sure to select the area before choosing the filter) or the entire picture.

2. In the dialog box that appears, drag the arrows at the bottom of the graph to adjust the low, mid, and high values. Shades to the left of the low arrow are black. Shades to the right of the high arrow are white. Highlights are the shades between the high and mid values, and shadows are the shades between the low and mid values.

3. Check the effects by clicking on Preview. Repeat step 2 as necessary.

4. When you are satisfied with the preview, choose OK.

If you decide to return to the original values (the default values do provide good results in most cases), choose Restore in the Equalize dialog box.

Image Transformations

The image transformations that are available in PHOTO-PAINT are similar (but not identical) to those available in CorelDRAW!. Review Chapter 13 if you are not familiar with CorelDRAW!'s image transformation features.

To transform the orientation or appearance of an entire picture (or a selected area of a picture), choose Image, Flip. The cascading menu that appears enables you to flip the image horizontally (along the side-to-side axis) or vertically (along the up-and-down axis). A vertical flip creates a mirror image of the picture; a horizontal flip creates an upside-down version of the picture.

To rotate the picture, choose Image Rotate. The cascading menu that appears enables you to rotate your image 90 degrees at a time in a clockwise or counterclockwise direction, or to rotate it 180 degrees. Choose Custom to rotate in 1-degree increments.

If you want to rotate your image manually by dragging it, choose Free Rotate. This option allows you to use the curved corner areas to rotate your image to the desired location. Freeform rotations are very similar to the rotation possible in Corel when you click a second time on an object. You can change the point of rotation exactly the same way you changed it in DRAW!, by moving the bull's-eye. A moving, dotted-line box surrounds the object, and to grab the corner arrows, you must move the image in the window. Select the arrow tool, and select an area in one of the corners of your window. When you see the corner of the dotted line appear, you can stop dragging. Place the cursor over the curved arrows and rotate the image as you wish. The screen redraw on this rotation is slow, so be patient. Also, when you use Custom at 45 degrees, it displays a new image box.

To manipulate an image by stretching it in one or more directions, choose Image Distort. The image is selected and bounded by a marquee with corner handles. Drag the corner handles in any direction to change your image into different shapes. Figure 16.12 shows the result of distorting a figure by dragging two corner handles in and leaving the other two fixed.

To create a new image of a different size (in pixels) and/or resolution, follow these steps:

1. Choose Image Resample. The Resample Image dialog box appears (see fig. 16.13).

2. Define the change by selecting the appropriate values in either the Resample By Size or Resample By Percentage box. The changes made in one box are reflected automatically in the other.

3. When the Maintain Aspect box is checked, the height-to-width ratio of the image is maintained through all changes. The height automatically changes in relation to the width and vice versa.

Deselect this box by clicking if you want to enter both values yourself.

4. To change the resolution (in dpi) for the image, change the value in the Resolution box. This procedure has an effect on your output, but does not change the on-screen image.

5. The Process box provides several tools that you can use to affect the quality of the resampled image:

> **Anti-alias** removes jagged edges, making a smoother image.
>
> **Average** blends the image together by averaging duplicated (overlapped) pixels.
>
> **Stretch** creates a jagged image by separating duplicated pixels.
>
> **Truncate** removes duplicated pixels, which creates a rougher image.

6. After making all your choices, choose OK. A new window opens and displays the resampled image (see fig. 16.14).

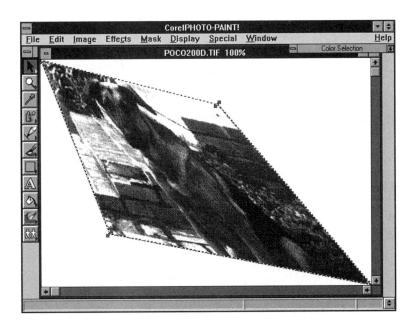

FIG. 16.12

A distorted image.

FIG. 16.13

The Resample Image
dialog box.

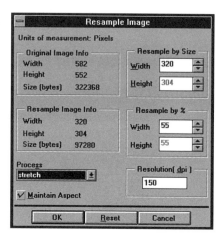

FIG. 16.14

A resample of a
PHOTO-PAINT window.

50% resample —

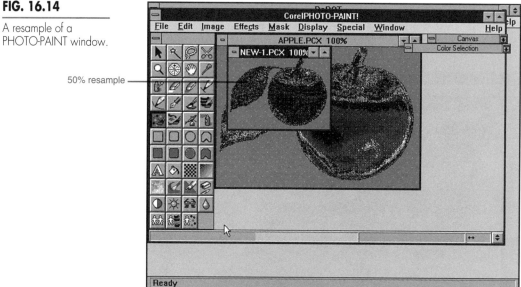

To change the resolution of the image (in dpi), choose **I**mage **R**esolution. This relates the image dimension in pixels to the image dimension in inches. This creates a new file and a separate window for the new image with the new resolution. You may not see a difference on-screen, but you will with the output and file size.

Working with Special Effects

PHOTO-PAINT comes with numerous special effects filters that can dramatically alter (and hopefully enhance) your images. To use any of these special effects on an entire image choose Effects and then the desired effect. To use the effect on only part of an image, select the appropriate area before choosing Effects and the desired effect. Some of the effects have cascading menus with multiple options. All of them are listed and described briefly in table 16.1. Click Display Screen Preview to see the results of the chosen effect. The Outline and Invert options, however, do not have a Preview button; when using these options, use Undo, Screen Preview to go to another clear full screen.

> **NOTE**
>
> All of these effects are only available when working with 24-bit color or grayscale images. Some of them do not apply to black-and-white or 256-color images.

Table 16.1 PHOTO-PAINT Effect Filters

Effect Name	Result
Artistic	Adds a brushstroke effect to a picture.
Pointillism	Adds colored dots to the picture so that the image appears to have been created with dabs of colored paint.
Impressionism	Adds colored brush strokes to the picture so that the image appears to have been created with big swathes of paint.
Edge	Affects how the boundaries of objects appear by making the edges more pronounced.
Edge Emphasis	Adds highlights along the edges of different colors and shades.
Edge Detect	Creates an outline effect by adjusting the sensitivity to edges.
Contour	Creates lines to outline the edges of a picture.
Outline	Outlines all or the selected parts of a picture.
Emboss	Creates a 3-D raised relief effect.

(continues)

Table 16.1 Continued

Effect Name	Result
Invert	Switches all colors to their opposites, like in a negative image.
Jaggie Despeckle	Scatters colors in a picture, making the image appear diffused.
Motion Blur	Creates the appearance of an image moving so fast that the picture is blurred.
Noise	Puts specks or textures across the image—the equivalent of visual *noise*.
Add Noise	Puts a granular texture on the image.
Add More Noise	Puts even more grainy texture on the image.
Remove Noise	Softens edges and reverses a grainy effect (like the unwanted noise from a bad scan).
Maximum	Lightens an image by adjusting pixel values to decrease the number of colors in an image.
Median	Removes noise from scanned pictures with a grainy texture.
Minimum	Darkens an image by adjusting pixel values to decrease the number of colors in an image.
Pixelate	Makes the block-like pixels of your image appear larger.
Posterize	Takes away the color gradations, re-creating the image as large sections of solid colors or solid grays.
Psychedelic	Creates a 1960s psychedelic look by randomly changing colors.
Solarize	Creates a negative (reversed image) of the image.

These effects cannot be adequately described with words. To see how they really work, apply them to images and consider the results. The following gallery of figures (16.15–16.18) shows images that have been treated with several of these effects.

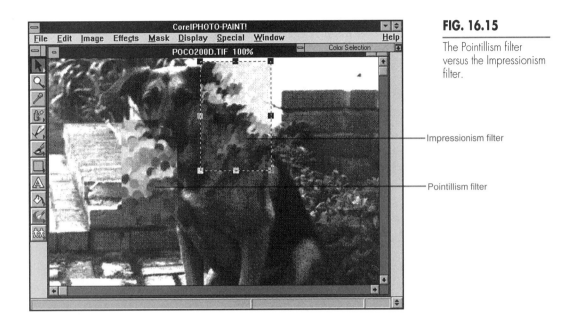

FIG. 16.15

The Pointillism filter versus the Impressionism filter.

Impressionism filter

Pointillism filter

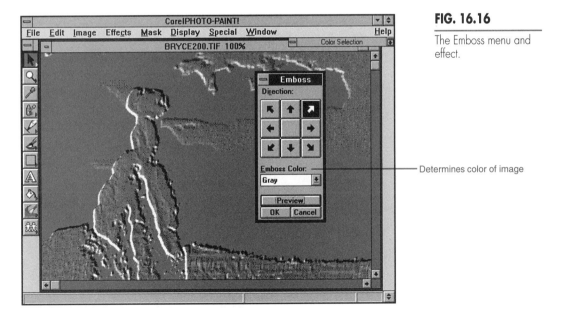

FIG. 16.16

The Emboss menu and effect.

Determines color of image

FIG. 16.17

The Motion Blur dialog box and effect.

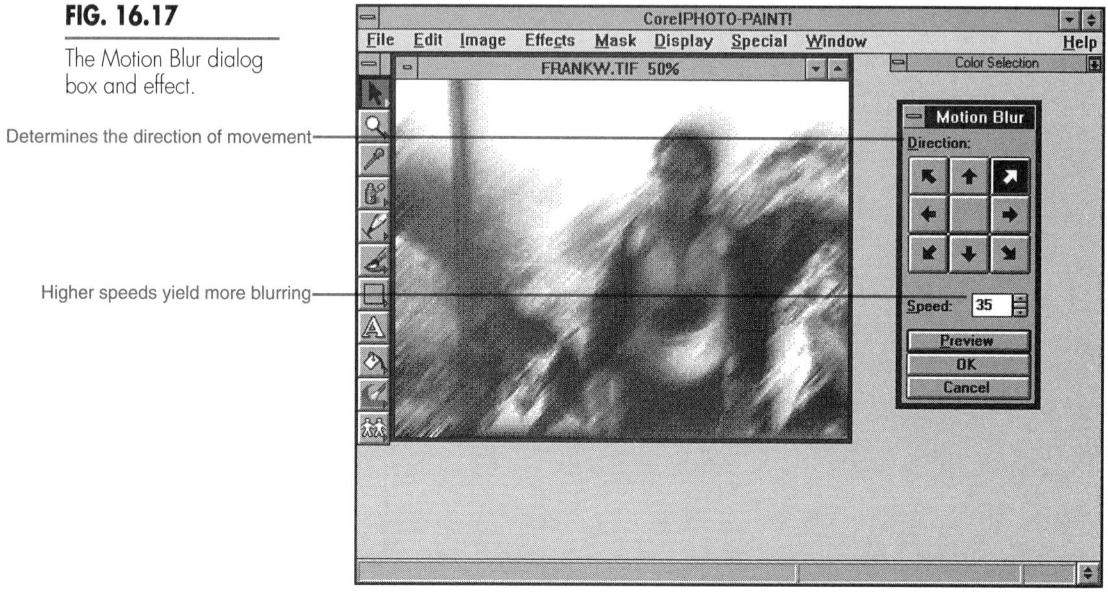

Determines the direction of movement—

Higher speeds yield more blurring—

FIG. 16.18

Adding the noise filter to an image.

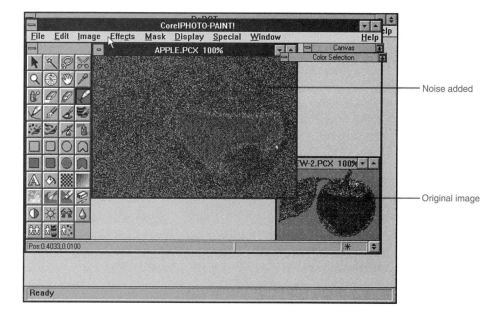

Noise added

Original image

Each of these effects employs a menu or a dialog box to determine how to transform the image. The best way to get to know them is to experiment and watch the image previews on-screen.

Using Masks with Special Effects

Sometimes you might want to *mask*, or separate, various portions of a picture from the effects of filters or tools, or from enhancements made to the masked area. Generally, you mask an area and only apply effects to it. You can do so with the Mask feature provided by PHOTO-PAINT. To mask an area, follow these steps:

1. Use any of the selection tools to select an area on the active image.

2. Choose **M**ask Cro**p** to Mask. A new window opens with the masked area selected.

3. Apply the desired effects to the masked image area.

Changing the Effects of Brushes and Tools

You can customize PHOTO-PAINT tools and brushes in numerous ways to meet your needs. Most of this customization is done using roll-up windows. To open a roll-up window, choose **D**isplay and then choose one of the four roll-up windows from the list.

> **NOTE**
>
> The Color Selection and Canvas roll-up windows are opened by default (but minimized to their title bars) when you start PHOTO-PAINT.

To change the shapes, sizes, and effects of Brushes and Tools, choose the Tool Settings roll-up window (see fig. 16.19). The options available in this window vary, depending on the tool you are working with.

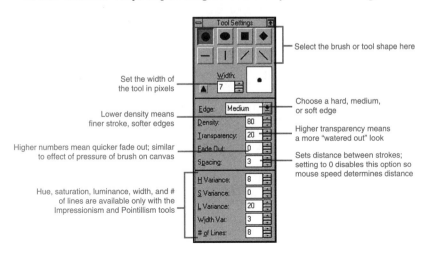

FIG. 16.19

The Tool Settings roll-up window for the Pointillism tool.

Labels in figure:

- Select the brush or tool shape here
- Set the width of the tool in pixels
- Choose a hard, medium, or soft edge
- Lower density means finer stroke, softer edges
- Higher transparency means a more "watered out" look
- Higher numbers mean quicker fade out; similar to effect of pressure of brush on canvas
- Sets distance between strokes; setting to 0 disables this option so mouse speed determines distance
- Hue, saturation, luminance, width, and # of lines are available only with the Impressionism and Pointillism tools

Tool Settings panel values:

Width: 7
Edge: Medium
Density: 80
Transparency: 20
Fade Out: 0
Spacing: 3
H Variance: 8
S Variance: 0
L Variance: 20
Width Var: 3
# of Lines: 8

To use bitmap patterns or textures as fills with the Tile Fill tool or Texture Fill tool, choose **Di**splay **F**ill Settings Roll-Up (F7). This roll-up window gives you access to all the texture and pattern fills used in CorelDRAW! (see Chapter 6); it also enables you to access almost any bitmap to create a pattern of your own.

 Here you can also set the color and gray-scale gradient fills available with the Gradient Fill tool. Again, each type of fill tool provides its own set of options. Figure 16.20 shows the Texture Fill dialog box that displays when you choose the Create Texture button in the Fill roll-up window.

FIG. 16.20

The Texture Fill dialog box.

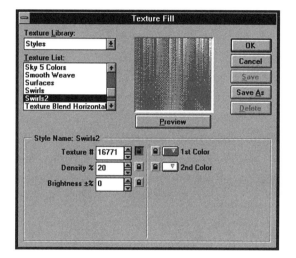

 You use the Flood Fill tool to fill enclosed areas. You choose the Fill tool, choose a color, adjust the color to differentiate it from any near matches, and click in the area where you want the color applied. If the color leaks outside the area, make sure that the border is solid and/or vary the color tolerance to create a greater differential. The left mouse button uses the active fill color, and the right mouse button uses the active outline color.

To load previously saved canvas patterns, choose **D**isplay **C**anvas Roll-Up (F6). PHOTO-PAINT gives you an error message unless canvas files are square, 8- or 24-bit color, and sized between 16 and 128 pixels (in multiples of 16) on each side. To use the canvas as your background or as an overlay on your image, click the Apply button. To view the canvas pattern, click the Load button. The Merge button only works if you are using the canvas as an overlay; it combines the canvas and the picture it overlays into one image which can then be painted because the image is now one file instead of two (see fig. 16.21). Until the picture and canvas are merged, they are treated as separate images. After they are merged, they become a single image with the characteristics of both.

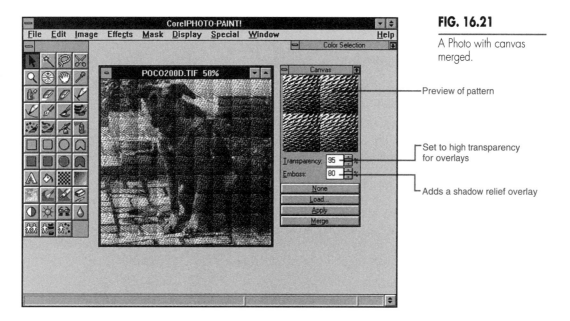

FIG. 16.21

A Photo with canvas merged.

Preview of pattern

Set to high transparency for overlays

Adds a shadow relief overlay

To select and revise your color palette, do the following:

1. Choose **D**isplay Colo**r** Selection Roll-Up (F5). The Color Selection roll-up window appears (see fig. 16.22).

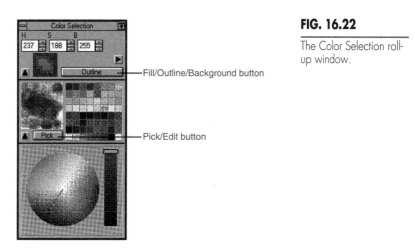

FIG. 16.22

The Color Selection roll-up window.

Fill/Outline/Background button

Pick/Edit button

2. Click the small black triangles (provided only when dealing with color images) to display the color palette choices and the palette display area.

3. Click the Fill/Outline/Background button to choose different colors for the outline, fill, and background. CorelPHOTO-PAINT uses the outline color with the painting, drawing, and text tools, but you can use the Color Replacer to fill the outline with the current fill color.

4. Click the Pick/Edit button to mix a new color by clicking and dragging existing ones. After creating a new color, you can click and drag it to the custom palette grid.

You can load and save palettes, as well as clear the paint area. You have many of the same color model choices as CorelDRAW!: RGB, CMYK, HSB, the standard palette (process colors), and a special image palette.

  The Eyedropper tool lets you pick up the color from one area of the picture and *drop* it into another area. After you select the Gradient Fill tool, the To and From buttons become active on the color roll-up window; use these to select the color range for the fill.

Scanning an Image

 One of the most useful features of CorelPHOTO-PAINT is its capability to retouch and edit photographic images with many sophisticated tools, effects, and color choices. And now you can use the File Acquire command to scan and place an image into PHOTO-PAINT in one step, rather than performing your scanning outside the program. (See Chapter 17 for further information on scanning.)

Scanning a Picture with PHOTO-PAINT

 You can still import photographs and other images into PHOTO-PAINT, but now you can also use PHOTO-PAINT's resident scanning program to capture images directly from a scanner attached to your PC. To access the scanning program, you must first make sure the driver software for your scanner is set up according to Microsoft Windows requirements. The options that appear under the File Acquire Image

Acquire dialog box (resolution, size, cropping, and so on) are deter-mined by the type of scanner and driver software you have. Some scan-ners require manual resetting of resolution or gray scale; others are controlled by software commands. Your scanner has to be supported by both Windows and Corel. Please consult your scanner documenta-tion for details.

After setting up your driver software, follow these steps to scan in a photograph or other artwork:

1. If using a flatbed scanner, place the photograph or artwork on the scanner bed. If using a hand-held scanner, have the scanner and photograph or artwork ready.

2. Choose File Acquire Image. A submenu appears.

3. Choose Select Source to specify the device (usually a Twain-compatible scanner).

4. Choose Acquire to activate the scanner attached to your PC. A scanning dialog box appears (see fig. 16.23).

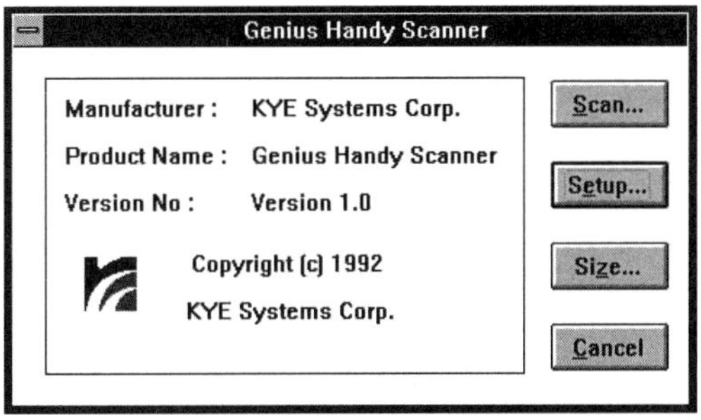

FIG. 16.23

A typical scanner dialog box.

The settings that appear in this window depend on the driver software you installed for your scanner.

5. Choose Setup, if available, to adjust resolution, gray scale, and so on (you may need to use manual controls on the scanner itself to reset these parameters). A Setup Scanner dialog box appears (see fig. 16.24).

   Make any necessary changes to the information in this dialog box (see your scanner documentation for detailed instructions), and then choose OK.

6. Click the Scan button to complete the scan of the image. The im-age appears in your PHOTO-PAINT window, ready for reworking.

FIG. 16.24

A typical scanner setup
dialog box.

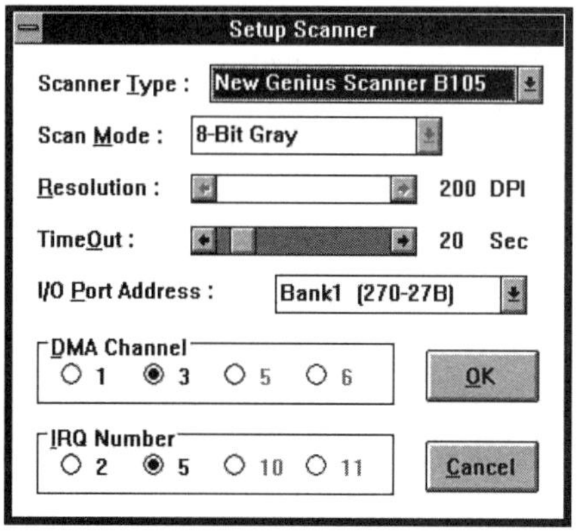

Scanned images come into CorelPHOTO-PAINT as bitmaps. Large bitmaps use a great deal of memory and disk space, so previewing them can be a very slow process. In general, the higher the resolution of the scan, the more detailed and accurate the bitmapped image and the larger the resulting file. You have to weigh the importance of having detail in your bitmap against the realities of working with large, memory-hogging files. An oversized file can cause problems with printing or importing, and after it is imported into PHOTO-PAINT, it may also be harder to edit.

After retouching the photograph in CorelPHOTO-PAINT, you may want to convert it to vector form using TRACE if you plan to use it in CorelDRAW! or another drawing or page layout program. See Chapter 17 for details on how to use TRACE to do this.

Scanning Considerations

A high-quality bitmapped image gives you better results when you are retouching photos. Though some flaws can be fixed after the image is imported, you should try to maximize image quality when scanning. A major disadvantage of bitmapped files is their size; scanning in a bitmap at a high resolution—at many dots per inch, or dpi—can create so large a file that you have difficulty importing it or reworking it. Too low a resolution, however, results in a loss of detail and an inaccurate image.

Scan black-and-white images at the highest resolution possible (while keeping the file a reasonable size) to ensure more accurate tracings. Experiment with settings to find a happy medium. Depending on the size of the bitmap, a scanner setting of 300 dpi may give you good results. Scan color and gray-scale images at 150 dpi or less because higher resolutions only increase the size of these files without giving you much improved quality.

The quality of the scanner is also a factor. Although some scanners detect only 16 levels of gray, others can pick up as many as 256 levels. In actuality, the file size of an image scanned at 256 levels of gray may be too huge to work with—up to four times the size of one scanned at 16 levels of gray. Usually 16 levels of gray or color are sufficiently detailed for any application short of commercially printing images with a four-color process using the electronic prepress tools available in PHOTO-PAINT and CorelDRAW!. If the shape of the image is more important than its colors, scan for 8 or 16 colors only.

The artwork you scan should be as clean and sharp as possible; sometimes scanner software has a *clean-up* function that can improve the quality of the image. In most cases, scanners also offer two different settings: one for black-and-white images and one for color and gray-scale images. Select the one most appropriate to the type of artwork you are scanning. When scanning black-and-white artwork, adjust the contrast or intensity controls of the scanner to get a sharper image. If fine lines in the original artwork do not appear when you scan, increase the contrast or intensity settings. These settings are also important when scanning color and gray-scale images; if the image is too dark, the tracing functions have difficulty distinguishing between shades of gray or color. (Remember that PHOTO-PAINT has a set of noise filters that enable you to clean up the image after scanning. See the "Working with Special Effects" section earlier in this chapter.)

For best results, original artwork should be no smaller in size than 4 by 5 inches and no larger than 10 by 10 inches. If the original image is smaller, enlarge it using a photocopier or the scanner's scaling feature. If you scale the image to more than 300 percent of its original size, however, the quality may suffer. Increase the scanning resolution to compensate in such cases. Make sure the artwork is positioned at right angles to the edges of the scanning bed so that straight lines scan in straight. If you are using a sheet-fed scanner, you may want to mount the artwork on a sheet of 8 1/2-by-11-inch paper.

Working with Color

CorelPHOTO-PAINT supports 24-bit color, gray-scale, and black-and-white pictures. The PHOTO-PAINT filters and retouch tools, however, work most quickly with 24-bit color or gray-scale. If you open a PHOTO-PAINT picture in gray or with fewer than the most common 256 colors, it is automatically converted into 256-color display. Even though your on-screen colors don't appear to change when you make color changes in CorelPHOTO-PAINT, the program remembers the underlying file changes. You can create and edit pictures that have more colors than your hardware supports because CorelPHOTO-PAINT simulates the enhanced colors on-screen.

TIP

To improve the way PHOTO-PAINT shows colors on-screen, choose Optimized Dithering from the Display menu. Optimized Dithering is discussed in detail in the "Advanced PHOTO-PAINT Operations" section of this chapter.

Working with Color Images

24-bit color mode is also called *true color*, because it supposedly gives you all the color choices found in nature (nearly 17 million). In CorelPHOTO-PAINT, 24-bit color has better detail and depth than the other color modes; all the retouch tools, painting tools, and filters work best in this mode. Even if your monitor doesn't display 24-bit color, PHOTO-PAINT simulates the colors on-screen and retains the original detail. The palette you see for 24-bit color contains 256 of the almost 17 million colors available.

A *256 colors* picture is made up of 256 solid colors, with a color set in the palette that defines the colors available for your picture. Use 256 Colors mode if you are creating pictures to view on-screen or if you don't have the memory to support 24-bit color. Even if your monitor doesn't support 256 colors, PHOTO-PAINT simulates all colors on-screen and retains the original detail.

No matter which of the color modes you choose, you can use the Color Selection roll-up window to adjust individual colors or to change all the colors in the palette together. The Eyedropper tool enables you to click a colored area in your picture and then change another spot in the picture to that color or recreate the color in another place.

Working with Gray-Scale Images

You can think of gray and black and white as shades of colors. Often, the output device is a monochrome printer, and working with grays is a good way to ensure output quality.

Grayscale mode is the best setting for providing tone shadings in your picture without adding the complexity of the color modes (or requiring the large amount of free RAM). A gray-scale picture is made up of 256 solid grays; any grays not supported by your monitor are simulated on-screen with the original detail retained. All the filters and tools of PHOTO-PAINT are available in Grayscale mode.

Another color choice is *Black and White* mode, which is useful for high-contrast pictures. Black and white also requires the least amount of memory. When you convert to black and white, you can choose a conversion type such as halftone or line art. Because most of PHOTO-PAINT's tools and filters are not available for Black and White mode, you might want to convert your image to another mode for editing purposes and then convert it back to black and white as a final step.

Automatically Changing Color Modes

To convert an image from one color format to another, choose the Image Convert To command. As mentioned earlier, your choices are Black and White [1-bit], Grayscale [8-bit], 256 Colors [8-bit], and True Color [24-bit]. If an application or device requires grayscale or 24-bit color images, you can convert the picture to the required format, edit it, then convert it back to the format you need.

If you convert to black and white, you have three more options from which to choose. If you don't care to have halftones, choose the Line Art setting. If you want gradations of black within a picture that has a coarser dot pattern, you can choose the Screen option for a finer dot pattern.

The converted picture is loaded into a window and named *New*; you can then save it using the Save As command from the File menu.

Painting the Photo

One of the most exciting and useful things about CorelPHOTO-PAINT is that it allows you to enhance any photograph you scan in or place as a bitmap. You can add and change colors, blend areas to simulate a motion blur, add artistic filters to transform a photograph into a painterly image, add contrast to brighten an image, or eliminate distracting images. You can skew, scale, or rotate images. You can also combine several photos or bitmap images into one compiled picture. You can rework your original photographic image in thousands of different ways.

At the most basic level, painting photographs using PHOTO-PAINT is quite simple. To paint a photograph, follow these steps:

1. Choose the tool you want to use for the job at hand.

2. Make desired adjustments using Tool Settings and menu commands to create precisely the effect you want.

3. Choose an outline color from the Color Selection roll-up window.

4. Point to the location in the image where you want to start, and paint away!

PHOTO-PAINT gives you fill tools as well as paintbrush and airbrush tools. You can use the Gradient Fill tool, for example, to create an effect where the color(s) filling an area change gradually from one shade or tint to another.

The Tile Fill tool lets you specify a tile pattern (PHOTO-PAINT gives you several to choose from) to fill an object. The Eyedropper tool makes it easy to pick up the color from one area of the picture and use it in another area. To paint an entire image with a few drags of the mouse, you can use the Cloning tools. They paint whatever portion of the image you have selected onto another area you specify, including special painting effects. You can enhance areas that are already the color you want by choosing the Airbrush tool, setting the color and the tool width/shape, then dragging over the area you want to shade. Other tool effects include smudging colors, smearing colors, and splattering colors with the Spraycan.

  You can also sharpen a fuzzy photograph or blur an in-focus photograph using the filters. The Smudge tool and Smear tool let you rework the edges of shapes pixel by pixel if you want. Use a blur effect to create motion, for instance. See the following section on filters for more details about these effects. PHOTO-PAINT also enables you to invert colors (from black to white, and from other colors to their numeric opposites) and fine-tune the color map.

Adding Shapes to the Photo

 You might want to add shapes to your picture, perhaps as background for text. CorelPHOTO-PAINT offers many of the same square, ellipse, line, and curve drawing tools provided by CorelDRAW!; the only difference is that in PHOTO-PAINT these tools create bitmap images instead of vector ones. That means you won't see any nodes or Bézier curves in

PHOTO-PAINT. Still, the process of drawing a rectangle or circle, whether hollow (no fill) or filled, is the same as it is in CorelDRAW! You simply click and drag your mouse to create the shape, using the Ctrl key to constrain it to a square. See Chapter 4 if you need to refresh your memory on these skills.

Adding Text to the Picture

CorelPHOTO-PAINT gives you very sophisticated control over the process of adding text to your pictures. You may want to add labels to images in your PHOTO-PAINT picture, or to add titles and author's names. PHOTO-PAINT gives you advanced control over the text size, font, and style; it supports all the installed Windows fonts. Text is entered in the outline color. To add text to your picture, follow these steps:

1. Click the Text tool to display the Enter Text dialog box (see fig. 16.25).

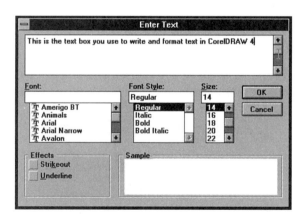

FIG. 16.25

The Enter Text dialog box.

2. Type your text in the Enter Text box. PHOTO-PAINT automatically wraps the text at the end of each line. If you want to create a line break, press Ctrl+Enter. If you want to use this dialog box to place and edit text that you have previously copied to the clipboard, press Shift+Ins.

3. After you enter all your text, click the OK button. A text frame containing your text appears on-screen.

4. Drag the handles of this text frame until the margins are set correctly. To move the entire text frame, place the pointer inside it and click and drag. If you decide you want to edit the text, press the space bar to return to the Enter Text dialog box.

5. To paste the text onto your image, click outside the text frame or choose another tool. After the text is pasted down, it becomes part of the image.

Advanced **PHOTO-PAINT** Operations

CorelPHOTO-PAINT offers many tools that serve needs beyond those of the beginning or occasional user. These advanced operations make PHOTO-PAINT the ideal application for rendering images for commercial printing. Be forewarned that this is very complicated information, treated in an overview fashion only in this chapter. For more detailed information, refer to references dedicated to printing and display design.

Various printing methods produce their own characteristic changes to the underlying images. CorelDRAW! includes the Prepress option under the File menu that helps to compensate for these characteristic changes. The Prepress Tools dialog box shown in figure 16.26 shows the available prepress options.

Fig. 16.26

The Prepress Tools dialog box.

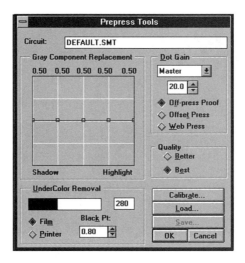

The Circuit name shown at the top indicates the compensation scheme used for this prepress situation. In general, you should find the DEFAULT.SMT compensation "circuit" adequate for most situation and output devices. If you have a custom need, you may need to define a special SMT file type for that device.

Cyan, magenta, and yellow combine to produce gray, and you control the respective combination of each using the Gray Component Replacement (GCR) chart. Dragging the tonal handles changes the values and the contribution of the component to the image gray for the shadow and highlight sections of the drawing. Experimentation is needed to find the proper combination for your situation.

Dot gain refers to the dot size used by various printing methods. Choose the output option that corresponds to your situation (web, offset, or off-press). You can select the dot gain (size) for each of the CMYK components, but this gets pretty sophisticated, and you are better served leaving the values between 18% and 24%.

Use the Quality option to test the acceptability of the output. Choosing Better shortens the time for printing the test because a looser correction is applied. Best increases the time and improves the quality, but with a considerable increase in printing time.

Undercolor Removal (UCR) removes the process colors and replaces them with Black. Choosing Film or Printer indicates which output device receives the output and compensates for the black appropriately. The Black Point option determines the level of opacity of the black printing.

Use Load and/or Save to save a custom circuit or to load it for use.

You can use Calibrate to compare the actual printer output with the colors as displayed on the computer screen. Clicking on any of the colors opens a Color dialog box in which you can set the colors.

The Edit Tone Map option is used to edit the color components of an image in either RGB or CMYK format. Choosing File Edit Tone Map opens the Tone Map dialog box shown in figure 16.27.

This dialog box allows you to set the level of red, green, or blue used in either highlights or shadows for any image. Click on the RGB buttons to set the amount of that particular color to use. The values are changed by dragging on the handles, just as with the Prepress option settings. Clicking on CMYK allows you to change their values in a similar way.

Fig. 16.27

The Tone Map dialog
box.

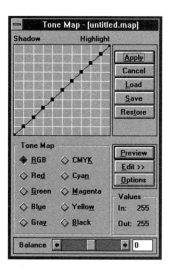

You also can use the following PHOTO-PAINT features for advanced
operations:

- **Display Optimized Dithering.** Used to improve the way the picture looks on-screen, especially if it has more colors than your
  monitor can support. The picture itself is not changed by this
  command, but CorelPHOTO-PAINT chooses the halftone pattern
  that yields the best look. But because optimizing your display
  slows down the response time of PHOTO-PAINT, you should save
  this feature for the final editing stages.

- **Split Channels To.** Used to separate the image into a different file
  in PCX format (or in BMP, TGA, or TIFF if you reset the default) for
  reworking each of the color components of its color model. The
  available color models are CMYK, RGB, HSV, HLS, and YIQ (see
  Chapter 11 for detailed coverage of these models). Choosing the
  CMYK model, for example, creates four files—one each for the
  cyan, magenta, yellow, and black inks a commercial printer would
  use to print the picture. You can then edit just one of these *channels* (or colors), or two, or all four at once. The YIQ setting creates
  separations similar to a video standard (like NTSC), with the Y
  component creating a very detailed gray-scale image.

- **Combine Channels.** Used to recombine an image that has been split, usually by way of the Split Channels command. You can also check options within this dialog box to select a different mode and reassign channels for special effects.

- **Display Calibrate.** Used to change the brightness of your on-screen display and to calibrate your monitor; enter or select a Gamma value.

Another way to affect the on-screen look of the picture is to go to change the brightness using the **Image Color Gamma** menu option. You can type a number from 1.0 to 2.0 in the Gamma text box, or use the mini-scroll bar to brighten your picture—all without changing the information on it. The higher the gamma number, the brighter your pictures. If you want to adjust your screen display, CorelPHOTO-PAINT also gives you a file called GAMMA.PCX (see fig. 16.28). Load this file; if you can see boxes inside of boxes, then your gamma value needs to be adjusted. In this case, change the gamma value and keep checking the image in Screen Preview until you see twelve solid boxes. You may not be able to adjust your gamma perfectly, but the more you can make the inside boxes disappear, the better your on-screen pictures look.

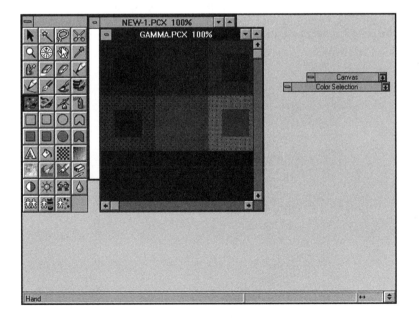

FIG. 16.28

The GAMMA.PCX File for adjusting screen display.

Summary

This chapter provided you with a basic understanding of PHOTO-PAINT, the PC painting utility program that comes with the CorelDRAW! package. Unlike the CorelDRAW! software, which creates vector-based images and illustrations, PHOTO-PAINT creates bitmap images which are essentially just arrangements of pixels. This chapter showed you how to create an illustration from scratch and how to import or scan in a photographic or other graphic images to retouch and rework. It introduced you to some of the more than 40 PC paint tools provided by PHOTO-PAINT, and discussed the ways that each can be customized. It also covered the PHOTO-PAINT commands that help you display, enhance, and control your picture and the series of roll-up windows that allow you to choose colors, tile fills, tool settings, and more.

This chapter covered the color mode choices available with PHOTO-PAINT, from 24-bit True Color to Black and White, and explained why some modes require more memory than others (but give you more color control and tool and filter options). It discussed the process of scanning from within the PHOTO-PAINT package and suggested ways for you to acquire the best image possible for your final PHOTO-PAINT picture. Finally, the chapter discussed some of the features that CorelPHOTO-PAINT provides to support the settings and parameters you need to print your picture commercially in spot color or four-color process.

Tracing Bitmap Images

CorelDRAW! helps you create sophisticated illustrations by allowing you to import images into your drawing from other sources. You can import, for example, images such as logos, architectural drawings, illustrations from paint programs, and scanned-in photographs and line art. These imported images, however, usually come in as bitmaps; they can be difficult to rework. If you convert your imported bitmap images into vector-based images (like those created in CorelDRAW!), they print smoother and faster, take up less disk space, and can be resized without distortion.

You can convert a bitmapped image to a vector-based image in one of these three ways (which range from fairly simple to very sophisticated):

■ Tracing an outline with the Pencil tool from within CorelDRAW!

■ Using the AutoTrace features of CorelDRAW!

■ Running the CorelTRACE utility program

A new feature of the CorelDRAW! package is the *Object Character Recognition (OCR)* function in CorelTRACE. This feature allows you to trace scanned text, convert it to vector form, and then edit the text using a word processing program or the text functions in CorelDRAW! or CorelPHOTO-PAINT.

Some Considerations Before Tracing

Tracing is a processor/memory-intensive operation. TRACE analyzes dot patterns and determines objects from the pattern's relationship. If the starting bitmap is very complex, then many objects will need to be created and the tracing time can be huge. If the bitmap is simple, the tracing time is reduced along with the number of objects created.

Try to capture the essence of your image when scanning and trace the bitmap so that the substance of the image is converted to vector form.

What Are the Advantages of Tracing?

You can trace imported images to turn them into vector form so that you still get high-quality resolution and sophisticated image manipulation features when working with those images in CorelDRAW!. Most non-CorelDRAW! images are created or imported as *bitmaps*, or arrangements of dots that form pictures of certain sizes.

The major drawback of bitmaps is that they have a fixed resolution. If you try to print to a high-resolution output device or to enlarge the image, fixed resolution often causes jaggedness and distortion. These problems occur because the bitmap contains no encoded information to tell how the dots are placed in relation to each other.

In comparison, each node and line in a vector-based object carries with it invisible data about its placement and connection with the other nodes and lines that make up the object. As a result, you can scale and even rotate the object without distortion because CorelDRAW! maintains a consistent relationship among all of its components. A vector-based image can still be revised and reworked even when it is placed in a page layout program or in a drawing program. Vector-based images also take up less disk space and print faster than bitmaps.

Generally, you want to trace an image to enhance and change it. When you edit bitmap images, you are limited to changing dots from black to white or vice versa (as you do in CorelPHOTO-PAINT). Tracing the bitmap image, on the other hand, enables you to rework it using the powerful editing features of CorelDRAW!. After an object is traced, it becomes an arrangement of lines and nodes that you can revise and edit using the features covered in previous chapters.

Tracing can also be used in other ways to enhance your work in CorelDRAW!. You can do initial rough sketches with pen and paper, for example, and then scan in the sketch, trace it, and develop it in CorelDRAW!. After the illustration has gone from paper to a vector-based computer image, you can also experiment more easily with outlines and fills, stretching and scaling, and other revisions.

Tracing text in the OCR mode in CorelTRACE converts it from a single bitmap image containing the text block into a set of individual vectors for each letter. This method is used in type management programs; it allows you to edit and format the resulting image as regular text. CorelTRACE can read many fonts (including artistic fonts); it also maintains to a high degree the position, style, and size of the scanned text.

Producing High-Quality Images through Scanning

A high-quality bitmapped image gives you better results when you are tracing. Though some flaws can be fixed after the image is imported, you should try to maximize image quality when scanning. A major disadvantage of bitmapped files is their size; scanning in a bitmap at a high resolution—at many dots per inch, or dpi—can create so large a file that you have difficulty importing it or tracing it. Too low a resolution, however, results in a loss of detail and an inaccurate image.

Scan black-and-white images (without gray-scale shading) at the highest resolution possible (while keeping the file a reasonable size) to ensure more accurate tracings. Experiment with settings to find a happy medium. Depending on the size of the bitmap, a scanner setting of 300 dpi may give you good results. Scan color and gray-scale images at 150 dpi or less because higher resolutions only increase the size of these files without giving you much improved quality.

The quality of the scanner is also a factor. Although some scanners detect only 16 levels of gray, others can pick up as many as 256 levels. In actuality, the file size of an image scanned at 256 levels of gray may be too huge to work with—up to four times the size of one scanned at 16 levels of gray. Although CorelTRACE does detect 256 levels of gray, scanning at 16 levels is usually sufficient for tracing.

TIP

CorelTRACE can detect a maximum of 256 colors, so never scan color images at a setting higher than this. In fact, if the shape of the image is more important than its colors, scan for 8 or 16 colors only.

The artwork you scan should be as clean and sharp as possible; sometimes scanner software has a *clean-up* function that can improve the quality of the image. In most cases, scanners also offer two different settings: one for black-and-white images and one for color and gray-scale images. Select the one most appropriate to the type of artwork you are scanning. When scanning black-and-white artwork, adjust the contrast or intensity controls of the scanner to get a sharper image. If fine lines in the original artwork do not appear when you scan, increase the contrast or intensity settings. These settings are also important when scanning color and gray-scale images; if the image is too dark, the tracing functions have difficulty distinguishing between shades of gray or color.

For best results, original artwork should be no smaller in size than 4 by 5 inches and no larger than 10 by 10 inches. If the original image is smaller, enlarge it using the scanner's scaling feature. If you scale the image to more than 300 percent of its original size, however, the quality may suffer. Increase the scanning resolution to compensate in such cases. Make sure the artwork is positioned at right angles to the edges of the scanning bed so that straight lines scan in straight. If you are using a sheet-fed scanner, you may want to mount the artwork on a sheet of 8 1/2-by-11-inch paper.

TIP

Bitmap editor programs such as CorelPHOTO-PAINT, PC Paintbrush, or Publisher's Paintbrush can correct problems such as broken or jagged lines that occur as a result of poor alignment.

You can decrease the file size of a bitmap scan by cropping any unnecessary white space around the image before tracing it. You can also scan a partial image, if your scanner supports this technique, or trace a partial area using the selection tools provided by CorelTRACE (described later in this chapter).

Working with Large Bitmap Files

Large bitmaps use a lot of memory and disk space and can be slow to preview. Tracing a large or complex bitmap can create a very large file. In general, the more detail in the bitmapped image—the more accuracy—the larger the traced file. You have to weigh the importance of having detail in your bitmap against the realities of working with large, memory-hogging files.

In CorelTRACE, resetting the various options under the Settings menu in the Modify dialog box affects both the detail and the accuracy of your tracing. These options also have an effect on the final size of the traced file. An oversized file can cause problems with printing or importing; it can also be more difficult to edit. Even the conversion process uses a fairly large amount of temporary disk space. If you do not have enough temporary disk space to accommodate tracing, CorelTRACE halts and notifies you of the problem.

CorelTRACE also uses up a great deal of memory. To cut down on conversion time and prevent computer lock-up problems, quit all other Windows applications when using CorelTRACE.

TIP

For a rough estimate of the kilobytes of RAM and temporary disk space it will take to convert an image, multiply the bitmap file size by ten.

Using Trace and AutoTrace

The Trace and AutoTrace features of CorelDRAW! were designed for simple black-and-white graphics. AutoTrace only traces images whose colors map to black, so color bitmaps give you unacceptable results. To avoid this problem, however, you can trace the object in CorelDRAW! using the Pencil tool. Or you can use AutoTrace to trace the inner and outer edges of an object and then define the fill and outline for that object. Color or gray-scale bitmaps may give you unacceptable results.

If you are working with a complex image, or a color image, you are better off using the CorelTRACE utility. CorelTRACE offers you greater speed and accuracy, and it requires less work on your part than the Trace and AutoTrace features of DRAW.

Manually Tracing an Object with the Pencil Tool

Tracing an object in CorelDRAW! is simply a matter of using the Pencil tool in either Freehand or Bézier mode to set nodes and/or draw the lines that make up the outline of the object (see fig. 17.1). This process works just like hand-tracing with a pencil and tissue paper, so it is appropriate for only the most simple objects (or when image accuracy is not very important). Remember to join the beginning and final nodes to make a closed path if you plan to fill or color the object later.

FIG. 17.1

Tracing an object by hand.

Tracing a Simple Drawing with AutoTrace

AutoTrace is a DRAW function of the Pencil tool in Bézier mode. You can scan the bitmap using CorelPHOTO-PAINT and then import it into CorelDRAW!.

To AutoTrace a simple drawing, follow these steps:

1. Choose the **Import** command from the **File** menu, and then find and select the bitmap image to be traced. The Import dialog box appears (see fig. 17.2).

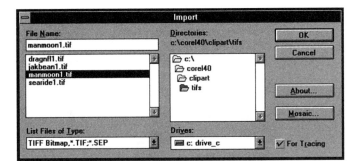

FIG. 17.2

The Import dialog box.

2. Select the For Tracing option to display the bitmap at a higher resolution so AutoTrace can be more accurate.

3. Choose OK to import the image into CorelDRAW!.

4. Use the Zoom tool to zoom in on the area to be traced—usually the outer edge of the bitmap. Then click the rectangular frame of the object that now appears to get the highlighting box for the bitmap. The word *Bitmap* appears on the status line to indicate that the bitmap has been selected.

5. Now click the Pencil tool in the Bézier mode (see fig. 17.3). This step automatically puts you in AutoTrace mode; the special AutoTrace cursor appears on-screen.

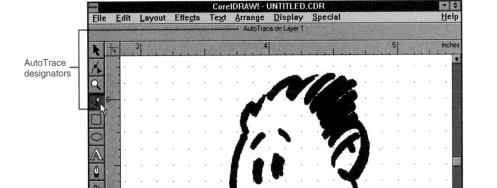

FIG. 17.3

Going to AutoTrace mode.

6. To begin the automatic tracing, click just to the left of the bitmap (see fig. 17.4). CorelDRAW! automatically finds the black bitmap image and begins to trace around it. If the bitmap has long curving lines, this may take several seconds. Nodes appear along the contour of the object created by the AutoTrace procedure.

FIG. 17.4

Click the left of the image to begin AutoTracing.

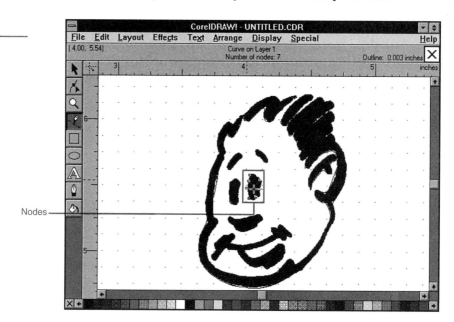

7. Trace as many regions of the bitmap as needed to define the major black-and-white areas of the image (see fig. 17.5). If you click to begin tracing and nothing happens, move your cursor slightly and click again. Usually this means there are hidden pixel clusters that do not appear at your current zoom factor. A hidden pixel cluster is a group of pixels large enough to be sensed during tracing but too small to show on the display. If problems continue, zoom in to find these hidden pixel clusters.

 To color the regions of your object after tracing, use the Pick tool to select all the curves, then choose Arrange, Combine. This procedure combines the curves into a single curved object. If you fill this object, CorelDRAW! fills in the closed paths with the selected color, leaving transparent holes between them. This process is especially helpful if you want the interior regions of your image to be transparent rather than opaque white.

 The other way to color the regions of your image is to select each of the closed paths, click the Fill tool, and choose the desired fill color.

To move quickly and easily from one part of the drawing to another, use the Arrange Order menu commands To Front, To Back, Forward One, Back One, and Reverse Order.

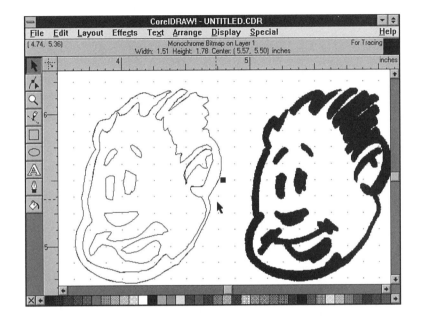

FIG. 17.5

Results after all shapes AutoTraced. The left image is the AutoTraced copy of the right image.

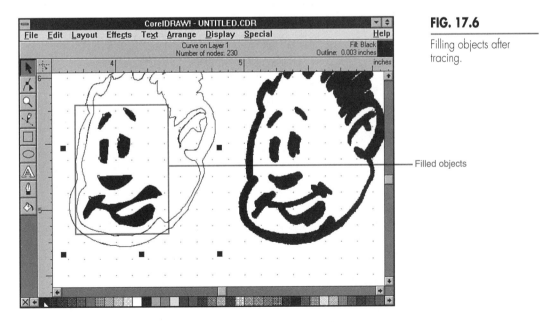

FIG. 17.6

Filling objects after tracing.

Filled objects

TIP

After you have traced a bitmap image, select the bitmap and delete it to keep your CorelDRAW! document small. If you want to keep the bitmap itself, assign it to a non-printable invisible layer in the drawing. Then select all the objects and group them using Arrange Group. This procedure keeps the components of the converted image from being dragged apart accidentally.

Customizing the AutoTrace Operation

Setting the options available under the Preferences command can make AutoTrace perform more accurately. To customize the AutoTrace operation, follow these steps:

1. Pull down the **S**pecial menu and select **P**references.

2. Click the Curves button to access the settings that affect AutoTrace. The Preferences-Curves dialog box appears (see fig. 17.7).

FIG. 17.7

The Curves dialog box for AutoTrace options.

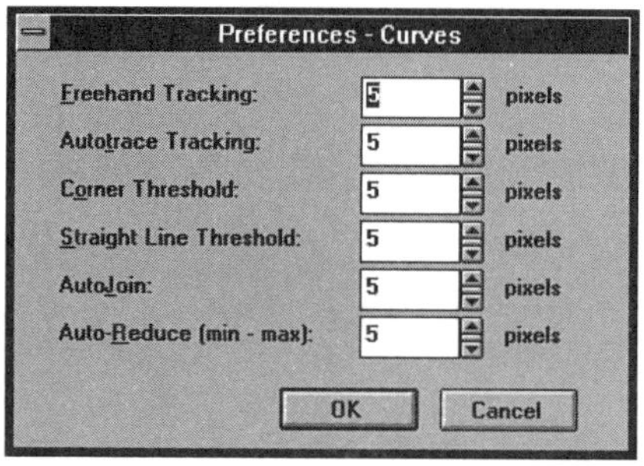

3. If desired, change the setting in the Autotrace Tracking, Corner Threshold, and Straight Line Threshold text boxes. See table 17.1 for explanations of the effects of these settings.

NOTE

The Corner Threshold and Straight Line Threshold settings apply to both AutoTrace and Freehand drawing modes.

4. Choose OK twice to return to the drawing screen.

Table 17.1 Curve Settings on AutoTrace.

Option	Low Setting	High Setting
Autotrace Tracking (see figure 17.8)	Rough curve with many nodes	Smooth curve with fewer nodes
Corner Threshold	More cusps for crisp changes in direction	Smooth corners for flowing look
Straight Line Threshold	More curves and fewer straight lines	More straight lines and fewer curves

FIG. 17.8

Autotrace Tracking at two pixels and eight pixels.

Tracing an Image with CorelTRACE

CorelTRACE provides much finer control over tracing options than hand tracing or the AutoTrace function of CorelDRAW!. In addition, CorelTRACE can trace color and grayscale images as well as mono-chrome bitmaps, and can extract words from a bitmap to convert them to editable text.

CorelTRACE is a utility program that installs automatically with CorelDRAW!. To access CorelTRACE, use the Windows Program Manager to open the COREL group window, then double-click the CorelTRACE icon.

To close the CorelTRACE window and application, choose **E**xit from the **F**ile menu.

TIP

Because CorelTRACE is memory-intensive, you should shut down your other Windows programs, including CorelDRAW!, before starting it.

Placing Images into CorelTRACE

Images in several bitmap file formats, including TIFF, TGA, BMP, and PCX, can be traced in CorelTRACE. Acceptable sources for these images include digital scanners, paint programs (such as CorelPHOTO-PAINT, PC Paintbrush, or Publisher's Paintbrush), bitmapped clip art, and screen capture programs (such as Hotshot).

TIP

HiJaak and PaintShop (shareware) are programs that convert images from a variety of formats into TIFF or PCX format.

The advantage of TIFF files is that they can be created at any resolution (whatever settings on your scanner you think best: 150 dpi, 300 dpi, and so forth) and can have any number of gray levels or colors. But TIFF files can also be very large; some scanners automatically compress monochrome TIFF images by as much as 75 percent. Because CorelTRACE expands these files to their original size before tracing them, large or complex images can take up a lot of disk space during the tracing process. You may need up to ten times the number of kilobytes in the bitmap file you are tracing. PCX is the format used by bitmap editors. PCX can also handle monochrome, gray-scale, and color images. Some scanners are limited to 16 levels of gray when saving in PCX format. Either format is usable by most graphics oriented packages, with PCX being a common favorite.

 You can import images to be traced, or you can use CorelTRACE's resident scanning program. This new option allows you to capture images for use in CorelTRACE directly from a scanner attached to your PC.

To access the scanning program, follow these steps:

1. Make sure the driver software for your scanner is configured according to Microsoft Windows requirements.

2. Choose **F**ile Acquire **I**mage.

3. Choose **S**elect Source to specify a standard image input driver (usually a Twain-compatible scanner); the Corel Image Source driver is a default, and the driver for your particular scanner should appear as an option.

or

Choose **A**cquire to control your scanner without having to leave the CorelTRACE program. A scanning dialog window like the one shown in figure 17.9 appears. The group of options (resolution, size, cropping, and so on) that appears in this window is determined by the scanner and driver software you are using. Some scanners require manual resetting of resolution or gray scale; others are controlled by software commands.

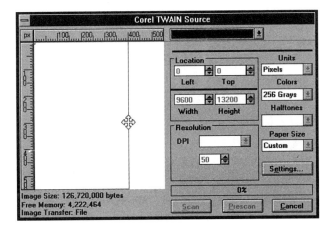

FIG. 17.9

A scanner dialog window in CorelTRACE.

4. Click one of the six different tracing method buttons, which are described in the sections that follow, to tell the scanner to complete the scan of the bitmap. The scanned image then appears in your CorelTRACE window.

Use **F**ile **O**pen to access a BMP, TIF, PCX, or TGA bitmap image for tracing. If you select more than one file, the Batch roll-up window automatically opens. The Open command brings up a dialog box with the options File Name, List Files of Type, Directories, Drives, Preview, Preview Window, and Options. Most of these options are self-explanatory.

To see a small bitmap picture of the selected file displayed in the Preview Window, click Preview. Choosing Options lets you sort by name, date, or other criteria, plus it gives you such information on the selected file as date, file size, file format, width, height, color, and depth.

Understanding the CorelTRACE Window

The CorelTRACE dialog window is basically a split screen; the left side displays the source image (to be traced) and the right side displays the new traced image. The CorelTRACE interface window also provides five pull-down menus, six icons across the top of the screen (plus Palette and Eyedropper buttons for selecting the Tracing Color), and five icons at the left side of the screen (see fig. 17.10).

 The Control menu in CorelTRACE is used the same way as it would be in any Microsoft Windows application. With it you can switch to other open applications, overlap windows, arrange icons, and so on.

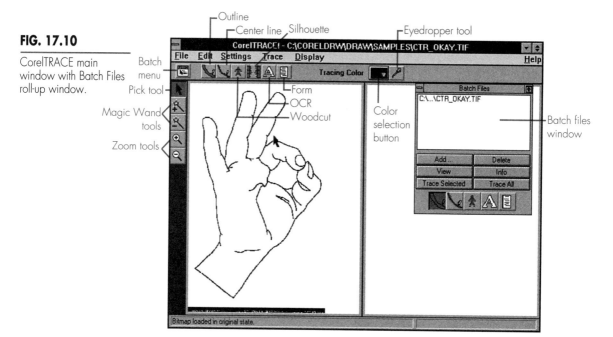

FIG. 17.10

CorelTRACE main window with Batch Files roll-up window.

The Tracing Method Icons

The Batch Menu icon (the leftmost icon below the menu bar) enables/disables the Batch Files roll-up window, which is used to trace multiple files (see the later section of this chapter called "The Batch Files Roll-Up Window" for details). The next six icons represent the six tracing methods used in CorelTRACE:

Outline. Used to trace the edge of each element or shape in the bitmap. The resulting outline can then be filled in to emulate the source image.

Centerline. Used to trace lines as lines instead of objects to fill.

Woodcut. Used to create a special effect on the traced image that emulates the lines across woodcuts; you can specify the angle of the lines.

Silhouette. Used to trace the outline of a specified area and fill it in with a single silhouette color.

OCR. Used to convert scanned text into editable format, maintaining most of the relationships between different font styles and sizes.

Form. Used to convert scanned text within a form or other ruled and lined document into editable format, keeping the boxes, rules, and so on.

The Color Selection Button

The color selection button gives you the color palette, from which you can choose a tracing color when in silhouette or woodcut mode.

The Eyedropper Tool

The Eyedropper tool lets you pick up color from the source image for use in the traced image.

The Pick Tool

The Pick tool is used to select certain areas of the source image for tracing. You can specify more than one area by holding down the Shift key while selecting.

The Magic Wand Tools

The Magic Wand tools are used to select (icon with a +) and deselect (icon with a -) areas of the source image for scanning that share a similar color. These are generally used when you want to simultaneously work with similar shades of a color.

The Zoom Tools

The Zoom tools are for magnifying (icon with a +) and minimizing (icon with a -) the display of the image.

The Batch Files Roll-Up Window

The Batch Files roll-up window allows you to select and control several files for tracing as a group, saving you time and allowing you to take care of other business (see fig. 17.11).

FIG. 17.11

The Batch Files roll-up window.

Some of the buttons and icons in this roll-up window perform the same functions as commands found elsewhere in CorelTRACE; others are unique to this menu.

The File Names box shows a list of the files you have selected. Clicking the Add button opens a dialog box that lets you open one or more files for tracing by way of an Open Files dialog box like the one provided under the File menu. To select groups of files to add, you can hold down the left mouse button and drag over several consecutive names or you can hold down the Shift key as you click file names in various locations. Ctrl-clicking allows you to select noncontiguous files.

If you choose an image file and then change your mind, simply highlight it and click the Delete button. To display a bitmap representation of a file, click the View button, then double-click any file in the File Names box. Click the Info button to see a given file's date, size, file format, width, height, color mode, resolution, and compression. This information is important if you want to export the tracing to CorelDRAW!.

To trace only one or a subset (choose multiple files using the Shift key with the mouse button) of all the files listed, click the Trace Selected button. To begin tracing all the files in the File Names box, click the Trace All button. The files chosen for batch tracing do not all have to be the same type of file. The tracing method and parameters must be the same, however, for all files traced by a single command. Five of the six tracing method icons—Outline, Centerline, Woodcut, OCR, and Form—appear at the bottom of the Batch Files roll-up window. Silhouette tracing is not available in batch mode.

The CorelTRACE Menus

The menus in CorelTRACE are different than the DRAW menus. At the far right corner of the CorelTRACE window is the On-line Help menu, which allows you to choose from a general overview, a list of commands, step-by-step instructions on different procedures under How To..., and a list of the tools and their functions. You access this menu by clicking Help in the upper-right corner of the screen or pressing F1. A Help Index gives an overview of the available topics; you can see detailed Help information on any of these topics by double-clicking it. Some topic explanations contain *hypertext entries*—underlined words or phrases— which you can click to get related information. You can also Browse the help topics or Search for a specific topic. To exit Help, click the Exit command in the File menu.

Choosing a Tracing Method

You can use the following guidelines to determine which CorelTRACE tracing method is appropriate for a job:

- To simply turn a bitmap image into a vector image, use either Centerline or Outline.

- To turn a bitmap image into a vector image with special effects applied to the traced outlines, use either Woodcut or Silhouette.

- To turn words into editable text, use either OCR or Form.

Centerline and Outline

The two basic tracing methods in CorelTRACE are Centerline and Outline (see fig. 17.12). Clicking a method's icon starts a trace of the currently active bitmap using that tracing method.

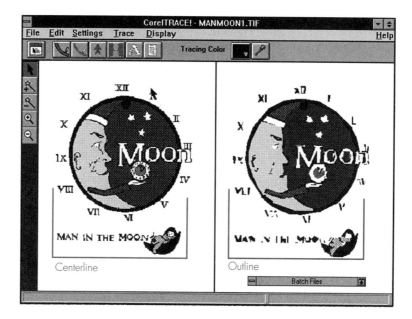

Both of these methods can be used with almost any image that contains solid areas, fine lines, or a combination of both. Centerline is the best choice for images with many thin black lines, such as technical illustrations or architectural drawings. The original bitmap image must consist of black lines on a white field.

Outline is the best choice for tracing images with many thick, filled objects, images in gray scale, color images, or images made up of white lines on a black background. The Outline method traces the edges of the elements in a bitmapped image—the equivalent of the Wireframe display—and then fills in the resulting outline. If tracing a black-and-white image, the areas that are black in the original will be black in the converted image also. If tracing color or gray-scale images, CorelTRACE decides which grays or colors are the closest match to the original.

The Centerline method treats thin bitmapped lines as objects having a certain thickness but no fill. As a result, the line itself is traced instead of its outline. Any filled objects, however, are treated using the Outline techniques.

When the Outline method is used, each element in a bitmap image is treated as a filled area. As a result, lines may appear as elongated ovals or rectangles when the vector image is exported to CorelDRAW!. The letter O, for example, becomes a black circle with a white inner circle layered on top.

Woodcut and Silhouette

To create special effects, try the Woodcut or Silhouette methods. Both of these methods add a special visual appearance to the vector version of the bitmap image that they create. The Woodcut method puts lines or *cuts* across the image at a specified angle (see fig. 17.13). You can control the appearance of these cuts, including whether they obscure or enhance the original image.

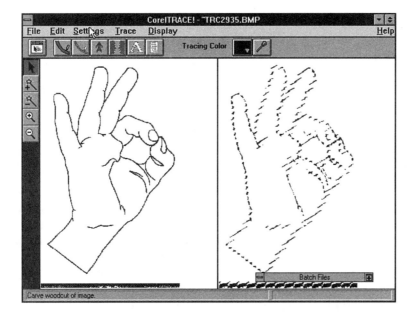

FIG. 17.13

The Woodcut special effect.

The Silhouette method drops out the interior of objects; it traces just an outline and fills it with a color that you specify using the color selection button (see fig. 17.14).

FIG. 17.14

The Silhouette special effect.

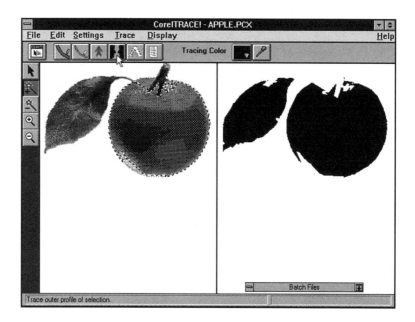

OCR and Form

To convert bitmap words to editable text, CorelTRACE now offers an Optical Character Recognition (OCR) feature. You can turn scanned text into vectors that can be manipulated as normal text. You can even re-create other graphic elements with editable text by using the Form setting. CorelTRACE scans text, then lines, and any remaining objects from a scanned form when done in the Form setting.

When using the OCR feature, you have several options from which to choose. To display these options, choose Settings Modify OCR Method. Clicking Spelling sets CorelTRACE to ignore all incorrectly spelled words—not a recommended procedure. The Source option defines the source of the original copy so that TRACE can apply special recognition features to improve accuracy: Normal is used for 300-dpi printed text such as text from a laser printer, Fax Fine is used to scan a fax and improve its readability, and the Dot-Matrix option improves the readability of dot-matrix printed text.

The Form option on the Trace menu converts a scanned bitmap of a preprinted form and changes it into text, lines, and objects so that the form can be reused or modified.

Defining the Accuracy of the Traced Image

CorelTRACE provides numerous parameters that enable you to control the results of its automated tracings. How you set these various parameters depends on the image to be traced and how you plan to use it. Which CorelTRACE settings are the best for your current tracing job? Use this four-step procedure to help you choose the settings that yield the best results in the least amount of time, but you will find the best method through trial and error:

1. Evaluate the composition. Is the image you are tracing made up of mostly lines, mostly filled shapes, or a combination of both? Are the lines thick or thin? Are the lines straight or curved? If you are scanning an image containing words, are the words the most important element and do you plan to edit the text later? Do you want only the text, or do you also want to trace some of the rules, lines, and boxes?

2. After analyzing composition, choose between Outline or Centerline tracing. Or if you want a special effect applied to the trace, choose Woodcut or Silhouette. If you are scanning text for editing later, choose between OCR and Form. Use the Form setting if you want to keep the graphic elements (lines, rules, and so on) with the text.

3. Decide how much detail you want to include in the traced image. As much as possible? Some detail, but a final image with smooth edges? Or just the general shape and features of the bitmapped image?

4. Determine how the traced image will be used. Will it be used as is, brought into a page layout program, or transferred into a drawing program for editing? Will it be used as text or as a graphic?

When you know answers to these questions, you can review the settings information provided next in this chapter to apply TRACE to your job.

Modifying Image Settings

To modify the settings in CorelTRACE, choose the **M**odify option from the **S**ettings menu. The list of settings that appears includes the following:

- Image Filtering
- Color Matching
- Line Attributes
- Centerline Method
- Woodcut Style
- OCR Method
- Batch Output

Image Filtering

CorelTRACE works best on high-resolution (300 dpi) black-and-white line art. This category includes technical illustrations, architectural drawings, and logos.

The shades of gray in a gray-scale image are converted by CorelTRACE into either black or white. This procedure may create problems; not all gray-scale images yield satisfactory results when traced. The best candidates are simple images with distinct outlines, rather than images where the object tends to blend into the background. You can improve the gray-scale tracing by using your scanner's 4-bit gray-scale scanning mode, reducing the scanner resolution to at least 150 dpi to get a smaller file, and adjusting your scanner's contrast and intensity to more sharply define the darker and lighter portions of the image.

Images made of solid color also trace well; when the colors change gradually instead of changing at clearly defined borders, tracing problems can arise. Smooth Dithering can help you avoid some of these problems. To access this setting, choose **M**odify from the **S**ettings menu, and then choose **I**mage Filtering. The Image Filtering dialog box appears (see fig. 17.15).

FIG. 17.15

The Image Filtering dialog box.

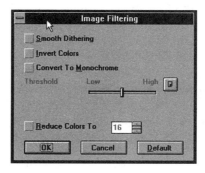

Image Filtering controls how CorelTRACE reads the source image. It provides the following setting options:

Smooth Dithering. Improves the traced image by smoothing the dithered pixels.

Invert Colors. Specifies a numeric inversion of the RGB values of the colors (reassigns each initial color value to the difference between that color value and 255). In actual color terms, this procedure turns white to black and other colors to their corresponding inverted colors.

Convert to Monochrome. Controls how colors are converted to a series of grays by letting you set values for various RGB shades.

Threshold. Activated with Convert to Monochrome; controls the darkness and lightness of the converted image. Low values tend to generate light conversions in which only the very dark colors convert to black. High values tend to generate darker conversions in which only very bright colors convert to white. Clicking the small page icon to the right of High Threshold toggles the display between the Low-High scale and Red, Green, Blue settings (RGB). You can also use the boxes provided with this setting to enter individual values for RGB—the default button specifies a RGB value of 128. These numbers are relative and vary the value at which the selected colors are recognized.

Reduce Colors To. Controls the number of colors used for the tracing. CorelTRACE examines all the colors in the image and selects the best ones to perform the reduction. With a setting of 8, for example, the image is displayed again using only eight representative colors.

Color Matching

Color Matching adjusts the Magic Wand tools and the tracing tolerance that enables CorelTRACE to distinguish objects. Use the slide control to set tolerance quickly. With low values, colors must be very close to one another to be treated as if they were the same color. With high values, many different colors fall into a limited number of color ranges. The default tolerance in CorelTRACE for the Magic Wands is plus or minus 48. Numbers lower than 48 give you a more detailed final image that takes longer to trace. You can also specify RGB values by clicking the RGB button; the RGB default value is 48.

Line Attributes

Line Attributes lets you select parameters for the Outline tracing method. It provides the following options:

Curve Precision. Controls how tightly the trace output follows the curves of the original image.

Line Precision. Controls how straight a line must be before CorelTRACE converts it to a line. CorelTRACE first attempts to convert all edges to simple uncurved linear paths. The default value captures as much detail in the source image as possible.

Target Curve Length. Limits the length of individual curves in the traced image (limits the distance between the nodes placed to emulate the bitmap curves of the source image). The default setting of Very Long is adequate for most types of images. For more detail, choose Short or Very Short. The shorter the curve length, however, the more nodes are required. Be aware that a short curve length generates a larger image file.

Sample Rate. Tells CorelTRACE how closely to match the bitmap. Medium is the default setting. Fine gives the closest match possible; Coarse averages some connecting points.

Minimum Object Size. Affects the way that CorelTRACE counts the pixels in the object outline. A higher number filters out small objects; a lower number gives greater detail.

Centerline Method

Centerline Method provides the following options:

Maximum Line Width. Defines the widest object that can be accepted for a centerline. If the ends of lines in the traced image look distorted, reduce the line width and retrace. If the curves have gaps, increase line width and retrace. If you want to trace all lines in the source image as lines instead of filled objects, set the line width to match the width of the heaviest line. If the majority of lines are wider than 20 pixels (in an image at 300 dpi), use the Outline method instead.

Create Lines of Uniform Width. Assigns a specific weight (1 to 50 pixels) to all lines in the image. The default is 4 pixels.

Horizontal and Vertical Line Recognition. Rotates the entire page to get the lines perfectly vertical and/or horizontal for better recognition. Used when the scan was slightly rotated, and you want the traced image perfectly vertical and horizontal.

Woodcut Style

Woodcut Style provides the following options:

Continuous Cut. Makes cuts with no breaks; otherwise the cuts fade in bright areas to give the illusion of highlights.

Tapered Ends. Creates a gradual narrowing effect at the end of each line.

Sample Width in Pixels. Specifies the width of each line. The lower the number, the more lines in the tracing.

Angle of Cut in Degrees. Determines the angle of the lines; a negative number creates a mirror image of the traced image.

OCR Method

OCR Method provides options enabling you to specify the source of the document and to have CorelDRAW! check the spelling of the traced text (misspelled words are not traced). OCR text can come from the following sources:

Normal. Documents with standard fonts and a resolution of 300 dpi.

Fax Fine. A standard scanned fax.

Dot Matrix. A scanned dot-matrix printout.

Batch Output

Batch Output works much like the Batch Files roll-up window discussed earlier in this chapter. The options are: Make file Read Only, Replace old versions (with new files of the same name), and Save text as *. TXT (see fig. 17.16).

FIG. 17.16

The Batch Output dialog box.

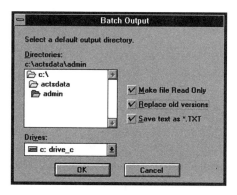

Saving the Traced Image

CorelTRACE allows you to save tracings in three different formats, depending on the type of image you are creating. All three choices are accessed by choosing Save from the File menu:

Trace As... Choose this option for a bitmap successfully traced and converted to vector form. It saves an EPS (encapsulated PostScript) file using the path and file name you specify.

Text As... Choose this option for scanned text successfully converted to an editable text file. It saves a TXT format file using the path and file name you specify.

Image As... Choose this option for an edited bitmap image that has not been scanned or converted to vector form. It saves a BMP document using the path and file name you specify.

Choose the Save Trace option to store the trace under the directory and path you specify. It saves an EPS (PostScript) file which is readable by DRAW and can be imported there and exported in whatever file format you need.

Tracing Only Part of a Bitmap

In many cases, you might want to trace only a part of a bitmap. Because bitmaps are such large files, selecting only part of the image to trace can save you time and disk space. CorelTRACE provides two ways to do so. You can use the Pick tool to draw a rectangular marquee around the area(s) you want to trace. You can select several areas at once by holding down the Shift key; all areas selected will be traced at the same time.

If you are working with unusual shapes, on the other hand, you can use the Magic Wand tools to select (or deselect) portions of the image that have the same or similar colors. The color tolerance for these selections can be set using the Color Matching option from the Modify Settings menu.

You can use the Magic Wand tools and the Silhouette setting to piece together a tracing using different colors for different shapes. This procedure enables you to approximate the source image without having to go back later and choose fill colors. To use it, follow these steps:

1. Click the + Magic Wand tool.

2. Click an area on the source (bitmap) image. A marquee appears around the area that is in the color tolerance range you set earlier (under the Modify menu).

3. Click the color selection button and choose a tracing color similar to the original bitmap color (or choose a different but appealing color, if you want to make changes).

4. Click the silhouette trace button. The tracing of the selected area appears as a solid filled shape.

5. Click the + Magic Wand tool again, and then click another area of the source image. Another marquee appears. Choose a color similar or complementary to the bitmap, and continue with the steps above.

6. After you piece together a complete image, you can save it to disk or copy it to the Clipboard and paste it into another program.

Tracing and Saving Multiple Files Simultaneously

CorelTRACE makes it easy for you to perform repetitive tasks using a few simple commands. You can trace and save multiple files at once, for example, by choosing all the bitmap files to be traced, specifying the path for the traced images, and then issuing a single command to start the tracing. CorelTRACE then scans the images consecutively, leaving you free to catch up on reading or eat dinner. CorelTRACE gives the tracings it produces the same root names as the original bitmap images, but changes each extension to EPS.

Batch Trace begins automatically with the same TRACE settings. TRACE loads the files and creates the traced images. Pressing Esc stops the batch process. To trace a complete batch of files at once, follow these steps:

1. Activate the Batch Files roll-up window by clicking its icon.

2. Take off Preview if you are using it. Click the Add button to get a list of directories and files. Double-click the names of the files that you want to trace. You can add several file formats (PCX, TGA, TIFF, BMP, and so on) to the list at the same time. After you are finished, click OK.

3. Click the Trace Selected button to trace the files in the list you have highlighted. Click the Trace All button to trace all the files listed in the roll-up window. All traced images must go to the same location.

4. To halt the entire process of tracing and saving, press the Esc button. To restart, repeat the steps beginning with step 3 above.

Using the Bitmap Header Information

A *header* is a bitmap representation of an image that is required by some programs (such as PageMaker 3.0 and Ventura 2.0) to correctly size and position the vector-based image. Without the header, you get a screened box in PageMaker. If you want to see the image on-screen and manipulate it, you need the header. After CorelTRACE finishes tracing a bitmap, it saves the vector image as an EPS file without a header. So when you look up CorelTRACE files in programs like PageMaker 3.0 or Ventura 2.0, your screen displays an X in the preview box instead of an image.

If you want to add a header to an EPS file created by CorelTRACE, follow these steps:

1. Import it into CorelDRAW!.

2. Export the image from CorelDRAW! as a PostScript file with an image header included.

3. Specify the size of the header you want to include (a dimension that affects the resolution of the bitmap only and has no impact on the quality of the printed image). See Chapter 9 for detailed information on exporting PostScript files.

To minimize the increase in document size, choose the 128 x 128 header setting (which adds only 2K or so). Size is important because some of the programs that use these image headers also have maximum importable file sizes of about 64K.

Using CorelTRACE Images with Other Applications

A traced bitmap rarely becomes the final document; the image is generally edited to its final form in CorelDRAW! or some other application. But the images created by CorelTRACE can be quite complex; at times they can lock up the program attempting to load them. Somewhat less complex images can still take several minutes to load, and may not print correctly after being loaded. To remedy these problems, experiment with the following suggestions:

1. Reduce the size of the file by tracing only a portion of the bitmap instead of the entire object. CorelTRACE reproduces fine details by creating many short line segments; some programs, like CorelDRAW!, have a maximum number of line segments and nodes that they accept in an imported document.

2. Scan the image to be traced at a lower resolution. You reduce the number of line segments and nodes this way; you also lose some of the detail of your image.

3. Choose the **I**mage Filtering option from the **S**ettings **M**odify menu and reset **R**educe Colors to 8 or less. Then choose **L**ine Attributes from the same menu, and reset **T**arget Curve Length to Very Long and/or Minimum Object Size to a higher number.

4. After the converted image is in CorelDRAW! or another vector-based drawing program, simplify it by deleting groups of nodes, breaking apart long lines, and eliminating unnecessary objects.

TIP

CorelDRAW! accepts a maximum of 3000 objects and limits the number of nodes to 1000–2000 per object, depending on your printer. You might have to trace a smaller portion of the image or adjust the parameters to lower the node and/or object count on complex bitmapped images.

Using Traced Images in CorelDRAW!

To import a CorelTRACE image into CorelDRAW!, quit CorelTRACE and launch CorelDRAW!. Choose Import from the File menu, and then click CorelTRACE as the import type. A list of EPS files appears; choose the one you want and click OK. After the image appears, you can rework it just like any object created within CorelDRAW!. If you want to make revisions, the first step is usually to Ungroup the elements. Then you can add a fill, change the outline, add or subtract nodes and line segments, or issue other desired object manipulation commands.

Using Traced Images in Other Applications

CorelTRACE is made expressly to be used with CorelDRAW!, but files created with TRACE can also be imported into other IBM PC programs. Sometimes it is best to use the graphics conversion capabilities of CorelDRAW! to put the traced image into a format acceptable to another program. Read the documentation for the source program to see what formats are needed. Printing CorelTRACE images placed into other programs usually requires a PostScript printer. If you have a non-PostScript printer, import the traced image into CorelDRAW! first and save it as a CDR file with an image header (see above) to get the traced image to print.

The OCR and Form settings turn scanned words into text that can be edited in CorelDRAW! or CorelPHOTO-PAINT using the Text tools. Text tracings made with the OCR and Form settings can also be exported as *ASCII text files* which can be opened and edited by most major word processing programs.

Conceptual Overview: Tracing a Logo

The scanning and placement of photographs or drawings rarely require tracing. If you are including a photograph of a product in a flier or brochure, for instance, the bitmap image, though large, works fine. Tracing is important, however, when converting a graphic image into a form that you want to scale, skew, and rotate without distortion. This process comes in handy, for example, when you create a new paper system—letterhead, business envelopes, business cards, pocket folders—and want to use your company's logo in many sizes and orientations. You want the logo to reproduce on your laser printer without jaggedness, and you want to be able to give your CorelDRAW! file to your commercial printer and know the logo will appear clear at any resolution. Most logos begin as black-and-white images, but maybe you can only find the already printed three-color version (green, red, and orange). How would you trace the logo?

If you only care about retaining the logo shape, the AutoTrace function in CorelDRAW! may be enough. As you remember, AutoTrace cannot see colors, so the logo will trace as an outline that you can then fill with colors from the color palette. If the logo is elaborate, delicate, or has great variations in color, use CorelTRACE and adjust the settings in the Modify menu for the best effect. If you use the Silhouette setting and the Magic Wand tools, you can even scan each of the red, green, and orange areas separately already in matching colors.

When you have your traced logo, you can place it at one-fifth the original size on your business card layouts, at six times the original size on the cover of your pocket folder, and rotated 45 degrees on your business envelopes. No matter how you treat it, you should get a crisp image with a smooth outline. Plus, each of these graphic files will be smaller than if they had the appropriately sized bitmap image included and will be easier and faster to rework in CorelDRAW!.

Summary

The capability to access and use bitmap graphics adds a great deal of versatility to any drawing program. This chapter showed you why bitmap images are more difficult to work with and explained how they can be easily converted into vector-based images. It discussed three methods of converting bitmaps to vectors, beginning with hand-tracing and ending with automated tracing using the sophisticated utility program CorelTRACE. It covered the process of scanning in images for more accurate conversion later, showing you how to get the best results from black-and-white, gray-scale, and color images. The chapter also explained the many tracing options and parameters available in CorelTRACE, and introduced you to two special effects settings—Silhouette and Woodcut. Finally, it covered the steps necessary to import CorelTRACE images to CorelDRAW! or other graphics programs.

The next chapter covers CorelCHART, an application used for creating professional-quality presentations of numerical data.

Creating Presentation Charts

CorelCHART integrates CorelDRAW!'s graphic capabilities with a versatile charting package. With its 12 basic chart styles, you can create dozens of variations to meet virtually any charting need. In addition to standard chart titles, headings, and legends, CorelCHART enables you to place text annotations anywhere on the chart to explain the data or highlight specific points. Custom graphics can be created within CHART or imported from other applications (such as CorelDRAW!) to give your charts visual interest and a personalized touch.

You can easily import data from many other applications into CHART. In addition, data created in Windows-based applications can be dynamically linked to CHART via dynamic data exchange (DDE) so that the chart is updated each time the source data changes. After a chart is created in CorelCHART, it can be exported or linked in graphic format to a number of other graphics and word processing packages including CorelSHOW.

CHART offers features that set it apart from the charting packages that come with spreadsheet, database, and word processing software.

Its capability for customizing chart presentations using graphics and text annotations, for example, represents a major advantage over other charting packages. CHART makes use of CorelDRAW!'s tools to allow you to move, size, color, and fill titles, backgrounds, and other chart elements. CHART enables you to store these basic characteristics as *templates* which can then be applied to charts you create later. This feature makes it easier for you to maintain consistency in your reports and presentations even when working with large numbers of charts. CHART's easy interface with CorelSHOW allows you to quickly produce professional presentations that integrate charts with images and text generated in other applications (such as CorelMOVE animation).

CHART does not have an integrated text editing capability, so bulleted text lists for use in CHART must be imported from another application like DRAW. In most cases, however, you will probably use CHART's tremendous flexibility to design and create your chart before transferring it to another application where it can be integrated with text lists and other images.

Understanding How CHART Works

CHART uses two windows to create a chart:

■ The *Data Manager window* contains the data which generates the chart, including chart titles and headings.

■ The *Chart View window* displays the chart and provides tools to customize the chart presentation.

Figures 18.1 and 18.2 show what a simple chart looks like in each of these windows.

Only two simple steps are required to create a chart. First, specify the type of chart that you want to create (a bar chart, pie chart, or line chart, for example). Second, you enter the data to be charted in the Data Manager window. After entering your data, you can view the resulting chart in the Chart View window.

If you want to change anything about the way the chart is presented, the Chart View window provides the tools. You can change almost any aspect of the chart presentation, including font styles and sizes, legend and title positions, colors and patterns, and many other elements. You can also add text and graphic annotations (imported or created in

CHART) to your chart. You might scan your company logo in
CorelPHOTO-PAINT, for example, and then add it to your chart.

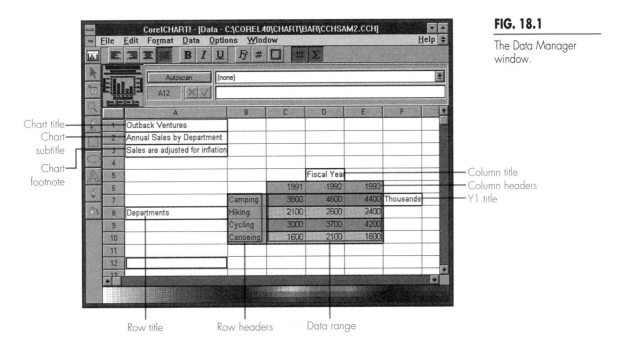

FIG. 18.1

The Data Manager window.

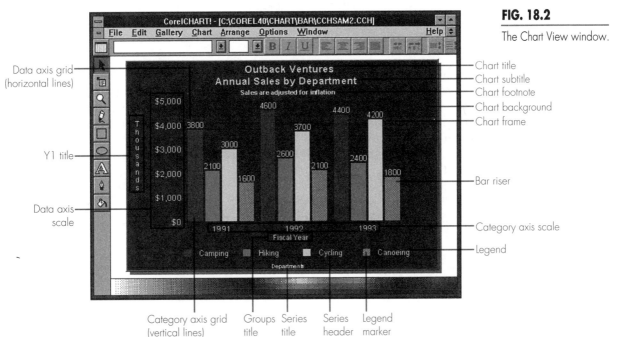

FIG. 18.2

The Chart View window.

Learning Basic CHART Concepts and Terminology

Before getting into the details of creating a chart, you should be familiar with some basic CHART terminology.

The Chart View window in figure 18.2 shows a chart with its numerous elements labeled. Charts are generally divided into several components. In this chart, the horizontal axis is the *category axis* and the vertical axis is the *data axis*. The category axis shows the different data groups that are being charted. The data axis allows you to read the value of each data point. The vertical bars which represent data points are called *risers*.

The chart also includes a *title*, a *subtitle*, a *footnote*, and *data labels*. The data classifications labeled along the category axis are called *groups*. Individual data items within each group are called *data series* and are labeled in the *legend*.

Each of the chart elements can be individually sized, placed, and colored. For the most part, these steps can be handled with simple point and click techniques. To change the color of the title, for example, click the title and then click the color you want to apply from the palette at the bottom of the screen. To move the title to a different location, click the title and drag it to the new location. See the "Modifying Chart Elements Using Chart View" section of this chapter for more details on these techniques.

All of the items shown in the sample chart came from data entered in the Data Manager worksheet. The Data Manager window in figure 18.1 shows a data worksheet with its various parts labeled. The Data Manager works much like a spreadsheet. Text, numbers, and formulas are first entered into individual cells and then are *tagged* or identified as titles, headings, data, and so on. If you use the Autoscan feature, data entered in the format shown in the figure is recognized and automatically tagged by CHART. If you need to analyze your data before charting it, CHART provides a formula editor with a full range of statistical functions. See the "Entering Data in the Data Manager" section of this chapter for the procedures to use when entering and importing data.

Starting CorelCHART

To start CorelCHART from the Program Manager window, open the Corel Application group and then double-click the CorelCHART icon. Click the **F**ile option, and the screen shown in figure 18.3 appears. Only the File and Help commands appear on the menu bar at this time; other menu items appear as needed, depending on the selections you make as you create your chart.

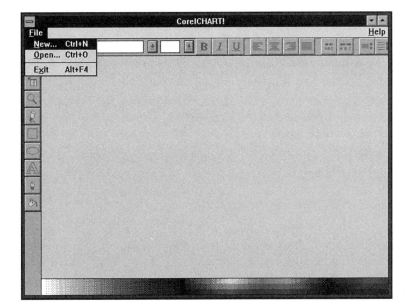

FIG. 18.3

The CorelCHART opening menu.

You can open a chart using the New or Open options from the File menu. The New option provides a series of standard templates, including sample data, to guide you through the process of creating a new chart. These materials are particularly handy when you are initially creating a chart. The Open option allows you to access an existing chart.

Creating a New Chart

To create a new chart, select the **N**ew option from the **F**ile menu. The dialog box shown in figure 18.4 appears.

FIG. 18.4

The New dialog box.

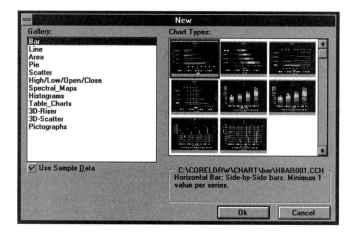

You must first specify the kind of chart that you want to create. The 12 *chart styles* supported by CHART are listed in the Gallery window on the left side of the dialog box.

Each of the basic chart styles may be modified in a number of ways. Data can be graphed horizontally rather than vertically, for example, or bars can be stacked instead of being placed side by side. These variations are called *chart types*.

To view the chart types available for a particular chart style, click the chart style in the Gallery window. Previews of each chart type appear in the Chart Types window at the right side of the dialog box. Table 18.1 summarizes the 12 chart styles and the chart types related to each style.

The file information box below the Chart Types window lists the path and file name of the selected chart as well as other basic information about the chart.

Table 18.1 Chart Styles and Types

Chart Style	Chart Types	Use
Bar Graph	Horizontal or Vertical, Stacked or Side By Side, Dual Y, Bipolar	Compare the behavior of several groups of data over time; best used for a limited number of data groups and observation points (usually not more than 4–5 of either); stacked bars show parts of the whole.

Chart Style	Chart Types	Use
Line Graph	Horizontal or Vertical, Absolute Lines or Stacked, Lines, Dual Y Absolute, Bipolar Absolute	Compare the behavior of several groups of data over time; especially good for long time periods; large numbers of data groups can be confusing on these charts.
Area Graph	Horizontal or Vertical, Absolute or Stacked, Bipolar Absolute, Bipolar Stacked	Show parts of the whole in a continuous fashion; can be more appealing visually than stacked bars.
Pie Graph	Standard or Ring Pie, Single or Multiple Pies, Percentage Pie	One of the most effective ways of showing parts of the whole; multiple pies allow comparisons over time or across different categories.
Scatter Graph	Dual Y, With or Without Data Labels	Show the correlation between two variables.
High/Low/Open /Close Graph	High/Low or High/Low /Open/Close Data, Dual Y	This is the standard stock market graph; works best for multiple data items at a single point in time or a single data item at a series of time points.
Histogram	Horizontal or Vertical	Show the individual values of each item in a data group; frequently used for reports on exam scores.
Table Chart	Colored by Row, Colored by Column or Not Colored	Show the actual data points in table form rather than a graph; good when there is a lot of disparity between sample points.
Spectral Map	No options available	Show the occurrence of an item across a geographic area; these maps are unique in that they show value using color intensities rather than numeric quantities.
Pictograph	Horizontal or Vertical, Dual Y, Bipolar	Strengthen the visual identity of data categories and increase interest in the chart; best used with a very limited number of data categories and observation points.

(continues)

Table 18.1 Continued

Chart Style	Chart Types	Use
3D-Riser	3D Riser, 3D Connected Group, 3D Connected Series or 3D Floating Bars, Ribbon, Floating Cubes or Area	Highlight the interrelationships among multiple data categories; rotating the chart with the 3D tool can create very dramatic presentations.
3D-Scatter	With or Without Tie Lines to Floor and Walls, With or Without Data Labels	Show the correlation among three variables; this is an extremely effective way of presenting these types of relationships.

To select a specific type of chart, click the preview sketch of the chart in the Chart Types window. Each chart type comes with sample data, so you can simply type your own information over the data provided by CHART. If you don't want the sample data included in your chart, click the Use Sample Data box to deselect it. But take care to match the overall data layout structure used by the CHART sample data; if you don't, you may get unpredictable results.

After you select the appropriate chart type, click OK to load the chart. If you have loaded the file with sample data, the Chart View window appears first. If you have loaded the file without sample data, the Data Manager window appears instead.

The Chart Types window shows files located in subdirectories in the CHART directory (the full path name, shown at the top of the file information box, is usually *C:\COREL40\CHART*, but it can be *C:\CORELDRW\CHART* as shown in figure 18.4 if the user defined that as the directory name during installation). Each of the 12 chart styles has its own subdirectory; another subdirectory contains sample charts which include graphic annotations and other customized features. You can customize the chart types provided by Corel or add your own chart type to this group simply by saving it in the appropriate subdirectory.

Opening an Existing Chart

To open an existing chart, choose **File Open**. The Open Chart dialog box appears (see fig. 18.5). All CHART files have a CCH extension. To list all the CHART files in a particular disk location, use the Drives and

Directories boxes to specify that location. CHART lists all files with the appropriate extension in the files window. Click a file name to view a sketch of the selected chart in the Preview box.

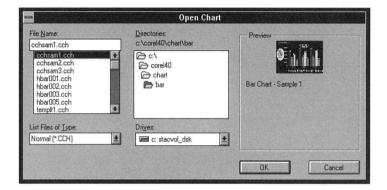

FIG. 18.5

The Open Chart dialog box.

Entering Data Using the Data Manager

The Data Manager window is used to enter data to be charted, chart titles, and labels. This information can be entered directly into the Data Manager spreadsheet, imported from another file, pasted from the Clipboard, or dynamically linked to files from other Windows-based applications. Figure 18.6 shows the Data Manager window.

TIP

If you start a new chart *without* sample data, CHART displays the Data Manager window. If you start a new chart *with* sample data, CHART displays the Chart View window. To get to the Data Manager window from the Chart View window, choose **V**iew Chart Data from the **E**dit menu, or click the View Chart Data button in the upper-left corner of the screen.

Entering Data

Entering information in the Data Manager is much like entering data in a spreadsheet. Information is entered in *cells* which are referenced by their column letter and row number (*A1*, *C6*, *F12*, and so on).

FIG. 18.6

The Data Manager
window.

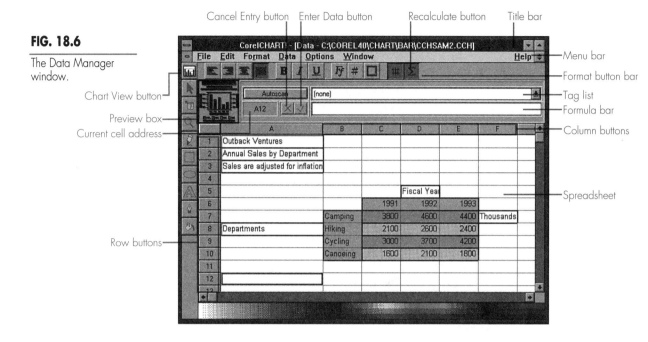

To enter information into a particular cell, follow these steps:

1. Click the cell and begin typing. As you type, the characters appear
   in the selected cell and in the Formula bar at the top of the Data
   Manager window.

2. To enter the information in the cell, press Enter, press one of the
   arrow keys, click the Enter Data button, or simply click another
   cell.

TIP

Clicking the Recalculate button (F7) causes all formulas to be updated to
reflect the most current values. If Options, Auto Recalc (Shift+F7) is activated, this button serves no purpose.

To make corrections to existing data, follow these steps:

1. Click the cell to be corrected; the contents of the cell are displayed in the Formula bar.

2. Click the text in the Formula bar at the point at which you want to
   make the change.

3. Make your corrections using the standard editing keys.

4. Press Enter.

To completely overwrite old information, simply click the cell and begin typing. The old information is replaced by the new information.

To clear the cell completely, click the cell and then press the Delete key or choose **E**dit Clear from the menu bar. The Cut and Clear dialog box appears. Click OK to clear all values and formatting from the cell.

Speeding Up Data Entry

You can substantially speed up the data input process by using CHART's data range entry feature. To do so, follow these steps:

1. Click and drag to highlight the data range.

2. Begin entering the data in the upper-left corner of the range, and press Enter after each entry.

CHART moves the cursor down the column for you until it reaches the end of the range. At the end of the column, CHART moves the cursor to the beginning of the next column. The process repeats itself until you reach the end of the selected data range.

Filling in Repetitive Data

The Edit, Fill Right, and Fill Down commands enter the same value in all cells within a highlighted range. For Fill Right or Fill Down to work, the fill value must be initially entered in the top or leftmost cell in the range. Follow these steps to fill a range with repetitive data:

1. Highlight the range including the cell with the fill value.

2. Click Fill **R**ight or Fill Dow**n**.

All cells in the range now are identical to the first cell.

Moving, Copying, and Pasting Data

You can easily move data within the Data Manager. To do so, follow these steps:

1. Highlight the desired data range.

2. Choose Cut from the Edit menu.

3. Click the cell that represents the upper-left corner of the new location for the data that was cut.

4. Choose Edit Paste.

The data is transferred from the Clipboard onto the data manager screen and all internal cell references are automatically updated.

To copy data, follow these steps:

1. Highlight the desired range of cells.

2. Choose Copy from the Edit menu to copy the cell data to the Clipboard.

3. Move the cursor to the location that corresponds to the new upper-left corner of the copied cell range.

4. Choose Paste from the Edit menu.

The data is copied to the new location; the initial data range is also left in place.

Paste Special is useful when you need to combine several existing sets of data. Sales, cost, and expense data for a number of products over a period of time might need to be combined to calculate annual total profit, for example. Instead of entering formulas to calculate the profit for each product, use Paste Special to copy all the data sets to a new location, one on top of the other, with Add selected as the operation and Paste All as the default. The values are combined by the operation selection, and the result displays as the new numbers.

Choose Paste Special from the Edit menu; the Paste Special dialog box appears (see fig. 18.7). Paste Special allows you to perform arithmetic operations on the data as it is transferred from one location in the Data Manager to another. This Paste Special operation performs a different function than within CorelDRAW!.

Manipulating Columns and Rows

To select a column or row, click the button that appears to the left of the row or above the column. The entire column or row is highlighted. Multiple columns and rows are selected by clicking and dragging across multiple buttons.

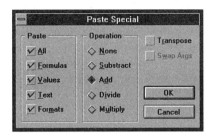

FIG. 18.7

The Paste Special dialog box.

Inserting and Deleting Columns and Rows

To insert a column or row, select the row below the desired location for the new row (or the column to the right of the desired location for the new column), and then choose **Edit Insert**. To delete a row or column, simply select the entire row or column and then choose Edit Delete.

Changing Column Widths and Row Heights

Although the column widths and row heights used in the Data Manager window do not affect the presentation of your chart, your data is much easier to work with when your column width settings match the types of data being entered.

To change the width of a column, move the cursor to the vertical line separating the header of that column from the one to its right. Notice that the cursor changes from a cross to horizontal bars with arrows. Click and drag the bar to the right until the column is wide enough to accommodate its longest data entry.

You can also change the column width by choosing Format Column **W**idth and setting the entry box to the desired value. You can change the row height following the same procedures; simply use the appropriate row selection button at the left side of the screen, or the Format Row Height menu selection.

Importing Data from Other Applications

If the data you want to chart has already been entered in another application, you can import the existing data to CHART instead of manually reentering it in the Data Manager window. You can also link your chart to the source application data so that changes to that data are automatically reflected in CHART.

CHART accepts data imported from Table (TBL), Excel (XLS), Lotus (WK1 or WKS), MS Works (WKS), and Comma Separated Values (CSV) files.

The imported data must be arranged in a specific fashion in order for CHART to make use of it efficiently. If the format of incoming data is not consistent with the standard CHART format, you may get unexpected results. See the "Automatic Tagging" section later in this chapter for tips on organizing your data once it arrives in CHART.

To import a data file, follow these steps:

1. From the Data Manager window, choose File Import. The dialog box that appears queries you for the drive and directory location of the source file to be imported.

2. Select the file and then click OK to import the file into the Data Manager.

CHART always starts entering imported data at cell A1; it erases anything that was in the Data Manager window prior to the import. If you need data from several files to produce a chart, combine the data in a single source file before importing it to CHART.

If the source application for your data is a Windows application such as Excel or Lotus for Windows, you can use *dynamic data exchange (DDE)* to link the data in the source program to CHART. DDE is helpful if you plan to update your source information frequently and want to have an updated chart available at all times. With DDE, all changes in the source document are reflected in the linked document.

To set up DDE links in CHART, use the Paste Link option as follows:

1. Start up both applications (CHART and Excel, for example) and open the files to be linked. Make sure that the Data Manager window is open in CHART. Before setting up the links, check your spreadsheet program documentation to be sure that it supports DDE.

2. Select the range of cells to be linked to CHART in the source spreadsheet program. Choose Copy from the Edit menu to copy these cells to the Clipboard.

3. Switch back to CHART and click the upper-left cell of the range location at which you want to place the linked data.

4. Choose Paste Link from the Edit menu. The linked data appears in the Data Manager.

> You can also use Paste Link to link together related CHART documents.
>
> **TIP**

Formatting Text, Numbers, and Cells

CHART's formatting options can make your data easier to understand in the Data Manager window (and easier to read on your printouts). You can change the font of any of the text items in the Data Manager window; you can also apply bold, italic, or underline type characteristics to these items. To do these things, first select the data range to be formatted. Then click the Font button to define typeface, size, and style, or else select **B** (bold), *I* (italic) or U (underline) from the Format button bar to apply the desired trait.

To define the way your numeric entries are displayed, select the range of cells to be formatted and then choose the Numbers (#) button (or choose Format Numeric from the menu bar). The Numeric Format dialog box appears. You can create your own format in this dialog box and then Add it to the list. The format you create will be available the next time you access the Numeric Format dialog box.

> The Display Grid selection on the Options menu allows you to turn the grid on or off (like clicking the Grid button on the toolbar).
>
> **TIP**

To define the formatting of the cells themselves, pull down the Format menu and choose **B**order (or click the Borders button on the toolbar). In the Borders dialog box which appears, you can define a border line style and color. You can also determine whether the border surrounds the highlighted cells or only appears on selected sides of the data range. To color the interior of your data range, click Shaded. In the Brush dialog box which appears, you can choose two shading patterns—one each for the foreground and background of your data range.

To align data in a cell or range of cells, select the data range and then click the appropriate button (left, center, right, or no justification) at the left side of the toolbar.

Formatting data in the Data Manager only affects the way text is displayed and printed in the Data Manager; it does not affect the way text appears in the chart itself.

Tagging the Data Cells

Different cells in the Data Manager window contain different types of data that serve different purposes. Some cells contain title data, for example, and others contain data to be charted. For CHART to work correctly, these data items must be correlated with their corresponding Chart View window components. CHART calls this correlation process *tagging* and allows you to perform it in either manual or automatic modes.

The Preview box is just below the toolbar and to the left. It represents a snapshot view of the overall chart layout based upon the most current settings. It provides a convenient means for you to quickly determine the macroscopic effect of any formatting changes you make. If you select a cell that has been tagged as one of the chart elements, the corresponding part of the Preview box is highlighted.

Manual Tagging

Using manual tagging to identify the elements of your chart is a simple and straightforward process. To tag your chart title, for example, follow these steps:

1. Click cell A1 (or whichever cell contains the title) to select the title.

2. Click the down arrow on the Chart Element box located just above the Contents box at the top of the screen. The drop-down menu lists the various chart elements (see fig. 18.8).

3. Click Title. The Chart Element box displays Title as the tag for this cell.

Repeat this procedure as often as necessary, tagging data items until all required chart components have been identified.

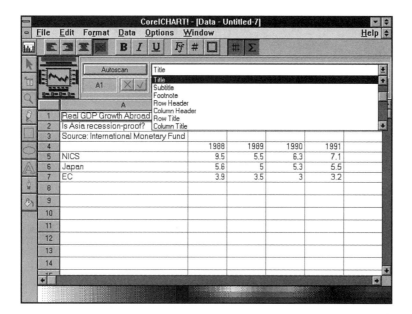

FIG. 18.8

Manually tagging the
chart title.

Automatic Tagging

Tagging data manually is a tedious process. But as long as your data is arranged within certain parameters, CHART can automatically tag the data for you using its Autoscan feature. The Sample Data provided with each chart type are arranged in a format that Autoscan can use; these formats are fairly consistent from one chart type to another. A typical data format is shown in figure 18.9.

Title					
Subtitle			Column Title		
Footnote		Column Headers			
	Row	Data Range	Data Range	Data Range	
Row Title	Headers	Data Range	Data Range	Data Range	Y (Z) Title #1
		Data Range	Data Range	Data Range	Y (Z) Title #2

FIG. 18.9

The Autoscan data
arrangement.

After your data is in the proper format, simply click the Autoscan button next to the Tag list box. CHART automatically tags the data and highlights the column headers, row headers, and the data range. Click some of the highlighted cells to see how the tags were assigned.

Printing Data from the Data Manager Window

To print the information you enter in the Data Manager without printing the chart it creates, choose the **P**rint command from the Data Manager **F**ile menu.

The Page Setup option allows you to set page margins and to control the printing of cell borders, grids, and highlights. The Print Setup option allows you to specify a printer and to set the characteristics of the printed page.

Print Preview allows you to interactively place your data on the page by using the mouse and drag-and-drop procedures. Both the Page Setup and Print Setup options are available from Print Preview.

Reversing the Orientation of Data

Data orientation refers to the way CHART presents information on the category, or horizontal, axis. *Data categories* are frequently points in time such as months or fiscal quarters. A *data series* is the item which is graphed at each point in the Data Categories. When there is more than one item graphed at each category point, those items form a *data group*. The Data Orientation command on the Data menu enables you to change which part of the chart data you want as a series and which part you want as a group (see fig. 18.10). Reversing the orientation of the data on your chart highlights different aspects of the data. Figures 18.11 and 18.12 show the results of reversing data.

FIG. 18.10

The Data Orientation dialog box.

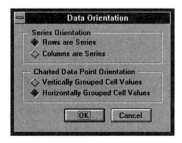

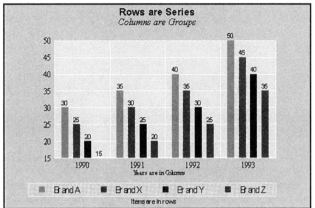

FIG. 18.11

Chart before data series reversal.

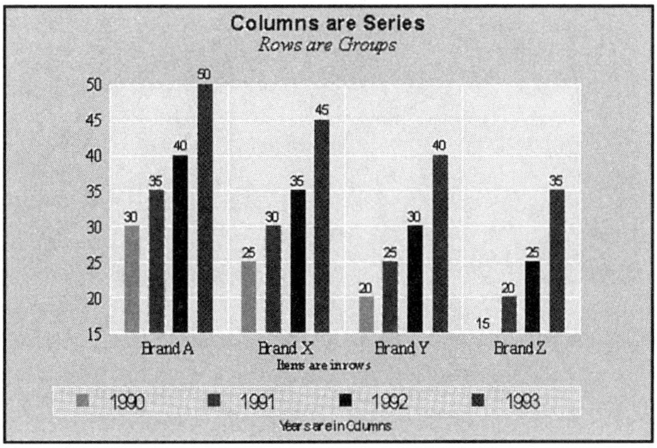

FIG. 18.12

Chart after data series reversal.

Sorting Data Items

Insert Sorted Item on the Data menu is a handy feature if you frequently add new items to your chart data. Click and drag over the range in which you want the new item inserted, choose **D**ata **I**nsert Sorted Item and type in the item you included. CHART automatically inserts the item in the correct alphabetic sequence and inserts a row or column as designated. The key defines the row/column at which the sort will start.

Modifying Chart Elements Using Chart View

The Chart View window displays the charted data (see fig. 18.13).

FIG. 18.13

The Chart View window.

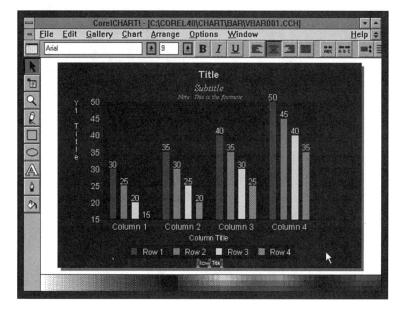

In this window, you can edit all aspects of the chart presentation and add text and graphic annotations. The toolbar found at the left side of the screen works almost exactly like the one in CorelDRAW!. It allows you to add, select, and move chart elements, graphic objects, and text. The Text Ribbon found at the top of the screen allows you to define fonts, point sizes, and text formats. The menu bar provides commands which enable you to change chart types and to rearrange the data within your chart. The commands on the Chart View menu bar are similar to those found on the Data Manager menu bar; the main difference is that they work with graphic files and objects rather than text.

Using the Toolbar

Most chart objects are edited or created by one of the tools found on the toolbar at the left side of the screen. Using toolbar devices, you can move and size objects, place graphic and text annotations, and select colors for chart elements. Table 18.2 provides a list of the toolbar devices and their functions. Most of them function just like their counterparts in CorelDRAW!.

Table 18.2 The Chart View Toolbar

Icon	Tool Name	Function
	Data Manager/ Chart View button	Toggles between the Data Manager screen and the Chart View screen.
	Pick tool	Selects, scales, and moves CHART objects.
	Pop-up tool	Provides a quick way to select and edit a CHART object; produces different pop-up dialog boxes depending on the element selected.
	Zoom tool	Magnifies or reduces the chart; unlike the CorelDRAW! Zoom tool, the CHART Zoom tool magnifies the entire graph as a unit.
	Pencil tool	Draws lines, curves, and arrows.
	Rectangle tool	Draws rectangles and squares on the annotation layer.
	Ellipse tool	Draws ellipses and circles on the annotation layer.
	Text tool	Adds and edits text information entered in the chart.
	Outline tool	Changes color, width, and pattern of borders around objects.
	Fill tool	Changes the interior color and fill of an object.

Several of these tools have fly-out menus which provide additional options.

The Zoom fly-out menu (see fig. 18.14) allows you to specify the degree of magnification or reduction you want to apply to the chart. You might find it helpful to magnify the chart when you are adding text or graphic annotations.

FIG. 18.14

The Zoom fly-out menu.

TIP

If you are working with several charts and want to see what they look like as a unit, reduce the charts to 25 percent, size the windows to fit the charts, select Window Tile. This method can be particularly helpful when several charts display related data.

The Pencil fly-out menu (see fig. 18.15) provides tools for drawing lines, polygons, curves, and arrows. All four tools work in the same general fashion. Click the tool to select it, click the chart where you want the line to begin, and then drag to the end point. The polygon tool is a little different because you don't hold down the mouse button as you drag. Instead, you click the end point of each side of the polygon and double-click to join the final side to the starting point.

FIG. 18.15

The Pencil fly-out menu.

The Outline fly-out menu (see fig. 18.16) allows you to specify an object's outline width, color, and pattern. You can control the outline width of chart elements, such as chart riser bars and frames, as well as objects drawn on the screen with the drawing tools. The menu works almost exactly like the comparable menu in CorelDRAW!.

FIG. 18.16

The Outline fly-out menu.

To change outlines, use the Pick tool to select the object that you want to modify, click the Outline tile, and then click the modification you want to make. The first row of the fly-out menu specifies the outline width; the first tile allows custom widths and the second tile removes the outline entirely. The second row specifies the color of the outline: white, black, a shade of gray, or a custom color.

The Fill fly-out menu (see fig. 18.17) allows you to fill any CHART element with the color, pattern, texture, or graphic of your choice. It includes two roll-up windows—the Fill roll-up and the Pictograph roll-up—which are discussed in detail later in this chapter in the "Adding Pictographs" section.

FIG. 18.17

The Fill fly-out menu.

The first row of tiles, from left to right, allows you to apply custom colors, use the Fill roll-up window, make an object transparent, apply fountain fills, two-color patterns, vector graphics, bit-map textures, and use the Pictograph roll-up window. The second row permits black, white, and various patterned fills. Except for the roll-up menus, the use of this menu is almost identical to its use in CorelDRAW! and so is discussed in Chapter 6.

Selecting Chart Elements

You can select most chart elements as objects, in much the same way as you select objects in CorelDRAW!. To use the Pick tool to select any item on the chart, click the Pick tool and then click the object you want to select. The object's outline and handles appear. You can select multiple objects by holding down the Shift key while clicking the additional items.

After you select an item, you can move it by clicking it and dragging it to the new location. You can resize the chart itself, as well as the titles and legends, by clicking on the object's handles and dragging the item to its new size.

Using the Context-Sensitive Pop-Up Menu

Although you can modify some chart elements directly by clicking and dragging the object frame, you must use menu selections to modify other chart elements. One way to modify these elements is to use the Pop-up tool. Like the Pick tool, this tool is used to select items on the chart. When you select an item with this tool, however, a menu pops up to give you access to various options that relate to that specific item. Figure 18.18 shows the pop-up menu for the data axis legend.

FIG. 18.18

The Data Axis pop-up menu.

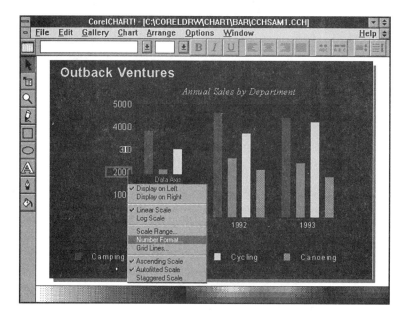

Choose the item modifications you want and then apply them to the chart element by ending the selected procedure.

TIP

Another way to access this pop-up menu is to position the cursor over any of the chart items and click with the right mouse button while using any of the other tools.

Moving and Sizing Text

Moving and sizing text in CorelCHART is similar to moving and sizing text in CorelDRAW!. With the Pick tool, click the text item you want to modify. The scaling handles appear around the text, indicating that it is selected. To move the text, click the text box and drag it to the new location. To size the text, click a scaling handle and drag the box to the desired size. CorelCHART adjusts the text to fit inside the box. Alternatively, once the box is selected, you can use the point size box at the top of the screen to enter the desired point size.

Occasionally, the box containing the text may be larger than actually required to hold the text, which may prevent you from repositioning the text because the frame of the box cannot extend past the edge of the chart. To correct this problem, click the text with the right mouse button. The context-sensitive pop-up menu appears. Choose Fit Box to Text. Now click the text again. The box is sized so that it exactly matches the text length. Click and drag the text to the desired chart position.

Formatting Numbers

To reformat numbers, highlight any of the values along an axis and click the right mouse button. The context-sensitive pop-up menu appears. Choose the Number Format menu option and scroll through the formats listed until you find the format you want. Choose it and click on OK. The highlighted numbers are now displayed in the desired format.

Adding Color with the Color Palette

To change the color of any chart item, select the item, and then click the desired color on the color palette located at the bottom of the screen.

To choose the outline color when working with objects such as a bar in a vertical bar chart, click the object and then choose the desired outline color from the palette by clicking it with the right mouse button.

Modifying a Chart Using a Template

Apply Template from the File menu is a handy tool for applying a standard chart format to the currently active chart. To use this feature, open a chart and insert the desired data using the Data Manager. Then choose File Apply Template to open a standard Windows file-directory dialog box in which you choose the desired CHART template file (which is another CorelCHART file with a CCH extension). CorelCHART applies the formatting and graphic information (but not the data) contained within the template file to the currently active chart.

Importing Graphics into a Chart

You can take advantage of the vast DRAW clip art library, or graphics created in DRAW or other graphics applications, to include graphic files into your chart. (The procedure is virtually identical to that discussed in Chapter 10.) To import a graphics file into a chart, follow these steps:

1. Choose Import from the File menu. The Import dialog box appears.

2. Choose the graphic you want to import and click OK. (A wide assortment of file types is supported.) The graphic appears on-screen.

3. Move and scale the graphic as needed.

Exporting Charts into Other Applications

The Export command on the File menu allows you to put the charts you create in CorelCHART into a format that other applications can use. CorelCHART provides a number of bitmap and vector graphic file formats; the one you choose should be determined by the application into which you want to insert the chart.

NOTE

To use the object linking and embedding (OLE) features, you must use the Clipboard or import the file into the client application using the Link features. For more information on OLE and exporting files, see Appendix B and Chapter 9, respectively.

Editing Chart Objects

The Edit menu options operate very similarly within CHART as they do with all other Corel applications. Undo only applies to the last action taken. Cut (Ctrl+X), Copy (Ctrl+C), and Paste (Ctrl+V) work with Clipboard data and function just as they do in other applications.

You can use the Paste Inside command to copy an object from the Clipboard and have CHART automatically size it to fit the inside dimensions of the CHART page. You can then move the object to the back using

Arrange To Back to create a backdrop against which the chart data is displayed. For example, if you were presenting a chart to investors concerning a new building, you could transfer a drawing of the building to the background of the chart by using Paste Inside.

Clear (Del) erases the highlighted information from the CHART screen. Duplicate (Ctrl+D) makes an exact copy of the highlighted information as long as the information is not created in, or used by, the Data Manager. For example, you can duplicate graphic objects and text annotation, but not the chart title.

Copy Chart automatically selects the entire chart and copies it to the Clipboard. You can then open another application (like CorelDRAW! or Word for Windows) and paste the chart information into that application.

Changing the Chart Style

You may want to change the chart style after the data has been entered to determine whether another style would better match your presentation needs. To do this, use the options on the Gallery menu. When you choose a chart style from this menu, a fly-out menu appears that lists the types associated with that style.

The Chart menu options deal with the attributes of the currently selected style. Use these options to edit the current chart.

Controlling the Display of the Underlying Chart Data

All options on the Chart menu deal with the display of the underlying chart data contained within the Data Manager. Remember that the category and data axes change from horizontal to vertical depending upon the style of chart selected.

Choosing the Category Axis option opens a menu you use to determine where and whether the category headings are displayed. A vertical bar chart provides a top and bottom choice, and a horizontal bar chart provides a left or right choice. Activating the Show Grid Lines option displays the lines that divide the different categories along the category axis. The line thicknesses are set using the Pop-up tool or the Outline tool. Autofitted Text, when selected, controls the type size of the legend data so that it all fits on a single line. Staggered Text displays alternate category titles on different horizontal lines so that very long titles can be displayed without overlapping each other.

Choosing the Data Axis option opens a menu with options that deal with the formatting and orientation of the data axis information. You can define the location of the axis (top/bottom, left/right), the scale (logarithmic/linear), the data scale range (lower-and-upper range bounds), the formatting of the numbers, and the grid line display characteristics.

Figure 18.19 shows the dialog box that appears when you choose the Grid Lines option. You can choose to display either or both of the major and minor grid lines. You can also determine whether the number of subdivisions within the major and minor grid lines should be automatically determined by CHART or conformed to a set number that you define in the text entry box. The Normal grid line display is simply a line that extends from one side to the other of the chart area. Normal with Ticks displays a small line outside of the chart across from the grid line and next to the data value. Inside and Outside Ticks remove the Normal Line and display the tick mark either inside or outside of the chart area, depending upon which is selected. Spanning Ticks span the chart frame barrier and do not include the Normal line. It is usual to include Normal for the major grid lines and to use Inside Ticks for the minor grid lines.

FIG. 18.19

The Grid Lines dialog box.

The options at the bottom of the Data Axis menu allow you to determine whether the scales are displayed in Ascending/Descending order, whether the scale ranges should be automatically determined by CHART (overrides the Scale Range option), and whether the scale labels should be staggered similarly to that described in the Category Axis section.

The 2nd Data-Axis command performs the same function as the standard Data Axis menu selection, except it deals with those instances when there is a dual, or Y1 and Y2, axis chart type. Be cautious of how you set your grid lines for the two axes; you want to be able to easily determine which grid lines are associated with which data axis. When working with dual axis charts, you can also define which scale range (Y1 or Y2) appears on the left or right axis by choosing the Axis Assignment menu option. The displayed dialog box allows you to switch the current axis assignment if you choose.

The Data Reversal option does not switch the series-group relationship; it only reverses the ordering of the information contained within the group or series. For example, choosing the Data Reversal Reverse Groups option causes the category heading on the left side of a vertical bar chart to swap with the heading on the right side, and all categories in between to swap positions accordingly. Using the Data Reversal Reverse Series option reverses the ordering of the series data displayed within each category, but the category location remains the same.

Clicking on a data series and then choosing Data Analysis displays the dialog box shown in figure 18.20. A number of different data analysis procedures are provided with CHART. Using these tools properly keeps you from having to perform this analysis in another spreadsheet type product and then importing the information into CHART for final display. You can work with the raw data within the CHART application's framework.

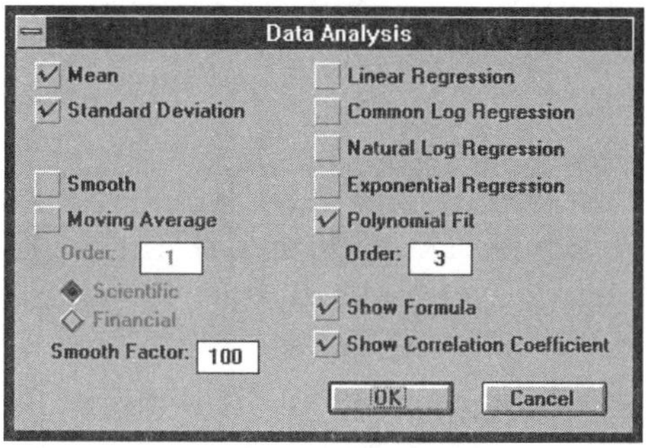

FIG. 18.20

The Data Analysis dialog box.

Choosing Mean and/or Standard Deviation displays the result of the calculation on the chart as straight lines. Both scientific and financial data series smoothing are provided, and you can set the order and smooth factor used in performing the calculations when you choose

Moving Average. Linear, common log, natural log, and exponential regression analysis are also available. If polynomial fit is chosen, you can define the order of the equation used in the text entry box. Choosing Show Formula and Show Correlation Coefficient displays the information used in calculating the equation fit (see fig. 18.21). You can then move the displayed correlation information to the desired location on the chart.

FIG. 18.21

The third order polynomial fit with regression coefficient.

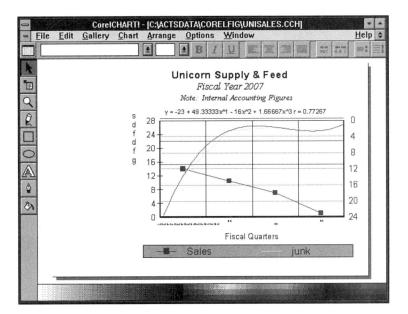

The content of the menu section below Data Analysis changes with the type of chart selected. In general, you can modify attributes associated with the display of the actual data (the bar chart riser thickness and spacing, line chart data markers, and so on). Clicking an attribute reveals a fly-out menu within which you can change the designs and preview the final effects on your chart.

The contents of the next section of the Chart menu also vary with the chart type selected. A bar chart type allows you to create a pictograph, which uses a graphic image such as an airplane in place of the bar. If you are working with a line chart, selecting a data series and then choosing Display As Bar allows you to make combination charts because one section will be a line chart and the other a bar chart. If you are working with a bar chart, this option becomes Display As Line and performs a comparable function. Emphasize Bar is also provided with bar charts, and allows you to select a data point out of a series and give it special emphasis by modifying the bar outline. This feature is useful for drawing attention to particular data points presented within your chart.

Clicking on Legend displays the Legend dialog box shown in figure 18.22. Display Legend allows you to enable/disable the legend function. When this option is enabled, you have a number of options provided with respect to orientation of the text to the legend marker. These options are displayed to the right of the dialog box; you can designate the orientation as left, right, below, above, or on the marker itself. Autofit Legend Text automatically fits the text to appear on the line in accordance with the Legend Layout criteria set at the bottom of the dialog box. You can set the legend to automatically determine its orientation, to display vertically, or to display horizontally. The Number of Markers per Row option defines the number of legend entries allowed on a single line and affects the legend text size.

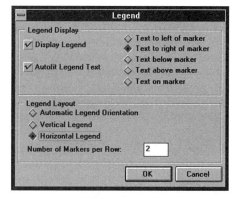

FIG. 18.22

The Legend dialog box.

Choosing Display Status from the Chart menu reveals a dialog box within which you determine which chart elements are displayed or hidden (see fig. 18.23). Most of the options are self-explanatory, but several of them require elaboration. Choosing ALL Text displays all chart related text items, and NO Text hides all text items. The Display option in the Data Values area affects the entire chart and allows you to display the numeric value of the data points at a number of different locations with respect to the specific data point. The location definition is consistent for all data points within the chart. Clicking on Format allows you to define the format in which the numbers are displayed.

The Zero Line option under the Data Axis section adds an emphasis to the zero line as either a different color and/or a different thickness.

FIG. 18.23

The Display Status dialog box.

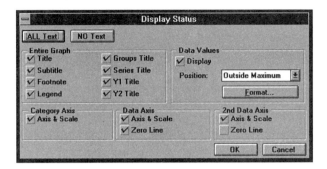

Controlling the Alignment of Graphics and Text

The Arrange menu allows you to control the presentation of graphic and text annotations on the chart. The upper part of the menu is used to order the layering of objects when there are multiple objects. Any number of objects can be arranged together. To change the order of a particular object, select the object with the Pick tool and then choose the desired option from the Arrange menu.

You can also align objects with each other or on the page. To align two objects, first select the item to be centered, and then hold the Shift key down while you select the object on which to center (when aligning more than two objects, the last item selected should be the object on which the other objects should be centered). With both items selected, choose **Arrange Align**. The Align dialog box shown in figure 18.24 appears. You can choose to align the items with each other horizontally or vertically (or both), matching tops, bottoms, or centers. Alternatively, the items can be aligned on the page. (This procedure is identical to that used in DRAW; see Chapter 5 for details.)

Refreshing a Window

The Refresh Window option on the Window menu is helpful when you are making custom annotations and text adjustments to a chart. CHART sometimes leaves ghosts on-screen when working with these types of changes. The Refresh Window option redraws the screen, eliminating these problems. (This works exactly the same way in DRAW, so refer to Chapter 15 for additional information.)

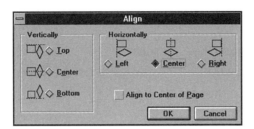

FIG. 18.24

The Align dialog box.

The Cascade and particularly the Tile options are also extremely helpful in allowing you to move from window to window when working with multiple charts. With the edges of each window displayed, you can click the window you want to make it current. All the currently active windows are listed at the bottom of the Window menu. You can make a chart current by clicking on its title in this menu. (This procedure is *not* available with DRAW.)

Formatting Text with the Text Ribbon

The Test Ribbon immediately above the chart screen allows you to choose the typeface and size of the chart text. The first text box on the left is the Typeface box. You click on the down arrow beside the box to choose from a list of available typefaces. The second text box on the Text Ribbon is the Point Size box, which also has a down arrow that you can use to choose from a list of point sizes.

The Text Ribbon also provides the ability to add emphasis with bold or italicized type. It also has icons you use to justify the text and control the spacing between letters and lines. The functions of the various Text Ribbon icons are describerd in table 18.3.

Table 18.3 Text Ribbon Button Functions

Icon	Function
B	Bold the selected text
I	Italicize the selected text

(continues)

Table 18.3 Continued

Icon	Function
U	Underline the selected text
	Left justify the selected text
	Center the selected text
	Right justify the selected text
	Fully justify (right and left) the selected text
	Decrease kerning (interletter spacing)
	Increase kerning (interletter spacing)
	Decrease leading (interline spacing)
	Increase leading (interline spacing)

To use these tools, you must first select the text to be modified with
the Pick tool or the Text tool. To select text with the Pick tool, select
the text box by simply clicking on the text to be changed. To select
with the Text tool, highlight the text to be changed by dragging the
cursor over it. After you select the text, click the appropriate button(s)
to change the text. Selected buttons appear darker than unselected
buttons.

Customizing Your Charts

When you have the basic data charted, you can add the final touches
that will draw attention to important characteristics. Text, graphic

objects, fill types, and other artistic features that are standard with DRAW are also available with CHART. These attributes make a conventional looking chart into something worth noticing. You apply them using Chart View.

Creating Text Annotations

Text annotations are text strings added to the chart that are in addition to the titles and legend. To enter the annotation, follow these steps:

1. Select the Text tool from the toolbar on the left side of the chart and click in the area to the left of the chart. The cross hairs become an I-beam cursor.

2. Type in the annotation, pressing Enter at the end of each line to preserve the line spacing. Don't worry about correct text sizing at this point.

3. When you have finished typing, choose the Pick tool. Click the text you just entered and drag the text box so that the first line is located in the desired chart position.

4. Position the cursor over the lower-left corner of the box until the cursor changes to a double-headed arrow. Drag the box corner until it is the desired size, and release the mouse button. The text size changes to fit into the box just as it did in DRAW.

The text formatting procedures outlined earlier can be applied to the text annotation to make it bold, italicized, a different font or color, and justified the way you want.

TIP

If the text does not change immediately after you apply the formatting, click anywhere on the chart background and then click on the text box again.

Creating Graphic Annotations

You can use the Pencil, Ellipse, Rectangle, Fill, and Outline tools just as they were used in DRAW. Together they combine to create as varied a combination of graphic objects as you can imagine.

To create a backdrop to highlight the text, for example, choose the Ellipse tool from the toolbar. Choose a bright yellow color from the Palette. Click and drag an ellipse around the text. Don't worry if they don't line up correctly. When you release the mouse button, a yellow ellipse covers most of the text. Choose **Arrange Backward One** from the menu bar. The text is now superimposed on the ellipse.

To center the text in the ellipse, choose the Pick tool, hold down the Shift key, and click on the text. Both the ellipse and the text are now selected. Choose **Arrange Align** from the menu bar. Click on Center Vertically and Center Horizontally in the Align dialog box, and then click on OK. The text is now centered within the ellipse.

Creating Customized Fills

Any CHART element, except text, can have any of the various DRAW fill types applied to it. For example, the bars on a bar chart can all contain a fountain fill or a bitmap pattern. The method of application is identical to that used in DRAW. For detailed information, refer to Chapter 6.

Fills fall into several basic categories:

- **Uniform.** The same percentage of shading occurs across the entire object.

- **Fountain.** The fill density varies in a linear or radial pattern across the object.

- **Two-color pattern.** The applied pattern contains two colors in a format consistent with any of the CHART-compatible formats.

- **Full-color pattern.** The color and pattern of the object virtually unlimited.

- **Bitmap textures.** A bitmap image is used to create a three-dimensional effect to the surface of the fill.

A wide variety of fill types, colors, and patterns are provided with DRAW, and you can use any of them to add an artistic effect to CHART objects.

To access the fill types, access the Fill roll-up window by choosing the Fill tool and then the Roll-Up icon. Once the roll-up is activated, you can access the fill types by clicking on the appropriate icon in the roll-up window.

Adding Pictographs

Bar chart and histograms allow you to add pictographs to them so that the conventional lines and rectangles associated with the chart are replaced by graphic images (see fig. 18.25). To add a pictograph, follow these steps:

1. After you have created your bar chart or histogram, choose Chart Show as Pictograph to divide the bars into smaller subsections that exist between the grid lines. CHART cannot insert your desired graphic image into these smaller grid subsections.

2. Using the Pick tool, click on a bar of the series to which you want to apply the pictograph and then open the Pictograph roll-up by clicking on the Fill tool and then selecting the upper-right-hand icon in the fly-out menu. The Pictograph roll-up now opens to display the currently active pictograph image.

3. If the pictograph image is acceptable, click on Apply to create the pictograph using this image.

   If it is not acceptable, click the small arrow in the bottom right of the image box to display the variety of images readily available for pictograph creation. Double-click the image you want, and then click Apply to create the pictograph using your selected object.

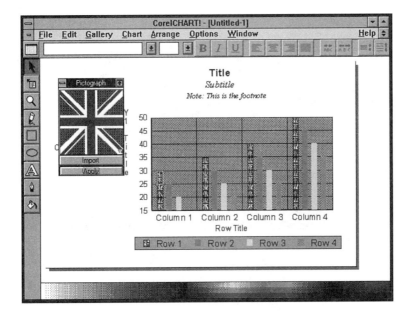

FIG. 18.25

A pictograph.

You can also import an image using the Import option provided in the Pictograph roll-up. Follow the standard importing procedures to import graphic objects such as logos, clip art, symbols, and other DRAW objects as you might want to use. (Importing is covered in the "Importing Graphics into a Chart" section earlier in this chapter and in Chapter 9.) When they are included in the roll-up, click on Apply to create the pictograph.

Creating 3-D Charts

The extent of CorelCHART's power becomes clear when you use the 3D Tool roll-up window. The features in this roll-up only work on 3-D charts.

To use this window, first create your 3-D chart using any of the Gallery 3-D menu options. Then open the 3-D roll-up by choosing the Chart 3D Roll-Up menu option, which appears on the menu only when you are working on a 3-D chart. The roll-up shown in figure 18.26 appears.

FIG. 18.26

The 3D Tool roll-up window.

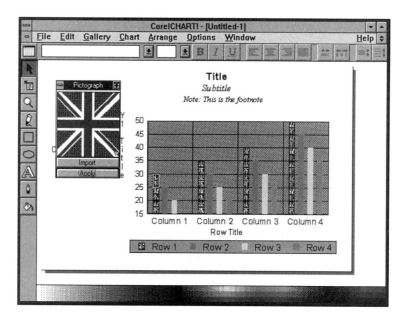

This roll-up is used to vary perspective effects, modify the thickness of walls and the length of chart axes, rotate the chart in virtually any direction, and move it diagonally on the chart surface. Using this roll-up window, you can modify most orientation and design features associated with a 3-D chart.

The upper-left icon moves the chart at an angle across the page, the next icon adds perspective to the chart, the third allows you to change the axes lengths and wall thicknesses, and the upper-right icon allows you to change the orientation of the chart in virtually any dimension. The procedure for operating these icons is to choose the icon and then click on the appropriate arrows attached to the center object to make the chart perform as you expect. Make sure that Show Graph is activated so that you can monitor the changes. When you are satisfied with the chart, click on Redraw to change your original 3-D chart to look as the preview does. If you click on Undo, no changes are made to your chart and you are returned to the Chart View.

Summary

CHART provides you with wonderful tools for making professional looking charts by taking advantage of the many artistic features associated with DRAW. You may find it advantageous to create your chart images in CHART, and then export them to another presentation graphics package to add any associated text. The OLE features make this a viable option. Remember, inserting your charts into SHOW is a natural option. From there, you can make a stand-alone presentation that does not require DRAW, SHOW, or CHART to display, which allows you greater flexibility on how your work is used.

You can combine your charts with other Corel images by using CorelSHOW, which is covered in the following chapter. You can use this program to make your work into a complete, unified presentation.

19

CHAPTER

Making Presentations Using CorelSHOW

The CorelSHOW application becomes a rallying point around which the other applications revolve. Quite often, the final reason for creating charts, logos, images, scanned images, animation, and screenshots is to make a formal presentation. Such a presentation can be in the form of a computer-based display, a set of 35mm slides, a set of overhead projections, or a collection of images on paper. SHOW allows you to combine materials created in all the other Corel applications into a single unified presentation. This chapter introduces you to the operation of CorelSHOW and covers some recommended procedures for making the most out of your presentations. Remember that CorelDRAW! objects can be used in SHOW presentations. Try to use the provided clip art and images that you have already created so that you can make the most efficient use of your time and effort.

A *show* consists of a series of *slides* containing images and text. The slides are generally unified in appearance by similar fonts, colors, and bullets. The graphic images used also share similar qualities. In many cases, certain information—such as a company logo—appears on every slide.

This chapter shows you how to build a SHOW file by defining the page size and orientation, defining a background, and finally incorporating the desired images and text into the presentation. It also explains the use of some of SHOW's more sophisticated features: slide-to-slide transition effects, event timing, interactive presentations, stand-alone presentations, and formal presentations. It also includes a brief section on the Windows 3.1 Object Linking and Embedding (OLE) and Dynamic Data Exchange (DDE) features.

NOTE

A drawback to SHOW is that it has little intrinsic processing power and relies on the source applications for all modifications other than simple sizing and moving. This means that you will often have several applications running at the same time, which drains processing power and makes computer operation very slow. If you plan to use SHOW along with the other Corel applications on a regular basis, you are encouraged to get a high power machine (486/33 type minimum) with at least 8M RAM (16 recommended) and at least 200M hard disk space. Otherwise, it is frustratingly slow working with the several applications at once.

Starting SHOW and the SHOW Screen

To start SHOW, double-click the CorelSHOW icon located in the Corel application group. The Welcome to CorelSHOW dialog box shown in figure 19.1 appears. You can choose either to open an existing presentation (if one exists) or to start a new presentation. Choosing Open and Existing Presentation opens the standard Windows file access dialog box, in which you find the desired file and double-click it to begin the editing process.

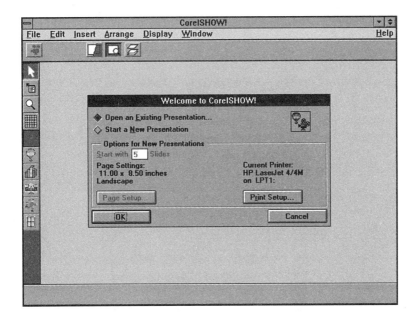

FIG. 19.1

The CorelSHOW
welcome screen.

Choosing Start a New Presentation provides access to the Options section of the dialog box. Here you can set the number of slides you want to include initially in your presentation, define the Printer Setup parameters, and define the Page Setup for the new presentation.

You set up the printer in much the same way you would in any of the other Corel applications. Simply click Print Setup to open the standard Corel Print setup screen. Here you can access the default printer, select a special printer for a particular operation, or make use of print options such as print orientation (see Chapter 10 for details).

To define the page size and characteristics for your presentation, follow these steps:

1. Choose Page Setup. The Page Setup dialog box appears (see fig. 19.2).

2. Choose the desired page size from the numerous Page Size options available. After you make your choice, the corresponding page dimensions are shown in the Horizontal and Vertical boxes. Switching from Portrait to Landscape (or vice versa) automatically switches the Horizontal and Vertical dimensions.

You should set the page size you intend to use at this point, because later changes will affect object layout on-screen and may require substantial rearrangement.

FIG. 19.2

The Page Setup dialog box.

3. After you have made your page size choice, click OK. The SHOW editing window appears with the desired page setup displayed (see fig. 19.3).

TIP

You will probably want to stick with a landscape page for on-screen presentations because most monitors are landscape.

Along the left side of the new display are a set of tools used to create SHOW objects and images. The Pick and Zoom tools operate much like those in DRAW. Choosing the Command pop-up tool and then clicking an object or the screen itself displays a pop-up menu with various options associated with the selection. The menu contains various framing options when an object is selected and contains page setup of background options when you click the screen itself (see fig. 19.4).

With this menu, you can access the Page Setup menu, select a Background, Edit Cues, Show Time Lines, and set up Transition Effects for objects and slides. You can, of course, use the Pop-up tool, icons, or menu selections to achieve the same results. At the bottom of the tool bar at the left of the screen are buttons that provide OLE access to objects created in DRAW, CHART, PHOTO-PAINT, MOVE, or other (non-Corel) OLE-compatible Windows applications.

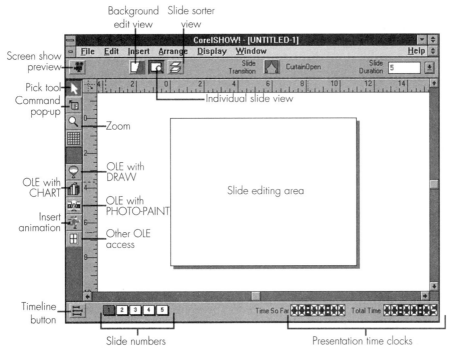

FIG. 19.3

The SHOW Screen.

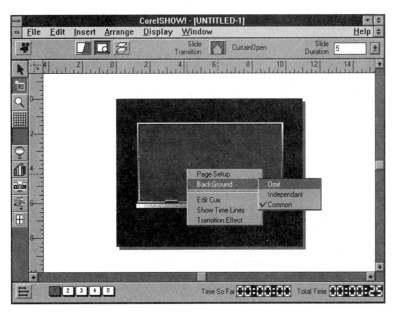

FIG. 19.4

The Background pop-up menu.

Information about total and elapsed presentation times, slide selection, cue management, and object timelines appear along the bottom of the screen. Icons related to background editing, slide viewing (individually or in groups), and slide and object transition effects associated with the currently active appear at the top of the screen, along with a box noting the slides viewing duration.

Creating SHOW Presentations

Easy access to slide show creation technology does not create an effective presentation in and of itself. You also need to observe effective design principles. This section is a small primer on the rules of good presentation design and some techniques that streamline the creation process.

Understanding Design Principles

No matter how effective you are with SHOW's operation, the presentation is only as effective as its basic design. Whenever you create a presentation, consider the following design principles:

- Know your audience and what its members expect from the presentation.

- Determine the three essential concepts that you want to drive home, and make sure that they are reinforced throughout the presentation.

- Outline the flow (storyboard) of the presentation before you create it in SHOW.

- Determine the proper output media type before you start designing. If the output will go to a monochrome printer, for example, color considerations do not apply.

- Keep the amount of slide text to a minimum. Use seven lines of text or less per slide and never more than seven words to a text line. Use bullets for emphasis and text of at least 18-point size. Check for grammar and spelling errors.

- Use charts, graphs, and graphic images to reinforce a point.

■ Keep the presentation flow consistent and on track toward your ultimate goals.

Adding Text and Graphic Objects

Text and graphic objects are not created in SHOW; they are created in another application, such as DRAW, and then added to the SHOW file. This section introduces you to the addition of text and graphic objects into a CorelSHOW project.

To add text to a SHOW file, click the toolbar's DRAW icon and drag a box on the slide display of the desired size and shape. CorelDRAW! opens and allows you to create the desired text string. When finished in DRAW, exit the program by choosing **File Exit** and return to SHOW to see the text included in the SHOW slide image. This procedure requires a great deal of experimentation to get it right; try to think ahead about the sizing of text and overall frames.

> **TIP**
>
> You might find it easier to work with artistic text instead of paragraph text because the number of characters and lines is generally small when working with slide text.

To add clip art from DRAW to individual slides, follow these steps:

1. Select the slide number by clicking the appropriate number shown in the lower-left corner of the screen.

2. From the **Insert** menu, choose **Object CorelDRAW! 4.0 (Ctrl+B)**.

3. Move your cursor to the SHOW screen, and create a box of approximately the size of the desired object by dragging one of the selector tools. DRAW opens, and you have access either to the DRAW editing window or the file management utilities that make it possible for you to choose the desired piece of clip art, object, or symbol.

4. Choose the clip art, symbol, or image you want using DRAW. After you make your choice and exit DRAW, the clip art or drawn object is included in the SHOW presentation at the previously specified location.

5. If necessary, resize the object by dragging the control handles or move it by dragging the object itself.

If you want to edit an object after placing it in SHOW, double-click the object. DRAW opens and enables you to edit the object using all of DRAW's formidable features. After completing your edit, choose File Exit to return to the SHOW editing window with the modified object.

Both objects shown in figure 19.5 were included from the DRAW clip art directory.

FIG. 19.5

A SHOW slide with DRAW clip art images.

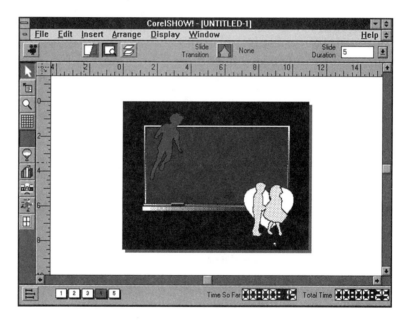

SHOW does not differentiate between DRAW objects. It treats the entire image as an object and imports it for use in the precentation. All previously defined DRAW features can be added to the objects before bringing them into SHOW.

Organizing the Presentation

To rearrange the order in which slides are presented during your screenshow, press the Slide Sorter View button at the top of the screen. A view showing thumbnail images of your slides in their current order appears (see fig. 19.6).

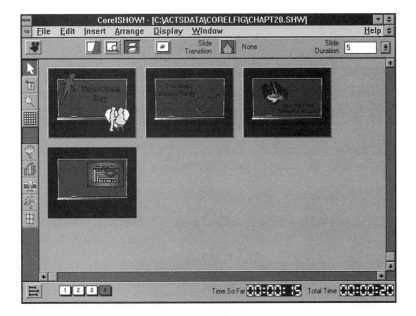

FIG. 19.6

The Slide Sorter view.

To place a slide in a new sequence position, simply drag it to the correct point relative to the other slides. Notice that a small gray bar appears on-screen at the point where the slide will now be located.

To rearrange the order of all slides at once, follow these steps:

1. Click the # button at the top of the Slide Sorter window. The prompt No: ??? appears on each slide.

2. Number the slides by clicking them in the desired presentation order.

3. Click the # button again to rearrange the slides in your prescribed order. To return them to the original order, choose **Edit Undo**.

Display and Timing of Slide Object Transition Effects

SHOW provides a number of transition effects that allow you to pre-scribe the way the show moves from one slide to the next. The opening effect for one slide is the closing effect for the preceding slide. To apply these effects to your slides, follow these steps:

1. Select a slide to work with (in either Slide Sorter view or Individual Slide view).

2. Click the Transition Effects button (the curtains). The dialog box shown in figure 19.7 appears. There are numerous effects pro-vided; experiment with them to see exactly what each one does.

FIG. 19.7

The Transition Effects
dialog box.

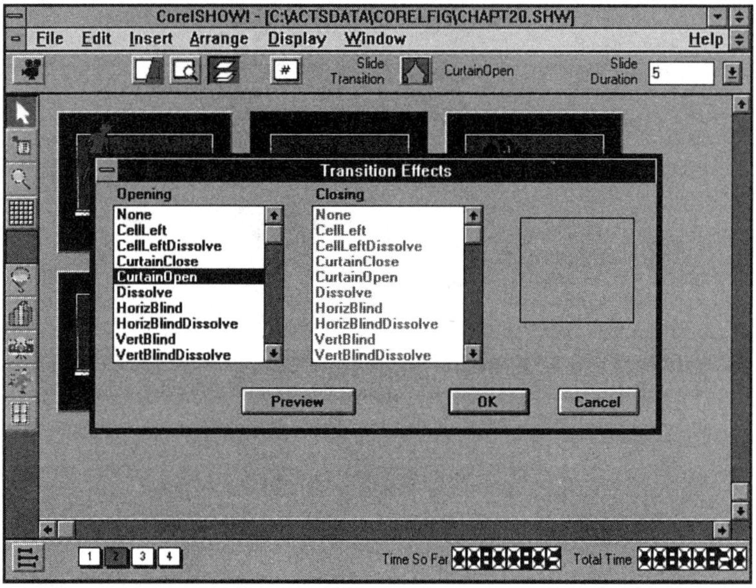

3. Choose Opening and Closing transition effects for your slide from the two list boxes provided. Click Preview to see the transition effect in action before applying it to the slides.

4. After making your choices, click OK. Repeat the process for as many slides as necessary.

To define transition effects for a particular object contained within a slide, simply select that object and then follow the same steps. In either case, the transition effects are applied when your screen show is created.

Finally, if you plan to run the screenshow in automatic mode, you should set the length of time that you want the slide to appear on-screen by clicking the Slide Duration box and setting it to the desired number of seconds. The slide opens with the defined transition effect, stays on-screen the designated number of seconds, and then closes with the transition effect defined for the opening of the following slide.

Remember that you determine the display duration in manual mode and must define the duration in automatic mode. The timing of events related to a particular slide are determined by the timelines in both modes. Manual mode only determines when the specific slide display starts and stops.

Working with Backgrounds

Information about the background appears on each slide of the presentation, unless you specifically choose to omit it. This feature helps you give overall consistency to your presentation; you are encouraged not to modify the standard backgrounds that come with SHOW until you are experienced enough to know the difference between effective and confusing background design.

To see the library of SHOW background files in thumbnail format, click the Background Library Access icon (see fig. 19.8).

To use one of the available backgrounds in your current presentation, simply double-click the design of choice. To view another library, choose Change Library and then select the directory and library file that contains your backgrounds.

To create a custom background, follow these steps:

1. Click the Background Edit View button located on the toolbar.

2. From the Insert menu, choose Object, and then indicate the application from which you plan to create the background (such as CorelDRAW! 4 or PHOTO-PAINT). Indicate whether you plan to use a piece of existing artwork or create a new one.

   SHOW sends you to the application of choice so that you can edit or create the image for your background.

FIG. 19.8

The background library.

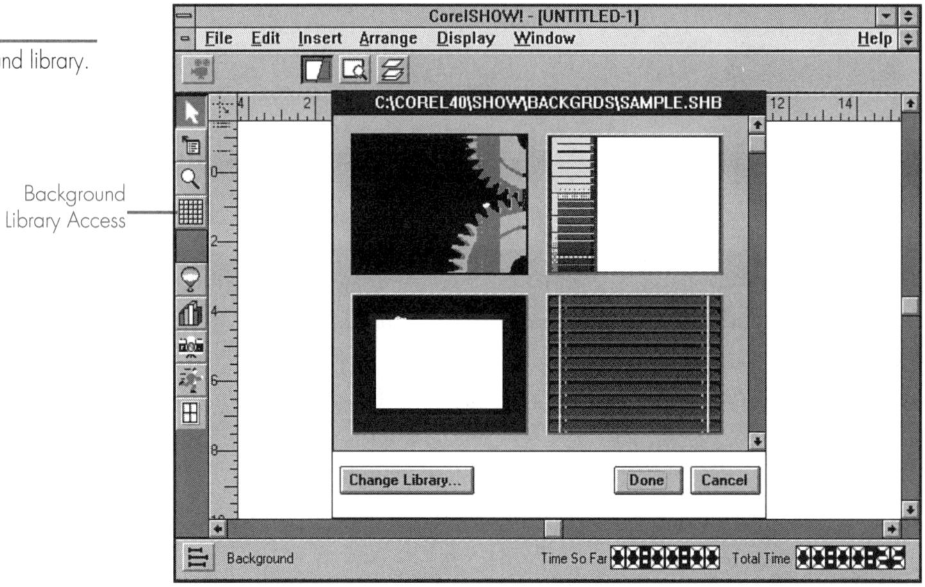

3. After creating the new object in the source application, choose File Exit to return to SHOW and see the object integrated as the background design.

4. Edit, size, and shape the background as needed while in Background Edit mode. After you return to Individual Slide view, you can no longer edit the background (without returning to Background Edit view once again).

The background shown in figure 19.9 was brought in from CorelPHOTO-PAINT as a TIF file and then resized to match the current presentation page size.

To turn off the background for a particular slide, select that slide by clicking the appropriate number shown in the lower-left corner of the screen, and then choose Edit Omit Background. The background is omitted only from the slide you have chosen; it remains in effect for all the other slides. To turn the background back on for the slide you chose, activate the slide and choose Edit Omit Background once again.

You can also use images in the DRAW clip art directory for your backgrounds. Try not to reinvent the wheel when working in SHOW. Use the extensive drawing capability (and the ready-made resources) of DRAW to make the presentation backgrounds, and other objects, look professional and attractive.

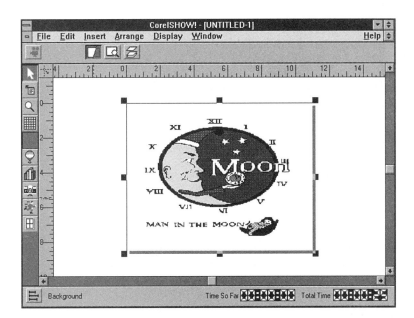

FIG. 19.9

A PHOTO-PAINT TIF
format background.

Using OLE with SHOW

Much of the power associated with SHOW comes from the Windows *Object Linking and Embedding (OLE)* feature. SHOW has very little object creation capability, but it provides tremendous flexibility for displaying objects created in other applications.

Applications that create objects for use in SHOW are called *source* applications; SHOW is the *destination* application for those objects. In similar fashion, the original file created by the source application is called the *source file* and the presentation file in SHOW is called the *destination file*. After an object is transferred to a destination file, it can be embedded so that the destination file retains a record of the source application and file name. Double-clicking the object in the destination file then automatically opens the source application, loads the source file, and enables you to edit the file or object within the source application. After you finish editing, the image of the object within the destination file is updated to reflect the most current changes. If you do not want the updates included, refuse to include the updates when asked by the Windows dialog box.

Object linking sets up a path between the source object and the destination object so that any time the source object is modified, the destination object is automatically updated. Linking makes life much easier when the underlying objects are going through substantial revision. Embedding ensures that you always have access to the original application so that object modifications are possible.

One critical thing to remember about links: *files should not be moved around after they are linked.* Doing so breaks the link because the computer has no way to recognize the change of locations and can no longer make the connection between the source and destination files and applications.

NOTE

See Appendix B for further details concerning OLE and the way that Windows applications work together. See Chapter 21 for a tutorial showing how to integrate several Corel applications using CorelSHOW.

Saving and Retrieving a Presentation or Background

You save a presentation just as you would save any Windows application file—by using the File Save and Save As options. You can save a complete presentation as an SHW file, or you can save the background only as an SHB file for use at a later time with other presentations. If you want to save the background for use with other presentations, use the File Save Background command rather than Save or Save As. This command enables you to save the background file as a stand alone file or to include it in the background library (choose Insert In Library) for easier access with less disk storage. If you save to the background library, your background appears as one of the options when you click the Background Library Access toolbox icon.

The Save option works just like it does in other Windows applications. A few special options appear, however, when you use the Save As option in SHOW (see fig. 19.10).

Most of the features of the Save As dialog box should be familiar by this point, with the exception of the options unique to SHOW. Because you are saving the file under a different name, and possibly to another directory, the OLE/DDE links must be updated for the new file. To update the location of all linked files relative to the file you are saving so that linked objects still appear in the new presentation, select the Move Links option.

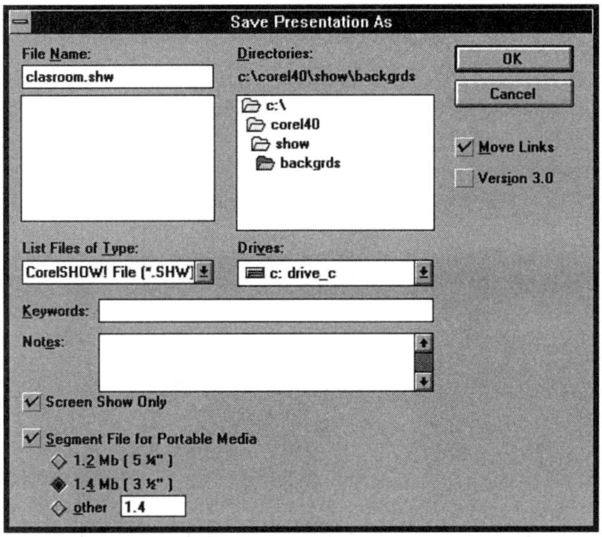

FIG. 19.10

The Save As dialog box.

To save your file in a CorelSHOW 3-compatible format, select the Version 3.0 option. To create a stand-alone presentation by saving to a file format that can be used in conjunction with SHOWRUN.EXE (see the coverage of this topic later in the chapter), select the Screen Show Only option. If your presentation file may be too large to fit on a single floppy disk, you can select the Segment File for Portable Media option.

CAUTION

Files saved in Screen Show Only format cannot be edited. Be sure to save your presentation file in SHOW (SHW) format before saving it as a Screen Show Only file.

Presenting Your Work

SHOW creates a screenshow from the slides contained within the currently active file. The recommended procedure for creating a screenshow involves the following steps:

1. Design the slides.

2. Place them in the desired presentation order using Slide Sorter view.

3. From the **D**isplay menu, choose Presentation Options and set the desired options within the dialog box that appears (see fig. 19.11).

FIG. 19.11

The Display Presentation
Options dialog box.

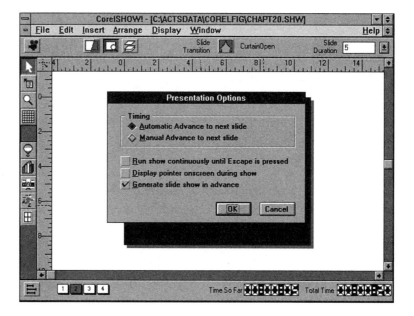

If you choose Automatic Advance, the slides change automatically after they are on-screen for the time you designated in the Slide Duration box. If you choose Manual Advance, you must indicate when to advance from one slide to the next by pressing the right cursor arrow, the down cursor arrow, the PageDown key, or the F10 key (or by double-clicking the left mouse button). You can also move backwards in this mode by pressing the up arrow, the left arrow, the PageUp key, or the F5 key (or by double-clicking the right mouse button). Pressing Home returns the presentation to the first slide, and pressing End takes it to the last slide.

The Run Show Continuously option simply loops the show back to the beginning when the final slide is reached. The Display Pointer option makes the pointer accessible during the show so that you can use it to address portions of the screen. The Generate screenshow in advance option instructs SHOW to process the entire show before displaying it, which is advisable when display-ing on a slower system where processing power is limited and creating each slide when it is displayed may cause flickering or slow transitions.

4. After setting your Presentation Options, save the presentation.

5. Click the Screenshow Preview button. SHOW assembles the screenshow, then asks if you want to see it. Click OK to watch your work come alive.

You can stop the presentation by pressing Esc whether you are in automatic or manual advance mode.

Adding Sound and Animation

You can add sound to your presentation just like you would add any other object type. Follow these steps to do so:

1. Select the slide to which you want to add the sound object.

2. Choose the Insert Sound menu option.

3. Click the sound object you want to insert; click Play to preview it before including it in the presentation.

4. To make your final choice, double-click the desired sound object, or click OK when it is highlighted.

The sound object is added to the SHOW timeline associated with this particular slide. You can move the sound object around on the timeline by dragging it as needed within the timeline display. If Embed is checked, the object is embedded in the presentation which allows ready access to the application that originally created it if sound editing is desired. Disable Embed if you want the object in nonembedded mode. As of this writing, only WAV file formats are accessible and supported. You must have a sound card installed with the proper Windows compatible drivers for the WAV files to play properly.

Animation is added in similar fashion. Select the slide before which you want the animation to begin, and then insert the animation object using Animation option on the Insert menu. Figure 19.12 shows the Insert Animation dialog box. You can select from CorelMOVE, Autodesk Animator, or Quicktime for Windows animation files by choosing the desired List File of Type option. Click the Options button to specify whether the animation repeats itself indefinitely (Repeat Forever), repeats a specified number of times (Repeat n times), or holds its position after completing its last frame (Hold after Last Frame). In addition, you can specify the speed of playback as a percent of the normal frame per second speed.

FIG. 19.12

The Insert Animation
dialog box.

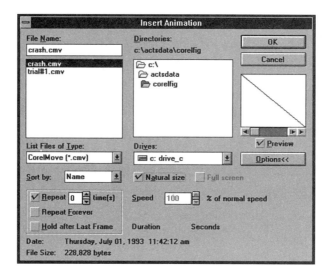

After the animation is on-screen, move its location by dragging the box
that outlines the animation. The animation plays at its normal size,
which means that you should try to size it appropriately in the source
application before adding it to your SHOW presentation.

Adding Cues and Using the Timelines

The overall timing of the presentation is recorded graphically on the
timelines. The Timelines chart shows the timing relationship between
the various slides used, including when they open and close, what objects each slide contains, and the transition effects applied to each. To
view or edit the timelines, click the Timelines button at the bottom left
of the screen. The window shown in figure 19.13 appears.

You can move the objects around on the timelines just as you did in
MOVE. To open a slide sooner, drag the left side of the appropriate
timeline. To make a slide stay on-screen longer, drag the right side of
the timeline. The duration time of the slide on-screen cannot be shorter
than the duration time of its underlying objects. To view the underlying
slide objects, click the black triangle to the left of the appropriate slide

on the clapboard. Notice that a timeline listing of the objects is displayed. These objects are adjusted just like the overall slide by dragging the endpoints around on the lines. As you move the slide timings around, notice that the overall presentation timing also changes.

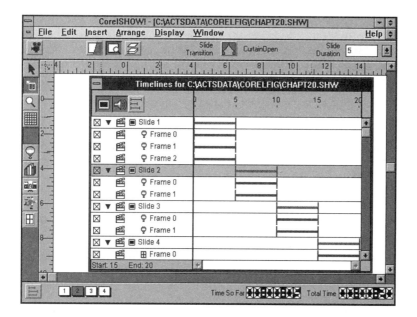

FIG. 19.13

The Timelines window.

Manual/automatic mode determines when a slide transition occurs, but the timing of events after the slide is displayed is determined by the timeline's relationship for that particular slide. Cues are included with each slide. A cue is an action that takes place when a certain set of conditions exist, such as the user clicks a tool to move the presentation in a different logical direction. If the clapboard is open, then there are no special cues included with a slide. If the clapboard is closed, then a special set of cue conditions exist for that particular slide. The logical cue procedure used with SHOW is identical to that used in MOVE, and you are referred to that section for a detailed discussion of its uses, operations, and options (see Chapter 20).

The interesting thing about the cues is that they allow for viewer interaction with the presentation. Based upon a user selection such as clicking on an icon, a cue can display another slide, play a sound object, or display an animation. The SHOW becomes more personalized due to the existence of the cues, and you should get to fully understand their capability after you become familiar with the other more conventional SHOW functions.

Running a Stand-Alone Screenshow

After you complete your presentation, you might want to distribute it for display on computers that do not have CorelSHOW loaded and are running Windows 3.0 or higher. This is often the case with canned sales presentations, where the sales rep has access to a computer, but not to SHOW. The *stand-alone* screenshow option provides a solution to this problem.

To prepare your stand-alone screenshow, follow these steps:

1. Save the presentation as Screen Show Only from the File Save As dialog box. Make sure that you save to a floppy disk, or to multiple floppies, depending upon the size of the presentation file. This way the file is easily copied and transported.

2. Copy the SHOWRUN.EXE file from the Corel SHOW subdirectory to a floppy disk that can be inserted into the target computer.

3. On-site, copy SHOWRUN.EXE and the screenshow to the hard disk of the target computer.

4. Start Windows 3.0 or higher, and then start the SHOWRUN.EXE application using any of the standard Windows techniques (pressing Alt+F, typing **SHOWRUN** and pressing Enter, or double-clicking SHOWRUN.EXE from within File Manager).

5. Choose the name of the presentation file from the Open Presentations dialog box, select the File Presentation Options desired (such as transition effects, timing, and so on); then choose OK. See earlier sections of this chapter for various timing parameters options and settings.

6. Click the ScreenShow icon to start the presentation.

The target computer must have the proper hardware to support the presentation objects included. If the computer does not have a sound card, for example, it cannot play the sound parts of your presentation. In addition, the presentation may play at different rates on different computers due to RAM and processor limitations.

Summary

Ultimately, the images and text that you create must be printed or displayed; SHOW provides a way for you to do that with flair. This chapter discussed the role that SHOW plays as a central clearinghouse for the other Corel applications.

SHOW acts as the hub of a wheel, with the various Corel applications acting as spokes. Images created in the other applications are brought together in SHOW to create a unified presentation.

This chapter covered the basics of effective presentation design, the use of OLE/DDE for adding text and graphic objects, various methods of displaying the presentation, and how to create a stand-alone presentation. The following chapters introduce you to animation (CorelMOVE) and methods of combining all the applications in a complementary way.

Adding Animation Using CorelMOVE

CorelMOVE unleashes the power of the Corel application group. By using this package, you can add movement to objects so that the graphics you created in DRAW now communicate to the viewer through action and sound. The concepts associated with animation are a little foreign and the jargon is new, but the fun and excitement this package generates is hard to describe. The complex process of creating animations requires prior planning. This chapter introduces you to the basic operational principles behind MOVE and shows you how to use CorelDRAW! to simplify the tedious yet rewarding task of animation creation.

Understanding CorelMOVE's Basic Concepts

Animations are essentially relationships between objects and paths of action that happen over a predefined timeframe. Animation objects fall into three basic categories: actors, props, and sound. Actors are objects that change location during the movie. Actors are either single cell or multicell. Single cell actors retain the same shape during their acting progression. Multicell actors change shape from one cell to another. Props are objects that remain stationary during the movie presentation, although they may appear or disappear during the movie. Sound objects are in the WAV file format that you can add to the movie timeline. Sound adds a lot to the presentation so consider adding sound to your animations when possible.

What Is CorelMOVE?

CorelMOVE is the application designed to create animation movies. It allows you to create and edit actors and props and provides a convenient mechanism for establishing the relationship between various objects. Say, for example, you want to create an animation about a magician, and you want the magician to make things appear and disappear. The timeline allows you to define the precise time at which a prop appears and disappears. The animated magician actor can snap his fingers and make a hat or other prop disappear. The timeline also enables you to determine what the hat looks like as it appears and disappears. You also can add music and sound effects to the animation for added drama. CorelMOVE provides the mechanism through which object creation, movement, and integration occur.

An Overview of the Animation Process

Think of an animation as a backdrop against which actor objects are superimposed. The backdrop can be anything related to your animation—a pasture, a mountain, or the surface of the moon. The backdrop is often a static object throughout the course of the movie and is one form of prop.

The actors move across the stage of the animation in a series of steps. Each step advances the actor in the desired direction. You can specify a different actor design for each step or allow the actor to remain the same shape from step to step.

A bird soaring across the screen, for example, is an actor with a shape that does not change. In this case, the actor is a single-cell actor following a path across the screen. You also can specify a different actor shape for each step, which adds lifelike attributes to your actors. You can animate the bird at each step, for example, to creating different wing shapes and giving a more lifelike illusion of a bird flapping its wings. Each cell appears at node points designated along the movement path. Each node represents a change to the next cell of the animation for that particular actor.

> Cells are called frames when editing an actor within CorelDRAW!.   **NOTE**

After you specify the objects, they are automatically or manually arranged along a timeline that sets the timing relationship among them during the movie's course. Prop objects move on and off the screen, actor objects interact as they move around and sound objects play as defined on the timeline.

Starting, Saving, and Retrieving a Movie

The animation procedure is useless unless you know how to start MOVE and how to save and retrieve the work you create. This section outlines these basic procedures.

To start CorelMOVE, double-click the CorelMOVE icon located in the Corel application group. When MOVE starts, the screen appears empty except for a few items on the menu bar. From this blank screen, you can start a new animation or open an existing animation you want to edit. MOVE displays at the bottom of the File pull-down menu a list of the last four files you edited while in MOVE.

Retrieving a Movie

After you've created an animated movie, you may want to make changes, such as changing your magician's bird from a dove to an eagle. To make changes, you must first learn how to retrieve a movie.

You can open an animation by using the **File Open** (Ctrl+O) command. You can open CorelMOVE (CMV) files or ProMotion (MWF) files by changing the file type selection that appears beneath the listing of file names. Selecting the proper directory and file name and then clicking OK opens the desired animation file. The MOVE screen shown in figure 20.1 appears.

FIG. 20.1

The CorelMOVE screen.

Pick tool
Path tool
Actor tool
Prop tool
Sound tool
Cue tool

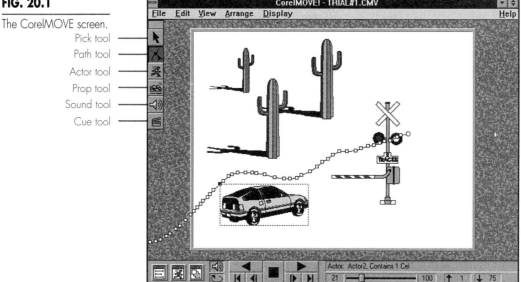

The following list explains how you can use the tools along the left margin of the CorelMOVE screen:

- *Pick tool.* Use this tool to select objects.

- *Path tool.* Use this tool to create and edit actor paths.

- *Actor tool.* Use this tool to create and edit actors.

- *Prop tool.* Use this tool to create and edit props.

- *Sound tool.* Use this tool to create and edit sound objects.

■ *Cue tool.* Use this tool to add and edit the insertion of events, or cues, to the timeline. A typical event is the display and removal of an object, the start and finish of an actor's actions, and the start or finish of a sound cue.

The center of the screen contains the editing area where you design the animation. Object placement and path definition happen in this screen.

Along the bottom of the screen are various other icons, controls you use to play or rewind the animation, and information about selected objects. Clicking the Timelines icon reveals the relationship among objects in the current animation as shown in figure 20.2. You will learn more about the Timelines window later in this chapter.

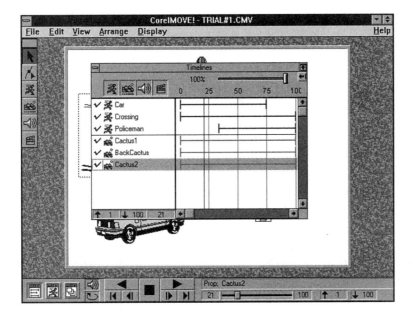

FIG. 20.2

The Timelines window.

Starting a New Movie

Choosing File New (Ctrl+N) opens the Select Name For New File dialog box (see fig. 20.3). Until you enter a name for the animation, the file name is UNTITLED.CMV. (The CMV extension indicates a CorelMOVE file.) Enter a file name, drive, and directory location, and click OK to save a spot for the animation where you specified. Now every time you save your movie, which you are encouraged to do frequently, MOVE stores the most recently edited animation file in the disk location you specified. Note that this procedure is the same as in DRAW.

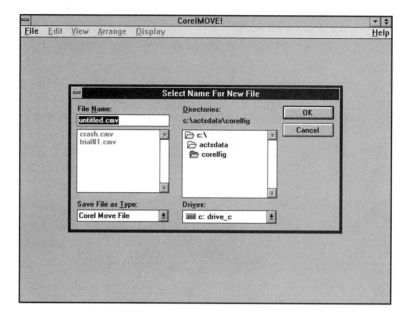

Saving a Movie

You can save animations by choosing File Save (Ctrl+S). MOVE stores the animation in the location you specify during the File New procedure. The File Save As command is more limited in MOVE as compared to other applications because you can only save a file in CMV format. You really use Save As to save the currently active animation under another name.

Setting the Animation Window Size and Playback Attributes

You should set the animation window size at the beginning of the animation process because the size of the window determines the amount of room available for props and actors. The default window size is

480-by-360 pixels (screen dots). Other standard sizes are 320-by-200 and 640-by-480 pixels. The smaller the window size, the less overall system demand it places on the computer.

You can set the animation window size by choosing the **D**isplay Animation Info menu option. Choosing this menu option displays the Animation Information dialog box shown in figure 20.4.

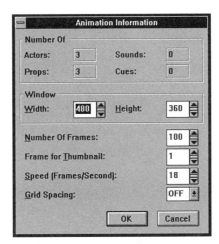

FIG. 20.4

The Animation Information dialog box.

The number of actor objects, prop objects, sound objects, and cues included in the current animation appear at the top of the window. Below this area are the boxes you use to enter the width and height of the animation window. Set the dimensions to the sizes mentioned previously in this section until you are familiar with MOVE's operational constraints.

The bottom portion of the Animation Information dialog box includes the Number Of Frames option, which determines the total number of frames in the animation. The default value is 100, but you can make the animation any length from 1 to 9,999 frames. Choose the frame number that best represents the contents of the animation and enter its number in this box. The frame number appears at the bottom of the screen when viewing the animation in the editing window. With the Frame for Thumbnail option, you can set the desired animation frame to display as the thumbnail (rough bitmap) image used in preview operations in MOSAIC and other Corel applications.

The Speed (Frames/Second) option determines the speed of the animation. The higher the setting, the faster the animation progresses. The lower the number, the slower the animation. The speed range extends from 1 to 18 frames per second, and the actual playback speed depends on the processor type, complexity of animation, hard disk access time, and amount of RAM memory.

TIP

If you divide the total number of frames by the number of frames per second, you can determine the length of your animation. If your animation includes 100 frames playing at 10 frames per second, for example, the animation plays in 10 seconds.

The Grid Spacing option determines the precise screen pattern along which objects and nodes are placed. If set to OFF, no grid is applied and objects can be placed anywhere. The other settings determine the pixel location closest to where you actually click and move the object to that location.

Clicking OK establishes these settings for the current animation.

Creating Props and Single-Cell Actors

You can create props and actors within MOVE using the Paint window. (Don't confuse the Paint window with the CorelPAINT application.) Or you can create the objects in another drawing application—such as CorelDRAW!—and transfer the object to MOVE. You start this section learning how to create a prop or actor, and then you move on to applying painting techniques for special effect.

Creating a New Prop or Actor

Props are stationary objects that transition on and off the screen. They do not move while on-screen. To begin the process of creating a prop, choose the Prop tool from the toolbox. The New Prop dialog box appears, as shown in figure 20.5.

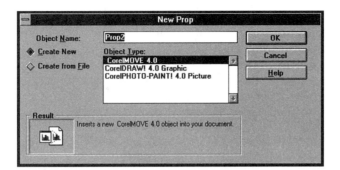

FIG. 20.5

The New Prop dialog box.

After you use the MOVE Paint facility to draw the object, choose **F**ile **E**xit and follow the instructions to save the prop object under its designated name and then add it to the current animation.

To name the prop or actor object you want to add to your animation, use the Object Name box located at the top of the New Prop dialog box. Always use a unique name to prevent the object from being confused later with other objects you create.

TIP

Give each object a unique name so that you know which to access when editing later in the timelines display.

The three options available in the Object Type window refer to the application you intend to use to create the prop object. CorelMOVE 4.0 uses the bitmap oriented Paint utility included with MOVE. CorelDRAW! 4.0 Graphic instructs MOVE to open CorelDRAW! so you can edit in DRAW using its more sophisticated tools. CorelPHOTO-PAINT! 4.0 Picture refers to a bitmap obtained from the PHOTO-PAINT application.

Create New indicates a new object is created after you open the application, and Create from File indicates you want to use an already existing image in the designated Object Type format.

To create a new actor, you follow an almost identical procedure except you begin by choosing the Actor tool instead of the Prop tool. The New Actor dialog box appears. It operates identically to the New Prop dialog box, and you perform the Paint-related editing operations identically for props or single-cell actors. Working with multicell actors is a little more complicated. You learn more about that topic after you learn about the basic operation of the Paint facility.

You can examine detailed prop information by double-clicking the prop or, after selecting the prop, by choosing Edit Object Info. The Object Information dialog box appears (see fig. 20.6).

FIG. 20.6

The Prop Information dialog box.

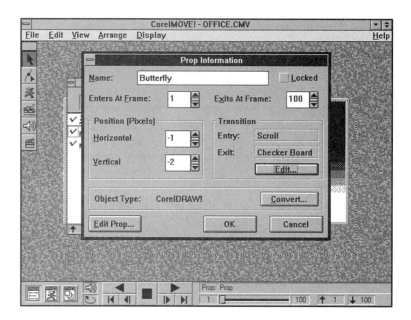

The Prop Information dialog box displays the prop's name, enter and exit frame numbers, pixel location relative to the upper-left corner (which is 0,0), and the type of prop object. You can edit any of these items. Choosing Locked, located in the upper-right corner of the dialog box, fixes the prop's screen position preventing you from dragging the prop around the window by using the mouse.

CorelMOVE provides several transition effects to control the style with which an object enters and exits the screen. They appear in the Transition option box, and you can edit them by clicking the Edit button. Selecting the desired transition type for Enter and Exit and then choosing Preview allows you to view the effect of your transition choice on that particular object (see fig. 20.7).

Using the Paint Facility

You will deal with object creation using DRAW later in the chapter. For now, assume you are going to create a new object using the CorelMOVE Paint facility. Follow these steps to create a new object:

1. Click the Prop tool to display the New Prop dialog box.

2. In the dialog box, choose CorelMOVE 4.0 from the Object **Type** drop-down list.

3. Choose **Create** New.

4. Click OK.

The Paint window shown in figure 20.8 opens so you can begin creating a prop object.

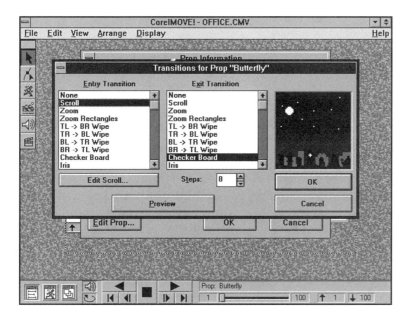

FIG. 20.7

The Prop Transitions dialog box.

To draw various objects, follow these steps:

1. Use the Background and Foreground tools to select the desired color.

2. Select the appropriate graphics tool.

3. Draw the object.

Remember that Paint works with bitmap images and does not have the same object-related orientation of DRAW. You need to shape the object properly the first time or erase and redraw the undesireable sections until the shape is as you want it.

FIG. 20.8

The MOVE 4 Paint
window and tools,
shown with an object
being created.

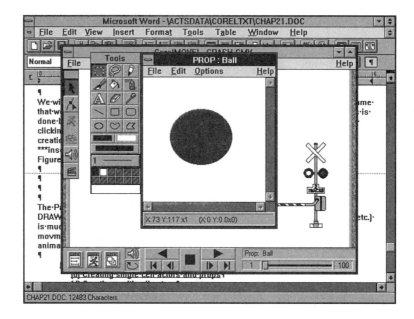

In the upper-left corner of the toolbox are the Marquee and Lasso tools. Marquee enables you to drag a square around the selected image sections, and with Lasso you can draw an irregular shape around the selected image sections. Paint selects all pixel dots contained within the selected area. When selected, the area can be dragged to other parts of the screen, deleted, cut, or copied.

You can use the Pencil tool to draw freehand lines, which adopts the color and line thickness set in the Line Width Selector and Foreground/Background tool sections. If you click the left mouse button, the line is drawn in the foreground color; the right mouse button draws in the background color.

The Brush tool draws where you drag the mouse, but uses the pattern and color defined by the Pattern Selector tool. You can edit the Paint Brush shape by double-clicking the Paint Brush tool icon. The fly-out menu displays a number of different shapes, which you can choose from by clicking the shape you want to use.

The Paint Bucket tool enables you to fill the interior of objects with the currently selected foreground color. The object you are filling should have a solid outline, or the fill spills onto the rest of the page and colors it as one object. If the fill does not work as desired, choose **Edit Undo** to return to the prior state. Then use the Options Zoom menu feature to find the break in the line, and use the Pencil tool to fill the break. Finally, you can refill the object.

The Spray Can tool acts just like a normal spray can. Double-clicking the icon displays a window with a setting for the thickness of the line (called the aperture) and the density of the color (called the pressure). Experimenting with these settings gets you the desired coverage and effect.

TIP

Pressing the Tab key toggles you between the current and previously used tool.

You can add text to the drawing by using the Font tool. Double-clicking the tool displays a familiar Font dialog box, which allows you to set the typeface, style, and size of any text added after you make this change. The text adopts the currently active foreground color. In addition, you must edit the text before clicking anywhere else on-screen. After you click the screen, the text becomes part of the bitmap image and must be erased and reentered.

The Eraser tool will likely become an old friend if you use the Paint utility regularly. You can use it to erase the pixels so that you can modify the image. To erase, drag the eraser icon over the desired area. Double-clicking the eraser removes the image currently in the Paint window. If you need to perform fine erasures, use Outline Zoom to increase the image size to eliminate the desired pixels without disrupting the rest of the image.

You use the Color Pickup tool to select a color from the drawing and to make it the currently selected color. This tool is most useful when working with complicated drawings that contain more than 12 colors—the limit of the Recent Color Pickup Log. After you select the color, it becomes the current default and exactly matches the color you selected it from previously from using the Color Pickup tool.

The next two rows of the toolbox contain tools used for drawing various shapes. These include, from top left to bottom right, drawing lines, rectangles, rounded corner rectangles, ellipse, curves, and polygons. All but the last two are simple click-and-drag operations to obtain the desired shape. You use the Curve tool by first dragging the desired shape and then releasing the mouse button. A straight line connects the starting and ending object points. You use the Polygon tool by clicking at the first corner point and then clicking at each other corner point. At the final point, you double-click to end the object.

TIP

> You can draw color-filled objects by first selecting the desired color from the Pickup Log and then double-clicking any of the object shape icons. They all fill in on the toolbox and draw with the selected interior fill color.

Creating Special Effects with Paint

You can rotate, scale, mirror, tint, define the opacity, or smooth out selected Paint image areas. These special effects are located under the Paint facility Options menu selection (see fig. 20.9).

FIG. 20.9

The Paint Options menu.

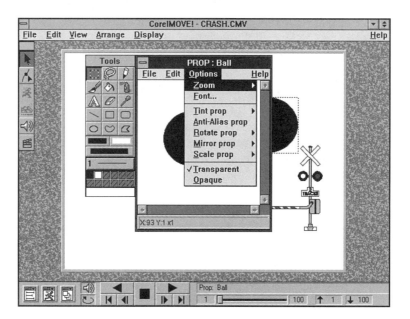

Zoom allows for x1, x2, x4, and x8 zoom in on the current Paint image. The keyboard shortcuts for the zoom options are Alt+1, Alt+2, Alt+3, and Alt+4, respectively. You can move to the desired section of the image using the scroll bars at the bottom and on the sides.

You define the desired default text font by choosing the Options Font menu selection and setting the font design, style, and size from the Font dialog box and clicking OK.

You use the Tint option to add a specific color tint to an entire object or to a specific section of the object. Towards Foreground adds a tint that shades the colors to that defined as the foreground color. Towards Background adds a tint that shades the colors to that defined as the background color. If you have selected a section of the Paint image, the Tint Selection designation appears. If you have not selected a section of the Paint image, Tint All Cells appears for an actor object and Tint Prop appears for a prop object.

The Anti-Alias prop option smoothes the outline of color objects and is most useful when printing to a video device.

Rotate, Mirror, and Scale deal with major movements of the object or a smaller subsection. You can rotate either the entire object or a smaller section of the object. You can rotate left by 90 degrees, right by 90 degrees, or by a specific number of degrees (By Degrees), clockwise, or counterclockwise. If you select a smaller section of the object, you can Free rotate the object around its center by dragging on the smaller handles in the corners of the selection outline border.

You use Mirror to change the object, or its selected subsection, into a mirror image of the original. Vertical turns the object upside down and Horizontal turns it left-to-right.

You use Scale to change the size of the object. You can change the size of the entire object from 0 to 200 percent of the original size by using the Scale By Percent dialog box. You also can scale by dragging the corner handles of the smaller subsection selection outline box.

The two provided translucency effects are Transparent and Opaque. If an object, or a selected subsection, is transparent, any object beneath it shows through. If it is opaque, any underlying object is not visible.

Adding Multicell Actors, Movement, and Sound

You create animation through a series of images with minor changes that, when displayed in rapid succession after each other, create the illusion of movement. Each separate image containing any modification is called a cell, and a number of cells together comprise an actor's animation. Consequently, a multicell actor is required to animate the actor. The actor can either remain in one place and animate, or it can move along a predefined path while displaying its animation contents. Finally, you can have a single-cell actor move along a predefined path. The actor itself does not change shape, but its location changes.

In summary, a multicell actor is animated in that its components change location and shape during replay based upon the image contained on each separate cell. The movement of the actor across the screen is caused by the relationship between the actor's cells, the predefined path that it is to follow and the number of path nodes compared to the number multiactor cells.

If you are getting the impression that creating animations requires a great deal of advance planning, you are right. Little happens spontaneously, although it looks that way on-screen. A great deal of creative effort goes into making animation look effortless. This section covers the actor creation procedures, actor path creation, object alignment, adding sound, and editing cues.

Creating Multicell Actors Using Paint

The process of creating a multicell object is the same as the process you already learned to create a single-cell object. You start with the basic object and copy it to the next cell of the animation. You then perform the desired changes and repeat the copying process for the next cell level until you have animated the actor as desired.

Because Paint is bitmap oriented, you must redraw much of the object for each cell. If you create actors in DRAW, you find that the node editing features greatly speed up the frame-to-frame editing process.

Follow this procedure to create a multicell actor object:

1. Open the Paint window by double-clicking the actor object you want to animate, or follow the preceding section's steps to create a new actor object. The Actor Info dialog box appears.

2. Click the Edit Actor button.

3. Choose Edit Insert Cels to reveal the dialog box shown in figure 20.10.

4. Choose Before Current Cel or After Current Cel to designate whether the additional cells are added prior to the current cell or after. In general, you add the cells after the current cell.

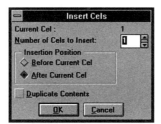

FIG. 20.10

The Insert Cels dialog box.

5. Enter a number in the **Number of Cels to Insert** text box to define how many cells you want to add in the direction you designated in step 4.

6. Choose **D**uplicate Contents if you want to copy the contents of the current cell to the inserted cells. This makes modification of the contents in the other cells easier because you don't create the initial object from scratch on each cell.

7. Click OK to insert the designated number of cells.

To delete cells, move to the cell just prior to those that you want to delete, and choose the **E**dit Remove Cels menu option to display the Delete Cels dialog box. Then, set the number of cells after the currently selected cell that you want to delete and click OK.

Viewing the prior cell's contents while creating the current cell is often useful to monitor the amount of change that takes place from one cell to the next. Choosing the Options Onion Skin menu option displays a menu with Previous Cel, Next Cel, and None as options. If you choose Previous Cel, the prior cell appears at 30 percent of its actual translucency. Thus, you can view the current cell's changes against the cell from which it is supposed to have moved. Choosing Next Cel performs the same function except that the following cell instead of the prior cell appears at 30 percent saturation. None displays only the current cell.

You can change the size and orientation of all cells associated with an object by applying the special effects to the entire image of any of the cells without selecting a subsection of the cell. After you apply these special effects, you can't remove or undo them. If you want to change a certain cell only, select a subsection of the cell and apply the desired change. You can verify the change based on the Onion Skin effect. The circle in cell one of figure 20.11, for example, has a dashed interior while the cell 2 contents were reduced by 65 percent in the vertical direction. Repeat this copy-modification process until you have the desired number of cells with the proper modifications. Choose File Exit to return to the editing window. Answer Yes, No, or Cancel as appropriate to the save related dialog box.

FIG. 20.11

Onion skin of a circle reduced by 65 percent.

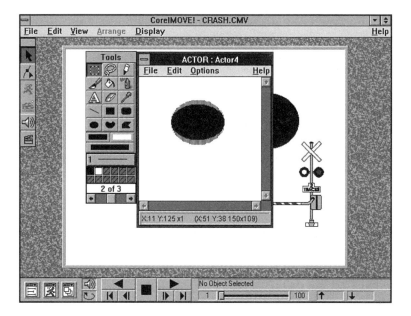

Setting the Path Registration Point

When an actor object moves along a path, it must have some orientation point that determines where the object lines up with respect to the path. This mark is called a Registration Point and appears in figure 20.12. You can move this registration point by opening the Paint window for the actor object in question and choosing Edit Registration (Ctrl+R), which creates a display similar to figure 20.1, appearing earlier in this chapter.

To move the registration point, simply click at the new registration point you want and again select Edit Registration to disable the registration operation. The object now aligns along the path using the new registration point location while moving. Notice that the registration point in the upper-left corner of the car actor object in figure 20.1 aligns along the path.

Arranging Object Orientation

CorelMOVE places every new object at a higher level than those you created previously. This feature can create problems for the actors as they move across the screen because they may be in front of or behind other objects simply because of the order of creation.

To remedy this situation, first select the object of interest and then use the Arrange menu selections, which operate similarly to those seen in CorelDRAW!. Forward One (Ctrl+PageUp) moves an object one layer forward than it is currently. Back One (Ctrl+PageDown) moves an object one layer back, or under, than it is currently. To Back (Shift+Page Down) moves the selected object to the very back of all other objects. To Front (Shift+Page Up) moves the object to the top of all other objects.

In addition, you can move the location of an object by simply clicking the object and dragging it to the new location.

Adding Actor Movement

Actors move along a path, which you define by using the Path tool. Each node of the path corresponds to a cell on the actors animation sequence. A correspondence between the number of nodes and the number of actor cells may be important for certain animated effects. If the actor only has one cell, it proceeds along the entire length of the path.

Start creating a path by first selecting the actor and then choosing the Path tool from the toolbox. The Path Edit roll-up window appears as shown in figure 20.12. Make sure you select Allow Adding Points before proceeding with the path-creation process. When you want to edit the path nodes, disable Allow Adding Points so that clicking with the mouse does not add another node point.

When you first create an actor, it is automatically given a path with only one node that is located at the actor-object's registration point. The Path Edit roll-up window automatically appears once the Path tool is selected. You use the Path tool to add more nodes to the path, which makes the object move. To add a node, simply click at the next location along the desired path of the actor's movement. A line forms to connect the two points. This second point is the next location for object display, which is the actor's second cell if it is a multicell actor. Continue to click along the desired path until the full extent of movement is defined. The last point along the path is a circle, and the other node points are all small squares.

FIG. 20.12

The Path Edit roll-up window.

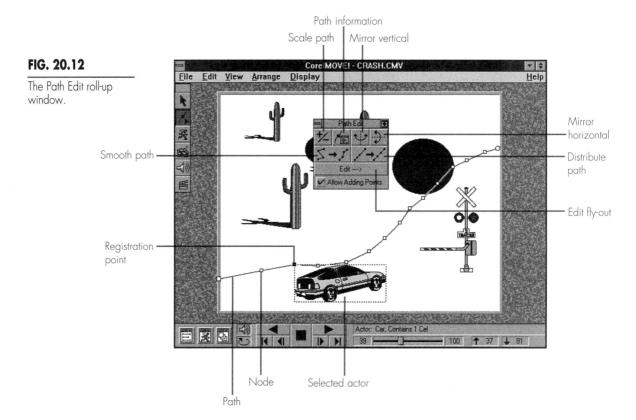

Choosing the Scale Path icon from the Path Edit roll-up window displays the Scale Path dialog box, which enables you to set the number of nodes you want along the path. The current number of points is displayed, and you change the number by entering a value in the desired box. Scale can be applied to the entire path by default or to a subsection of the path by selecting the starting and ending node points and scaling the points in between.

TIP

You can make an actor stop during your animation by inserting a large number of points between two existing ones along the path. Select the two points by clicking the first point and then pressing Shift while clicking the second point. Now choose Scale and add a large number of points between the two you selected. The actor takes a long time to traverse this large number of points, giving the impression that it has stopped.

Clicking on the Path Information icon displays the dialog box shown in figure 20.13. The Point Information box shows the total number of nodes, the number of the node currently selected, and its location in pixels on the editing window. The zero point is in the upper-left corner of the editing window. Selecting Loop To Here causes the actor to continuously loop back to this point after it has traversed the entire path. This process continues until the actor's timeline ends or the animation terminates. Double-clicking any point displays the Path Information window for that particular node.

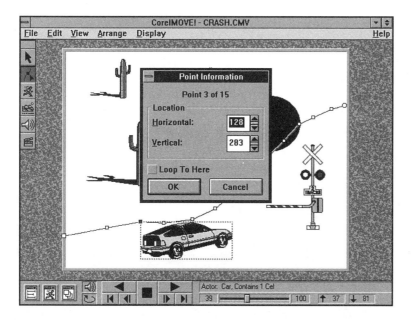

FIG. 20.13

The Path Information dialog box.

Mirror Vertical and Horizontal simply replace the original path with a mirror copy in their respective directions.

The Smooth Path option removes the sharp changes from the path. If it is selected several times, the curve begins to flatten. You use Distribute

Path to evenly distribute the nodes along the entire path or the subsection using the point-selection process. The Edit fly-out menu provides access to point-editing tools that allow for copying, cutting, pasting, clearing, and selecting points.

Adding Sound to the Animation

Sound adds a professional touch to animation. In traditional animation, you first create the sound track and then animate the actors to go along with the soundtrack. You must have properly working sound capture and playback equipment for the CorelMOVE sound features to work.

To start the Sound Editor, either click the Sound Icon located in the toolbox or choose the **E**dit Insert **N**ew Object **S**ound menu option. The New dialog box appears. Make sure to give the sound a distinct object name by typing in the Object Move text box for use when working with the timelines. Select the desired sound editing application, such as Sound Editor. If you select another sound editing application, it will now open for your use in creating the desired sound object. When you close that application, CorelMOVE inserts the object in the MOVE animation. For your purposes, use the Wave Editor included with MOVE (see fig. 20.14).

FIG. 20.14

The MOVE Wave
Editor.

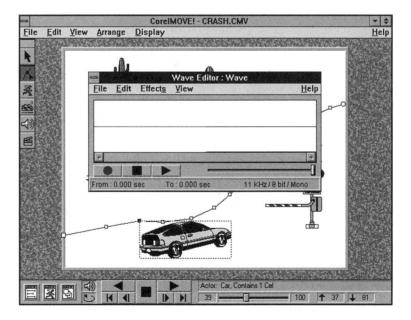

Sounds are recorded by clicking the Record button. To stop recording, click the Stop button, and choose Play to hear the recording. Choose File Exit to return to the editing window and save the sound object under its currently active name.

The Effects menu provides numerous special effects including the ability to flatten the sound (Silence), Fade Up from zero to a set percentage of the total volume, Fade Down to an established percentage of the current volume level, and Amplify from 0 to 9,999 percent. (Numbers less than 100 percent make the sound quieter and those more than 100 percent make it louder.) Other special effects include Reverse, which plays the sound backward (sometimes with amusing effects), and Echo, which makes the sound echo as though it originated in a cave. CorelMOVE applies these effects to the entire wave by default but you also can apply them to subsections of the sound by first selecting the section by dragging the mouse over the desired area and then selecting the desired effect.

After you exit from the Wave Editor, you can retrieve information regarding a sound WAV file by opening the timeline, by clicking the Timeline icon, and then double-clicking the sound object of interest. The Sound Information dialog box appears as shown in figure 20.15.

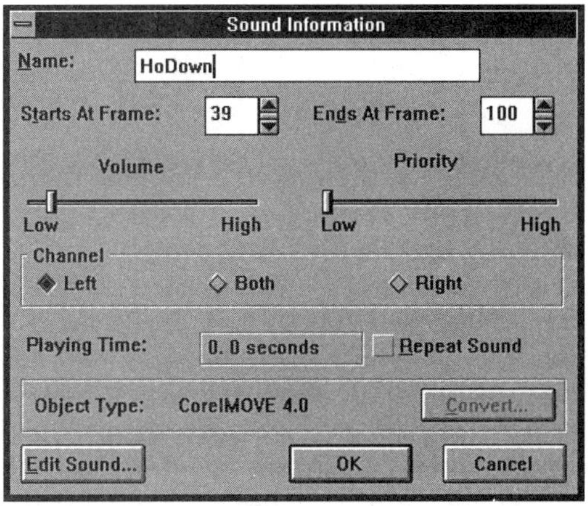

FIG. 20.15

The Sound Information dialog box.

The name of the sound object appears at the top of the window. You can edit this name if you desire. The Starts At Frame and Ends At Frame numbers indicate the animation frame numbers at which the sound starts and stops playing. The Start frame cannot be a number greater than the total number of frames in the animation. The end frame can be any number greater than the start frame. If less than the total number of animation frames, though, the sound terminates before the end of the animation unless you choose the Repeat Sound option. If the sound length is greater than the total number of frames, the animation ends and stops the sound replay at that point.

You can designate the sound as left, right, or both channel resident. If you want to play more than one sound at a time, you may consider putting one sound on the left channel and the other on the right channel. Putting it on both provides stereo sound but does not allow for flexible overlay of multiple sound signals. The Volume control sets a volume level for the sound wave and relates to the Priority setting. The higher the priority, the higher the sound volume relative to lower priority items. You may keep background music, for example, at a low priority (lower sound level) while you make the narrator's voice a higher priority (louder sound level). The length of recording time appears in the Playing Time section of the dialog box. Choose Edit Sound to display the Wave Editor or other generating application as shown in the Object Type dialog box section.

NOTE

Remember, the Wave Editor is not very sophisticated and cannot perform some special functions such as merging two sounds into one soundtrack. You may want to look around for more extensive sound-editing packages, such as Microsoft Quick Recorder, or EZ Sound FX for more capability—and more fun!

Adding and Editing Cues

You use cues to initiate segments of the animation. They provide a way for the person viewing the animation to interact with it and guide it in desired directions. Each Cue has its own name, which allows for its own specific definition. The basic Cue insertion sequence is to open the Cue tool, name the cue, define its enter and exit frame locations, designate the conditions under which events should happen (for example, clicking a prop), and finally define the action you take after meeting the predefined conditions.

Choosing the Cue tool opens the Cue Information dialog box shown in figure 20.16.

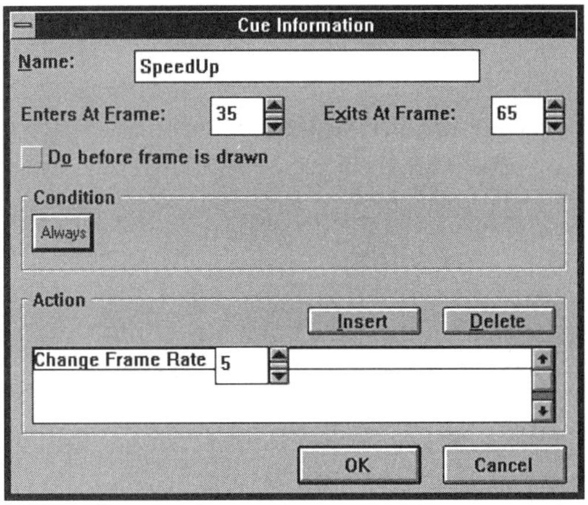

FIG. 20.16

The Cue Information dialog box.

The Name field contains the name under which the cue is accessed for later editing. The Enters At Frame and Exits At Frame fields designate the animation frames at which the designated cue starts and stops. Do before frame is drawn tells MOVE to begin the cue before the Enters At Frame number is drawn on-screen. A special effect, for example, may require that an object appears on-screen before CorelMOVE draws the designated frame on-screen.

You use the Condition field to define the criteria used to determine if and when to initiate the cue. Clicking the displayed button presents a listing of various condition types. Each of these conditions, except for Always, leads to other conditional lists. You can initiate actions after a time delay, after a mouse click anywhere on-screen, or after pressing a key.

Wait For stops the animation until one of the actions shown in the Second List (Time Delay, Mouse Click, or Key Down) occurs. Choosing Time Delay displays another box that allows for entry of the desired time delay (up to a 30-second maximum). Choosing Mouse Click displays the Anything, Actor Named, and Prop Named options. These three options define which mouse click type initiates the designated action.

Anything means that a click anywhere on-screen initiates the actions. Actor Named opens another list where you can specify the actor upon which a mouse click initiates the action. Prop Named opens another list where you can specify the prop upon which a mouse click initiates the action. Key Down, from list two, opens a third-level entry point that designates the pressed key action that starts the action.

The If Then Else option says that the cued action only starts when the designated conditions are met. If the conditions are met, the action designated with the Then diamond highlighted is initiated. If the conditions are not met, the action designated with the Else highlighted is initiated. If no action is selected, nothing happens.

The action field provides several options: Continue with the animation as it is; Goto Frame, which jumps the animation to a specific frame from which it continues; Pause Until, which causes the animation to pause until the previously defined conditional statement becomes true; End Animation, which stops the animation completely; Change Frame Rate, which changes the speed at which the animation plays to the frame rate set in the attached box; Play a Sound object, Stop a Sound object's playback, or Execute another Cue.

CorelDRAW! inserts cues on the timeline just like the other prop and actor objects, but grouped with the Cue icon. Make sure that the Then button is selected when you are setting the first action or confusing results may occur.

Viewing and Editing Animation Timing

The timing of when props appear, actors start, and sounds play are all related in the timelines. This timing relationship is graphically displayed, which allows for easy modification.

Clicking the Timelines icon from the main CorelMOVE screen reveals the Timelines dialog box. Clicking the expansion arrow at the top right of the Timelines dialog box displays the relative timing of each animation event on a timeline as shown in figure 20.17.

FIG. 20.17

The Timelines dialog box displaying the timing of each animation event.

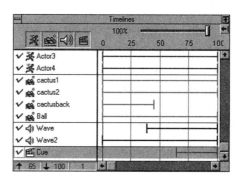

Along the left side of the display are the objects with the object-type icon shown to the left of the object name (such as *prop* or *actor*). To the right of the objects is a timing display that shows the starting and ending point for each of the objects. The frame numbers are at the top of the timeline window, and the Enter and Exit frames for each selected object appear at the bottom left of the window on the status line. The up arrow indicates the Enter frame, and the down arrow indicates the Exit frame. The currently selected frame number appears to the right of the Exit frame number.

Above the object names are icons representing, from left to right, actors, props, sound, and cues. If you click one of these icons, CorelMOVE displays that type of object or removes it from the display depending upon the current display status. The Zoom Slider displays a specified percentage of the timeline. When you set the Zoom Slider to 100 percent, you can view the entire timeline. If you set it to 50 percent, only half of the timeline appears, but it is in much finer detail. This Zoom In mode is useful when precise timing between objects is critical.

The left side of an object's timeline represents its enter frame, and the right side represents its exit frame. You can move the left and right ends of the timelines to new locations by dragging the left or right side of the line to the desired location. In addition, you can drag the entire line to a new location by dragging at the center of the line.

You delete an object from the timeline by first selecting it and then pressing Delete.

Animation Design Considerations

Planning goes a long way in creating an effective animation. Remember that animated objects appear more real when they have realistic characteristics. To compress a ball in the vertical direction when it hits a wall, for example, is one way to animate, but a real ball compresses vertically and expands horizontally. This combined effect makes animated objects appear more real.

You also can have fun with animation by setting up the characters—and the audience—for the next action. A slight pause, for example, may be very effective in increasing the awareness of the next activity. A slight wavering indicating the intention to walk makes the actual walking actions more effective. Don't be afraid to exaggerate an actors movements, and do not minimize the number of frames at the expense of adequate follow through on the actor's part. It also helps to keep things less square—more rounded. Real objects are rarely square but because computers make squares so easily, many computer generated objects have square edges. Try to avoid this tendency.

Timing also is a critical aspect of animation. You make things slow down or speed up based upon the number of frames contained within that particular part of the animation. The more frames included along the path, the slower the object moves. The fewer points, the faster the object will move. If you want a man to move slower than a dog that is chasing him, for example, you give the dog actor's path fewer points than the path for the man and adjust the point spacing so that the dog moves a larger distance with each path point compared to the dogs distance.

The more appealing the characters, the more fun the audience has in watching them in their excursions. Take the time to make the characters meet your desired audience objectives, and your viewers will receive the animations better.

Using DRAW Images in MOVE

The Paint facility included with MOVE is bitmap oriented, and has only a fraction of DRAW's editing capabilities. In addition, moving the object's parts (the feet or hands, for example) is much more difficult in Paint than in DRAW. DRAW allows for object node movements where Paint requires a substantial redraw effort for each frame of an actor's animation movie since it does not use a vector graphic approach.

The layering aspects of DRAW allow for easy copying of information from one layer (or frame) to another while showing the previous or following layer in a specially selected outline color. You are strongly encouraged to use the editing capabilities of DRAW while making your animated actors. In addition, the extensive DRAW clipart and symbol library provides a tremendous base from which to create professional yet simple animations.

This section shows how DRAW is used to create actors and why you are better served working with DRAW than Paint.

To create a prop or actor in DRAW, choose the Edit Insert New Object Prop or Actor menu option to display the New Actor or Prop dialog box. Choose the Create New and CorelDRAW! 4.0 Graphic options;

then click OK. DRAW opens and prepares for creation or editing of the desired object. In figure 20.18, a kangaroo was pulled into DRAW's symbols library. We will work with this symbol.

You have access to the CorelDRAW! symbols library and drawing tools while creating and modifying your actor and prop objects. Having this access makes life simpler when creating actors because moving object nodes around is much easier and faster than redrawing the object for each frame of the animation as is required with Paint.

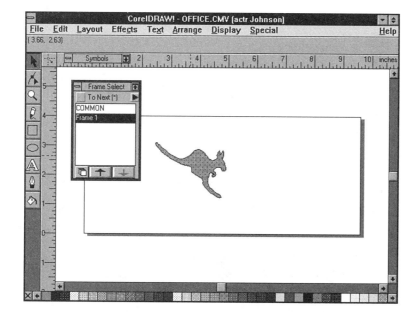

FIG. 20.18

The CorelDRAW! Frame Editing window (with kangaroo symbol included).

The animation opens with a single frame, as shown in the Frame Select roll-up. You use the Common layer to create objects that will be cloned to all other frame layers. To add an object to this layer, select it and create the object. It automatically appears on the other layers. To create an object's first frame, choose Frame 1 and create the object. In figure 20.18, you can see the kangaroo from the CorelDRAW! Animals symbol library. The To Next option, when selected, copies certain of the effects added to the object on the current layer to the next layer.

The process for adding objects to frames includes adding a frame and then copying the object to that frame. To add objects to frames, follow these steps:

1. To add a frame, first select Frame 1 in the Frame Select window.

2. Click the black triangle in the upper-right corner of the Frame Select window to display the drop-down list.

3. Choose New to display the Insert New Frames dialog box into which you can define the number of new frames to insert. When the frames are inserted, they have no objects on them. You add the objects after the frames are inserted.

4. Click OK to add a single frame, or change the number and then click OK.

5. To copy an object from one frame to another, first move the frame containing the object for copying.

6. Select the object(s).

7. Select Copy To from the drop-down list in the Frame Select window. The cursor changes to an arrow.

8. Move the arrow to the desired destination frame and click to copy the object to that frame level. Notice that the same object now appears on each frame level.

Alternatively, choosing Move To from the drop-down list moves the selected object(s) to the destination frame.

Seeing the prior frame's contents is often valuable when editing the current frame's objects. You can determine the level of desired change from one frame to the next. DRAW provides an easy way of determining one frames contents from the next by allowing you to view the underlying, or following, frame in another color and at a reduced intensity. These settings are provided under the drop-down list's Options selection, which displays the Frame Options dialog box (see fig. 20.19).

The Onion Skin is like a transparency that allows you to view the underlying (Previous) or following (Next) frames in a color you select by clicking the small triangle in the color boxes to the right. In Front tells DRAW to display the other layer's object outlines in front of the objects on the currently selected layer. Selection Wire Color defines the color used to display an object selected on a specific layer while viewing another layer of the actor's animation. If you set Wire Color to green, for example, and you have selected an object on frame 4 but are currently viewing frame 2, the frame 4 object appears in green. You can activate Previous and Next at the same time. Figure 20.20 displays the frame 2 view of the kangaroo symbol copied to frame 2 and reduced in vertical height and then copied to frame 3 and reduced again.

The Preview icon is located in the bottom left corner of the Frame Select dialog box. Clicking it displays the Previewing Frame dialog box and plays the animation for this particular actor. The arrows move the animation frame display forward and backward. This is a convenient way to survey the effect of the various editing changes between frames. Click OK to return to the Frame Edit display. Click the desired Frame level, and perform any editing necessary to get the actor into the desired form.

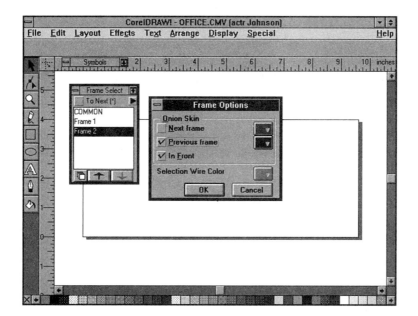

FIG. 20.19

The Frame Options dialog box.

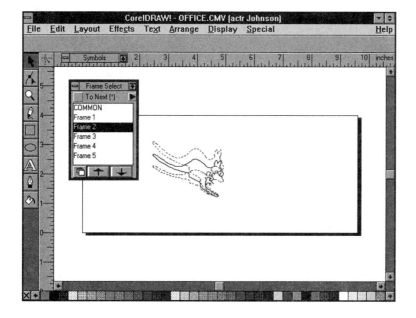

FIG. 20.20

The Onion Skin view of multiple frames.

Choose File Exit Revert To to save the actor under its designated name and return to the MOVE editing window. The DRAW actor is now treated as an OLE (Object Linking and Embedding) object while in MOVE. Double-clicking the object instructs MOVE to open DRAW so that you can edit the object. Changes made to the object in DRAW are automatically updated and added to the MOVE animation.

TIP

> If you want to save a copy of the object while in DRAW and in a DRAW format, choose File Save As, type a file name and directory, and then choose OK.

You are encouraged to use the power of CorelDRAW! to create and edit animation objects. The clip art library is extensive, and the node-editing tools make object modification much more efficient. The drawback is that to make it work at a reasonable speed requires a substantial amount of system resource. If your system is not powerful enough to perform up to desired speeds, you may be better off importing the objects into the Paint editor and making modifications there. A drawback is that the standard CDR format is not accepted by MOVE, so you may need to export the image from within DRAW into a PCX or other compatible format before using it in Paint. Importing is accomplished by selecting File Import Actor/Prop/Sound and then selecting the desired file.

Exporting Animation Objects

You can save your animation as a movie and view it without even operating CorelMOVE. This type of feature is useful for KIOSK displays or sales presentations where you only need the movie, not the editing capability. Choose the File Export To Movie command. After you type the name of the movie, make a drive selection and click OK. MOVE makes a CMV movie playable by using the CorelPLAYER application. Installing the CorelPLAYER involves copying the executable files and modifying the INI files.

You can export animated movies in a CorelMOVE (CMV) or Movie for Windows (MWF) file format. You can use the animation in another application as long as that application supports the CMV or MWF file format. You can use MOVE animations in CorelSHOW or export them as a stand-alone presentation when you use them in conjunction with the SHOWRUN.EXE file.

Summary

CorelMOVE provides extensive animation capability that adds a high level of fun and excitement to presentations. You can create your animation objects completely from within MOVE, but you are encouraged to use the Windows OLE capability and employ the extensive power of CorelDRAW! in object creation. In addition, you can use CorelPHOTO-PAINT images as backdrops for the presentations. You can import and modify CorelTRACE vector images within DRAW and then use them in MOVE. You then can use MOVE animations in conjunction with CorelCHART files to add a special—and unforgettable—touch to a CorelSHOW presentation.

By this time, you have extensive experience with the various Corel applications, and you can begin thinking of ways to use them in conjunction with each other. Scan your picture into TRACE and scan it into a vector graphic that is imported into DRAW for editing as a MOVE actor. Animate the actor and have it introduce an object from within MOVE combined with your voice-over.

The combinations are endless. Let your imagination go wild, and turn your DRAW images into animations with life.

Combining the Applications

Although each application performs a powerful function, the true power of CorelDRAW! comes from integrating the applications into a uniform set of complimentary graphic tools. This chapter leads you through the creation of a simple presentation that includes components from DRAW, CHART, TRACE, MOVE, PHOTO-PAINT, and SHOW. When finished, you should have a clear picture of how the applications compliment each other and truly make a whole that is more than the sum of the parts.

Summary of the Application Functions

CorelDRAW! is a drawing package. You use it to create various vector-based graphic images that can then be used for actors or props in MOVE animation, logos or other objects that accent CorelCHART's graphs, and backgrounds in SHOW. PHOTO-PAINT is used to touch up bitmapped images such as photographs so that they match the artistic effect desired. TRACE converts bitmapped images into vector graphic images that can be scaled or easily modified in DRAW.

For example, you can scan a person's photograph in PHOTO-PAINT, convert it to a vector image in TRACE, finalize the vector image design in DRAW, and use that image as an actor in MOVE. Ultimately, the MOVE animation could be pasted into a SHOW presentation as an introduction to a particular slide. The total scope of effects possible with the Corel suite of applications is limited only by your imagination.

Overall Scope of the Project

For our purposes here, we are going to create a presentation for Merlin's Unicorn Grain and Feed store. We will create a unicorn logo in DRAW, transport it to CHART for a representation of last year's grain sales, create a MOVE animation using a clip art wizard as Merlin, and then combine the pieces into a SHOW presentation. The overall scope of the project is not complex, but will illustrate the complimentary use of the applications. If you do not have a CD-ROM drive, select any of the images from the standard clip art included under the C:\COREL40\CLIPART subdirectory. The procedures are identical, only the file names change.

Creating the Unicorn Logo

The first main procedure is to create the logo in CorelDRAW!. Follow these steps to create the logo:

1. Open DRAW and choose **File** **I**mport.

2. Insert CD-ROM 1 into your optical drive and then select the D:\CLIPART\FANTASY subdirectory.

3. Open the IUNICORN.CDR file to bring it into DRAW. Reduce it in size.

4. Choose the Text tool, and click at the bottom-center of the unicorn image and type **Unicorn**<Enter>**Supply & Feed**. Use an Arabian typeface, normal style at 24-point size with black outline and interior fill.

5. Select both the text and the image and choose **Group** from the **Arrange** menu (Ctrl+G) to ensure alignment remains intact. This group becomes the logo.

6. Save the logo under the name UNIFEED.CDR and close DRAW to conserve processing power for the CHART section.

Your logo should look something like figure 21.1 when finished.

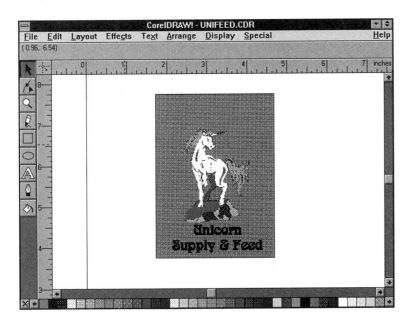

FIG. 21.1

The unicorn logo.

If you want to modify the clip art (for example, remove the background), you select the clip art, choose **Arrange Ungroup** (Ctrl+U), and make the desired modifications. You can also add other pieces of clip art to the drawing to enhance the logo effect. Once again, do not take this example as a limitation of your possible drawing options.

Creating the Feed Sales Chart

The second major task is to create a chart depicting the feed store's sales. Follow these steps to create the sales chart in CorelCHART:

1. Open CorelCHART.

2. Choose File New (Ctrl+N). For Chart Type, use vertical line chart design. Do not include the sample data.

3. Enter the data shown in figure 21.2 into its respective cell location, and then click Autoscan to assign the proper chart component names.

The data in cells A1, A2, and A3 is truncated in figure 21.2 because the column is too narrow. CHART does not truncate the data itself, just the display of the data. Click the cell to verify that the underlying text is there. If you choose, you can change the column to a wider size by dragging the line between the A and B columns. See Chapter 18 for more details.

FIG. 21.2

The Chart Data
Manager display.

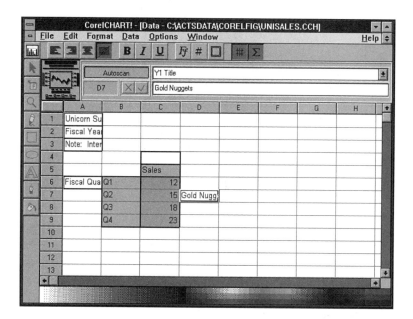

Cell A1 data is Unicorn Supply & Feed, cell A2 data is Fiscal Year 2007, and cell A3 data is Note: Internal Accounting Figures. Click the chart icon to return to the chart display screen. Choose File Import; then select the UNIFEED.CDR file we created in the previous section and click OK to include it as part of the chart. Finally, scale and relocate the chart and logo components as shown in figure 21.3. Save the chart design as UNISALES.CCH. Notice that this procedure did not take advantage of the OLE features and that double-clicking in the logo does not open DRAW and modifying the UNIFEED.CDR file does not change the logo design in the CHART file.

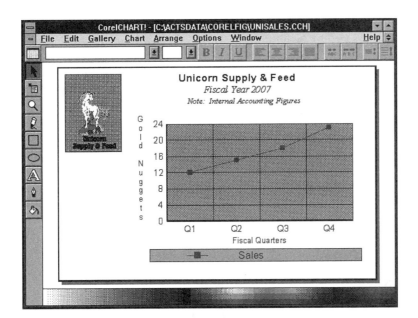

FIG. 21.3

The chart display with logo.

Animating the Wizard

Now include an animation of Merlin walking across the screen to introduce the latest Fiscal Year 2007 sales figures. To do this, use a piece of clip art from the DRAW clip art library (\FANTASY\th3_2.cdr). Don't make him walk; have him float around on-screen and get everyone's attention before the big sales numbers are released.

Open MOVE and choose **File New**. Name the file MERLIN.CMV. Click the Actor icon and choose New CorelDRAW! 4.0 File to open CorelDRAW!. Notice that DRAW now expects us to create an actor. Use the **File Import** command to bring in the \CLIPART\FANTASY\TH3_2.CDR file. Once you've brought the file into DRAW, use **Arrange Ungroup** to free the backgrounds, and then select and remove the rectangular background and the diamond. Select the entire figure, and use **Arrange Group** (Crtl+G) to once again form it into a group. Finally, choose **File Exit** to return to MOVE with the new actor. A dialog box appears that asks whether you want to update your OLE object. Click Yes. Be sure drive and directory are set to where you want to save the file or it won't work.

Click the Path icon (it looks like the DRAW Shape tool icon) and then click the new actor. Create a series of points beginning with the current location and circling around on the screen until Merlin moves off the screen to the right (see fig. 21.4). Next, select the beginning and end points; then click the roll-up's +/- button and insert 100 nodes between the two to give our actor a slower motion. Notice that this actor does take advantage of the OLE capability, and that you can double-click the actor and edit it using DRAW. This would be particularly handy if you wanted to make your actor change shape between frames during his migration.

FIG. 21.4

Making Merlin move.

Remember that you could also have included background props, sound objects, and additional actors to achieve your desired point. The sound could have been music followed by Merlin's voice announcing the next slide. Once again, your imagination is the limit.

Combining into a Show

Now that you have your chart and introductory animation, the final step is to integrate the two in SHOW for the final presentation. Follow these steps:

1. Open SHOW and choose **File New** (Ctrl+N) presentation with a total of two slides.

2. Select the first page, and then choose **Insert Animation**.

3. Choose the CorelMOVE file type and then the MERLIN.CMV file you just created. Size the animation to fit on-screen once it is displayed.

4. Select the second slide, and choose **Insert Object** Create From CorelCHART 4.0 File; then choose the UNISALES.CCH file you created in the last section. Drag the cursor for the projected chart size, and the CHART design is inserted as slide 2 with the dimensions you defined.

5. Choose File Save **As** and save the file under the name UNIPRESO.SHW. Click the Screenshow icon and watch the fun start (see fig. 21.5).

TIP

Make sure that the duration of the animation matches the duration of the slide display or you may end the presentation prematurely or see blank pages at the end.

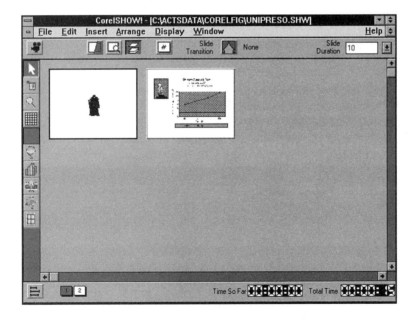

FIG. 21.5

The slide sorter view of the presentation.

Efficiency Tricks and Tips

The more powerful your computer, the easier time you will have in making the applications work with each other because you will be able to open more of them without seriously degrading system performance. Once you have the applications open, use the Alt+Tab feature to cycle between them, or access the Windows Task List by pressing Ctrl+Esc and then selecting the desired open application. In addition, try to use the provided support art work provided by Corel. There are literally thousands of different designs provided, from bitmaps to CDR files to animation. Bringing them into the proper application and modifying them as opposed to creating them from scratch will greatly increase your efficiency when creating images and artwork.

Finally, you may find it better to create your presentations in stages as opposed to all at once. The more complicated the design, the more characteristics need to overlap in a complimentary way. You may find it useful to create a timeline onto which you can map the relationship between the various objects.

No matter how you do it, have fun! CorelDRAW! 4 provides you with wonderful tools for releasing your imagination. It has been a pleasure leading you through its operation, and I hope to see some of your handiwork in the future.

Installation Considerations

This section of the book is designed to provide you with the overall information you need to perform an initial installation of CorelDRAW! 4. If you have very specific problems with the installation procedure, refer to the *CorelDRAW! 4 Installation Guide*, or review the README.WRI file located on floppy disk 1 or on the CD1 root directory. Also check the various application subdirectories for additional README files which contain the most current information available at the time of product shipment.

You can also call Corel Technical Support at (613) 728-1990. Be aware that a file named LOGFILE.TXT is created during installation and stored under the \WINDOWS directory. This file includes a listing of all options selected during the installation procedure. Print this file before calling Corel Tech Support because many of their questions will be answered by this information.

Finally, to run DRAW at an adequate speed, you need a system with at least a 80386/33 processor with 4M RAM, particularly if you plan to open more than one application at a time, such as DRAW and CHART. To achieve acceptable performance, use a super VGA monitor with 1M video memory, upgrade your RAM to 8M (16M ideal), and run on a 80486DX processor with at least a 200M hard disk drive and one high-density 3 1/2" drive. You need a sound card, such as the Pro Audio Spectrum, to play sound objects.

Windows 3.1 is required for CorelDRAW! 4 operation, and the SHARE.EXE file must be installed unless running under Windows for Workgroups. In addition, you can store the various sections of CorelDRAW! on different disk drives, but the first fixed disk drive (usually C) must have 1151K free for use by the ~COREL.T temporary file. This file is deleted automatically after the installation is completed. Finally, make sure the SMARTDRV.EXE is installed with your Windows installation, or loading CorelDRAW! can take an eternity (about two and a half hours). To install SMARTDRV.EXE, add the following line to your AUTOEXEC.BAT file:

C:\WINDOWS\SMARTDRV

The Basic Installation Options

You can install CorelDRAW! 4 from floppy disks or from the CD-ROM. You can install CorelDRAW! 4 to run from a hard disk or from the CD-ROM.

To install from floppy disks or a CD-ROM, follow these steps:

1. Insert floppy disk 1 or CD disk 1 in the 3 1/2" drive (usually A or B) or your optical drive (for example, D).

2. Open Windows Program Manager.

3. Choose **File Run** and type **<drive letter>:\SETUP**. The setup program starts and leads you through the rest of the installation procedure.

The program asks you to choose between Full Install or Custom Install. The following sections detail these options.

NOTE

You can run earlier versions of DRAW (1.2, 2.x, or 3) and 4 on the same system if they are stored in separate directories. If you are installing to a system that already has release 3 installed, delete the PROGMAN.COR, REG.COR, and WIN.COR files from the \WINDOWS subdirectory before performing the installation so that the version 4 installation will create the proper files and backups. Corel makes backups of prior files by leaving them with the same file name but adding a BAK extension to designate it as a backup.

Full Installation

Full Install installs all applications and offers a choice of specific import and export filters, fonts, and scanner drivers. Files are installed under the COREL40 subdirectory on the default drive upon which Windows is installed, unless you specify otherwise at the beginning of the installation procedure. If you choose to install a scanner, the TWAIN.DLL file is copied to the \WINDOWS\TWAIN directory. The directory is created if it does not already exist. A full installation requires around 34M of hard disk space.

Custom Installation

Custom Install allows you to specify precisely which applications are installed and where they are installed. If you decide to install CHART, DRAW is automatically installed because the two share some files. At the bottom of the dialog box is a reading of the total disk space free on the target disks, the amount of disk space required for the installation selected, and the amount of disk space anticipated free after installation. You are provided with three options for each of the applications: All, Some, or None. *All* installs the total application. *Some* allows you to select the various aspects of that application by displaying another Options dialog box. *None* does not install any aspect of that particular application. You can also specify the disk drive and directory under which the application will be stored.

A minimum installation of DRAW only requires between 10 and 15M of hard disk space. Loading only DRAW makes the installation procedure faster and easier. So if you don't plan to use the other applications, don't install them.

If you need to change your installation at a later date, choose Custom Install option and only install the options you want.

SETUP makes changes to the AUTOEXEC.BAT, CONFIG.SYS, and WIN.INI files as needed to make the packages run correctly.

Installing Fonts

Because Windows applications scan the TrueType font listing while loading, a large number of installed TrueType fonts can slow down your applications. You may want to keep the number of fonts to a minimum and only load those you need.

Full Install installs up to 50 TrueType fonts under the \WINDOWS\SYSTEM subdirectory. Note that CD-Disc 1 contains over 750 other TrueType fonts that can also be installed using the FONTINST.EXE file located on the CD-ROM root directory. You may find that the larger the number of installed fonts, the slower your system will run.

The TrueType fonts are installed from the Windows File Manager. Follow this procedure:

1. Open the Windows File Manager.

2. Insert CD-DISC 1 in your optical drive.

3. Choose File Run and type **D:\FONTINST.EXE** (assuming D is the letter for your optical drive). The TrueType font options dialog box appears with a number of different font categories.

4. Choose the typeface category you want, or select Customize to pick exactly the typefaces for your needs.

5. Click OK to install the fonts you selected as FOT files in the \WINDOWS\SYSTEM subdirectory.

The Adobe type fonts are stored on Disc 7 under the \Fonts\ATM directory and are installed using Adobe Type Manager, a non-Corel, non-Windows application. Refer to Adobe Type Manager's manual for installation instructions.

Installing CorelDRAW! To Run from the CD-ROM

The CD-ROM installation has a multimedia QuickTour tutorial on CorelDRAW! 4 that is accessed by running the SETUP program located under the \QTOUR directory of the CD-ROM Disc 2. You run this program using the following procedure:

1. Open the Windows Program Manager. Make sure Disc 2 is in your optical drive.

2. Choose **F**ile **R**un and then type the CD-ROM drive letter (such as, D:)**\QTOUR\SETUP**. The on-screen instructions lead you through the rest of the installation procedure.

To install CorelDRAW! to run from the CD-ROM, which saves hard disk space, follow these steps:

1. Insert CD-ROM Disc 1 into the CD-ROM.

2. Open the Windows File Manager and choose **F**ile **R**un.

3. Type **<driveletter>:\SETUP2**, where <driveletter> is the CD-ROM drive.

The CD-ROM Disk 1 must remain in the CD drive while running the applications because the program files are not on the hard disk, but on the CD.

Although running CorelDRAW! directly from the CD-ROM gives you access to features that you don't get on the floppy disks, the access times are so slow that it is impractical in many situations. CD-ROM access times are 10 to 15 times slower than a standard IDE hard drive. In addition, SMARTDRV does not cache CD-ROMS, so you should get a drive-caching program for CD-ROMs. The best way to take advantage of the CD-ROM and still achieve acceptable performance is to install the program to the hard drive using SETUP and then access the CR-ROM as needed for clip art, and so on.

Network Installation

CorelDRAW! 4 comes completely local area network (LAN) ready. LAN users can concurrently access all modules once they are installed. To perform the installation, you must have access to Windows and the intended CorelDRAW! installation subdirectories. When you want to network install, run \SETUP /A. Without the /A, a non-network installation is accomplished.

After CorelDRAW! is installed on the server, you must run \COREL40\SETUP\SETUP.EXE on the server from the user's station. This action installs the necessary files onto the user's hard disk. This procedure takes around 3M of hard disk space. You can also install CorelDRAW! on the server so that the users can install a stand-alone version on their own PC from the server. The CorelDRAW! license allows this type of operation.

Working with Other Applications

Images created using the Corel applications are often used by other applications in the creation of their documents. For example, you might create a logo design in DRAW and then incorporate that design into a PageMaker newsletter document or a Freelance Graphics presentation. This section covers the basic procedures to follow to best ensure that your files transfer easily and accurately.

Windows 3.1 provides tremendous capabilities for connecting information between different applications through the use of Object Linking and Embedding (OLE). Prior to Windows OLE implementation, you needed to understand the intricacies associated with file formats and directory paths. Connecting files was a manual task heavily dependent upon the user's level of expertise. With OLE, the process is substantially automatic and you can get back to the task at hand, which is creating a document or drawing.

Object Linking and Embedding

Object Linking and Embedding refers to the Windows procedures for relating files and information to each other. Your final objective is to automate the connections between data files so that the updating of information between files is achieved with minimal impact on you. Before getting too involved with OLE use, you need to learn some terminology.

Objects are any information that is created in one Windows application and transferred to another. An object can be an image, a text file, a sound file, a chart, or even an animation move. There are two basic types of OLE applications: servers and clients. A *server* supplies objects which are used by the clients. Most applications can be both clients and servers, but that is not always the case. CorelSHOW, for example, is never a server and is a client because the information created in other applications comes together in SHOW for final presentation, but the SHOW files are never linked to other applications.

The source document is the file that contains the server application's information. The destination document is the file that will use the source document information. Using the earlier Corel logo-PageMaker newsletter document example, CorelDRAW! would be the server and the DRAW CRD file would be the source document. PageMaker would be the client and the PageMaker PM4 newsletter document would be the destination document.

An object becomes embedded in the destination document once it is filed following the proper embedding procedures. Once embedded, it is used by the destination document just as any other component of the document except with an important exception: if you want to edit the embedded object, you simply double-click it and the server application automatically opens and loads the embedded object for editing purposes. Once the editing in the server application is finished, you exit the server and return to the client application with the newly edited object information. The connection between the object and the server application is the file extension, which makes that information critical for any Windows application.

Objects become linked when the object is inserted into the destination document using the proper linking procedures. Linking means that any time the underlying source document is modified, the destination document is automatically updated. This feature can save you hours of time updating information and keep you from making mistakes of omission when working in a dynamic environment.

Coming back to the logo-newsletter example, suppose that the final logo design is still under review. You have completed the newsletter, which includes the most current logo design, and the boss tells you that the logo should be modified and included in the final newsletter design. Without linking, the logo would be modified in DRAW and then copied manually to each of the newsletter pages. Using linking, the logo is modified in DRAW, and all other occurrences of the logo are automatically updated without your intervention. The underlying file is linked to those files that use the information. Once the underlying source file information changes, all destination files automatically update.

Windows applications, including the Corel applications, make extensive use of these OLE features, and you should be aware of some limitations. Once a link is established, it includes the source document's file name and path. If you move the file, the link is useless, so try not to move things around after links are established. You probably will not remember what is linked to which files unless you establish a structured data storage procedure and stick with it to ensure proper linking operation.

Working with the Corel Applications

CorelSHOW would be a client for other objects; CorelDRAW! would be both a client and server, as would CorelMOVE and CorelCHART. Corel-PHOTO-PAINT and CorelTRACE would generally be server applications.

For example, you may use CorelPHOTO-PAINT to create a bitmap design. That bitmap could be used by DRAW as part of an image that is then used as a background in MOVE. That MOVE animation might then be used by SHOW. If you changed the PHOTO-PAINT image, the DRAW, MOVE, and SHOW files would automatically update to reflect the changes.

The basic embedding and linking procedures are very similar between Windows applications. The illustrations in this section use DRAW. Realize that the procedures are directly transferable to Corel applications and other Windows applications that support OLE.

To embed an object, choose **File** Insert Object to display the dialog box shown in figure B.1.

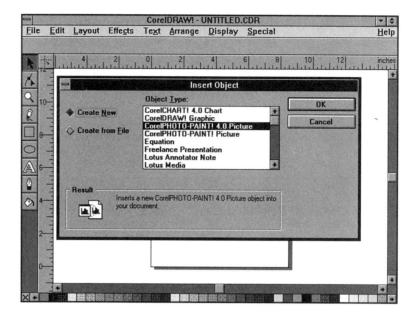

In the Object Type list box are all applications registered with your
system's Windows operation system as supporting OLE. If you want to
open the server application and create a new object that will then be
inserted in to DRAW as the destination document, choose Create New.
To display another dialog box, choose Create from File, which allows
access to an already existing file (see fig. B.2). To apply the Windows
linking between the source and destination files, choose Link. If the
underlying file is modified, the DRAW image that will use that information is automatically updated.

Clicking Browse in the Create from File dialog box opens a standard
Windows file management window so that you can review the various
directories and files until you find the desired source document.
Clicking OK brings the object into DRAW for your use. If Link is not
selected, there is no automatic updating of information provided, but
the object is still embedded, meaning that double-clicking it will open
PHOTO-PAINT so that the bitmap object can be edited.

You can also transfer file information between applications using the
Windows Clipboard. This method requires that both applications be
running at the same time. It also might require substantially more system resource, but it is fast and convenient. The general procedure is to
open start applications and open the respective source and destination

files. Highlight the desired information within the source application and choose **E**dit **C**opy to transfer a duplicate of the information to the Clipboard. Using Alt+Tab, or any of the other applicable Windows options, make the destination document active and choose **E**dit **P**aste **S**pecial to display the dialog box shown in figure B.3.

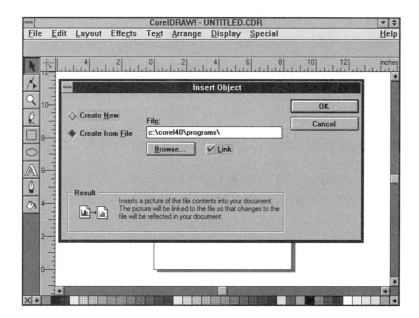

FIG. B.2

Linking to an existing file.

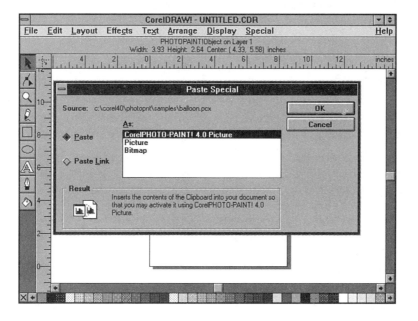

FIG. B.3

The Paste Special dialog box.

Paste Special differs from a standard paste in that linking and embedding is attached to the pasted information, where a conventional paste only transfers the information without regard to the OLE features. Selecting Paste in the Paste Special dialog box transfers the information to the destination file without linking, but retains the embedding information. Selecting Paste Link activates the linking so that any subsequent changes to the source file are automatically reflected in the destination. Click OK to complete the procedure.

The picture and bitmap options do not retain the linking and embedding information, but allow you to paste the image so that it can be rotated and modified using DRAW's features. OLE objects cannot be rotated, so you may occasionally want to paste an object without using the OLE features.

Once the object is embedded, you can edit it at a later date by simply double-clicking the object. Close any unnecessary applications before performing this procedure because you will be opening another application which uses system resources. Closing the other applications makes the overall system performance more acceptable.

The basic procedure presented here should apply to any Windows-based application that supports OLE. Refer to that particular application's manual for specific information.

File Transfer Compatibility

CorelDRAW! provides a wide variety of file conversion filters. In general, try to work with vector-based graphic file formats, such as the Windows Metafiles or PostScript so that the image quality is not compromised in the transfer process. Many times, this will not be convenient or possible, and you will need to create bitmap files such as PCX and TIFF. Always size the image in DRAW to the closest possible dimensions ultimately needed before performing the export operations.

The recommended procedure is to size the image in DRAW, select the objects to be exported, and choose **F**ile **E**xport to display the File Export dialog box. Then choose the desired file format from the List File of **T**ype box check **S**elected Only, define the path and file name, and click OK. The file will be exported in the format you define. You will probably see another dialog box with EPS (Encapsulated PostScript) and bitmap files which requests additional information pertaining to the export operation. Refer to Chapter 9 for detailed information on dealing with these settings.

Macintosh Considerations

Although you can export an image in a Macintosh file format, remember that the Macintosh uses a different disk format than that used by the PC. Consequently, you will need extra utilities on the Macintosh, such as PC-to-Mac, to read the PC-formatted disk.

Special Characters

You will often need to include characters other than the standard alphabetical and numeric (alphanumeric) characters in your Corel documents. You can insert any of the characters from any Windows, TrueType, or Adobe (if you have Adobe Type Manager) font you have installed. You can also insert any of the characters from the Corel WFN fonts you have installed. The WFN fonts are font versions of the symbol sets. (See Chapter 3 for details on working with symbols.)

There are three ways to enter a character in Corel:

- Type it from the keyboard.

- Enter the three- or four-digit Corel character code.

- Use the Windows Character Map.

Because not all characters are on the keyboard, the second two methods are needed for the extended (nonkeyboard) characters.

To enter a character using the three- or four-digit Corel code, choose either the artistic or paragraph text tool, and press and hold the Alt key while typing the character code from the numeric keypad. Release Alt after you type the code, and the character is inserted at the text insertion point. The character codes for a typical character set are shown in figure C.1. Blank spaces in the table indicate that there is no character in this font for that code. Remember, different fonts may have different characters.

FIG. C.1

Character codes for a
typical font (Times New
Roman).

033	!	071	G	0109	m	0147	"	0185	¹	0223	ß
034	"	072	H	0110	n	0148	"	0186	º	0224	à
035	#	073	I	0111	o	0149	•	0187	»	0225	á
036	$	074	J	0112	p	0150	–	0188	¼	0226	â
037	%	075	K	0113	q	0151	—	0189	½	0227	ã
038	&	076	L	0114	r	0152	˜	0190	¾	0228	ä
039	'	077	M	0115	s	0153	™	0191	¿	0229	å
040	(	078	N	0116	t	0154	š	0192	À	0230	æ
041	)	079	O	0117	u	0155	›	0193	Á	0231	ç
042	*	080	P	0118	v	0156	œ	0194	Â	0232	è
043	+	081	Q	0119	w	0157		0195	Ã	0233	é
044	,	082	R	0120	x	0158		0196	Ä	0234	ê
045	-	083	S	0121	y	0159	Ÿ	0197	Å	0235	ë
046	.	084	T	0122	z	0160		0198	Æ	0236	ì
047	/	085	U	0123	{	0161	¡	0199	Ç	0237	í
048	0	086	V	0124			0162	¢	0200	È	0238	î
049	1	087	W	0125	}	0163	£	0201	É	0239	ï
050	2	088	X	0126	~	0164	¤	0202	Ê	0240	ð
051	3	089	Y	0127		0165	¥	0203	Ë	0241	ñ
052	4	090	Z	0128		0166	¦	0204	Ì	0242	ò
053	5	091	[	0129		0167	§	0205	Í	0243	ó
054	6	092	\	0130	‚	0168	¨	0206	Î	0244	ô
055	7	093	]	0131	ƒ	0169	©	0207	Ï	0245	õ
056	8	094	^	0132	„	0170	ª	0208	Ð	0246	ö
057	9	095	_	0133	…	0171	«	0209	Ñ	0247	÷
058	:	096	`	0134	†	0172	¬	0210	Ò	0248	ø
059	;	097	a	0135	‡	0173	-	0211	Ó	0249	ù
060	<	098	b	0136	ˆ	0174	®	0212	Ô	0250	ú
061	=	099	c	0137	‰	0175	¯	0213	Õ	0251	û
062	>	0100	d	0138	Š	0176	°	0214	Ö	0252	ü
063	?	0101	e	0139	‹	0177	±	0215	×	0253	ý
064	@	0102	f	0140	Œ	0178	²	0216	Ø	0254	þ
065	A	0103	g	0141		0179	³	0217	Ù	0255	ÿ
066	B	0104	h	0142		0180	´	0218	Ú		
067	C	0105	i	0143		0181	µ	0219	Û		
068	D	0106	j	0144		0182	¶	0220	Ü		
069	E	0107	k	0145	'	0183	·	0221	Ý		
070	F	0108	l	0146	'	0184	‚	0222	Þ		

NOTE

The Quick Reference booklet provided with the Corel package lists
character codes for six of the Corel fonts, including symbol fonts.

If you are working with a Windows, TrueType, or Adobe font, the Windows Character Map is an easy way to insert characters, especially characters from nonalphanumeric fonts like Symbol or Wingdings. To use the Character Map to insert a character, follow these steps:

1. Open the Accessories group and start Character Map.

2. Choose the font containing the characters you want to work with from the Font drop-down list.

3. Select the character (or characters) to insert. The selected characters are shown in the box at the upper right of the Character Map window (see figure C.2.).

4. Choose Copy when you have all the characters you want selected.

5. Then return to the Corel document you are working on and choose Paste from the Edit menu. The characters are pasted into place. You can then edit or move them as any other Corel text.

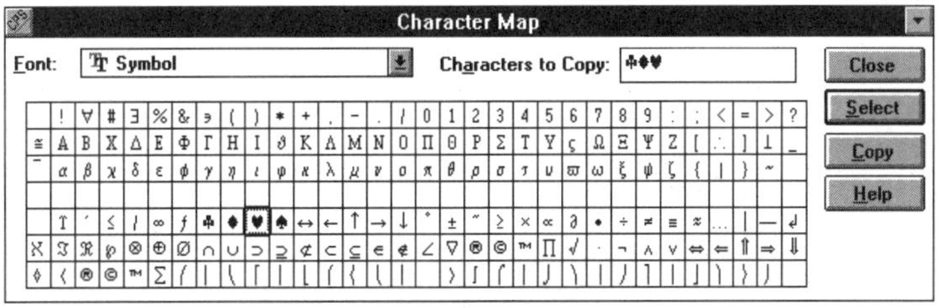

FIG. C.2

Windows Character Map.

Glossary

active window   A region of the display that is ready and waiting to receive user input.

actor   An object in CorelMOVE contained within an animation that moves during the animation. Composed of a number of cells.

actor cel   A series of images that create the illusion of movement in CorelMOVE when displayed quickly in succession.

additive primary colors   Red, green, and blue. The three colors used to create all other colors if direct or transmitted light is used (as on television, for example). See also *primary colors* and *subtractive primary colors*.

alignment   The positioning of lines of text on a page or in a column: aligned left (flush left, ragged right), centered, aligned right (flush right, ragged left), or justified (flush on both left and right).

animation path   The path over which the actor moves during the animation.

animation path points   The prompting point for displaying the next cel in the actor's movement.

annotations   Text added to a chart to further explain its contents.

anti-alias   The process of adding dots adjacent to existing dots to make a jagged line appear more smooth.

artistic text   Strings of text in CorelDRAW! that can be manipulated as objects.

ascender   The part of a lowercase letter that rises above its main body. Technically, only three letters of the alphabet have ascenders: b, d, and h. Uppercase letters and the lowercase letters f, k, l, and t also reach the height of the ascenders. See also *descender*.

ASCII   A standard format for storing text files, which stands for American Standard Code for Information Interchange. The form in which text is stored if saved as Text Only, an Export/Import command option, as well as a Save command option, available for most databases, spreadsheets, and word processors. ASCII files include all the characters of the text itself (including tabs and carriage returns) but not the non-ASCII codes used to indicate character and paragraph formats. See also *text-only file*.

aspect ratio   A fractional number that represents the ratio between horizontal and vertical measurements of dots relating to printing and screen display resolutions.

attributes   The characteristics applied to an object in CorelDRAW!, including font, size, spacing, style, color, line thickness, and fill.

Autoflow   Text placement in which the text continuously flows from column to column and page to page.

AutoTrace   The conversion by CorelTRACE of a fixed resolution bitmap image into a structured graphic that is not of fixed resolution.

bad break   Term referring to page breaks and column breaks that result in widows or orphans, or to line breaks that hyphenate words incorrectly or separate two words that should stay together (for example, *Mr. Smith*).

baseline   In a line of text, the lowest point of letters, excluding descenders. (The lowest point of letters such as *a* and *x*, for example, but not the lower edges of descenders on *p* and *q*.)

Bézier curve   A curve created in CorelDRAW! comprised of nodes connected by line segments whose slope and angle can be altered by moving related control points.

bitmap   A graphics image or text formed by a pattern of dots. PC Paint, Windows Paint, and PC Paintbrush documents produce bitmapped graphics as well as scanned or digitized images. Low-resolution images are sometimes called *paint-type* files, and these images usually have a lower number of dots per inch (dpi) than high-resolution images.

bitmap texture   A representation of surface irregularity that can be applied to an object in CorelDRAW! to change its appearance.

bleed   Term used to describe a printed image extending to the trimmed edge of the sheet or page.

blend   Changing one image into another over a series of steps to provide a transition type of visual illusion. Used for highlighting objects.

block   See *text block*.

blue lines   A preliminary test printing of a page to check the offset printer's plates. This test printing is done by using a photochemical process (instead of printer's inks) that produces a blue image on white paper. See also *prepress proofs* and *press proofs*.

blue pencil/blue line   Traditionally, a guideline drawn with a blue pencil or printed in light blue ink on the boards and used as a guide for manually pasting up a page layout. The blue ink is sometimes called *nonrepro blue* because the color is not picked up by the camera when a page is photographed to make plates for offset printing. In CorelDRAW!, you can create nonprinting margins, column guides, and ruler guides on-screen to help you position text and graphics; these lines do not appear when the page is printed.

board   A sheet of heavyweight paper or card stock onto which typeset text and graphics are pasted manually. See also *blue pencil/blue line*.

body copy   The main part of the text of a publication, as distinguished from headings and captions. See also *body type*.

body type   The type (font) used for the body copy. See also *body copy*.

boilerplate   See *template*.

bounding box   The dashed outline that appears around an object after selection.

brochure   A folded pamphlet or small booklet.

callouts   In CorelDRAW!, text that points out and identifies parts of an illustration. Also, headings that appear in a narrow margin next to the body copy. See also *pull-out quote*.

camera-ready art   The complete pages of a publication assembled with text and graphics and ready for reproduction. Literally refers to pages ready to be photographed as the first step in the process of making plates for offset printing. See also *mechanicals* and *offset printing*.

CDR   File name extension that indicates CorelDRAW! as the associated tool.

center of rotation   A point relating to an object or group in CorelDRAW! around which any rotational transformations occur.

chained text   Blocks of text that are connected across the columns on a page and across pages from the beginning to the end of an article. CorelDRAW! chains all text blocks that are part of a story. As you edit chained (or threaded) text, CorelDRAW! moves words from one text block into the next text block in the chain to adjust to the new text length. See also *text block*.

chart   The graphical display of data as a line, bar, or other type of chart design.

check box   The small square to the left of certain options in dialog boxes; you click the check box to turn an option on or off (to select or deselect it). An x appears in the check box after it is selected, or turned on. The check box is empty if is it deselected, or turned off.

child object   A member of a group that is individually selected without ungrouping that object.

cicero   A unit of measure equivalent to 4.55 millimeters, commonly used in Europe for measuring font sizes.

click   To press and release a mouse button quickly.

clip art   Originally, predrawn art ready for cutting from a book to be pasted into a design layout. Now, ready-to-use art provided for easy paste-up into designs and projects.

Clipboard   A feature of Microsoft Windows, the Clipboard temporarily stores text or graphics cut or copied by the commands on the Edit menu. The Paste command brings the contents of the Clipboard to the page. The Clipboard command displays the contents of the Clipboard. See *Copy*, *Cut*, and *Paste*.

clone   In CorelDRAW!, a command used to create an exact copy of the original including the attributes of the original. Clones are actively linked to the original and reflect any changes made to the original object. See also *duplicate*.

Close   To choose the Close command from the Control menu and leave CorelDRAW!. Close is also used to close some dialog boxes.

coated stock   Paper that has a light clay or plastic coating. A glossy or slick paper is often coated.

collated　Printed in numerical order with the first page on top of the stack that comes out of the printer. This is an option in the Print dialog box. Multiple copies are grouped into complete sets of the publication.

color keys　A color overlay proofing system produced by the 3M Company. See also *overlay proofs*.

color separations　In offset printing, separate plates used to lay different colors of ink on a page printed in multiple colors. You can create masters for color separations by preparing the drawing by choosing the Print Separations option from the Options dialog box in the Print menu of CorelDRAW!.

column rules　Vertical lines drawn between columns.

command button　A large rectangular area in a dialog box that contains a command such as OK or Cancel. You can activate command buttons surrounded by a thick black line by pressing the Enter key.

comp　Traditionally, a designer's comprehensive sketch of a page design, showing the client what the final page is to look like after being printed. Usually a full-sized likeness of the page, a comp is a few steps closer to the final than a pencil rough and can be composed by using ink pens, pencils, color markers, color acetate, pressure-sensitive letters, and other tools available at art supply shops. The comp is used as a starting point in building the final document.

composite　Printing process that includes all colors on a page, as in CorelDRAW!'s Print Options feature.

condensed type　A narrow typeface having proportionally less character width than a normal face of the same size. Although you can achieve this effect by graphically scaling characters from the normal font, condensed characters are usually individually designed as a separate font. Condensed typefaces are used where large amounts of copy must fit into a relatively small space (such as in tabular composition). See also *kerning*.

constrain　To restrict an object's movement while drawing or moving it to an angle that is a multiple of degrees. You constrain the movement by holding the Ctrl key as you drag the mouse. See also *X axis* and *Y axis*.

continuous-tone image　An illustration or photograph, black-and-white or color, composed of many shades between the lightest and the darkest tones and not broken up into dots. Continuous-tone images usually need to be converted into dots, either by scanning or by halftone, in order to be printed in ink or on a laser printer. See also *halftone*.

contour   A blend that an object performs on itself.

Control menu   The Microsoft Windows menu listing commands for working with Windows, getting help, using the Clipboard, and leaving an application.

Control menu box   Small square displayed in the upper-left corner of a window. You click this box to display the Control menu.

Control Panel   A Microsoft Windows application program used to add or delete fonts and printers, change printer connections and settings, and adjust mouse and screen settings.

control point   A point relating to a node whose position determines the shape of the object containing that node.

Copy   To place an exact copy of an object or text to the Clipboard. See also *Clipboard, Cut,* and *Paste.*

copy fitting   Determining the amount of copy (text set in a specific font) that can fit in a given area on a page or in a publication. Making copy fit on a page in CorelDRAW! by adjusting the line spacing, word spacing, and letter spacing.

CorelCHART   The Corel charting application.

CorelDRAW!   The Corel drawing and illustration application.

CORELDRW.INI file   The file used to define many of the attributes used by DRAW while it is running. Changing some defaults requires modifying the INI files. Only experienced users should make such changes.

CorelMOSAIC   Visual file manager used to organize, manage, manipulate, and view graphic files.

CorelMOVE   The Corel animation application.

CorelPHOTO-PAINT   The Corel bitmap modification application.

CorelSHOW   The presentation application that allows for integration of CHART and MOVE images into a unified presentation.

CorelTRACE   The Corel application that converts bitmap images into vector images.

corner style   Rectangular objects that have either square or rounded corners.

crop   Trim the edges from a graphic to make the image fit into a given menu or to remove unnecessary parts of the image.

crop marks   Lines printed on a page to indicate where the page is to be trimmed after the final document is printed. These marks are printed if the page size is smaller than the paper size and if the Crop Marks option is selected in the Print options dialog box.

cross hairs   The shape of the pointer after a tool has been selected. See also *pointer*.

cues   Decision points within a timeline that steer the sequence of events in particular directions based upon user actions.

curve object   A Bézier or Freehand curve created with CorelDRAW!.

cusp node   A node where the line is independently controlled on each side.

custom   A word to describe attributes or characteristics that do not conform to an existing standard reference.

custom color   An ink color that you assign to objects in your publication. Using custom color, you produce one negative for each color used in your artwork. Treated the same as spot color.

Cut   To remove an object or text from the working page to the Clipboard. See also *Clipboard, Copy,* and *Paste*.

cutout   See *knockout*.

cyan   The subtractive primary color that appears blue-green and absorbs red light. Used as one ink in four-color printing. Also known as process blue. See also *subtractive primary colors*.

CMYK   Shorthand notation for cyan (C), magenta (M), yellow (Y), and black (K). See also *subtractive primary colors*.

data range   A group of neighboring cells in a column and/or row in the Object Data Manager in CorelDRAW!.

default   The initial setting of a value or option when you first display or create it (as when a dialog box opens). You can usually change default settings.

descender   The part of a lowercase letter that hangs below the baseline. Five letters of the alphabet have descenders: g, j, p, q, and y. See also *ascender* and *baseline*.

deselect   To select another command or option or to click a blank area of the screen to cancel the current selection. Also to turn off (remove the X from) a check box. See also *select*.

desktop publishing Use of personal computers and software applications to produce a copy that is ready for reproduction.

dialog box A window that appears in response to a command that calls for setting options. See also *window*.

digitize To convert an image to a system of dots that can be stored in the computer. See also *scanned-image files*.

dimension lines Lines and labels adjacent to a drawing that describe the object's dimensions.

Dingbats Traditionally, ornamental characters (bullets, stars, flowers) used for decoration or as special characters within text. The laser-printer font Zapf Dingbats includes many traditional symbols and some untraditional ones.

directory A named area reserved on the hard disk where a group of related files can be stored together. Each directory can have subdirectories. See also *hierarchical filing system*.

display type Type used for headlines, titles, headings, advertisements, fliers, and so on. Display type is usually a large point size (several sizes larger than body copy) and can be a decorative font.

dot-matrix printer A printer that creates text and graphics by pressing a matrix of pins through the ribbon onto the paper. These impact printers usually offer lower resolution (dots per inch) than laser printers and are used only for draft printouts from CorelDRAW!.

dots per inch (dpi) See *resolution*.

double-click To quickly press and release the main mouse button twice in succession.

drag To hold down the main mouse button, move the mouse until the object is where you want it, and then release the button.

drag and drop Dragging a selected item from one open publication to another open publication.

drawing window Window appearing after you start DRAW. Displays a view of one or two pages, page icons, pointer, scroll bars, title bar, menu bar, and toolbox window.

drop-down menu See *pull-down menu*.

dummy publication Traditionally, a pencil mock-up of the pages of a publication, folded or stapled into a booklet, that the offset printer uses to verify the correct sequence of pages and positions of photographs.

duplicate   In CorelDRAW!, a command used to create a copy of an object, not linked to the original. See also *clone*.

edit   To alter the text of a written work. See also *Copy, Cut,* and *Paste*.

Editable Preview   The default display mode in CorelDRAW! that allows you to interactively work with objects, and which shows outlines, fills, and text attributes as they appear when printed. See also *Wireframe view*.

ellipse   A regular-shaped oval created by using the Ellipse tool.

em   Unit of measure equaling the size of the capital letter M. The width of an em dash or an em space. See also *en*.

emulsion   The photosensitive layer on a piece of film or paper. Emulsion side up or down may be specified in the Print command dialog box.

en   One-half the width of an em. The width of an en dash or an en space. See also *em*.

Encapsulated PostScript (EPS) format   A file format that describes a document or graphic written in the PostScript language and that contains all the codes necessary to print the file.

end node   A point at the end of a line or curve. In CorelDRAW!, it is denoted as a small square.

Enter key   Key you press to break a line if the Text tool is active or to confirm the selected options in a dialog box. Also called the Return key. Usually has the same effect as the Return key on a typewriter.

envelope   A shape which is applied to objects in CorelDRAW! that acts like a mold to form that object.

export   To convert text or an image to another file for use with another application.

export filter   A process that defines how to convert its files so that the files can be understood by the program that imports them.

extrude   To give an object the illusion of depth by adding dynamic three-dimensional forms in CorelDRAW!.

facing pages   The two pages that face one another if a book, brochure, or similar publication is open. Also an option used in double-sided publications.

fill   To paint an area enclosed by a border with a gray shade, pattern, and/or color. You can fill a closed path.

Fill tool   The toolbox item used to define the object interior fill attributes.

film   Photosensitive material, generally on a transparent base, that receives character images and may be chemically processed to expose those images. In phototypesetting, any photosensitive material, transparent or not, may be called film.

flow text   Place text on a page.

flush   Aligned with, even with, coming to the same edge as. See also *alignment.*

flush right (or right justified)   Text in which lines end at the same point on the right margin. Opposite of ragged right or left justified. See also *alignment.*

folio   Page number on a printed page, often accompanied by the name of the document and date of publication.

font   One complete set of characters (including all the letters of the alphabet, punctuation marks, and symbols) in the same typeface, style, and size. A 12-point Times Roman font, for example, is a different font from 12-point Times Italic, 14-point Times Roman, or 12-point Helvetica. Screen fonts (bitmapped fonts used to display text accurately on-screen) can differ slightly from printer fonts (outline fonts used to describe fonts to the laser printer) because of the differences in resolution between screens and printers.

footer   See *folio* and *running foot.*

format   Page size, margins, and grid used in a publication. Also, the character format (font) and paragraph format (alignment, spacing, and indentation).

formatting   Using the type and paragraph attributes to modify the page.

fountain fill   This fill pattern is applied to objects in CorelDRAW! to create three-dimensional effects.

four-headed arrow   Shape of the pointer if used to drag a selected text block or graphic. See also *pointer.*

fractal texture   A representation of surface irregularity that is applied to an object in CorelDRAW!. This effect is based on the fractal number set for chaotic events.

frame   In CorelDRAW!, this defines the boundaries for paragraph text on the drawing page.

Freehand drawing mode   A mode of drawing in CorelDRAW! appropriate for rough sketches, analogous to pencil-on-paper techniques.

ghosting   The shift in ink density that occurs when large, solid areas interfere with one another. Also, a procedure in which two images are combined together electronically. The images are given specific weight in relation to each other to create the effect.

graphic   A line, box, or circle that you draw in CorelDRAW!. An illustration brought into a CorelDRAW! publication from another application.

graphic boundary   The dotted line around a graphic that limits how close text can get to the graphic.

greek text (greeked text)   Traditionally, a block of text used to represent the positioning and point size of text in a designer's comp. Standard greeked text used by typesetters looks more like Latin: "Lorem ipsum dolor sit amet. . . ." See also *greeking*.

greeking   The conversion of text to symbolic bars or boxes that show the position of the text on the screen but not the real characters. Text usually is greeked in the Fit in Window view in CorelDRAW!; small point sizes may be greeked in closer views on some screens. See also *greek text*.

grid   The underlying design plan for a page. You can use the grid for object alignment by using the Layout Snap To Grid option.

grid origin   The intersection of the two CorelDRAW! rulers at 0 (zero). The default zero point is at the intersection of the left and top margins, but can be moved.

gripper   The top part of a page.

group   Several objects that are combined into a single group that accepts some modifications as a single unit.

guide   A nonprinting line (margin guide, ruler guide, or column guide) created to help align objects on a page. Nonprinting guides look like dotted lines, dashed lines, or blue lines, depending on the screen's resolution and color settings.

gutter   The inside margins between the facing pages of a document; sometimes describes the space between columns in a frame setting. In some word processors, the gutter measure is entered as the difference between the measures of the inside margin and the outside margin. See also *margin*.

hairline   The thinnest rule you can create. (Some laser printers do not support hairline rules.)

halftone   The conversion of continuous-tone artwork (usually a photograph) into a pattern of dots or lines that look like gray tones when printed by an offset printing press. See also *continuous-tone image*.

handles   The eight small, black rectangles enclosing a selected shape; the two small rectangles at the ends of a selected line; the small black rectangles at the four corners and the loops at the center of the top and bottom of a selected text block. You can drag the handles to change the size of the selected object. Also called sizing squares. See also *windowshades*.

hanging indent   A paragraph in which the first line extends to the left of the other lines. You can use a hanging-indent format to create headings set to the left of the body copy. See also *indentation*.

hard disk   Disk storage that is built into the computer or into a piece of hardware connected to the computer. Distinguished from removable floppy disk storage.

Header   See *running head*. See also *folio* and *running foot*.

hierarchical filing system   A disk storage system in which files can be stored in separate directories, which, in turn, can contain subdirectories. See also *directory*.

highlight   To distinguish visually. Usually reverses the normal appearance of selected text, graphics, or options (black text on a white background, for example, appears as white text on a black background after it is highlighted).

hyphenation   The dividing of text words as they reach the end of a line (the right margin). If the hyphenation is not used, the entire word moves to the next text line. Using hyphenation divides the word in accordance with accepted conventions, and keeps the first half of the word (pre-hyphen) or the initial line and moves the post-hyphen word section to the next line. A "Hot Zone" is defined within which hyphenation application is determined.

icon   Graphic on-screen representation of a tool, file, or command.

image header   Part of an EPS graphics file that allows the screen viewing of the image in a page layout program.

import   To bring text or graphics into an image from other programs, such as text from a word processing program or clip art from a graphics program.

import filter   A processor that tells how to convert files from other programs.

increment   Distance between tick marks on a ruler. See also *measurement system.*

indentation   Positioning the first line of paragraph text (or second and following lines) to the right of the left-column guide (to create a left indent), or positioning the right margin of the paragraph text to the left of the right-column guide (to create a right indent), relative to the other text on the page.

insertion point   A blinking vertical bar where text is to be typed or pasted.

inside margin   Margin along the edge of the page that is to be bound. In single-sided publications, this is always the left margin. In double-sided publications, the inside margin is the left margin of a right-hand page or the right margin of a left-hand page. See also *gutter* and *margin.*

integral proof   A color proofing system that bonds all four process colors to a single sheet. Also called a *composite.*

Invert   A Photo-PAINT filter used to produce a negative photo offset. See *Reverse.*

italics   Letters that slope toward the right, as distinguished from upright, or Roman, characters.

jump line   Text at the end of an article indicating on what page the article is continued. Also, the text at the top of a continued article, indicating from where the article is continued. Also called a *continued line.*

justified text   Text that is flush at both the left and right edges. See also *alignment.*

kern   To adjust the spaces between letters with the Shape tool, usually to move letters closer together. See also *kerning.*

kerning   The amount of space between letters, especially certain combinations of letters that must be brought closer together to create visually consistent spacing around all letters. The uppercase letters AW, for example, may appear to have a wider gap between them than the letters MN unless a special kerning formula is set up for the AW combination. See also *kern.*

knockout   A generic term for a positive or overlay that "knocks out" part of an image from another image. The most obvious example of this is white type on a black background. The white type is knocked out of the background.

landscape printing   The rotation of a page to print text and graphics horizontally across the longer measure of the page or paper (usually 11 inches).

laser printing   Term used to describe printing on a toner-based laser printer. These printers use laser technology—light amplification by stimulated emission of radiation—to project an intense light beam in a narrow band width (1/300 inch in 300-dpi printers). This light creates on the printer drum a charge that picks up the toner and transfers it to the paper. Some typesetters (such as the Linotronic 300 and 500) also use laser technology in their photochemical processing but usually are referred to as phototypesetters rather than as laser printers. See also *phototypesetting*.

layer   One plane that contains one object or group of objects in CorelDRAW!. Used to place objects in front of other objects to provide depth.

layering order   Order in which overlapping text and graphics are arranged on the page and on-screen.

layout   The process of arranging text and graphics on a page. A sketch or plan for the page. Also the final appearance of the page. (In plate making, a sheet indicating the settings for the step-and-repeat machine.)

leaders   Dotted or dashed lines that can be defined for tab settings.

leading   Historically, the insertion of thin strips of metal (made of a metal alloy that included some lead) between lines of cast type to add space between the lines and to make columns align. In modern typography, the vertical space between the baselines of two lines of text. Leading is measured from ascender to ascender between two lines of text and is entered in points or percentage in the Type Specifications dialog box. To give an example of the terminology, 12-point Times with 1 point of leading added is called 13-point leaded type, also called 12 on 13 Times, and sometimes written as 12/13 Times.

letterspacing   Space between letters in a word. The practice of adding space between letters.

Library   A collection of commonly used text and graphic elements stored in a Library, displayed in the MOSAIC palette.

ligatures   Character combinations that are often combined into special characters in a font. Some downloadable fonts, for example, come with the combinations fi and fl as special characters.

line spacing　See *leading*.

line style　The width or point size and type of a line, as in dotted, dashed, or solid lines.

linked file　A graphic or text file that has been imported using the Place or Paste command in conjunction with the option to Link the original file to the current publication, rather than store it as part of the publication. Linked files can be managed through the First Links command. See also *Object Linking and Embedding*.

list box　Area in a dialog box that displays options.

lock　Using the Lock Guides on Layers command to anchor column guides and ruler guides on the current page or to anchor the zero point of the rulers. Locked guides cannot be inadvertently moved while laying out text and graphics.

logo　A company trademark. Also, the banner on the front cover of a magazine or newsletter. See also *masthead*.

magenta　The subtractive primary color that appears blue-red and absorbs green light. Used as one ink in four-color printing. Also known as *process red*. See also *subtractive primary colors*.

manual text flow　Manually placing text on the page so that the text flows to and stops at the bottom of the column or the first object that blocks the text. See also *Autoflow*.

margin　Traditionally, the distance from the edge of the page to the edge of the layout area of the page. The margins are normally used to define the limits of text. See also *gutter* and *inside margin*.

margin guides　Dotted nonprinting lines displayed near the borders of the screen page to mark the margins of a page as specified in the Page Setup dialog box. See also *margin* and *nonprinting master items*.

marquee　A dashed rectangular region that appears when you drag the Pick tool to select objects.

marquee select　The process of using a marquee to encircle and thus select an object or group of objects.

mask　A shape which can be applied to an image in Photo-PAINT to isolate a region from/for effects of filters.

master items　Items on a master page; may include text (running heads), graphics (rules), and nonprinting guides (column guides). See also *master page* and *nonprinting master items*.

master layer   A plane which holds all objects common to all layers or pages of a project.

master page   Page containing text, graphics, and guides you want repeated on every page in a publication. See also *master items*.

masthead   Section of newsletter or magazine giving its title and details of staff, ownership, advertising, subscription, and so on. Sometimes the banner or wide title on the front cover of a magazine or the front of a newsletter or newspaper. See also *logo*.

measurement system   Units chosen through the Preferences command on the Edit menu: inches, decimal inches, millimeters, picas and points, or ciceros and points. The chosen units appear on the rulers and in all dialog boxes that display measurements. You can enter a value in any unit of measure in many dialog boxes. See also *pica*.

mechanicals   Traditionally, the final pages or boards with pasted-up galleys of type and line art, sometimes with acetate or tissue overlays for color separations and notes to the offset printer. See also *camera-ready art* and *offset printing*.

mechanical separations   Color separations made based on black-and-white art. If using CMYK process color separations, for example, each of four plates represents a different color (cyan, magenta, yellow, and black) but is given to the press/printer as a black-and-white print on paper or film.

memory   Area in the computer where information is stored temporarily while you work; also called *RAM*, or random-access memory. You can copy the contents of the memory onto disk by using the Save or Save As command.

menu   A list of choices presented in a fly-out, pull-down, or pop-up window.

menu bar   Area across the top of the publication window where menu titles are saved.

merge   Combining text information with an image so that the resulting merged file is a combination of the two.

Mirror   To create a mirror image of an object.

Moiré pattern   An undesirable grid pattern that may occur if two transparent dot-screen fill patterns are overlaid or a bit-mapped graphic with gray fill patterns is reduced or enlarged.

MOSAIC　See *CorelMOSAIC*.

mouse buttons　The main, or primary mouse button (usually the left button) is used to carry out most actions. Use the Control Panel to specify the main button as the left or right button of a two- or three-button mouse. Some commands also use the secondary mouse button on a two- or three-button mouse. See also *Control Panel* and *secondary mouse button*.

movie　A completely finished and self-contained animation.

multiple select　To choose more than one object in sequence with the Shift key as a modifier.

negative　A reverse image of a page, produced photographically on a clear sheet of film as an intermediate step in preparing offset printing plates from camera-ready mechanicals.

node　Object locations that designate the start and end of line segments and a possible change in curve direction. Nodes can be moved to change object shapes.

nonprinting master items　The ruler guides and column guides on a master layer. See also *margin guides*, *master page*, and *ruler guides*.

Object Data Manager　The DRAW feature that correlates database information with an image so that clicking on the image displays the information.

Object Linking and Embedding (OLE)　A feature of Windows 3.1 (and later versions), whereby objects created in one application that supports OLE can be pasted into another application that supports OLE either as embedded objects (that is, part of the document into which they are pasted) or as linked objects (that is, linked to the external source and updated when the source changes). In either case, the objects can be edited by double-clicking on them, thereby activating the application that originally created them. See also *linked file*.

object-oriented files　Draw-type vector graphic files consisting of a sequence of drawing commands (stored as mathematical formulas). These commands describe graphics (such as mechanical drawings, schematics, charts, and ad graphics) that you would produce manually with a pencil, straightedge, and compass. Usually contrasted with paint-type files or bitmaps. See also *bitmap*.

offset printing　Type of printing done using a printing press to reproduce many copies of the original. The press lays ink on a page according to the raised image on a plate created by photographing the camera-ready masters. See also *camera-ready art*, *laser printing*, and *mechanicals*.

OLE   See *Object Linking and Embedding*.

onion skin   A special view of the animation actor's cells so that the underlying or following cells can be viewed while modifying the currently active cell.

option button   The round area to the left of certain options in a dialog box; you click the option button to turn on, or select, its option. Click it again to deselect the option. See also *Control Panel* and *secondary mouse button*.

orientation   Refers to the portrait or landscape page position options. Portrait pages and columns run down the longer measure of the page. In landscape orientation, text runs horizontally across the wider measure of the page, and columns run down the shorter measure of the page. See also *landscape printing* and *portrait printing*.

outline font   A printer font in which each letter of the alphabet is stored as a mathematical formula, as distinguished from bit-mapped fonts that are stored as patterns of dots. PostScript fonts, for example, are outline fonts. See also *bitmap* and *font*.

Outline tool   The toolbox item used to define the object outline attributes.

outside margin   The unbound edge of a publication. In single-sided publications, the outside margin is the right margin. In double-sided publications, the outside margin is the right margin of a right-hand page and the left margin of a left-hand page. See also *inside margin* and *margin*.

overhead transparency   An image printed on clear acetate and projected onto a screen for viewing by an audience.

overlay   A transparent acetate or tissue covering a printed page; contains color specifications and other instructions to the offset printer. Also, an overhead transparency that is intended to be projected on top of another transparency. See also *color separations*.

overlay proofs   A color-proofing system that uses transparent overlays for each of the four process buttons in the group.

overprint   To specify that a colored object show through another colored object that overlaps it. Normally, the object underneath is hidden by the object in front.

oversized publication   Publication in which page size is larger than standard paper sizes. See also *page size* and *Tile*.

Page Control box   An icon displayed in the bottom-left corner of the Publication window. Icons represent the master pages and every regular page. See also *icon*.

page size   The dimensions of the pages of your publication as set in the Page Setup dialog box. Page size can differ from paper size. See also *margin* and *paper size*.

paint-type file   See *bitmap*.

pair kerning   The process that changes the amount of space between two letters to create visually consistent spacing between all letters.

palette   The color bar located at the bottom of the screen that is used to define outline and interior colors.

PANTONE Matching System   A popular system for choosing colors, based on ink mixes.

paper size   The size of the printer paper. Standard paper sizes are letter (8 1/2 by 11 inches), legal (8 1/2 by 14 inches), European A4 (210 by 297 millimeters), and European B5 (176 by 250 millimeters).

paragraph text   A block of text in CorelDRAW! to which many attributes can be applied, always placed in a text frame. See *artistic text*.

Paste   To move cut or copied objects or text from the Clipboard to the working page.

Pasteboard   The on-screen work area surrounding the pages on which you are working. You move text and graphics to the pasteboard, where they remain after you turn to another page or close the publication.

paste-up   See *mechanicals*.

perspective   Provides the illusion of depth by forcing all lines to merge at a selected vanishing point.

phototypesetting   Producing a page image on photosensitive paper, as when documents are printed on a Linotronic 300 or 500. This process is sometimes referred to as cold type to distinguish it from the older method of casting characters, lines, or whole pages in lead (called hot type or hot metal). See also *laser printing*.

pica   A unit of measure equal to approximately 1/6 inch, or 12 points. See also *cicero*, *measurement system*, and *point size*.

Pick tool   The tool used for selecting and manipulating text and graphics. If the Pick tool is selected, the pointer looks like an arrow. See also *pointer*.

PICT format   A format used to store graphics on a Macintosh computer. Usually converted to PIC format when transferred to an MS-DOS/Windows system.

pictographs   Creating bar charts with outlines and fills derived from images instead of patterned or shaded interior fills.

pixel   The smallest unit on a computer display. Monitors can have different screen resolutions (pixels per inch) and different sizes (total number of pixels).

point   To place the mouse pointer on an object on-screen.

point size   The smallest unit of measure in typographic measurement and the standard unit of measure for type. Measured roughly from the top of the ascenders to the bottom of the descenders. A pica has 12 points; an inch, approximately 72 points; a point equals 1/12 pica, or 1/72 inch. See also *cicero*, *measurement system*, and *pica*.

pointer   The on-screen icon that moves as you move the mouse.

portrait printing   The normal printing orientation for a page: horizontally across the shorter measurement of the page or paper (usually, 8 1/2 inches).

PostScript   A page-description language developed by Adobe Systems.

PostScript textures   A representation of surface irregularity defined in a PostScript printer that can be applied to an object to alter its appearance.

PowerLines   A CorelDRAW! tool used to give lines a hand-drawn look or to give lines a variable line width.

PPD and PDX files   PostScript Printer Description and Printer Description Extensions files. These files provide information used to set the default information for the type of printer you are using.

Preferences   The command on the Special menu used to select the unit of measure displayed on ruler lines and in dialog boxes, display character, mouse option, and others. See also *measurement system* and *pica*.

prepress proofs   Sometimes called blue lines, these proofs are made by using photographic techniques. See also *blue lines* and *press proofs*.

press proofs   A test run of a color printing job through the printing press to check registration and color. See also *blue lines* and *prepress proofs*.

Preview   A CorelDRAW! mode that allows viewing the work as it will appear when printed.

primary colors   The elemental colors of either pigments or light. Red, green, and blue are additive primaries. White light is produced when red, green, and blue lights are added together. Cyan, magenta, and yellow are subtractive primaries, the inks used to print in the three-color process (or four-color process with black). See also *additive primary colors* and *subtractive primary colors*.

print area   The area on a piece of paper where the printer reproduces text and graphics; always smaller than the paper size. See also *margin*.

Print Manager   A Microsoft Windows application for sending files to the printer. The Print command sends the publication to the Print Manager, which is a spooler, not directly to the printer. The Print Manager holds files in the print queue and prints them in the order in which they were received. You can continue working on other files while a file is being printed. The Print Manager is Windows spooler. See also *print queue*.

print queue   Files in the spooler waiting to be sent to the printer. Files are sent in the order received. See also *Print Manager*.

printer font   A bit-mapped or outline font installed in the printer or downloaded to the printer as a publication is printed. Usually distinguished from the screen font, which displays the text on the computer screen. See also *bitmap*, *font*, and *outline font*.

process separations   Four-color separations made from color artwork.

proofread   To read a preliminary printout of a page and check for spelling errors, alignment on the page, and other features that are not related to the technical accuracy of the content.

prop   Background objects for animation.

pull-down menu   A list of commands that appears after you select a menu item. The menu items appear on the menu bar along the top of the screen, and the menu commands drop down in a list below the selected menu title.

pull-out quote   Quotation extracted from the text of an article and printed in larger type, often set off by ruled lines.

radio button   See *option button*.

ragged right   Text in which lines end at different points near the right margin. Opposite of flush right or justified text. See also *alignment* and *flush right*.

RAM   See *memory*.

Rectangle tool   The tool used to create squares and rectangles.

registration   The accuracy with which images are combined or positioned, particularly in reference to multicolored printing where each color must be precisely aligned for the accurate reproduction of the original.

registration mark   A mark that is added to a document for color printing line-up copies of the same page to aid the printer in positioning color overlays.

release   To let go of a mouse button.

resolution   Number of dots per inch (dpi) used to create an alphanumeric character or a graphics image. High-resolution images have more dots per inch and look smoother than low-resolution images. The resolution of images displayed on the screen is usually lower than that of the final laser printout. Laser printers print 300 dots per inch or more; typesetters print 1,200 dots per inch or more.

reverse   Text or a graphic on the printed page that appears opposite of normal. Usually, text and graphics are black on a white background; if reversed, they are white on black.

RGB   Shorthand notation for red, green, and blue. See also *additive primary colors* and *primary colors* .

right justified.   See *alignment* and *flush right*.

roll-up windows   Various small windows that provide quick access to a number of related object attributes, which can be applied quickly to selected objects.

roman   Upright text styles, as distinguished from italic.

rotate   To revolve an object about a given point.

roughs   Traditionally, the preliminary page layouts done by the designer using pencil sketches to represent miniature page design ideas. See also *thumbnail*.

ruler guides   Nonprinting extensions of the tick marks on the rulers, which form horizontal and vertical dotted, dashed, or blue lines on the page. Used to align text and graphics on the page. See also *nonprinting master items*.

rulers   Electronic rulers are displayed across the top of the publication window and down the left side. Rulers show measurements in inches, picas, millimeters, or other undefined units. Increments (tick marks) on the rulers depend on the size and resolution of your screen, as well as on the view. See also *measurement system*.

running foot   One or more lines of text appearing at the bottom of every page. The running foot is entered on the master pages. See also *folio*.

running head   One or more lines of text appearing at the top of every page. The running head is entered on the master pages. Also referred to as the header. See also *folio*.

sans serif   Typefaces without serifs, such as Helvetica and Avant Garde. See also *serif*.

scale   To change the size of an object vertically, horizontally, or both. You scale a graphic by selecting it with the pointer tool and then dragging one of the square handles.

scanned-image files   Bitmapped files created by using hardware that digitizes images (converts a two- or three-dimensional image to a collection of dots stored in the computer's memory or on disk). See also *bitmap* and *digitize*.

scanner   An electronic device that converts a photo, illustration, or other flat art into a bitmap. A video camera is a scanner that converts three-dimensional objects into bitmaps.

screen font   See *font*.

screen ruling   The number of lines per inch in a screen tint or halftone. See also *halftone*.

screen tint   A screened percentage of a solid color.

script fonts   Type designed to look like handwriting or calligraphy, such as Zapf Chancery.

scroll bar   Gray bars on the right side and bottom of the publication window. Scroll arrows at both ends of each bar enable you to scroll the document horizontally or vertically. Each scroll bar has a scroll box that you drag to change the view within publication window. List boxes also can have scroll bars for viewing long lists of files or options.

secondary mouse button   On a multiple-button mouse, the button that is not the main button. (Usually the right button.) See also *mouse buttons*.

select   To click or drag the mouse to designate the location of the next action. Also, to turn on (or place an X in) a check box (or other options) in a dialog box. See also *deselect*.

selection area   Area of a text block or graphic defined by the handles displayed after you select that text block or graphic.

selection marquee   A dashed rectangular region drawn by dragging the Pointer tool to enclose and select more than one graphic or text block at a time. See also *drag*.

serif   A line crossing the main stroke of a letter. Typefaces that have serifs include Times, Courier, New Century Schoolbook, Bookman, and Palatino. See also *sans serif*.

shape   A drawn object such as a square, a rectangle, a circle, or an oval.

Shape tool   A toolbox icon used to modify object shapes and attributes primarily by working with the nodes.

signature   In printing and binding, the name given after folding to a printed sheet of (usually) 16 pages. The term is sometimes applied to page spreads printed adjacent to each other in the sequence required for offset printing of smaller booklets.

size   To make a graphic smaller or larger by dragging the handles. See also *handles*.

skew   To slant an object vertically or horizontally.

slide   A CorelCHART image.

Smooth node   A node where the line enters and leaves the node at the same angle.

snap   To force objects to a predefined point on grid lines or guides for alignment purposes.

Snap To   The effect of various types of alignment options to align such as margin guides, object, and column guides. These guides exert a "magnetic pull" on the pointer, text, or a graphic that comes close to the guides. Useful for aligning text and graphics accurately.

Snap To guides   Command that, after turned on, causes margin guides, column guides, and ruler guides to exert a "magnetic pull" on the pointer or any text or graphic near the guides.

sound icon   A small picture that represents a sound file for use in CorelSHOW.

spacing   The amount of space, in points, that is added or removed between every pair of characters or lines in a type block. Spacing affects the amount of white space in a type block. See also *leading* and *white space*.

spooler   See *Print Manager*.

spot color   A process that adds solid areas of colored ink to a publication.

spot-color overlay   A page prepared so that each color on the page is printed separately and then combined by a commercial printer to form the completed page.

standoff   Distance between the graphic boundary and the graphic.

start node   A point at the beginning of a line represented by a hollow square larger than an end node square.

story   All the text from one word processing file; all the text typed or compiled at an insertion point outside existing text blocks. Can be one text block or several text blocks threaded together. See also *text block*.

stretch   The application of horizontal or vertical expansion to an object, usually by use of sizing handles.

style[1]   One of the variations within a typeface, such as roman, bold, or italic. See also *font* and *typeface*.

style[2]   A list of all the tag formats that can be applied to text or a graphic in a document. See also *format* and *tag*.

subpath   A segment or line which is drawn by CorelDRAW! between nodes.

subtractive primary colors   Cyan, yellow, and magenta. The three colors used to create all other colors if reflected light is used (for example, in printed material). See also *additive primary colors*, *CMYK,* and *primary colors*.

Symmetric node   A node where the curve is exactly the same on each side of the node.

tag   Formatting applied to a particular paragraph. See also *format* and *style*.

target printer   The printer on which you intend to print the final version of your publication. If no target printer is selected, CorelDRAW! uses the default printer chosen when Windows was installed.

template   A collection of text and object styles that are then applied to newly created objects; text to provide design consistency between drawings.

text block   A variable amount of text identified, when selected with the text pointer tool, by handles (small squares at the four corners of the text block) and windowshades.

text box The area in a dialog box in which you type text.

text-only file   Text created in another application and saved without type specifications or other formatting. See also *ASCII*.

Text tool   Tool used to insert text into an image.

text wrap   Automatic line breaks at the right edge of a column or at the right margin of a page. Also, the capability to wrap text around a graphic on a page layout. You can wrap text around a graphic by changing the envelope of a text block.

texture fill   The application of bitmap, fractal, or PostScript pattern to the interior of an object.

thumbnail   A miniature version (mosaic) of a page that is created by using the Thumbnails option in CorelMOSAIC.

tick marks   Marks on the rulers showing increments of measure. See also *measurement system*.

Tile   Used in oversized publications. A part of a page printed on a single sheet of paper. For a complete page, the tiles are assembled and pasted together.

timeline   The overall timing sequence of events for animation and presentations.

Time-out error   Printer stops because it has not received information for a while. Usually occurs while you print complex pages and the printer takes a long time to print a large bitmapped image. Saving before printing helps reduce chances of data loss.

tint   A percentage of one of the process or custom colors.

toggle switch   An on/off switch, command, or option. Used to describe cases in which the same command is invoked to turn a feature on and off. These commands display a check mark if they are on.

tones   The shades of a photograph or illustration that are printed as a series of dots. Tones are percentages of black; lower percentages produce lighter tones.

toolbox window   Window that overlaps the publication window and contains icons for the tools you use to work with text and graphics.

Transitions   The process of adding or removing an image from the screen. This applies to animation props and CHART slides.

transparency   See *overhead transparency* and *overlay*.

trap   Overlap needed to ensure that a slight misalignment or movement of the color separations does not affect the final appearance of the job.

TRUMATCH   A standard method of exactly matching colors in the print industry.

TrueType   Font definitions from Windows that allow sizing and alteration of text without losing resolution quality.

TWAIN   An industry-standard scanning image driver that allows for various manufacturers to provide compatible scanning devices.

typeface   A single type family of one design of type, in all sizes and styles. Times and Helvetica, for example, are two different typefaces. Each typeface has many fonts (sizes and styles). Sometimes the terms typeface and font are used interchangeably. See also *font* and *style*.

unit of measure   The units marked on display rulers, and division files such as inches, picas and points, millimeters, or ciceros.

vector graphics   See *object-oriented files*.

welding   The process of reducing many overlaid objects into a single object with a combined outline of the previous group of objects.

WFN   The font used with early versions of DRAW. You can convert it to Adobe Type using the WFNBoss utility.

white space   Empty space on a page, not used for text or graphics.

window On-screen area in which a Windows application runs, or a dialog box. Each application window has a title bar, a menu bar, and scroll bars. Some dialog boxes also include a title bar. See also *dialog box*.

windowshades   Horizontal lines, each with a small hollow square at each end, that span the top and bottom of a text block.

Wireframe view   View in which only the outline of objects is shown and the fill is not displayed.

word spacing   The space between words in a line or a paragraph. See also *kerning* and *letterspacing*.

word wrap   The automatic adjustment of the number of words on a line of text according to the margin settings. The carriage returns that result from automatic word wrap are called soft carriage returns to distinguish them from hard carriage returns, which are entered to force a new line after you press the Enter key. See also *text wrap*.

wrap   See *text wrap* and *word wrap*.

WYSIWYG   "What You See Is What You Get" (or *wizzy-wig*). Term describes systems that display all text and graphics on-screen in a good facsimile of how it will actually look when printed. The Corel applications are good WYSIWYG programs. Some systems are more WYSIWYG than others in the accuracy of the display.

X axis   The horizontal reference line to which objects are constrained. See also *constrain*.

X-height   A distinguishing characteristic of a font. The height of lower-case letters without ascenders or descenders, such as *x*, *a*, and *c*. Also called the body of the type.

Y axis   The vertical reference line to which objects are constrained. See also *constrain*.

Yellow   The subtractive primary color that appears yellow and absorbs blue light. Used as one ink in four-color printing. See also *subtractive primary colors*.

zoom   To magnify or reduce your view of the current document.

Symbols

A

F

F6 (Rectangle tool) function key, 36
F7 (Ellipse tool) function key, 32
F9 (Preview) function key, 52
F10 (Shape tool) function key, 40
F12 (Outline tool) function key, 38
FaceLift typeface, 225
facing pages, 20, 392, 633
Field Editor dialog box, 398
fields (databases), 397, 399
fields (merges), 271
File Acquire Image Acquire dialog box, 458
File Import dialog box, 43, 199
file management, *see* MOSAIC
File menu commands
    Export, 224, 238
    Import, 43, 199, 243
    New, 507
    New from Template, 421
    Print, 52, 258
    Print Files, 254
    Print Merge, 275
    Print Setup, 263
    Print Thumbnails, 253
    Save, 42, 230
    Save As, 231-232
    View Directory, 249
File Name dialog box, 44
file names
    extensions
        CDR, 17
        CLB (library), 253
        CLC (catalog), 253
        PRN, 262
        TXT, 271
    MOSAIC, 249
file transfer, 244-247, 618
    see also Clipboard
files
    backups, 230, 235-236
    bitmap files, 475

copying
    MOSAIC, 250-251
    to library, 252
CORELDRW.INI, 630
    customizing, 421-422
exporting and naming, 238
finding, 233-234
formats
    CDR, 230
    CMF (CorelMetafile), 246
    Metafile, 245
    RTF file format, 246
    saving drawings, 231
    TIFF, 241
    WAV files, 566
formatting, 234-235
hierarchical filing system, 636
images
    headers, 230
    merges, 271-272
keywords, 232
linking, 639
LOGFILE.TXT, 607
merges, creating, 271-274
    see also merges
MOSAIC
    catalogs, 252
    libraries, 252-253
moving
    MOSAIC, 250-251
    to library, 252
naming, 44
    exported files, 238
notes, 232
object-oriented, 641
pattern files, saving drawings as, 232
printing, 259-265
    MOSAIC, 11, 254-255
README.WRI file, 607
retrieving, 229-235
saving, 229-235
    autosaving, 235-236
    copies, 231-232
    formatted, 234-235
    keywords, 232
    notes, 232

U

UCR (Undercolor Removal), 467
unconstrained envelope, 371
Undercolor Removal (UCR), 467
underexposed photos, 447
underlying chart data, 529-534
Undo command (Edit menu), 61
undoing transformations, 172
Ungroup command (Arrange
  menu), 45, 112
ungrouping objects, 112
Uniform Fill dialog box, 139, 282
uniform fills (charts), 538
unit of measure, 651

V

vanishing point, 349, 352-353
vector graphics, 21, 186
vector-based images, 472
vertical dimension line, 342
vertical grid frequency, 101-103
Vertical node mapping option,
  373
vertical ruler guidelines, 108
vertical scroll bar, 18
View Chart Data command (Edit
  menu), 511
View Directory command (File
  menu), 249
View Directory dialog box, 249
viewing
  animation, 590-591, 642
  directories, 249
  fills, 284
  grid, 101
  keywords, 232
  notes, 232
views
  Editable Preview, 18
  Preview, 18
  Wireframe, 18-19, 88, 652
Visual Selector wheel (color),
  292, 302

W

Wave Editor (animation), 587
Weld command (Arrange
  menu), 118
welding text, 118
welding objects, 117-118, 651
WFN fonts, 186, 621, 651
What-You-See-Is-What-You-Get
  (WYSIWYG), 27, 652
white space, 142, 651
Windows
  Clipboard, 628
  objects, 614
  Print Manager, 645
windows, 651
  active window, 625
  animation, 570-572
  cascading in PHOTO-PAINT,
    434
  Chart Types, 508
  Chart View, 522
  charts, 535
  drawing window, *see* drawing
    window
  duplicate windows in PHOTO-
    PAINT, 435
  Gallery window (charts), 508
  maximizing, 17
  Paint window (MOVE), 575
  restoring, 17
  roll-up, *see* roll-up windows
  scrolling, 18
  sizing in PHOTO-PAINT,
    432-434
  switching in PHOTO-PAINT,
    433
  tiling
    PHOTO-PAINT, 434
    vertically, 248
  Toolbox, 651
  TRACE, 484-487
Windows 3.1, 608
Windows Character Map, 623
Windows Dithering
  (Preferences), 411